CSWE's Core Competencies Practice Behavior Coverage in t

Competency	
Professional Identity	
Practice Behavior Examples...	
Serve as a representative of the profession, its mission, and its core values	3
Know the profession's history	
Commit to the profession's enhancement and to ones own professional conduct and growth	
Advocate for client access to the services of social work	
Practice personal reflection and self-correction to assure continual professional development	
Attend to professional roles and boundaries	6
Demonstrate professional demeanor in behavior, appearance, and communication	
Engage in career-long learning	
Use supervision and consultation	
Ethical Practice	6, 7
Practice Behavior Examples...	
Conduct oneself ethically and engage in ethical decision-making	
Understand the value base of the profession, its ethical standards, and relevant law	
Recognize and manage personal values in a way that allows professional values to guide practice	7
Make ethical decisions by applying standards of the National Association of Social Workers Code of Ethics and, as applicable, of the International Federation of Social Workers/International Association of Schools of Social Work Ethics in Social Work, Statement of Principles	6
Tolerate ambiguity in resolving ethical conflicts	
Apply strategies of ethical reasoning to arrive at principled decisions	8
Critical Thinking	1, 4, 5, 10, 11, 12
Practice Behavior Examples...	
Understand the principles of logic, scientific inquiry, and reasoned discernment	
Use critical thinking augmented by creativity and curiosity	
Synthesize and communicate relevant information	
Distinguish, appraise, and integrate multiple sources of knowledge, including research-based knowledge, and practice wisdom	4, 5, 11, 12
Analyze models of assessment, prevention, intervention, and evaluation	1
Demonstrate effective oral and written communication in working with individuals, families, groups, organizations, communities, and colleagues	10

CSWE's Core Competencies Practice Behavior Coverage in this Text

Competency	Chapter
Diversity in Practice	1, 2, 7, 9, 10, 11
Practice Behavior Examples...	
Understand how diversity characterizes and shapes the human experience and is critical to the formation of identity	2
Understand the dimensions of diversity as the intersectionality of multiple factors including age, class, color, culture, disability, ethnicity, gender, gender identity and expression, immigration status, political ideology, race, religion, sex, and sexual orientation	10
Appreciate that, as a consequence of difference, a person's life experiences may include oppression, poverty, marginalization, and alienation as well as privilege, power, and acclaim	11
Recognize the extent to which a culture's structures and values may oppress, marginalize, alienate, or create or enhance privilege and power	1, 5, 7
Gain sufficient self-awareness to eliminate the influence of personal biases and values in working with diverse groups	
Recognize and communicate their understanding of the importance of difference in shaping life experiences	5, 9
View oneself as a learner, and engage others as informants	
Human Rights & Justice	2, 8
Practice Behavior Examples...	
Understand that each person, regardless of position in society, has basic human rights, such as freedom, safety, privacy, an adequate standard of living, health care, and education	
Recognize the global interconnections of oppression and are knowledgeable about theories of justice and strategies to promote human and civil rights	
Incorporate social justice practices in organizations, institutions, and society to ensure that these basic human rights are distributed equitably and without prejudice	8
Understand the forms and mechanisms of oppression and discrimination	2
Advocate for human rights and social and economic justice	
Engage in practices that advance social and economic justice	
Research Based Practice	1, 4, 12
Practice Behavior Examples...	
Use practice experience to inform research, employ evidence-based interventions, evaluate ones own practice, and use research findings to improve practice, policy, and social service delivery	1, 4
Comprehend quantitative and qualitative research and understand scientific and ethical approaches to building knowledge	
Use practice experience to inform scientific inquiry	
Use research evidence to inform practice	12

Competency	Chapter
Human Behavior	2, 4, 7, 9, 11, 13
Practice Behavior Examples...	
Understand human behavior across the life course; the range of social systems in which people live; and the ways social systems promote or deter people in maintaining or achieving health and well-being	
Apply theories and knowledge from the liberal arts to understand biological, social, cultural, psychological, and spiritual development	2
Utilize conceptual frameworks to guide the processes of assessment, intervention, and evaluation	4, 7, 11, 13
Critique and apply knowledge to understand person and environment.	4, 9, 13
Policy Practice	9, 11, 12
Practice Behavior Examples...	
Understand that policy affects service delivery and they actively engage in policy practice	
Know the history and current structures of social policies and services; the role of policy in service delivery; and the role of practice in policy development	
Analyze, formulate, and advocate for policies that advance social well-being	9, 12
Collaborate with colleagues and clients for effective policy action	11
Practice Contexts	5, 7, 12
Practice Behavior Examples...	
Keep informed, resourceful, and proactive in responding to evolving organizational, community, and societal contexts at all levels of practice	
Recognize that the context of practice is dynamic, and use knowledge and skill to respond proactively	
Continuously discover, appraise, and attend to changing locales, populations, scientific and technological developments, and emerging societal trends to provide relevant services	7, 12
Provide leadership in promoting sustainable changes in service delivery and practice to improve the quality of social services	5

CSWE's Core Competencies Practice Behavior Coverage in this Text

Competency	Chapter
Engage, Assess, Intervene, Evaluate	2, 3, 6, 8, 10, 13
Practice Behavior Examples...	
Identify, analyze, and implement evidence-based interventions designed to achieve client goals	
Use research and technological advances	
Evaluate program outcomes and practice effectiveness	
Develop, analyze, advocate, and provide leadership for policies and services	
Promote social and economic justice	
A) ENGAGEMENT	
Substantively and effectively prepare for action with individuals, families, groups, organizations, and communities	3
Use empathy and other interpersonal skills	13
Develop a mutually agreed-on focus of work and desired outcomes	
B) ASSESSMENT	
Collect, organize, and interpret client data	3
Assess client strengths and limitations	2, 6
Develop mutually agreed-on intervention goals and objectives	8
Select appropriate intervention strategies	
C) INTERVENTION	
Initiate actions to achieve organizational goals	
Implement prevention interventions that enhance client capacities	6
Help clients resolve problems	
Negotiate, mediate, and advocate for clients	8
Facilitate transitions and endings	
D) EVALUATION	
Critically analyze, monitor, and evaluate interventions	3, 10

SECOND EDITION

Mental Health in Social Work

A Casebook on Diagnosis and Strengths Based Assessment

Jacqueline Corcoran
Virginia Commonwealth University

Joseph Walsh
Virginia Commonwealth University

PEARSON

Boston   Columbus   Indianapolis   New York   San Francisco   Upper Saddle River
Amsterdam   Cape Town   Dubai   London   Madrid   Milan   Munich   Paris   Montreal   Toronto
Delhi   Mexico City   São Paulo   Sydney   Hong Kong   Seoul   Singapore   Taipei   Tokyo

Editorial Director: Craig Campanella
Editor in Chief: Dickson Musslewhite
Executive Editor: Ashley Dodge
Editorial Product Manager: Carly Czech
Director of Marketing: Brandy Dawson
Executive Marketing Manager: Jeanette Koskinas
Senior Marketing Manager: Wendy Albert
Marketing Assistant: Jessica Warren
Media Project Manager: Felicia Halpert

Production Editor: Meghan DeMaio
Creative Director: Jayne Conte
Cover Image: VladisChern/Shutterstock
Cover Designer: Suzanne Behnke
Editorial Production and Composition Service:
   Chitra Ganesan/PreMediaGlobal
Printer/Binder: Edwards Brothers Malloy
Cover Printer: Lehigh-Phoenix Color

Library of Congress Cataloging-in-Publication Data

Corcoran, Jacqueline.
Mental health in social work : a casebook on diagnosis and strengths based assessment /
   Jacqueline Corcoran, Joseph Walsh. — 2nd ed.
     p. cm.
   Includes bibliographical references and index.
   ISBN-13: 978-0-205-05504-3
   ISBN-10: 0-205-05504-4
  1. Community mental health services—Case studies.   2. Psychiatric social work—Case studies.
3. Medical social work—Case studies.   I. Walsh, Joseph.   II. Title.
   RA790.6.C64   2011
   362.2'0425—dc23

2011025836

10 9 8 7 6 5 4 3 2   14 13 12

ISBN-10: 0-205-05504-4
ISBN-13: 978-0-205-05504-3

Contents

PART TWO: DISORDERS USUALLY FIRST DIAGNOSED IN INFANCY, CHILDHOOD, OR ADOLESCENCE

PART THREE: COGNITIVE DISORDERS

PART FOUR: SUBSTANCE-RELATED DISORDERS

PART FIVE: PSYCHOTIC DISORDERS

PART SIX: MOOD DISORDERS

9. Depressive Disorders   126

10. Bipolar Disorder   142

PART SEVEN: ANXIETY DISORDERS

PART EIGHT: EATING DISORDERS

PART NINE: PERSONALITY DISORDERS

Preface

Mental Health in Social Work: A Casebook on Diagnosis and Strengths-Based Assessment is a graduate-level textbook that will help students and professionals learn to understand clients holistically as they proceed with the assessment and intervention process. A major purpose of *Mental Health in Social Work* is to familiarize readers with the *American Psychiatric Association Diagnostic and Statistical Manual* (DSM) classification of mental disorders. The primary reasons that social workers need to become conversant with the DSM are the following: (1) to offer clients appropriate referrals and treatment; (2) to communicate effectively with other mental health professions; and (3) to be eligible for third-party reimbursement.

The learning in *Mental Health in Social Work* primarily occurs through a **case study method**; students are asked to respond to case illustrations that are presented in each chapter. Cases (two to three in each chapter) have been selected to represent the diversity of people with whom social workers intervene. Answers to the questions posed about each case are provided in an instructor's manual and should be discussed in class and/or through feedback on case study assignments.

While gaining competence in DSM diagnosis, the reader is also taught to maintain a critical perspective on the various DSM diagnoses and the medical model as promulgated through the DSM. The field of social work has a focus not just on the individual, but on the person within an environmental context, and concerns itself with strengths as well as problems. Additionally, social work has a traditional commitment to oppressed and vulnerable populations. Because the DSM is limited in these areas, *Mental Health in Social Work* **includes the biopsychosocial risk and resilience perspective, which takes into account both risks and strengths at the individual and environmental levels**. Each chapter then explores the relevant risk and protective influences for each disorder, highlighting some of the particular risks for special populations, including children, women, the elderly, minorities, people with disabilities, gay and lesbian individuals, and those from low socioeconomic strata. **Students are asked to complete risk and resilience assessments for the case studies presented**.

Another emphasis in *Mental Health in Social Work* is **evidence-based treatment**, a recent movement in social work and various other health and mental health disciplines. The meaning of evidence-based practice can be debated (Norcross, Beutler, & Levant, 2006), but has been generally defined as the prioritization of research evidence when social workers consider how to best help clients. However, client preferences and available resources must also be part of the process of clinical judgment in addition to research studies (Sackett, Straus, Richardson, Rosenberg, & Haynes, 2000). In considering the hierarchy of evidence, whenever possible we rely on systematic reviews and meta-analyses, which are considered "first-line evidence" (Petticrew & Roberts, 2006). These systematic reviews aim to comprehensively locate and synthesize the treatment outcome literature in a particular area. If the review lends itself to combining the results of primary studies in a quantitative way, then it is referred to as meta-analysis (Petticrew & Roberts).

From these reviews of the literature, *Mental Health in Social Work* **presents treatment guidelines for each disorder covered in the book, and through the case studies, students will learn how to form evidence-based treatment plans**. At the same time, in keeping with the importance of the environmental context, interventions address the broad nature of the concerns that people bring to social work professionals. For instance, if socioeconomic problems, such as lack of health insurance and unemployment, are part of the client's presenting problems, then intervention will appropriately address these concerns, as they are critical to a person's well-being and healthy functioning.

Since the last edition of this volume, the Council on Social Work Education has implemented new educational policy and accreditation standards that involve competencies and the practice behaviors associated with them that social workers are to learn. As a result, *Mental Health in Social Work* has become part of the *Advancing Core Competencies* series. The following table demonstrates how the competencies and practice behaviors are an integral part of this book. Further, within each chapter,

In summary, this book takes a case study approach, with students applying evidence-based information on mental disorders to build their social work competency in terms of assessment and treatment of mental illness.

Table | **Social Work Competencies Addressed in Casebook Exercises**

Competency	Practice behaviors	Casebook application
Competency **2.1.1—Identify as a professional social worker and conduct oneself accordingly**	P.B. 2.1.1a: Readily identify as social work professionals P.B. 2.1.1c: Manage assessment interviews with clients, using the person-in-environment perspective	The social work perspective is balanced with the biomedical perspective of DSM with the risk and resilience biopsychosocial assessment and an overall critique of DSM is offered in chapter 1 and for each DSM disorder.
Competency **2.1.4—Engage diversity and difference in practice**	P.B. 2.1.4a: Research and apply epidemiological knowledge of diverse populations and their mental/behavioral disorders	A chart for each mental disorder with a discussion of socially diverse populations.

Table

Social Work Competencies Addressed in Casebook Exercises

Competency	Practice behaviors	Casebook application
	P.B. 2.1.4.Fa: Recognize the extent to which a culture's structures and values may oppress, marginalize, alienate, or create or enhance privilege and power.	A critique of the DSM and its association with our culture's power structures is presented in chapter 2. Directions for each case study include **Critical Perspective:** Formulate a critique of the diagnosis as it relates to the case example. Questions to consider include the following: Does this diagnosis represent a valid mental disorder from the social work perspective? How does oppression, discrimination, and trauma play in the development of the disorder? Your critique should be based on the values of the social work profession (which are incongruent in some ways with the medical model) and the validity of the specific diagnostic criteria applied to this case (i.e., is this diagnosis significantly different from other possible diagnoses?).
Competency **2.1.3—Apply critical thinking to inform and communicate professional judgments**	P.B. 2.1.3c: Identify and articulate clients' strengths and vulnerabilities as part of the BPSS assessment	**Directions for each case study include Biopsychosocial Risk and Resilience Assessment:** Formulate a risk and resilience assessment, both for the onset of the disorder and for the course of the disorder, including the strengths that you see for this individual and the techniques you would use to elicit them.
Competency **2.1.5—Advance human rights and social and economic justice**	P.B. 2.1.5a: Use knowledge of the effects of oppression, discrimination, and trauma on development of clients' mental/ emotional/behavioral disorders	**Directions for each case study include Critical Perspective:** Formulate a critique of the diagnosis as it relates to the case example. Questions to consider include the following: Does this diagnosis represent a valid mental disorder from the social work perspective? How does oppression, discrimination, and trauma play in the development of the disorder? Your critique should be based on the values of the social work profession (which are incongruent in some ways with the medical model) and the validity of the specific diagnostic criteria applied to this case (i.e., is this diagnosis significantly different from other possible diagnoses?).
Competency **2.1.6—Engage in research-informed practice**	P.B. 2.1.6a: Use research knowledge to inform clinical assessment/ diagnosis	Evidence-based assessment and practice guidelines are presented based on the latest research for each disorder.
Competency 2.1.7— **Apply knowledge of human behavior and the social environment**	P.B. 2.1.7a: Synthesize and differentially apply biological, developmental, social, and other theories of etiology associated with specific mental, emotional, and behavioral disorders	The latest research on etiological factors associated with mental disorders in general (chapter 2) and for each mental disorder is presented.

(Continues)

Table	**Social Work Competencies Addressed in Casebook Exercises (*Continued*)**	
Competency	**Practice behaviors**	**Casebook application**
	P.B. 2.1.7b: Use a biopsychosocial-spiritual perspective and multiaxial diagnostic classification system to formulate differential diagnoses	**Directions for each case study include Multiaxial Diagnosis**: Prepare the following: a multiaxial diagnosis, the rationale for the diagnosis and global assessment of functioning (GAF) score, and additional information you would have wanted to know in order to make a more accurate diagnosis.
	P.B. 2.1.7.Fa: Utilize conceptual frameworks to guide the processes of assessment, intervention, and evaluation.	Strengths-based assessment techniques, solution-focused therapy, and motivational interviewing are covered in chapter 2. Theories of evidence-based intervention are covered for each mental disorder.
Competency 2.1.3—Apply critical thinking to inform and communicate professional judgments **P.B. 2.1.3.b:** Analyze models of assessment, prevention, intervention, and evaluation (S)	**P.B 2.1.7b:** Critique and apply knowledge to understand person and environment	Directions for each case study include **Biopsychosocial Risk and Resilience Assessment**: Formulate a risk and resilience assessment, both for the onset of the disorder and for the course of the disorder, including the strengths that you see for this individual and the techniques you would use to elicit them.
	P.B. 2.1.3.a: Distinguish, appraise, and integrate multiple sources of knowledge, including research-based knowledge, and practice wisdom (S)	Directions for each case study include **Goal Setting and Treatment Planning**: Given your risk and resilience assessments of the individual, your knowledge of the disorder, and evidence-based practice guidelines, formulate goals and a possible treatment plan for this individual.
Competency 2.1.10—Assess with individuals, families, groups, organizations, and communities	**P.B. 2.10.d:** Collect, organize, and interpret data (P)	Directions for each case study include **Multiaxial Diagnosis**: Given the case information, prepare the following: a multiaxial diagnosis, the rationale for the diagnosis and GAF score, and additional information you would have wanted to know in order to make a more accurate diagnosis.
	P.B. 2.10.e: Assess client strengths and limitations (P)	Directions for each case study include **Biopsychosocial Risk and Resilience Assessment**: Formulate a risk and resilience assessment, both for the onset of the disorder and for the course of the disorder, including the strengths that you see for this individual and the techniques you would use to elicit them.
	P.B. 2.10.g: Select appropriate intervention strategies (P)	Directions for each case study include **Goal Setting and Treatment Planning**: Given your risk and resilience assessments of the individual, your knowledge of the disorder, and evidence-based practice guidelines, formulate goals and a possible treatment plan for this individual.

Acknowledgments

The case studies that make up this book are based on our clinical practice and the contributions of our students and other professionals. As the application of assessment competencies is a core element of this book, we are truly grateful to the following students who offered case contributions.

Susan Bienvenu, Treva Bower, Lindsay Doles, Martha Dunn, Gidget Fields, Lisa Genser, Carolynn Ghiloni, Christine Gigena, Dana Gilmore, Kristine Kluck, Elizabeth Lincoln, Pamela McDonald, Jodee Mellerio, Cynthia Ormes, Kristi Payne, Constance Ritter, Zoe Rizzuto, Heather Roberts, Anne Ross, Amelia Schor, Tina Shafer, Rebecca Sorensen, Megan Vogel, Raquelle Ward, and Dallas Williams. We are also indebted to the following social work professionals: Kim Giancaspro, Kris McAleavey, and Adina Shapiro. Most of all, we want to thank Shane Fagan for tirelessly reading over case studies and offering her valued clinical opinions.

Moreover, we thank the reviewers for their suggestions: Chrystal Baranti, California State University; Laura Boisen, Augsberg College; Daphne S. Cain, Louisiana State University; Rebecca T. Davis, Rutgers University; and Judith H. Rosenberg, Central Connecticut State University.

As always, thanks to Patrick Corcoran for his diligent and conscientious proofreading, helping us to prepare the best book we can put forward.

1

Diagnosis and the Social Work Profession

Competencies Applied with Practice Behaviors — in this Chapter				
■ Professional Identity	■ Ethical Practice	✖ Critical Thinking	✖ Diversity in Practice	■ Human Rights & Justice
✖ Research-Based Practice	■ Human Behavior	■ Policy Practice	■ Practice Contexts	■ Engage, Assess, Intervene, Evaluate

Henry Williams, a 59-year-old African American man, was in the hospital after undergoing surgery for removal of a brain tumor. His past medical history included seizures, insulin-dependent diabetes mellitus, and pancreatitis (an inflammation of the pancreas that causes intense pain in the upper abdomen). Currently, Mr. Williams was taking several medications, including Dilantin (used to treat epilepsy), insulin, and steroids (to decrease swelling around his tumor).

About six days after the surgery Mr. Williams woke up in the middle of the night and was very loud in "casting the demons out," as he called it. The nurse tried to calm him, but Mr. Williams was so incensed that he picked up a small monitoring machine next to his bed and threw it at her. Security officers and the on-duty physician assistant were called to calm the patient.

The next morning the neurosurgery team requested a psychiatric exam, but because it was a Friday Mr. Williams was not examined until the following Monday. His family visited over the weekend, and he repeatedly became agitated, even accusing his wife of cheating on him. He was upset and emotional during those visits, and it took him a while to calm down after his family left.

On Sunday night, Mr. Williams got up at midnight and threatened his roommate. Mr. Williams yelled that his roommate was cheating on him with his wife and they were plotting to kill him. Because his roommate feared for his safety, he was moved to another room, while the nurse tried to calm Mr. Williams.

When the psychiatric team, accompanied by the social work intern, finally examined Mr. Williams, he said he felt great but was hearing voices, most prominently that of his pastor. He reported that he saw demons at night and was attempting to fight them off. He also stated that he thought someone wanted to kill him to benefit from his life insurance policy. In addition, Mr. Williams told the psychiatrist that his wife had not come to visit him for some days (this was not true; she had been there twice over the weekend) but that his son had been at his bedside in the morning and that he had enjoyed the visit.

Mr. Williams's wife heard about the incident with the roommate and said she would not take Mr. Williams home because she was afraid of him. She told the social work intern that Mr. Williams had behaved similarly in the past. She would sometimes wake up in the middle of the night and find him standing next to the bed or leaning over her body, staring at her. When she confronted her husband, he would pass it off as a joke, saying he was making sure she was really in bed and had not gone out. (They had separate bedrooms.) She also told the intern that although she had never cheated on her husband, he had had an affair several years ago. After she found out, they went to marriage counseling together, but the marriage had been "rocky" ever since.

The case described earlier is one in which the client, Mr. Williams, appears to have a mental disorder. Almost half of all Americans (46.4%) meet the criteria for a mental, emotional, or behavioral disorder sometime during their lives (Kessler, Berglund, Demler, Jin, & Walters, 2005). The various disorders are catalogued and described in the *Diagnostic and Statistical Manual of Mental Disorders* (DSM), published by the American Psychiatric Association (APA). The DSM is the standard resource for clinical diagnosis in the United States. The first edition of the DSM was published in 1952, and the manual has undergone many revisions during the last 59 years. The latest version is *DSM-IV-TR* (Text Revision) (American Psychiatric Association [APA], 2000), and another revision is planned for 2013.

The definition of *mental disorder* in the DSM is a "significant behavioral or psychological syndrome or pattern that occurs in an individual and that is associated with present distress (e.g., a painful symptom) or disability (i.e., impairment in one or more important areas of functioning) or with significantly increased risk of suffering death, pain, disability, or an important loss of freedom" (p. xxxi). A disorder ". . . must currently be considered a manifestation of behavioral, psychological, or biological dysfunction in the individual" (p. xxxi). The DSM represents a medical perspective, only one of many possible perspectives on human behavior. The medical definition focuses on underlying disturbances *within* the person and is sometimes referred to as the *disease model* of abnormality. This model implies that the abnormal person must experience changes within the self (rather than create environmental change) in order to be considered "normal" again.

In its desire to promote the "objectivity" of its manual, the APA does not recognize the notion of mental illness as a *social construction*. A social construction is any belief system in a culture that is accepted as factual or objective by many of its members, when in fact the belief system is constructed by influential members of that society (Farone, 2003). The medical profession holds great influence in Western society, so when mental health diagnoses are presented as scientifically based disorders, many people will accept them as such. Social constructionism asserts that many "accepted" facts in a society are in fact ideas that reflect the values of the times in which they emerge.

The foregoing information may explain why the DSM classification system does not fully represent the knowledge base or values of the social work profession, which emphasizes a transactional, person-in-situation perspective on human functioning. Still, the DSM is extensively used by social workers, for many positive reasons. Worldwide, the medical profession is preeminent in setting standards for mental health practice, and social workers are extensively employed in mental health settings, where clinical diagnosis is considered necessary for selecting appropriate interventions. In fact, social workers account for more than half of the mental health workforce in the United States

(Whitaker, 2009). Competent use of the DSM is beneficial to social workers (and clients) for the following reasons:

- Social workers are employed in a variety of settings, not just mental health agencies and facilities, where they meet people who are vulnerable to mental health disorders because of poverty, minority status, and other social factors. No matter what their setting, social workers should be able to recognize the symptoms of possible disorders in their clients and appropriately refer them for treatment services.
- The five-axis diagnostic system (which considers mental disorders, developmental disorders, medical problems, environmental stressors, and a global assessment of client functioning) provides the basis of a comprehensive bio- (Axis III), psycho- (Axes I, II, and V), and social (Axis IV) assessment.
- An accurate diagnosis facilitates the development of a suitable intervention plan.
- The diagnostic categories enable social workers to help clients, and possibly also their families, learn about the nature of the client's problems. Although some stigma is often attached to the assignment of a diagnostic label, many people take a certain comfort in learning that their painful experiences can be encapsulated in a diagnosis. It validates their experience, lets them know that other people suffer from the same disorder, and offers hope that their problems can be treated.
- Use of the DSM allows practitioners from various disciplines to converse in a common language about clients.
- The DSM perspective is incorporated into professional training programs offered by a variety of human service professions and portions of state social worker licensing examinations.
- Insurance companies usually require a formal DSM diagnosis for client reimbursement.

For these many reasons, social workers need to gain competence in DSM diagnosis, and enabling them to do so is a major purpose of this book. To that end, each chapter covers a particular mental disorder and is illustrated with two to three case studies on which readers can practice their skills and knowledge. Cases have been selected to represent the diversity of people with whom social workers intervene. The disorders chosen for this book are those that social workers may see in their employment or field settings and that have sufficient research information behind them. For instance, reactive attachment disorder is not included, even though child clients may carry this diagnosis, because there has been little research on the disorder itself, despite the fact that many data have been gathered throughout the years on attachment theory and attachment styles.

We will now turn to an overview of the DSM multiaxial classification system, using the case that opened the chapter as an illustration. (We note that the next edition of the DSM may include significant changes to the classification system, possibly reducing the number of axes used [APA, 2010]). We will then describe some of the tensions involved in DSM diagnosis as practiced by social workers and discuss how this book will help develop social workers' skills in ways that will overcome some of the limitations of the DSM approach for clinical practice.

THE DSM CLASSIFICATION SYSTEM

Following is a description of the DSM five-axis classification of mental disorders, along with some general guidelines for its use (APA, 2000).

Axis I   Beginning with the problem that is most responsible for the current evaluation, the mental disorder or other condition that may be a focus of clinical attention (a V-code diagnosis) is recorded under Axis I. The mental disorders, including adjustment disorders, will make up the chapters of this book. Although they are typically not given on their own, because they are not reimbursed by insurance, the V-codes are given in three different situations: (a) when no mental disorder is present but a problem needs clinical attention, (b) when there is a problem unrelated to the mental disorder, or (c) when a problem related to the mental disorder is sufficiently severe to warrant clinical attention of its own (APA, 2000).

When uncertain if a diagnosis is correct, the social worker should use the provisional qualifier. If a person no longer meets criteria for a disorder that may be relevant to his or her current condition, the qualifier "past history" can be given. For example, if a woman seeks help for depression while she is pregnant, it may be important to note if she had an eating disorder history.

Axis II   This axis includes the disorders that are considered to have more of a constitutional basis and includes the personality disorders and mental retardation. They are considered to represent relatively chronic conditions that can put the person at risk for a variety of Axis I disorders. If a personality disorder is the most important reason for the client's request for evaluation, the social worker should add the term *principal diagnosis*.

Axis III   This axis includes the person's general medical conditions, which may have a direct bearing on an Axis I diagnosis or may affect (or be affected by) management of an Axis I or II diagnosis. The source of the information should also be listed here, such as "according to the client" or "confirmed in the chart by a physician."

Axis IV   This axis is used to record psychosocial and environmental problems that have occurred in the last year and are a focus of clinical attention. These involve problems with the following: primary support group, economic or social environment, access to health care services, educational system, interaction with the legal or criminal systems, occupational setting, housing problems, and any other psychosocial stressors, such as phase-of-life and acculturation problems. The social worker should record the formal term and also add descriptive information about the stressor, such as "educational problem—failed past year of school."

Although Axis IV does not relate to problems within the individual, but only to environmental conditions, no differentiation is made between environmental problems that are contributing to a person's disorder (risk influences) and those that are consequences of the disorder. For example, educational problems in a child with oppositional defiant disorder (ODD) often arise because of disruptive behaviors displayed at school; it is not that the educational problems result in ODD.

Axis V   Global assessment of functioning (GAF) indicates the level of a client's social, occupational, and psychological functioning on a 100-point scale reflecting a continuum of mental health and illness. It comprises two scores: one reflecting the client's current GAF (the past week) and another reflecting the client's highest level during the past year. The DSM includes anchor descriptions for each 10 points on the scale. The reader should note that GAF scores, like many aspects of the DSM, are subject to interpretation. GAF scores tend to have low reliability, as individual clinicians vary widely in their assignment of scores.

Following is a list of "hierarchical principles" that can help the practitioner decide which diagnoses to use in situations where several might be considered:

Critical Thinking

Practice Behavior Example: *Analyze models of assessment, prevention, intervention, and evaluation.*

Critical Thinking Question: Which, if any, of the five axes in the DSM classification system represents attention to environmental influences on a client's mental, emotional, or behavioral status? Are the ones you have selected (if any) adequate for this purpose? How will your focus on each axis influence your perception of the client's problem?

- "Disorders due to a general medical condition" and "substance-induced disorders," which include not only substances people consume but also medications they are prescribed, preempt a diagnosis of any other disorder that could produce the same symptoms.
- The fewer diagnoses that account for the symptoms, the better. This is the rule of "parsimony." Practitioners need to understand the "power of the diagnostic label," in its negative as well as positive aspects, and use diagnostic labels judiciously. For example, posttraumatic stress disorder (PTSD) and reactive attachment disorder are sometimes diagnosed simultaneously in children. Although they share some presentation, when they are used together, the diagnostic picture becomes imprecise and does not lead to a coherent treatment plan.
- When a more pervasive disorder has essential or associated symptoms that are the defining symptoms of a less pervasive disorder, the more pervasive disorder is diagnosed if its criteria are met. For example, if "oppositional defiant disorder" and "conduct disorder" are both present, the social worker should use the "conduct disorder" diagnosis, because its range of criteria overlaps with the former diagnosis (see chapter 5 for case examples).
- When the client's presentation seems to match several diagnostic categories, the social worker should use the least severe diagnosis possible, to treat the client with respect and to avoid stigma and the negative social effects of labeling. Though there is no official ranking of diagnoses by severity, some categories do seem to be less stigmatizing than others, in that they are more common and shorter term in nature (such as an adjustment disorder versus depression, or depression versus a psychotic disorder or a personality disorder). Thus the social worker may assign a client an adjustment disorder diagnosis or a V-code (although the latter is not usually reimbursable by insurance companies).

The principles outlined earlier are, of course, applied only after a comprehensive client assessment is carried out. Each chapter in this book includes assessment principles relevant to specific disorders, but here we present some general guidelines for the assessment of a client's mental, emotional, and behavioral functioning.

MENTAL STATUS EXAMINATION

A Mental Status Examination (MSE) is a process by which a social worker or other human services professional systematically examines the quality of a client's mental functioning. Ten areas of functioning are considered individually. The results of the examination are combined with information derived from a client's social history to produce clinical impressions of the client, including a DSM diagnosis. An MSE can typically be completed in 15 minutes or less. One commonly used format for an MSE evaluates the following areas of client functioning (Daniel & Gurczynski, 2003):

- *Appearance.* The person's overall appearance in the context of his or her cultural group. These features are significant because poor personal hygiene or grooming may reflect a physical inability to care for one's physical self or a loss of interest in doing so.

- *Movement and behavior.* The person's manner of walking, posture, coordination, eye contact, and facial expressions. Problems with walking or coordination may reflect a disorder of the central nervous system.
- *Affect.* This refers to a person's outwardly observable emotional reactions and may include either a lack of emotional response or an overreaction to an event.
- *Mood.* The underlying emotional tone of the person's answers.
- *Speech.* The volume of the person's voice, the rate or speed of speech, the length of answers to questions, and the appropriateness and clarity of the answers.
- *Thought content.* Any indications in the client's words or behaviors of hallucinations, delusions, obsessions, symptoms of dissociation, or thoughts of suicide.
- *Thought process.* The logical connections between thoughts and their relevance to the conversation. Irrelevant detail, repeated words and phrases, interrupted thinking, and illogical connections between thoughts may be signs of a thought disorder.
- *Cognition.* The act or condition of knowing. The social worker assesses the person's orientation with regard to time, place, and personal identity; long- and short-term memory; ability to perform simple arithmetic (counting backward by threes or sevens); general intellectual level or fund of knowledge (identifying the last five presidents, or similar questions); ability to think abstractly (explaining a proverb); ability to name specified objects and read or write complete sentences; ability to understand and perform a task (showing the examiner how to comb one's hair or throw a ball); ability to draw a simple map or copy a design or geometrical figure; ability to distinguish between right and left.
- *Judgment.* The social worker asks the person what he or she would do about a commonsense problem, such as running out of a prescription medication.
- *Insight.* A person's ability to recognize a problem and understand its nature and severity.

Abnormal results for an MSE include any evidence of brain damage or thought disorders, a mood or affect that is clearly inappropriate to its context, thoughts of suicide, disturbed speech patterns, dissociative symptoms, and delusions or hallucinations.

> **Directions:** Now that you have read a description of the multiaxial system, hierarchical principles, and an MSE, can you work out a multiaxial diagnosis for Henry Williams before reading ahead?

Multiaxial Diagnosis

Axis I:
Axis II:
Axis III:
Axis IV:
Axis V:

Multiaxial Diagnosis of Mr. Williams

Axis I: 292.12 Psychotic disorder with hallucinations induced by steroids
             V61.10 Partner relational problem
Axis II: V71.09 (no diagnosis on Axis II)
Axis III: 250.01 Insulin-dependent diabetes mellitus
             225.2 Meningioma (cerebral)
             345.10 Seizure disorder
             577.1 Pancreatitis

Axis IV: Problems with primary support group (marital problems)
Axis V: GAF score: 35

Rationale for the Diagnosis

Psychotic disorder with hallucinations induced by steroids was diagnosed because the symptoms began a few days after Mr. Williams started to take the medication. Steroids can affect the limbic system, causing aggression and emotional outbursts. Although this diagnosis would have to be made by medical personnel, the social worker should be aware that the symptoms of apparent mental disorders may result from a medical condition or from medication used to treat the condition.

The specifier "with hallucinations" was used because the patient's hallucinations (casting out the demons) seemed to predominate over his delusions (thinking that his wife was cheating on him). The latter appeared to have a basis in reality, even though he was the one who had had an affair. Projection of his own behavior onto his wife may have caused the delusion. It should also be noted that Mr. Williams had just had a brain tumor removed; changes in mood and affect are fairly common in these patients. A diagnosis of psychotic disorder due to a medical condition can be excluded, however, because Mr. Williams did not show symptoms before or right after the craniotomy was performed. Instead they developed six days after the surgery. The V-code, partner relational problem, was also diagnosed due to the long-standing marital problems that have recently resurfaced due to Mr. Williams's accusations.

The GAF score of 35 was given because Mr. Williams is experiencing major symptoms, including impaired reality testing, hallucinations, and delusions, which cause him to behave aggressively and seriously impair his relationships with others. Although Mr. Williams's current GAF score is very low, there is considerable hope that he will be able to return to his previous level of functioning, because his symptoms appear to be the temporary side effects of the steroids he was given in the hospital.

LIMITATIONS OF THE DSM

Any classification of mental, emotional, and behavioral disorders is likely to be flawed, as it is difficult for any system to capture the complexity of human life. As noted earlier, the DSM classification system is based on the medical model of diagnosis, while the profession of social work is characterized by the consideration of systems and the reciprocal impact of persons and their environments on human behavior (Walsh, 2010). That is, for social workers the quality of a person's social functioning should be assessed with regard to the interplay of biological, psychological, and social factors in his or her life. Three types of person-in-environment situations likely to produce problems in social functioning include life transitions, relationship difficulties, and environmental unresponsiveness (Carter & McGoldrick, 2005). Social work interventions, therefore, may focus on the person; the environment; or, more commonly, both. Some other limitations of the DSM from the perspective of the social work profession are described on the following pages. Additionally, each chapter offers critiques of the particular DSM diagnosis and/or the medical perspective underlying it. Readers are encouraged to offer a critical perspective when presented with each of the case illustrations.

One of the criticisms of the DSM is that the reliability of diagnosis (agreement among practitioners about the same clients) is not

Diversity in Practice

Practice Behavior Example: *Recognize the extent to which a culture's structures and values may oppress, marginalize, alienate, or create or enhance privilege and power.*

Critical Thinking Question: Consider Mr. Williams's cultural context. In what ways might his cultural context affect the way he is assessed for a diagnosis by a majority culture practitioner? Give an example of how an oversight in this regard might result in an inappropriate intervention.

Practice Behavior Example: *Use practice experience to inform research, employ evidence-based interventions, evaluate ones own practice, and use research findings to improve practice, policy, and social service delivery.*

Critical Thinking Question: How do you think the editors of the DSM might best determine the validity and reliability of diagnoses? Consider Mr. Williams's diagnosis—how might you attempt to assess its validity?

high for some disorders, and generally has not risen since DSM-II (Duffy, Gillig, & Tureen, 2002). Second, psychiatric diagnoses are often based on cultural notions of normality versus abnormality and mental health versus illness (Maracek, 2006). For example, homosexuality was considered a mental disorder until 1974, when political pressure on the creators of the DSM was successfully applied (Kutchins & Kirk, 1997). Today, some question the validity of the diagnosis of gender identity disorder, claiming that it represents an unusual but valid gender orientation (Hill, Rozanski, Carfagnini, & Willoughby, 2005).

Third, arising as it does from the psychiatric profession, the DSM may overstate the case for biological influences on some mental disorders (Cooper, 2004; Healy, 2002; Johnston, 2000). For instance, heritability for both major depression and anxiety is about 30 to 40% (Hettema, Neale, & Kendler, 2001; Sullivan et al., 2000); for substance use disorders heritability is about 30% (Walters, 2002). Although other biological factors may play a role in the development of mental disorders aside from genetics (e.g., complications at birth, exposure to lead), social factors (family environment, community, social support, income levels) certainly play a large role as well.

Fourth, in a related vein, the DSM tends to view clients in isolation and decontextualizes the disorder from the person and the life circumstances that have given rise to it (Westen, 2005). Generally speaking, the DSM does not highlight the roles played by systems in the emergence of problems. Some parts of the DSM do so, however, primarily with the "adjustment disorders," in which people are seen as having difficulty adjusting to environmental stressors. Further, the V-codes allow practitioners to articulate relational issues, and Axis IV is also helpful in balancing the personal and the social aspects of life.

Fifth, some feminists argue that the DSM is gender-biased, according a higher prevalence of many disorders to women (notably depression, anxiety, and many of the personality disorders) (Wiley, 2004). The DSM has been criticized for blaming women for their responses to oppressive social conditions (Blehar, 2006).

Sixth, because not all symptoms need to be met for any diagnosis to be made, two people with the same diagnosis can have very different symptom profiles. There is also an acknowledged abundance of "subthreshold cases" (those that do not quite meet the minimum number of symptom criteria), even though these may produce as much impairment as those that meet full diagnostic criteria (Gonzalez-Tejara, Canino, & Ramirez et al., 2005). This problem of a lack of specificity has been dealt with in part by the addition over time of new subtypes of disorders, and also by the introduction of severity qualifiers (mild, medium, severe).

Due to this limitation of the DSM, many people have argued that mental disorders should be assessed through a dimensional approach on a continuum of health and disorder. (Some such changes may in fact appear in DSM-V, for example in the chapter on personality disorders [APA, 2010]). Measurement instruments assess symptoms in a dimensional context rather than through a categorical system like the DSM, in which a person either meets certain criteria or does not. In this book we may occasionally mention some measures that might be useful for assessment, but the focus is on DSM diagnosis. The interested reader is encouraged to refer to other books that focus on measurement instruments (e.g., Corcoran & Walsh, 2006; Fischer & Corcoran, 2007; Hersen, 2006).

Seventh, the problem of comorbidity, in which a person may qualify for more than one diagnosis on an axis, is a point of significant confusion among practitioners. The reader will note that, throughout this book, comorbidity rates for disorders are often substantial. The DSM encourages the recording of more than one diagnosis on an axis when the assessment justifies doing so. But many disorders (e.g., anxiety disorders and depression) correlate strongly with one another (Kessler, Chiu, Demler, & Walters, 2005). It may be that an anxious depression differs from either a "pure" major depressive disorder or anxiety disorder in critical ways. In addition, research on treatment generally confines itself to people without comorbid disorders, so that results are often not generalizable to the treatment population at large.

Finally, the DSM makes no provisions for recording client strengths. Strengths-oriented practice implies that practitioners should assess all clients in light of their capacities, talents, competencies, possibilities, visions, values, and hopes (Guo & Tsui, 2010; Saleeby, 2008). This perspective emphasizes human *resilience*—the skills, abilities, knowledge, and insight that people accumulate over time as they struggle to surmount adversity and meet life challenges. In chapters 2 and 3, we will discuss the appraisal of strengths—both at individual and environmental levels.

PRACTICE TEST The following questions will test your knowledge of the content found within this chapter. For additional assessment, including licensing-exam type questions on applying chapter content to practice behaviors, visit **MySocialWorkLab.com**

1. Which of the five axes of the DSM diagnostic system is most consistent with the perspective of the social work profession?

    a. Axis I

    b. Axis II

    c. Axis IV

    d. Axis V

2. A major disparity between the social work perspective and the medical model of mental illness is:

    a. The medical model ignores the impact of environmental events on human functioning

    b. The medical model sees disorders as existing within the person

    c. Social work deemphasizes the role of biology in the development of mental disorders

    d. Social work prefers psychosocial to medication interventions

3. Lynda experienced a crisis during the seventh week of classes of her first semester at the university. She had been having trouble in her courses but was shocked to receive two Cs and two Ds. Her chronic sense of sadness became worse and for the first time in her life she started having thoughts of suicide. Before making a diagnosis for Lynda, the social worker should first:

    a. Interview her parents

    b. Review several of her school assignments

    c. Assess for the existence of any medical conditions

    d. Speak with her academic advisor

4. Assessment of a client's global assessment of functioning takes into account the present situation as compared to the recent past. In Lydia's situation, it is likely that:

    a. Her current score would likely be lower than that of her previous-year score

    b. Her current score would likely be higher than that of her previous-year score

    c. Her current and previous-year scores will likely be similar

    d. These cannot be assessed until she has been in treatment for one month

5. Diagnoses of medical conditions take priority over mental health diagnoses, but social workers often perform client assessments in agencies where medical practitioners are not available to assist. With what types of clients do you think a medical assessment is absolutely necessary?

6. Given that the DSM reflects a medical model of mental illness, construct an alternative diagnostic system consisting of three to five axes. Which may be more consistent with the social work person-in-environment perspective?

SUCCEED WITH

2

Biopsychosocial Risk and Resilience and Strengths Assessment

Competencies Applied with Practice Behaviors — in this Chapter				
■ Professional Identity	■ Ethical Practice	■ Critical Thinking	✖ Diversity in Practice	✖ Human Rights & Justice
■ Research-Based Practice	✖ Human Behavior	■ Policy Practice	■ Practice Contexts	✖ Engage, Assess, Intervene, Evaluate

This book is organized with a biopsychosocial risk and resilience framework for understanding and intervening with persons who have mental disorders. In this chapter, we first describe this framework and its advantages for social work assessment. Then we detail a number of risk and protective factors at the biological, psychological, and social levels that may contribute to mental disorders. In the last section of the chapter, we cover techniques that social workers can use to elicit and build upon strengths of individuals and their social environment, going beyond naturally occurring protective factors.

DEFINITIONS AND DESCRIPTION

Although the biological and psychological levels relate to the individual, the social aspect of the framework captures the effects of the family, the community, and the wider social culture. The processes within each level interact, prompting the occurrence of risks for emotional or mental disorders (Shirk, Talmi, & Olds, 2000) and the propensity toward resilience, or the ability to function adaptively despite stressful life circumstances. Risks can be understood as hazards occurring at the individual or environmental level that increase the likelihood of impairment developing (Bogenschneider, 1996). Protective mechanisms involve the personal, familial, community, and institutional resources that cultivate individuals' aptitudes and abilities while diminishing the possibility of problem behaviors (Dekovic, 1999). These protective influences may counterbalance or buffer against risk

11

(Pollard, Hawkins, & Arthur, 1999; Werner, 2000) and are sometimes the converse of risk (Jessor, Van Den Bos, Vanderryn, Costa, & Turbin, 1997). For instance, at the individual level, poor health presents risks while good health is protective. It must be noted that research on protective influences is limited compared with information on risks for various disorders (Donovan & Spence, 2000).

The biopsychosocial emphasis expands one's focus beyond the individual to a recognition of systemic factors that can both create and ameliorate problems. The nature of systems is such that the factors within and between them have transactional and reciprocal influence on one another, with early risk mechanisms setting the stage for greater vulnerability to subsequent risks. The development of oppositional defiant disorder and conduct disorder is a case in point that shows how the presence of certain risk or protective mechanisms may increase the likelihood of other risk and protective influences.

Although precise mechanisms of action are not specified, data have begun to accumulate that four or more risk influences may overwhelm an individual and represent a threat to adaptation (Epps & Jackson, 2000; Frick, 2006; Garmezy, 1993; Runyan et al., 1998). Although some have found that the more risks, the worse the outcome (Appleyard, Egeland, van Dulmen, & Sroufe, 2005), others have argued that risk does not proceed in a linear, additive fashion (Greenberg, Speltz, Deklyen, & Jones, 2001). Nor are all risk factors weighted equally. The associations between risk and protection and outcomes are complex and may involve changing conditions across a person's development.

The biopsychosocial framework holds a number of advantages for the assessment of mental disorders. It provides a theoretical basis for social workers to conceptualize human behavior at several levels and can assist them in identifying and bolstering strengths as well as reducing risks. The framework offers a balanced view of systems in considering both risks and strengths, as well as recognizing the complexity of individuals and the systems in which they are nested.

The chapters in this book delineate the risk and protective influences for both the onset of particular disorders and an individual's adjustment or recovery. Some of the influences discussed in each chapter are nonspecific to that particular disorder; in other words, certain risks and protective mechanisms play a role in multiple disorders. These common mechanisms, discussed at the individual and social levels, are good targets for intervention and prevention and are given an overview here.

INDIVIDUAL FACTORS

Individual factors encompass the biological and psychological realms. Within biology we will discuss genes, neurotransmitters, temperament, health, developmental stage, and intelligence. At the psychological level we will explore individual patterns of behavior.

Biological Mechanisms

Genes and heritability

Genes determine the extent of internal risk for the development of disorders (Bulik, 2004). Although information on the genetic influences of all mental disorders is not available, the disorders differ in the extent to which they are attributed to genetic causes. For instance, heritability for major depression ranges from 31 to 42% (Sullivan, Neale, & Kendler, 2000); similarly, anxiety disorders seem to be moderately heritable. Certain other disorders, such as bipolar disorder and schizophrenia, are more heritable (U.S. Department of Health & Human Services [DHHS], 1999).

For most disorders, specific genetic markers have not been delineated, and genetic models for many disorders increasingly include a number of genes rather than a single-gene theory (Williams et al., 2005). Even for disorders assumed to have genetic causes, those conditions result not only from abnormalities in inherited genes but also from certain gene combinations or other errors in genes caused during pregnancy by such events as infections and exposure to x-rays (Arc, 2007). Finally, it is widely hypothesized that a genetic vulnerability may be activated by the presence of adverse environmental events (Williams et al., 2005).

Neurotransmitters

Many people describe mental disorders as caused by "chemical imbalances in the brain." Neurotransmitters are the chemicals that convey communication between neurons. These substances are naturally regulated by breaking down in the spaces between cells or through reuptake into transmitting cells. Problems with neurotransmitter action have been associated with various mental disorders. For example, low levels of serotonin have been associated with depression, anxiety (Ebmeier, Donaghey, & Steele, 2006), and borderline personality disorder (Ni, Chan, & Bulgin, 2006), while high levels have been linked to autism (Waldman & Gizer, 2006). Inflated levels of norepinephrine have been associated with borderline personality disorder (Gurvits, Koenigsberg, & Siever, 2000), and problems with dopamine have been correlated with schizophrenia (Finlay, 2001) and attention-deficit hyperactivity disorder (ADHD) (Levy, Hay, & Bennett, 2006). However, the notion of a "chemical imbalance" as the cause of a mental disorder is a reductionistic way to view disorders, as most arise from a complex interplay of biological, psychological, and social processes. In addition, correlation should not be confused with causality. That is, psychosocial events can affect brain functioning and the action of neurotransmitters (Andreasen, 2001; Cozolino, 2002).

Temperament

Temperament provides the foundation for personality. It includes qualities that are biologically driven, observed from infancy, and moderately stable across the life span and in different contexts (Deater-Deckard, Ivy, & Smith, 2005). Temperament involves activity level, intensity, attention span, quality of mood (irritability or explosiveness), adaptability, flexibility, and rhythmicity (the regularity of sleep-wake cycles, eating, and elimination) (Barkley, 2000). To a certain degree, a child's temperament will elicit behaviors from caregivers that will crystallize these traits, which will increase the likelihood that these behavior patterns endure over time (Johnson et al., 2005). "Children who are irritable, easily distressed by changes in the environment, and more distractible may be less able to cope with adversity and more likely to attract or elicit harsh and rejecting parenting" (Deater-Deckard et al., 2005, p. 52). On the other hand, positive temperamental traits, such as good-naturedness, precociousness, maturity, inquisitiveness, willingness to take risks, optimism, hopefulness, altruism, and personableness, help people cope with life stress and attract others to them (Henggeler et al., 1998).

Another temperamental style associated with mental disorders is temperamental sensitivity, which is characterized by a range of emotional reactions toward negativity including fear, worry, sadness, self-dissatisfaction, and hostility (Donovan & Spence, 2000). This tendency predisposes people to both anxiety and depression, which often occur together. Certain temperaments may present risk or protection. For example, behavioral inhibition, which involves timidity, shyness, emotional restraint, and withdrawal when introduced into unfamiliar situations (Kagan et al., 1988, as cited in Donovan & Spence, 2000), puts a person at risk for anxiety disorders but protects against the development of oppositional defiant and conduct disorders (Burke, Loeber, & Birmaher, 2002).

Physical Health

Good physical health is a protective mechanism for many disorders; this includes perinatal health (defined as the absence of pregnancy) and birth complications (Werner, 2000). Complications during pregnancy and delivery may place individuals at risk for mental disorders, including ADHD (Bhutta, Cleves, Casey, Cradock, & Anand, 2002; Root & Resnick, 2003); eating disorders (Favaro, Tenconi, & Santonastaso, 2006); bipolar disorder (Kinney, Yurgelum-Todd, Tohen, & Tramer, 1998); and schizophrenia (Verdoux et al., 1997). Further, certain maternal behaviors during pregnancy may increase the child's risk for some disorders. A pregnant mother's prenatal drug use, excessive alcohol intake, and malnutrition during pregnancy are risk influences for the onset of mental retardation (Arc, 2007).

Cigarette smoke exposure is associated with a higher risk of school-aged children developing behavioral problems, such as hyperactivity, attention deficits, or peer relationship problems (Rückinger et al., 2010). Controlling for other social influences, children who were exposed to tobacco smoke only prenatally have a 1.9 times higher risk of developing abnormal behavioral symptoms in comparison to children without any exposure. The risk for such children first exposed to tobacco smoke after birth is 1.3 times higher. Further, children who were exposed to tobacco smoke while in the womb and while growing up had twice the risk of developing abnormal behavioral symptoms. Similarly, Ekblad, Gissler, Lehtonen, and Korkeila (2010), in a Finnish study, found that the rate of psychotropic medication use in young adults was highest in those whose mothers smoked more than 10 cigarettes a day while pregnant (16.9%), followed by youths whose mothers smoked fewer than 10 cigarettes a day (14.7%) and unexposed youths (11.7%).

Developmental Stage

Mental disorders usually emerge early in life. About 50% of cases have their onset by age 14, and 75% begin by age 24 (Kessler et al., 2005). The risk of mental disorders continues to be high through the age category 30 to 44; prevalence then declines for people who have matured out of this high-risk age range. For example, borderline personality disorder (Paris, 2003) and antisocial disorder may remit as afflicted individuals mature into their 40s.

In Werner and Smith's (2001) longitudinal study on resilience, many people whose lives had been characterized by adversity and mental health or learning disabilities in their teens were able to make a positive adjustment by age 40. Protective influences for positive adaptation involved education at community colleges, educational and vocational skills garnered during military service, a stable marriage, active participation in a religious faith, and the experience of life-threatening accident or illness.

Intelligence

A high intelligence quotient (IQ) is a protective factor, resulting in higher school performance despite life stress and more effective problem solving in peer social situations (Wachs, 2000). Conversely, low IQ is a central risk factor for antisocial behavior, over and above socioeconomic status (SES) and race. More specifically, reading and reasoning skills have been identified as critical to a child's long-term development (Werner & Smith, 2001). Parental education is also key, extending from adjustment in childhood, all the way into middle age (Werner & Smith, 2001).

Psychological Mechanisms

Self-Efficacy and Self-Esteem

Children with positive self-concepts and a self-perception, characterized by an internal sense of control, a belief that they can influence their environment, and effective coping strategies, are better equipped to face life stressors (Wachs, 2000; Werner & Smith, 2001).

Human Behavior

Practice Behavior Example: Apply theories and knowledge from the liberal arts to understand biological, social, cultural, psychological, and spiritual development.

Critical Thinking Question: Given that social workers are not proficient, by the nature of their education, in assessing clients' biological functioning, to what extent should they address biological issues in their assessments? What should be the limits of their activities in this way? Whom should they rely on for assistance in this regard to best meet the needs of a client?

Self-regulation and emotion regulation

A child who can listen, pay attention, follow instructions, and persist on a task, even if faced with stressful life events, will achieve greater success in school (Sektnan, McClelland, Acock, & Morrison, 2010). When controlling for other risk factors, children whose parents and teachers reported that they had strong self-regulation in preschool and kindergarten did significantly better on math, reading, and vocabulary at the end of first grade.

Emotional regulation refers to the ability of the child to identify, tolerate, express a range of emotions, and to be able to recover from a challenging emotional state and return to a level of equilibrium (Davila, Ramsay, Stroud, & Steinberg, 2005). The ability to self-regulate is generally assumed to evolve from secure caregiving. When caregivers are unable to regulate their children's and their own emotional states, the children do not have opportunities to develop effective strategies for responding to their own emotions or those of others.

Coping Strategies

A tendency toward rigid belief systems and certain cognitive distortions puts people at risk for mental disorders. For example, depression is related to significant cognitive distortions, such as Beck's conceptualization of the "cognitive triad" of depression: thoughts about the self as worthless, the world as unfair, and the future as hopeless (Beck, Rush, Shaw, & Emery, 1979). In addition, youth with conduct problems display distortions in how they perceive and code their social experiences (called cognitive processing) (Kazdin, 2001). These conduct problems include the inability to produce a variety of strategies to manage interpersonal problems, difficulty figuring out ways to achieve a particular desired outcome, difficulty identifying the consequences of a particular action and its effects on others, a tendency to attribute hostile motivations to the actions of others, and misunderstanding of how others feel. The combination of perceived threat and limited options for managing social situations makes antisocial youth more likely to respond with aggression rather than with more productive problem-solving strategies.

The nature of one's coping strategies is also a general risk or protective mechanism. For example, certain coping strategies are problematic for the development of anxiety and depressive disorders. One type of problematic coping pattern involves avoidance coping. For instance, anxiety disorders develop partly because individuals avoid situations that trigger anxiety. They do not allow themselves to tolerate a situation until the anxiety begins to dissipate. Unfortunately, a style of avoidance for dealing with depression might lead a person to experience more life stress and depressive symptoms as a result (Holahan, Moos, Holahan, Brennan, & Schutte, 2005).

Rumination is another detrimental coping pattern. Rumination is the proclivity to focus on the symptoms of a distressed mood, or to mull over the reasons for its occurrence in an incessant and passive way (Nolen-Hoeksema, 2002), rather than using problem-solving strategies to resolve it (Hino, Takeuchi, & Yamanouchi, 2002). It is not only the internalizing disorders that are linked with problematic coping; conduct problems in girls have also been associated with poor coping skills (Burke et al., 2002).

Interpersonal skills can also be subsumed under the category of coping strategies. These skills involve the ability to create and maintain relationships and to communicate effectively and assertively (Henggeler, Schoenwald, Borduin, Rowland, & Cunningham, 1998).

SOCIAL MECHANISMS

Family factors have a major influence on whether an individual with a biological vulnerability develops a mental disorder. For instance, family characteristics explain more of the variance in conduct disorder (Dekovic, 1999) and adolescent substance use than do any other factors (Hopfer, Stallings, Hewitt, & Crowley, 2003). Families transmit both genetic material and an environmental context for children (Wachs, 2000), although the extent to which heredity or the family environment explains its influence is not always well understood. Other important influences in the social environment include neighborhood, church, school, and other community resources available to families. The influence of each of these mechanisms will be discussed, although it is important to point out that these aspects of the community context interact with one another (e.g., schools are part of the neighborhood) and with other levels (e.g., individuals and families make up neighborhoods).

Family

Family Functioning

Several patterns are indicative of families in which mental disorders develop, among them hostility, conflict, isolation, low cohesion, enmeshment, and an absence of nurturing. Certain family variables center on the parent-child relationship. Parental rejection of the child, inconsistent and ineffective discipline, lack of supervision, and lack of involvement in the child's activities are also mechanisms of risk.

Parent-infant attachment is especially central. The developing child requires a sense of security that caregivers will respond in warm, consistent, and sensitive ways to his or her needs (Bowlby, 1969, 1973, 1980). Early attachment is hypothesized to result "in the development of 'working models,' schemata about the self, others, and relationships that will guide functioning across the life span" (Davila et al., 2005, p. 216). Indeed, attachment style has been shown to afford stability into adulthood (Hazan, Campa, & Gur-Yaish, 2006).

Further risks in the context of the family involve instability and parental conflict, such as discord, separation and family violence, and high parental stress (Loeber et al., 1998). Chronic marital discord and family violence are associated with risks to maternal mental health, increased incidence of depression and PTSD (Golding, 1999), aversive parenting practices (Krishnakumar & Buehler, 2000), and the development of mental health disorders in children (Briggs-Gowan et al., 2010). Any psychopathology afflicting parents that compromises their abilities also constitutes a risk (Steinberg, 2000). Serious mental illness in parents relates to an increased risk of mental health disorders in children (Milne et al., 2009).

Conversely, family stability, a stable parental relationship (including parental agreement on values and discipline), and social support for parents are seen as protective. Families that have effective discipline skills, healthy cohesion, and positive communication help buffer their children against the development of mental disorders. Further, adolescents whose parents provide emotional support and structure the environment with consistent rules and monitoring tend to group with peers who share similar family backgrounds (Steinberg, 2000). Supportive parenting in turn affects the characteristics of the child, in that he or she learns to regulate emotional processes and develop cognitive and social competence (Wachs, 2000). Individual characteristics of parents are also key; parents who have problem-solving ability and resourcefulness, experience low stress, and demonstrate frustration tolerance and patience are more effective in their role as parents (Henggeler et al., 1998).

Household Composition

Household composition refers to familial structure and includes size of the family, the number of parents in the home, and the spacing of children's births. Larger family size (more than three children) is a risk factor, as precious family resources are then spread among many children (Werner, 2000). Living in a single-parent family has also been identified as a risk factor. Compared to teens with married or cohabiting parents, those with divorced parents are at higher risk for a mental health disorders, especially anxiety, behavior, and substance use disorders (Merikangas et al., 2010). Whereas in two-parent families two adults can provide financial security, guidance, and emotional support, single parents are more likely to work full time and therefore are not as available for supervision, monitoring, or time spent with their children. Rapid childbearing (defined as less than a two-year spacing between children) further presents risk, as it limits the amount of time devoted to the first child (Klerman, 2004).

Another risk for some mental disorders is the structure of Western society, in which the upbringing of most children is limited to one or two primary caregivers, without additional consistent parent figures available to "fill in" when these caregivers prove to be inadequate (Alarcon, 2005). In contrast, in some cultural groups, such as Latinos and African-Americans, extended family may routinely provide major parenting roles. Western society's reliance on the nuclear family fails to provide opportunities for children to have "second chances" to develop healthy attachments when these might be developmentally beneficial. Characteristics of the extended family that offer protection include the provision of material resources, child care, supervision, parenting, and emotional support to the child (Henggeler et al., 1998).

Traumatic Events and Loss

These experiences are grouped with family factors because events such as sexual abuse and physical abuse often occur in the context of the family. Child maltreatment is a risk factor for mental health disorders in both childhood and adulthood (Scott, Smith, & Ellis, 2010). When abuse and neglect are severe, children may be removed from their own homes and placed into foster care, and these situations put them at further high risk for mental health problems (Fazel, Doll, & Langstrom, 2008). Childhood adversities (defined as physical and sexual abuse, neglect, family violence, parental mental illness, substance use disorders, and criminality) may be associated with up to 45% of all mental disorders that have an onset in childhood, and at least 25% of disorders with later onset (Green et al., 2010).

Neighborhood

Although individual and family characteristics are major contributors to child and young adult outcomes, neighborhood factors are also key (Ellen, 2000; Leventhal & Brooks-Gunn, 2003). Living in poor and disadvantaged communities creates substantial risks of antisocial behavior in children. Such risks include poverty, unemployment, community disorganization, availability of drugs, the presence of adults involved in crime, overcrowding, community violence, and racial prejudice (Hill, 2002; Loeber et al., 2000; McGee & Williams, 1999). Parenting abilities are often challenged by the many stressors that attend to living in a low socioeconomic stratum, among them unemployment, underemployment, the lack of safe child care, the lack of transportation, inadequate housing, and exposure to crime. These stressors may not only negatively affect parenting but may also inhibit access to general health and mental health care services.

An extensive review of the literature on neighborhood effects (Leventhal & Brooks-Gunn, 2003) found evidence that living in a disadvantaged neighborhood had negative consequences for young children's mental health functioning. Moreover, a large-scale study of 2,805 children found that those living in poor neighborhoods were more likely to have mental health problems, particularly internalizing disorders (Xue, Leventhal, Brooks-Gunn, & Earls, 2005). Over time, as children mature, effects become more deleterious. For adolescents, not only impaired mental health but also criminal behavior, early sexual activity, and teenage pregnancy are associated with living in poor neighborhoods (Leventhal & Brooks-Gunn, 2003).

Neighborhoods can, however, represent a source of protection. Although neighborhood peers may exert negative influences on such behaviors as drug and alcohol use and criminal activity, some studies have found that adult neighbors who offer structure and monitoring can be an important source of support for children experiencing risks in their own families (Werner & Smith, 2001). In addition to providing informal social control and social cohesion, neighbors involved in local organizations help to sustain the mental health of children who live in neighborhoods marked by disadvantages (Xue et al., 2005). Studies have also shown that middle-class and affluent neighborhoods have generally positive effects on educational attainment and achievement for adolescents, and neighbors of high SES contribute to younger children's verbal ability, IQ, and academic achievement.

Finally, frequent changes in residences while growing up is associated with poor outcomes in youth in terms of attempted suicide and suicide completion (Qin, Mortensen, & Pedersen, 2009). Repeated separations from peers and familiar activities, the stress of facing a new environment, and the potential unavailability of parents due to their own stress may overwhelm a youngster's ability to cope.

Social Support Networks

"Social support is widely viewed as a multidimensional concept and is commonly defined as the availability of a network of people on whom a person can rely in times of need. There are different types of social support (e.g., emotional, financial, informational, or enacted support)" (Hankin & Abela, 2005, p. 265). Social support networks can provide risk or protective influences. Although positive social support acts as a buffer against the development of many mental disorders, it also plays a strong role in adjustment for all the disorders discussed in this book. The number and variety of social supports (extended family, friends, neighbors, coworkers, and church members) appear to be important (Henggeler et al., 1998). For youths, such supports encourage involvement in a peer group that is engaged in prosocial activities, hobbies, and interests.

A particular type of social network involving church or religious participation has been associated with positive physical and mental health, as well as with buffering the effects of neighborhood risks (Taylor, Ellison, Chatters, Levin, & Lincoln, 2000; Werner & Smith, 2001). Religious attendance and religiosity have also been significantly associated with a decreased likelihood of drug use among adolescents (Miller, Davies, & Greenwald, 2000). In addition, for African-American youth, religious involvement may buffer the impact of neighborhood risk on criminal offending (Johnson, Jang, Li, & Larson, 2000). Research further indicates a positive relationship between religious involvement and adult health outcomes and coping with stress (McCullough, Larson, Hoyt, & Koenig, 2000).

More formal support systems may also enhance protection. Research has shown that participation in out-of-school activities and availability of community supports have positive outcomes for children in terms of educational attainment and health status. Empirically validated programs, such as Big Brothers and Big Sisters (e.g., Thompson & Kelly-Vance, 2001), Head Start (e.g., Currie & Thomas, 1995), and other youth organizations present substantial protective factors (Werner, 2000).

SOCIETAL CONDITIONS

The United States has "overarching social, political, legal, economic, and value patterns" (Greene & Livingston, 2002, p. 79) that can both contribute to individual problem situations and provide protection against risk. These macro-level influences, however, do not occur in isolation from risk and protective mechanisms at the other levels. For example, employment may open opportunities for interactions with others and expansion of social support networks, which in turn may help the family provide a safe and secure home. As noted earlier, the nature of systems is that the processes within each system influence one another.

On the protective side, social policies can have positive effects on the income and employment of individuals. For example, Social Security payments to older adults have a significant effect on reducing the percentage of those who are poor, while Medicare covers many of their major health care costs. For the working poor, economic supports include such programs as the earned income tax credit and food stamps, which help them meet household expenses (for a review of income support policies, see Scholz & Levine, 2000). Strong child-support policies have also been shown to improve the income of single-mother families (Garfinkel, Heintze, & Huang, 2001).

Poverty, discrimination, and segregation are risks that affect individual-level functioning, whereas social and income supports, tax policies, and legal sanctions provide protection against these risks. We will now explore further some of the risks associated in U.S. culture with being poor, being a member of an ethnic minority, and being female.

The Health and Mental Health Care System

In the United States, the system of mental health care consists of a patchwork of ad hoc services (DHHS). There are four chief sectors for mental health care:

1. The specialty mental health sector, including mental hospitals, residential treatment facilities, psychiatric units of general hospitals, and specialized community agencies and programs (e.g., community mental health centers, day treatment programs, and rehabilitation programs). The Substance Abuse and Mental Health Services Administration (2009) indicated that an average of 28.8 million adults received traditional types of mental health treatment (i.e., inpatient care, outpatient care, or prescription medication) in the past year. In their survey of child and adolescent mental health disorders, Merikangas and colleagues (2010) found that overall, 55% of those with a disorder had consulted with a mental health professional, which is seen as an improvement in treatment seeking from the past.

2. The general medical and primary care sector. This sector is responsible for regular prenatal care, childhood immunizations, and routine developmental screenings that protect against the development of disorders, such as mental retardation (Arc, 2007) and for the early detection of others, such as the pervasive developmental disorders. General practitioners are responsible for a great deal of medication care for persons with certain disorders, such as ADHD, depression, and anxiety. Often this means that people receive substandard care. For example, ethnic disparities in the diagnosis and treatment of depression are present in the primary care system, where many people from ethnic minority groups are served for their mental health needs (Stockdale et al., 2008).

3. The human services sector, which comprises social welfare (housing, transportation, and employment), criminal justice, educational, religious, and charitable services. It is not until some adolescents reach the juvenile justice system that they are identified as having a mental illness (Fazel et al., 2008).

4. The voluntary support network, including self-help groups and organizations devoted to education, communication, and support. An annual average of 2.4 million adults aged 18 or older (1.1% of the population) received support from a mental health self-help group in a year (Goldstrom, Campbell & Rogers, 2006; Substance Abuse and Mental Health Services Administration [SAMHSA], 2009).

Human Rights & Justice

Practice Behavior Example: *Understand the forms and mechanisms of oppression and discrimination.*

Critical Thinking Question: Consider the means by which clients are currently referred to your field placement or agency of employment. Do some types of persons experience disadvantages in their potential to be referred to the agency? Can you think of any outreach practices the agency might devise in order to attract qualifying clients who do not have easy access to its services?

Unfortunately, there is no systematic way for people to obtain needed mental health services. Often those with the greatest and most complex needs, and the fewest resources, are underserved. The lack of access to health care and health insurance is a principal factor in limiting adequate treatment for serious and chronic conditions (Tondo, Albert, & Baldessarini, 2006). For example, among people who made an effort to get treatment for substance use disorders, 42.5% reported cost or insurance barriers (SAMHSA, 2006).

Typically, people do not receive timely treatment for mental disorders. The median delay across disorders for receiving treatment is nearly a decade (Wang et al., 2005). If people are left untreated, they may be more vulnerable to future episodes that may be even more severe in nature and more resistant to treatment.

Several factors have been associated with treatment delay (Wang et al., 2005). Early onset of a disorder, defined as child or adolescent onset, is of particular concern, because untreated early-onset disorders can result in school and subsequent occupational failure, early childbearing and marriage, and marital problems. Other factors associated with treatment delay include male gender, minority status, lower education (except for substance use disorders), being married, and having social support (presumably because of lesser need for support from formal sources).

Poverty

Low SES is associated with the development of a number of mental disorders, such as oppositional defiant disorder and conduct disorder (Hill, 2002), anxiety disorders, depression, and schizophrenia (Wadsworth & Achenbach, 2005; Mulvany, O'Callaghan, Takei, Byrne, & Fearon, 2001). People of the lowest SES have a two- to threefold likelihood of having a mental disorder compared with the general population (DHHS, 2001) and this is also true of children and adolescents (Merikangas et al., 2010). Those living in poverty are more exposed to stressful circumstances such as crime; violence; availability of drugs; and lack of safe child care, convenient transportation, quality health care, and adequate housing. Poverty is a risk factor for mental retardation (MR) because of its association with malnutrition, disease, inadequate prenatal and general medical care, and environmental health hazards (Arc, 2007). The poor are also less likely to be protected against these stressors by social or material resources. Finally, because the presence of a mental disorder, such as schizophrenia, usually results in academic and occupational impairment, those with mental disorders may end up living in poverty.

Ethnicity

Overall, ethnic minorities have rates of mental disorder similar to those among the White mainstream population. Some minorities, however, especially African Americans, are overrepresented among certain subgroups that are vulnerable to mental disorders, including people who are homeless, incarcerated, or in the foster care system (DHHS, 2001). Many people in these subpopulations are not counted in national surveys of mental disorders. In addition, ethnic minorities are disproportionately poor and are therefore subject to the attendant risks that have been detailed earlier. Further, "minorities' historical and present day struggles with racism and discrimination . . . affect their mental health and contribute to their lower economic, social, and political status" (DHHS, 2001, p. 4). Perceived discrimination has a strong association with measures of stress and mental health (Kessler, Mickelson, & Williams, 1999). Moreover, "racial stereotypes and negative images can be internalized, denigrating individuals' self-worth and adversely affecting their social and psychological functioning" (DHHS, 2001, p. 39).

Even though the prevalence of mental disorders among most ethnic minority groups is similar to the White mainstream, minorities are underserved when it comes to treatment (e.g., Merikangas et al., 2010; Meyer, Zane, Cho, & Takeuchi, 2009).

As well as a lack of access to health care, minorities may hold even more stigmatizing attitudes toward mental illness than the general population, making them less likely to seek treatment (DHHS, 2001; Vegas, year). Moreover, minorities are more likely to turn to the general health care system for problems they experience. Primary care providers typically do not have the time or the expertise to diagnose and treat mental disorders, especially when their patients already have physical disorders that they can recognize and treat (DHHS, 2001). Minorities may also seek help from informal sources such as family, friends, religious leaders, and indigenous healers.

Other barriers to the treatment of mental illness include the fragmented organization of mental health services in the United States, providers' "lack of awareness of cultural issues, bias, or inability to speak the client's language, and the client's fear and mistrust of treatment" (DHHS, 2001). In addition, although the helping professions have recently begun to move toward evidence-based practice, there is a shortage of research on treatment outcomes for the major mental disorders among people from different ethnic groups (DHHS, 2001). Further, there has been a call for "cultural competence," which involves sensitivity to culture and the development of "skills, knowledge, and policies to deliver effective treatments" (p. 36). Few models of culturally sensitive services have been tested, however, so we know little about either the key ingredients needed or their effect on treatment outcomes for ethnic minorities.

Diversity in Practice

Practice Behavior Example: *Understand how diversity characterizes and shapes the human experience and is critical to the formation of identity.*

Critical Thinking Question: Consider a client who comes from a racial or ethnic group much different from your own. Do you currently have resources available that can help you better understand this client's lifestyle? Where else could you find valid information about the client's race or culture that would help you better evaluate his or her strengths and limitations?

GUIDELINES FOR ELICITING AND ENHANCING CLIENT STRENGTHS

Thus far, we have been focusing on the biopsychosocial perspective for understanding human functioning, and the fact that the risk and resilience framework is useful for providing social workers with a means of assessing the occurrence of problems, as well as strengths. We now more greatly elaborate upon the latter to prepare the social worker to help people recognize and build upon strengths they may have so that they may recover from or functionally adapt to any mental health disorders. Our view, reflected in Table 2.1, is that we must assess for both problems and strengths in the clients we see.

The first guideline for the social worker is to develop an awareness of strengths and recognize them in clients. Many possible strengths and protective influences have been identified earlier in this chapter, and each subsequent chapter lists protective mechanisms pertinent to particular disorders. These strengths should be openly conveyed to clients. Often, by the time people seek help from a social worker, the problem may have enveloped them to such an extent that they have lost sight of their resources. For example, if a person

Table 2.1	**Balanced Assessment of Strengths and Risks**	
Presenting problem	**List of symptoms** **Onset and duration**	**Emphasis on client's language** **Coping strategies** **Exceptions to the problem**
Treatment history	Previous treatment history	What was helpful/not helpful?
Personal history	Developmental milestones Medical history Diet, exercise Physical, emotional, sexual abuse	Physical, psychological, social, spiritual, environmental assets How did you cope? How were you able to survive that time? What needs to happen so that you are safe?
Substance abuse history	Patterns of use: onset, frequency, quantity Drugs/habits of choice: Consequences: physical, social, psychological	Periods of using less and periods of abstinence. What are the advantages/disadvantages of use?
Suicide risk	Previous suicide attempts Current suicidality	If you've had thoughts of hurting yourself, what did you do to get past that point? Things sounded really hard then. How did you manage? How did you stop things from getting even worse? What needs to happen now so that you feel a bit better?
Family history	Description of relationships; history of illness, mental illness	Supportive relationships
Community involvement	Legal history Neighborhood risk Problematic relationships	Cultural and ethnic influences Community participation Spiritual and church involvement Other social support Neighborhood assets
Employment and education	Educational history Employment history	Achievements, skills, and interests
Goals	Goals	Future without the problem What do you want to get out of treatment? What will your life look like when treatment is successful?

Sources: Bertolino & O'Hanlon, 2002; Graybeal, 2001.

seems to have a solid social support system, he or she needs to be told (or reminded) that this is a strength critical to adjustment. One could take this intervention a step further and ask about the resources people have used to develop these strengths. Such a client could be asked, "What would your husband say makes you a good partner?" or "Why do your friends like to be around you?"

The social worker must further be alert to the strengths individuals bring to other contexts, such as work settings (e.g., organizational skills, assertiveness, problem-solving abilities), hobbies (e.g., gardening, crafts, handiwork, sports), and pastimes (churchgoing, socializing with friends). The social worker can also ask directly about strengths: "What do you do well?" "What are your best qualities?" "What would other people say you do well or is good in you?"

It must be emphasized that when people talk about the suffering and pain they have undergone, these experiences need to be validated. They can then be asked about the resilient qualities they have shown to "make it this far, despite the pain in their life." The social worker can inquire about aspects of the client's life that are still intact despite the problem, such as relationships, hobbies, interests, employment, and academics. The social worker can plumb for the resources that were drawn upon in these areas. Inquiry can further center on personal or family qualities or strengths that have developed as a result of dealing with the illness. A quantitative review found that when people are able to find benefits after a major stressor, they experience less depression and a greater sense of well-being (Helgeson, Reynolds, & Tomich, 2006). These lines of inquiry show that many facets of difficult circumstances can be explored to find the strengths that arise with them.

Another way of validating the extent to which people have struggled is through the use of the solution-focused intervention strategy of coping questions (deJong & Berg, 2008). Questions such as the following encourage clients to reflect upon the resources they have used to manage their struggles:

- "How have you coped with the problem?"
- "How do you manage? How do you have the strength to go on?"
- "This has been a very difficult problem for you. How have you managed to keep things from getting even worse?"

A major intervention using solution-focused therapy is exception finding (deJong & Berg, 2008), which involves inquiry about symptom-free periods or times that were "a little bit better." Even the most severe mental illnesses include periods of remission or at least a reduction in symptom severity. On a daily basis, there may be at least brief periods when the problem is not as bad.

When people are seeing a social worker for help with a possible mental disorder, they tend to experience their symptoms as all-encompassing and all-consuming. For example, a depressed person typically sees the past as depressing and the future as hopeless. These are biased perceptions based on present mood. By asking questions about what the person did during these times that made a difference and the supports that were used, people get in touch with the strengths and resources on which they have drawn to deal with difficult circumstances.

Sometimes people will respond by crediting situations, events, and people outside themselves for any improvements they have made. But the social worker should find a way to allow clients to recognize their own responsibility for any changes made. For instance, if a client says he or she remained sober only while incarcerated, the social worker can respond that people who are interested in abusing substances seem to be able to still find a way to do so, even when they are "inside." So what caused them to commit to sobriety this time?

Another way to identify problem-free times is through a technique called externalizing the problem (Bertolino & O'Hanlon, 2002; White & Epston, 1990), in which a linguistic distinction is made between the presenting problem and the person. Through language, the problem behavior is personified as an external entity (*the* depression, *the* mood swings, *the* voices), rather than being seen as a dysfunction integral to the individual. The purpose is to free the person from the belief that the problem is a fixed and inherent quality. It introduces fluidity into a problem that may have become rigid and seemingly fixed, so that the oppressive nature of the problem is lifted, and more options for behavior may be revealed.

After identifying the externalized entity, the next step is to empower people to fight against it by asking what are referred to as *relative influence* questions (when do they have influence over their problems and when do their problems have influence over them?). Individuals can be invited to extend their awareness of how they combat their problems through the following questions:

- What's different about the times you're able to control the (the mental health symptoms, the diagnostic label)?
- When are you able to overcome the temptation to . . . ?
- What percentage of the time do you have control over . . . ? What are you doing during these times?

An additional technique of solution-focused therapy is to inquire about past help seeking. People with mental health problems are often demoralized by extensive treatment histories. A line of questioning such as the one detailed next offers several benefits. First, it validates people's efforts to help themselves. It acknowledges that they have been trying to overcome their problems. Second, it informs the social worker about what the client has already tried. If one already knows what is not helpful for a client, that particular intervention should not be repeated. Third, it conveys that the client is the expert on himself or herself. The following questions convey the resources people bring to past help-seeking efforts:

- What did you find helpful about previous therapy (individual, couples, family, group, etc.)?
- What did the therapist do that was helpful?
- How did that make a difference for you?
- What wasn't so helpful?

Although medication is a critical element of the treatment protocol for many mental disorders, the case for medication has sometimes been overstated. For example, less than half of consumers experience a 50% reduction in depressive symptoms as a result of being on antidepressants (Trivedi et al., 2006), and most (74%) discontinue antipsychotic medications because of the side effects they experience (Lieberman et al., 2005).

Many consumers have an external locus of control toward medication; that is, they attribute changes in their behavior to the effects of medication rather than being empowered to see the changes as a result of their own efforts and qualities. The social worker can ask questions such as these if the client is currently or has previously been on psychotropic medication:

- How was the medication helpful to you? How was it not helpful?
- What, if anything, did the medication allow you to do that you wouldn't have been able to do otherwise?
- What percentage of the change you've experienced is a result of the medication, and what percentage do you think is your own doing?
- What qualities do you possess that enabled you to work with the medication to improve things for yourself?

The social worker should further be alert for opportunities to build client motivation. Motivational interviewing, a brief treatment model (one to four sessions), was formulated to produce rapid change by mobilizing the client's motivation. It was designed for substance use disorders but adapted to other problems in which there is ambivalence about change (Miller & Rollnick, 2002).

Empathic listening and affirming statements are used in a systematic way to direct the process toward building client motivation. The social worker selectively reflects and affirms change talk and asks the client to elaborate on statements about change. Additionally, to bolster one's motivation for change (Miller & Rollnick, 2002), the social worker highlights any discrepancies between the client's values and goals, such as long-term mental health, and the problem (failing to do things that one knows will help resolve the disorder) that stands in the way of these goals.

The interested reader is encouraged to pursue other sources for more information about motivational interviewing (see Miller & Rollnick, 2002); we will emphasize one technique here, called the decisional balance, which is aimed at getting the client to weigh the advantages and disadvantages of the problem behavior. In this technique, the social worker asks the client to recount some of the pros of the problem behavior: "What do you get out of drinking?" "How is the eating disorder working for you?" When people feel someone else understands the reasons they seek out problematic behaviors, they are less likely to show defensiveness against change. The practitioner can then switch to asking about "the not so good things" about drinking/purging/isolating from social contact/not taking medication. The client then details the advantages and disadvantages of changing. The process of gathering this information provides a great deal of information about the problem behavior necessary for diagnosis. It also makes it easier for clients to argue for their own change as they weigh the pros and cons of their current behaviors and their perceptions about change.

As the final part of the assessment, the social worker can help clients to orient toward the future and build a vision of a problem-free future. Sometimes when people are mired in their symptoms, they have difficulty seeing beyond their current unhappy circumstances. Asking people what their lives will look like after their problems are solved frees them from these circumstances to consider a different future. This process may fuel a sense of hope and may also help individuals develop a blueprint for what changes need to be made. Future-oriented questions include the following:

- Imagine yourself in the future when the problem is no longer a problem. Tell me where you are, what you are doing and saying, and what others around you are doing and saying.
- When you do succeed in getting past this and are looking back on it now, what most likely is it that worked? How did it happen?

These techniques show how the social worker, while collecting relevant information for the formulation of a diagnosis, can also keep focused on the strengths and resources of the individual. People who are empowered with regard to their strengths are more likely to feel a sense of hope about themselves and their future. If strengths and resources are galvanized during the assessment process, the client can begin a process in which a different perspective (about the self, about the problem) can inspire changes in behavior. People who feel empowered and hopeful are also more motivated to engage in intervention.

Engage, Assess, Intervene, Evaluate

Practice Behavior Example: Assess client strengths and limitations.

Critical Thinking Question: Think about one or two clients you have seen in the past whose capacity for social functioning was severely impaired. Reflect on, and list, the strengths they possessed in themselves and their social contexts for making positive changes in their lives. Were you aware of these at the time you worked with them? How might you have better helped those clients become aware of their strengths?

CONCLUSION

The social work profession is distinguished by its holistic attention to the biological, psychological, and social influences on the functioning of all people. With this broad perspective, social work practitioners can complete comprehensive assessments to determine the nature of their clients' problems, which may include the mental disorders described in this book. Additionally, the social worker's knowledge of the risk and resilience influences associated with the mental disorders helps focus his or her intervention onto the relevant areas of the client's life. Finally, the strengths perspective encourages social workers to build on the client's areas of real or potential resilience in recovering from, or adapting to, mental disorders, and in so doing helps the client develop a greater sense of self-efficacy. All of these themes will be incorporated into the subsequent chapters of this book.

PRACTICE TEST

PRACTICE TEST The following questions will test your knowledge of the content found within this chapter. For additional assessment, including licensing-exam type questions on applying chapter content to practice behaviors, visit **MySocialWorkLab.com**

1. Which of the following is a strengths-based technique?
   a. Having the client consider how to manage a problem in the future
   b. Inquiring when the client feels worst, and what is different then
   c. Asking how long the problem has persisted
   d. Asking what has been helpful and not helpful about previous treatment

2. Which of the following reflects the biopsychosocial perspective toward mental disorders?
   a. Genes are the primary cause of mental disorders
   b. The balance of risks and protective factors determine a person's experience of a mental disorder
   c. Mental disorders stem from situational stresses
   d. Mental disorders are largely due to internal conflicts

3. Felicia was a single female who wanted to overcome her inability to express feelings toward men. Felicia's current boyfriend, whom she loved, was talking about breaking up with her. He complained that she did not seem to care about him. Felicia explained to the social worker that she had had a lifelong problem of being unable to express feelings of affection to men, but on the other hand, she had many close female friends and had no trouble communicating with them. With regard to the presenting problem, which of the following represents a strength of this client?
   a. She is seeking help for her problem
   b. She is managing a job responsibly
   c. She is able to communicate well to women
   d. She cares deeply about her boyfriend

4. The social worker was alert to the kinds of questions she might ask to stimulate Felicia's awareness of strengths. Which of the following questions or comments from the social worker represents a strengths perspective?
   a. Can you allow yourself some additional time to work out a solution to your problem?
   b. Have you had relationships with men in the past that have been disappointing to you?
   c. Many women experience this same problem
   d. When in the past have you been able to communicate to a man?

5. Psychological risk and resilience factors have been identified in the areas of self-efficacy and self-esteem, self-regulation and emotional regulation, and coping strategies. Describe how each of these factors may influence an 18-year-old student's transition from high school and home life to college and dormitory life.

6. Think about a time when a friend has come to you with a personal problem. How might you have utilized the strengths perspective described in this chapter to help that person feel more capable of dealing with the problem? Do you typically (although informally) use a strengths perspective when dealing with friends?

3

Autistic Disorder

Emmanuel is a five-year-old Guatemalan boy who has just started kindergarten. He is an artistic and active child who enjoys playing in the playground, listening to music, and doing puzzles. On his first day of school, Emmanuel had a hard time separating from his parents. He cried almost continuously through the day, tried to run away from the classroom and playground, and threw tantrums when the classroom teacher tried to redirect him. Emmanuel continually asked for his mom or dad and could not be calmed down. The teacher reported that he seems to have difficulty with transitions, such as from the classroom to the cafeteria, and he does not follow directions unless the teacher or her assistant directs him through the individual steps. The teacher also noted that Emmanuel appears to have difficulty in other areas of development. His speech is functional but not pragmatic, meaning that he is able to form the words necessary for speaking but cannot use them as a social tool to interact verbally with others. He does not approach other children and does not react to their attempts to play or talk.

The range of autism spectrum disorders (ASDs) includes autistic disorder itself, Asperger's disorder, childhood disintegrative disorder, Rett's disorder, and pervasive developmental disorder not otherwise specified (PDD-NOS). The *Diagnostic and Statistical Manual of Mental Disorders* (DSM-V) work group will likely recommend that the term *autistic disorder* be used to encapsulate all of these other disorders as subtypes, while removing the diagnosis of Rett's disorder from the manual (American Psychiatric Association [APA], 2010).

Autism is a neurological-developmental disorder with an onset during the first three years of life. The child with autism demonstrates severe impairments in social interaction and communication, as well as odd repetitive behaviors and restricted interests (Schreibman, Stahmer, & Akshoomoff, 2006). More than anything else, autism is characterized by impairments in social relatedness (Volkmar, Charwanda, & Klin, 2004). These include a lack of awareness of the feelings of others, an inability to express emotions, and the absence of a capacity for social and symbolic (imaginative) play. On the other hand, persons with autism often possess impressive isolated skills such as memorization, visual and spatial awareness, and attention to details.

Two other major ASDs are described here. Asperger's disorder is sometimes used to describe higher functioning individuals with autism (Akshoomoff, 2006). In Asperger's disorder, early cognitive and language development are apparently normal, but the child has unusual interests that he or she pursues with intensity. The child's attachment patterns to family members are well established, but he or she does not tend to attach to peers and new adults. Because the behavioral abnormalities are less pronounced, the child's referral for assessment is usually later than with suspected autism. The social difficulties of Asperger's disorder are lifelong, but such persons are more likely to secure employment, live independently, and establish a family (Volkmar, Charwanda, & Klin, 2004).

PDD-NOS is diagnosed in cases where there is impairment in the three areas that are "core" to autism, but the full features of autism or another PDD are not met (Koyama, Tachimor, & Osada, 2006). The deficits in social and other skills are less severe than in classic autism. The issue of whether meaningful subtypes might be defined within the broad PDD category remains a topic of debate. The limited data available suggest that such persons have a better prognosis than persons with autism (Howlin, 2005).

PREVALENCE AND COMORBIDITY

The reported incidence of autism has increased worldwide in recent years. This increase may be due to a broader application of the criteria, more frequent inclusion of other PDDs in the diagnosis, and an increased alertness to assessing children for the disorder (Shattuck & Grosse, 2007). There is even some diagnostic variability across states (Mandell & Palmer, 2005), which is believed to be an indicator of differences in the training of education professionals, the availability of pediatricians, and the accessibility of health care resources.

A review of prevalence studies indicates that autism occurs at a rate of about 7.1 per 10,000; the rate for all ASDs is about 20 per 10,000 (Williams & Brayne, 2006). The Centers for Disease Control and Prevention (Rice, 2007) found that the prevalence of ASDs was 6.6 per 1,000 children in the United States. The number of students aged 6–21 years identified in the ASD reporting category in United States special education grew between 1994 and 2005 from 18,540 to 165,552 (Safran, 2008). Autism occurs in all social classes and races, although Caucasian children are more likely to be diagnosed than African American children. The reason for this difference is not understood, but may be due to a greater likelihood for Caucasians to be evaluated for an ASD. Studies consistently find that ASDs occur more often in males than in females, with a ratio of 4.3:1 (Rice, 2007).

On average, the rate for ASDs in eight-year-old males is 11.5 per 1,000 and 2.7 per 1,000 for females. The available data suggest that children and adolescents with ASD experience a range of comorbid disorders. Precise data are not available on these rates, however, because there are no formal ASD assessment instruments that include attention to comorbid disorders (Matson & Minshawi, 2006). Common comorbid disorders include mental retardation (severe in 50% of cases, mild to moderate in 30% of cases), seizure disorders

(25 to 30%), depression (4 to 57%), anxiety disorders (7 to 84%), overactivity and attention problems (21 to 72%), and tic disorders (7 to 29%) (Bernard, Young, Pearson, Geddes, & O'Brien, 2002; Matson & Minshawi, 2006; Rice, 2007; Shopler, 2001). The likelihood of comorbid disorders is largely due to the broadly debilitating features of the ASDs, their associated medical disorders, and the problematic life experiences related to having autism. Aggression and self-injury (head banging, finger or hand biting, head slapping, and hair pulling) are common behavioral symptoms for children with comorbid pathologies. These behaviors are rarely intentional, but are due to biological factors (such as seizures), cognitive and emotional impairments (leading to impulsivity and low frustration tolerance), inability to communicate anger verbally, difficulty managing change, learned behaviors to avoid certain tasks or situations, and misreading of others' intent as threatening (Gadow, DeVincent, & Schneider, 2008).

ASSESSMENT OF AUTISM

With autism the goals of assessment are to determine first whether a child has the disorder and then to offer appropriate interventions to maximize the child's potential for change (Rogers & Vismara, 2008). Professionals must set the stage for a long-term collaborative relationship with parents and help them become better informed advocates for their child.

A recent thrust in health care is the early diagnosis of autism, so that intervention can begin as soon as possible. Early diagnosis is associated with urban residence, middle socioeconomic status (SES), pediatric referral to a specialist, having a child with severe language deficits, having an IQ of 70 or lower, and symptoms such as hand flapping and toe walking (Shattuck et al., 2009). Later diagnosis is associated with rural residence, low SES, oversensitivity to pain, hearing impairment, female gender, and having seen at least four primary care providers (Landa, Holman, & Garret-Mayer, 2007). Parental concern is a more important factor than pediatric testing in identifying a child with autism (Mandell et al., 2005). Studies show that 90% of parents of autistic children recognize a significant abnormality in the child by age 24 months (Volkmar, Lord, Bailey, Schultz, & Klin, 2004).

The symptoms of autism do not usually appear until the child is 6–12 months of age (Ozonoff et al., 2010). During the first year of life the child typically displays unusual social development, being less likely to imitate the movements and vocal sounds of others, and exhibits problems with attention and responding to external stimulation (Landa et al., 2007). Between one and three years of age, when parents are most likely to seek evaluation, differences from peers are readily apparent, and the child's idiosyncratic, self-absorbed behaviors and communication problems are striking (Harrington, Rosen, Garnecho, & Patrick, 2006). Parents report their child's regression from a higher level of functioning in 20 to 40% of cases (Volkmar, Lord, et al., 2004). Often, neurologists and developmental pediatricians are responsible for diagnosing ASDs, with primary pediatricians doing so only 12% of the time (Harrington et al., 2006). Some reasons for the low rate of pediatrician diagnosis include the physician's feeling unequipped to do so, time constraints on conducting screens, and fears of labeling a child prematurely (Dosreis, Weiner, Johnson, & Newschaffer, 2006).

Researchers at the Centers for Disease Control and Prevention found that children with ASDs were initially evaluated at a mean age of 48 months but were not diagnosed until 61 months (with no differences by gender or SES) (Wiggins, Baio, & Rice, 2006). More severely impaired children were diagnosed earlier. Most practitioners (70%) did not use a diagnostic screening instrument in the process, and 24% of children were not diagnosed until after entering school.

Professional Identity

Practice Behavior Example: *Serve as a representative of the profession, its mission, and its core values.*

Critical Thinking Question: Timely assessment is a key to the effectiveness of autism intervention. What range of needs does Emmanuel display that may require a social worker's advocacy with outside systems? In what ways can a social worker prepare to advocate for the prompt assessment of a client who is suspected of having autism?

Assessment is a challenging process, because no biochemical tests are available to assess for the disorder; nor does a single behavior or set of behaviors unequivocally denote autism (Holter, 2004). Assessment should be multidisciplinary in nature, including evaluations by a clinical or school psychologist, medical doctor, and speech and language pathologist as well as a social worker. A core assessment for autism comprises the following (Bishop, Luyster, Richler, & Lord, 2008; Johnson & Myers, 2007):

- Information from parents about the mother's pregnancy, labor, and delivery; the child's early neonatal course; the parents' earliest concerns about their child; family history of developmental disorders; symptoms in the areas of social interaction, communication/play, and restricted or unusual interests; the presence of problem behaviors that may interfere with intervention such as aggression, self-injury, and other behavioral oddities; and the child's prior response to any educational programs or behavioral interventions.
- Direct observations in structured (school) and unstructured settings (home) and in interactions with peers, parents, and siblings.
- A medical evaluation, which includes information about possible seizures, visual and hearing examinations for possible sensory problems, and testing for lead levels if the child has had exposure.
- Cognitive assessment to establish the level of intellectual functioning.
- An assessment of adaptive functioning and social skill development.
- A speech and language assessment.

Neuropsychological testing might also be indicated for children with some verbal ability in order to gain a sense of their strengths and limitations for treatment and education planning (Ozonoff, Rogers, & Hendren, 2003).

Professionals are encouraged to use formal instruments to assist in their diagnostic assessments. A variety of instruments are available for this purpose (Ozonoff et al., 2005; Volkmar, Charwanda, & Klin, 2004; Volkmar, Lord, et al., 2004). Two instruments, both clinician-administered, are considered the gold standards for assessment of autism: the Autism Diagnostic Interview-Revised (Lord, Rutter, & LeCouteur, 1994) and the Autism Diagnostic Observation Schedule (Lord, Risi, & Lambrecht, 2000). Another recommended measure is the Social Communication Questionnaire, which is a parent report version of the Autism Diagnostic Interview-Revised (Berument, Rutter, Lord, Pickles, & Bailey, 1999; Rutter, et al., 2003). Another well-known assessment tool for general disability is the Checklist for Autism in Toddlers (Baron-Cohen, Ring, & Bullmore, 2000), whereas the Pervasive Developmental Disorders Screening Test (Siegel & Hayer, 1999) and the Screening Tool for Autism (Stone, Coonrod, & Ousley, 2000) are used to assess the specific disorder of autism. Some newer instruments that assess general developmental disabilities include the Social Responsiveness Scale (Constantino & Todd, 2003) and the Children's Communication Checklist (Bishop, 1998).

Engage, Assess, Intervene, Evaluate

Practice Behavior Example: Collect, organize, and interpret client data.

Critical Thinking Question: Autism is a biologically based disorder; accurate assessment requires the expertise of many health professionals. What knowledge do social workers have that can contribute to the comprehensive assessment of autism? How might a social worker best communicate this knowledge to members of the assessment team?

Although Emmanuel started kindergarten this year and has never been in a preschool setting, he can write all letters of the alphabet, as well as his own and his sister's name. He is also able to write numbers and recite up to three-digit numbers. His spelling is artistic and almost looks like a form of calligraphy, especially his numbers. His family states that they never taught him any of these skills.

Emmanuel uses very few of his own words and sentences but repeats what other people say and sometimes recites whole conversations from cartoons (echolalia). An example of echolalia is when he answers questions like, "Are you hungry?" with "Are you hungry?"

instead of giving an affirmative or negative answer. This affects his interaction with people, as he responds the same way to questions they pose. For example, if asked, "What is your name?" his answer would be, "What is your name?" Further, Emmanuel confuses pronouns (he says, "You want to go home" instead of "I want to go home"). When upset, Emmanuel makes guttural noises or screams unintelligibly. He also seems very sensitive to certain sensory inputs, especially loud noises, such as laughter or the hubbub of many people speaking at the same time. These seem to bother him greatly, and he reacts by covering his ears and screaming as if in pain.

Generally, Emmanuel seems to have no interest in his peers. He maintains very little eye contact and does not pick up social cues. For example, he is unable to play tag because he does not understand what to do when he is it; he cannot follow his classmates' example of getting in line. He prefers to play on his own and does not engage in imaginative play. When Emmanuel gets excited, he will flap his hands rapidly, clap his thighs and crotch, and tap his face. In comparison with his peers he appears aloof or in a world of his own.

Despite his lack of social skills, Emmanuel can manage many one-on-one situations with adults. He is able to interact in a limited way with one person at a time and participates in activities suggested by that person if those activities interest him. It is in these situations that he displays what resembles a sense of humor, although he seems to be amused only by his own jokes and does not react to other people's funny remarks or faces. The social worker who assisted him during the first two days of school reports that he has very limited interests. He is content with writing numbers and letters over and over and was willing to take turns with the social worker. He appeared to enjoy naming the numbers she wrote but showed distress when she did not use the same calligraphic style of spelling that he himself used. The social worker also reported that Emmanuel frequently writes down numbers to soothe himself after getting upset.

Emmanuel's parents report that he acts rather impulsively at times. They state that he likes to "help" with chores at home. On one occasion he attempted to do the laundry and emptied a whole bottle of bleach on a basket of colored clothes, thus ruining them. They say he is not aggressive, however.

Emmanuel's school personnel completed a thorough assessment, which included a review of his medical history. They conducted a series of tests, including a speech and language evaluation, the Wechsler Intelligence Scale, the Childhood Autism Rating Scale, the Developmental Behavior Checklist, the Vineland Adaptive Behavior Scale, educational evaluation and observation, and collected his social history. These revealed an average IQ (95) but below-average language skills. Instead of using words of his own, Emmanuel employs idiosyncratic expressions. He lacks social skills and shows some developmental delays in areas of self-help and adaptation. For example, he becomes easily frustrated when he cannot unzip his jacket and does not accept certain school rules, like putting his backpack in his locker, if they go against his usual pattern of behavior.

Emmanuel comes from a caring family. Family members have been aware of Emmanuel's atypical development but related it to his lack of schooling and interaction with peers. They also report that his language development was delayed—he didn't babble until the age of two and a half. He started imitating others and reciting sentences by age four. His parents attributed this delay to the fact that two languages (English and Spanish) are spoken in the home. They assumed that this lack of consistency led to Emmanuel's difficulties with language development. At this point, his mother speaks to him in Spanish, while all other family members go back and forth between English and Spanish. Emmanuel himself speaks English, which he started using at the age of two and a half. He understands Spanish, but speaks it only when distressed.

The parents are open to treatment and agreed to the special education eligibility process. All family members demonstrate affection toward and concern for Emmanuel. His mother and sister report some inconsistency in parenting, however, as his father seems to give in to all of Emmanuel's wishes. Emmanuel is clearly his father's favorite child. His father carries Emmanuel home from school although he is a physically strong and healthy boy, and he will always interrupt his activities if Emmanuel demands his attention. His mother tries to use a more structured approach to discipline and reports letting him cry if he does not get what he wants, such as when he demands candy in a store. According to Emmanuel's mother, these differences in parenting are also a source of marital disputes.

The family resides in a three-bedroom apartment in a working-class neighborhood. The family is living in the United States legally and receives disability benefits due to the father's medical condition (a job-related leg injury). Up to this point, Emmanuel stayed at home with his father while his mother worked as a maid. His sister (age 17) attends the local community college and his brother (age 13) is a seventh grader at a public middle school. The parents understand little English and need the assistance of their daughter or a translator to engage in meetings with school personnel. Extended family live in the area, and large family gatherings are common. The family is also involved in their Catholic church and has access to support services there.

> **Directions Part I, Multiaxial Diagnosis**   Given the case information, prepare the following: a multiaxial diagnosis, the rationale for the diagnosis and global assessment of functioning score, and additional information you would have wanted to know in order to make a more accurate diagnosis.

Multiaxial Diagnosis

Axis I:
Axis II:
Axis III:
Axis IV:
Axis V:

Rationale and Differential Diagnosis

Additional Information Needed

BIOPSYCHOSOCIAL RISK AND RESILIENCE INFLUENCES

Onset

Autism is at its core a genetic, neurobiological disorder, although its specific causes have not yet been identified (Lam, Aman, & Arnold, 2006). There is no association of autism with any psychological or social influences in the absence of biological mechanisms. Still, certain populations are more at risk for the disorder because of their biological characteristics or tendency to have a later age of diagnosis (see Box 3.1). Although autism has many potential causes, in this discussion we will explore risks due to heredity and brain abnormalities.

Heredity

Evidence that autism is a neurodevelopmental disorder is indicated by the high rates of heredity transmission that have been found for ASDs. The concordance rate for autism in identical twins ranges between 36 and 91%, depending on the diagnostic criteria used (Veenstra-Vanderweele & Cook, 2003). In other family studies, 2 to 4% of siblings also

Engage, Assess, Intervene, Evaluate

Practice Behavior Example: *Substantively and effectively prepare for action with individuals, families, groups, organizations, and communities.*

Critical Thinking Question: Is it likely that a social worker will be able to engage a client with autism in a working relationship? Further, how can the social worker best engage the family of a client, given the ongoing family system stresses that arise due to the disorder? What kinds of responses from the client and family would indicate that a positive connection has been made?

Box 3.1 • Autism in Vulnerable and Oppressed Populations

Females

- Overall, ASDs are more prevalent in males than females (except for Rett's disorder), but females tend to be more severely affected because of a greater likelihood of mental retardation.[1]

Low SES

- Low SES is one of the factors associated with later diagnosis of autism.[2]

[1]Smith, Magyar, & Arnold-Saritepe, 2002.
[2]Mandell et al., 2005.

develop autism, which is 50 times more likely than in the general population, and up to 90% of siblings of children with autism are diagnosed with one of the spectrum disorders (Matson, Nebel-Schwaim, & Matson, 2007).

The research suggests that different genes (perhaps 3 to 10 of them) and the variety of ways they can be manifested contribute to the symptoms of ASD (Liu, Paterson, & Szatmari, 2008). To date there is some evidence for three loci, in chromosomes 7q, 13q, and 15q (Happe & Ronald, 2008). In general, the strongest evidence points to the following chromosomes:

- #2, which includes genes that control growth and development early in life.
- #7, which includes a region that pertains to speech and language.
- #13 and #15, both of which include genes that, when damaged, can cause behavioral symptoms associated with autism.
- #16, which is associated with tuberous sclerosis, a rare genetic multisystem disorder characterized by seizures, mental retardation, and skin lesions.
- #17, deficiencies that are associated with metabolic and serotonin deficiencies.
- The X (or sex-specific) chromosome, associated with Rett's syndrome and fragile X (a syndrome of mental retardation that features a variety of physical abnormalities).

In one recent study of several hundred subjects, it was found that advanced paternal age (over 40), when the mother was under 30, was associated with an increased risk of ASD (Reichenberg et al., 2006). A subsequent study found that advanced maternal age is also a factor, regardless of the father's age, with an 18% increase in risk for every five years of maternal age, beginning in the mid-20s (Shelton, Tancredi, & Hertz-Picciotto, 2010). Possible biological mechanisms include mutations associated with advancing age or alterations in genetic imprinting.

Brain Abnormalities

Approximately 60 to 70% of persons with autism experience distinct neurological abnormalities and some degree of mental retardation (Ozonoff, Goodlin-Jones, & Solomon, 2007). Several relevant brain abnormalities have been identified. Brain imaging studies indicate that autism is associated with enlarged overall brain size (as much as 10% larger than nonautistic toddlers) and decreased size and activity in specific areas of the brain (Hutsler & Zhang, 2010; Volkmar, Lord, et al., 2004). These areas possibly include the midsagittal area of the cerebellum, thought to be involved in the sequencing of motor activities; the lower hippocampus (in the midbrain), associated with complex learning processes; the amygdala (located in the temporal lobe), which is believed to contribute to the recognition of faces and emotional expression; and a portion of the brain stem associated with attention. Children with autism may have an overgrowth of neurons, coupled with an underdeveloped organization of neurons into specialized systems in some areas of the brain, although findings have not received consistent replication.

Problems in a number of neurotransmitter systems (the chemicals in neurons that send messages to each other) include serotonin, dopamine, norepinephrine, acetylcholine, oxytocin, endogenous opioids, cortisol, glutamate, and gamma-aminobutyric acid (GABA) (Lam et al., 2006). Overall, the most empirical evidence for a role in autism points to serotonin. There is less support for the notion that dysfunctions of norepinephrine or the endogenous opioids are related to autism. The role of dopamine has not been shown to be compelling thus far, though conflicting findings suggest a need for further study. Promising new areas of study include possible dysfunction of the cholinergic system, oxytocin, and amino acid neurotransmitters. There is also a need for studies that control for subject variables such as race, gender, and pubertal status.

With regard to deficits in brain functioning, autism has been conceptualized in various ways (Volkmar, Lord, et al., 2004), among them the following:

- A disorder of *central coherence*, in which the person is unable to process information holistically and instead develops a bias toward part-oriented processing.
- A disorder of executive function, in which the person is unable to process bits of information or regulate behavior, and is thus inclined toward rigid, repetitive behaviors and impoverished interactions.
- A deficit in social cognition, in which the person fails to understand the internal mental states of other people and has difficulty making attributions of mental states to others and themselves.

Course of Autism

Advances in nervous system assessment may eventually facilitate more effective interventions for autism's core symptoms, but for now social workers can best focus on the adjustment of persons with autism. With early detection and intervention, the prognosis for autism seems to improve.

Currently, one third of children with autism ultimately achieve some level of independence and self-sufficiency in adulthood, while two thirds require intensive care (Billstedt, Gillberg, & Gillberg, 2005). Studies on the course of ASD over time show variable results that depend on the severity of the condition. Several relevant prospective studies have been conducted in Sweden. In one study, children who had been diagnosed with autism or atypical autism (N = 120) were assessed in adulthood (Billstedt et al., 2005). The majority (57%) was categorized as having a very poor outcome. No statistically significant differences existed between the autistic and the atypical autism group. The next common outcome was "poor" (21%) followed by "restricted" (13%), and "fair" (8%). None of the persons from the autistic or the atypical autism groups had a "good" outcome. In another prospective study, Swedish men with Autism or Asperger's disorder were followed for five years after diagnosis (Cederlund, Hagberg, Billstedt, Gillberg, & Gillberg, 2008). In the majority of cases of persons with Asperger's disorder the diagnosis was still valid (84%), and even those without the ongoing diagnosis showed impairment. About a quarter of the Asperger's sample had a poor outcome, despite their having average IQs. Outcomes were worse for persons in the autism group, with the majority (76%) having poor to very poor outcome. The intellectual level was much lower among those in the autism study group, where only five (7%) persons had a normal intellectual capability at follow-up.

In the United States, a sample of 48 children diagnosed with autism was followed up in late adolescence (McGovern & Sigma, 2005). Almost all persons were still diagnosed with an ASD, but their parents described improvements in the areas of social interactions, repetitive, repetitive or stereotyped behaviors, adaptive behaviors, and emotional responsiveness to others' distress. Adults with autism who were able to live independently and hold jobs typically had high levels of cognitive and communication skills despite their persistent social deficits. Barnhill (2007) studied the course of Asperger's disorder into adulthood and found that those persons who achieved adaptive functioning levels continued to experience some impairment in employment, perception, social isolation, motor skills, and mood, with depression being a common condition.

Other than the timing of intervention, protective influences for the course of autism and other ASDs include later age of onset (after 24 months) as well as the child's early acquisition of nonverbal communication, functional play skills, and speech capacity (Volkmar, Lord, et al., 2004). Unfortunately, 50% of the autistic population does not develop speech, and a majority fails to use speech in a functional manner. Another protective influence on the course of the disorder is the quality of parents' interactions with their children, which may affect the development of language skills over time. In one 16-year longitudinal study, parents' level of parallel participation during play with their children had a positive impact on the development of the child's language skills (Siller & Sigman, 2002).

> **Directions Part II, Biopsychosocial Risk and Protective Factors Assessment**
> Formulate a risk and protective factors assessment, both for the onset of the disorder and for the course of the disorder, including the strengths that you see for this individual.

INTERVENTIONS FOR AUTISM

Comprehensive interventions for children with ASDs include small-group or one-on-one behavioral and educational interventions, delivered for at least 10 to 15 hours per week for periods of time ranging from months to years (Shattuck & Grosse, 2007). Unfortunately, no intervention has been shown to change the core features of ASD to an extent that the person is able to achieve normative levels of functioning. After a thorough diagnostic evaluation, however, steps may be taken to help the individual function with significant gains. The range of interventions should include special education, family support, behavioral management, and social skills training (for persons with higher functioning ASD). Medications may be used to control behavioral symptoms, but considerable caution should be exercised when doing so. Some complementary and alternative medicines are available that some parents find appealing.

Special Education

Federal law mandates the provision of an Individualized Educational Plan (IEP) for all children with autism. Ancillary services such as speech or language therapy, occupational therapy, and physical therapy are often required as a part of this plan (Volkmar, Lord, et al., 2004). Continuous programming, including summer programming, is more effective than episodic intervention, because children with autism often regress in the absence of services. Professionals should be prepared to collaborate with teachers and other school personnel and to work with parents to obtain appropriate educational placements and other community resources (Holter, 2004).

Family Education, Support, and Involvement

Parents should always be encouraged to participate in programs for their ASD children, to enhance consistency in intervention at home and at school and to facilitate the child's generalization of skills across settings (Rogers & Vismara, 2008). Further, grandparents often play major roles in the detection of symptoms and family support

(Hillman, 2007). Family members can also be invited to join various parent and family groups for information and support. Many programs are parent-mediated, meaning that the parental caregiver takes on a primary intervention role. A systematic review of parent-implemented early intervention for ASD was undertaken by McConachie and Diggle (2007); 12 studies were located. The authors concluded that parent training leads to improved child communicative behavior, increased maternal knowledge of autism, enhanced maternal communication style, enhanced parent-child interaction, and reduced maternal depression.

Behavioral Management

Applied behavior analysis (ABA), first developed by Lovaas (1987, 2003) involves the examination of the antecedents of a problem behavior (the event or situation that precedes the behavior) and its consequences (the event or situation that follows the behavior). Any avoidable antecedents for a problem behavior are removed, and desirable behaviors are taught, followed by positive reinforcement for the child's performance. Seida et al. (2009) conducted a review of the meta-analyses and systematic reviews for autism interventions. The review supported ABA in terms of improvements in adaptive, cognitive, and language skills, as well as reductions in problem behavior. A later systematic review also found that cognitive behavior therapies consistently yielded positive outcomes (Lang, Register, Lauderdale, Ashbaugh, & Haring, 2010).

Rogers and Vismara (2008) conducted a review of the last 10 years of research on autism interventions, and two were found to be "probably efficacious." One of these is the intensive behavioral treatment program developed by Lovaas (1987, 1993), involving one-on-one assistance 40 hours a week. The other intervention is known as pivotal response training (PRT), a type of ABA taught to parents that focuses on "pivotal" aspects of the child's functioning, including motivation, self-management, initiation of interactions, and the ability to select cues that are relevant in a given situation. PRT earned its rating based primarily on single-subject studies, although a recent larger study was done on a diverse sample (Baker-Ericzén, Stahmer, & Burns, 2007).

Still, the results of studies of treatment programs for autism in general indicate that they are not as effective as once hoped (Matson & Minshawi, 2006). One limitation involves the challenge for families of maintaining the intensity recommended by some programs (such as the number of hours of face-to-face involvement and regular use of specific exercises). Still, despite various methodological flaws, a sufficient number of replications exist to declare ABA methods "promising."

Medication

The core features of autism do not respond to medication. Drug intervention, however, may help control the symptoms of aggression, self-injury, inattention, and stereotyped movements (Volkmar, Lord, et al., 2004). It is estimated that 27% of persons with autism take one medication, and 46% of those persons receive two medications (Matson & Hess, 2011). A majority of persons with autism take either a psychostimulant drug or risperidone, although side effects for the latter drug (weight gain and drowsiness) are a concern.

The effectiveness of the selective serotonin reuptake inhibitor (SSRI) medications for adults (but not children) supports evidence that autism and ASDs are associated with abnormalities in serotonin function (Leskovec, Rowles, & Findlay, 2008). For repetitive and maladaptive behavior in adults, fluvoxamine has been found effective, and fluoxetine has been validated for children's repetitive behavior (Posey, Erickson, Stigler, & McDougle, 2006). Still, children appear to be more sensitive to the adverse effects of the SSRI medications (including agitation), and the weight of evidence to support their use is weak. Other medications, such as the anticonvulsants, have been used to regulate the behaviors of persons with autism, but there is no compelling evidence for their utility at present (Oswald & Sonenklar, 2007). Empirical evidence for significant reductions in hyperactive symptoms is strongest for the antipsychotic drugs (particularly risperidone) and the psychostimulants. There is some evidence of the effectiveness of risperidone in treating irritability, aggression, self-injury, and temper tantrums, often without inducing severe adverse reactions (Jesner, Aref-Adib, & Coren, 2007).

Social Skills Training

Interventions emphasizing social skills developments for persons with autism have emerged as a major theme in the treatment literature in recent years (Matson & Minshawi, 2006). Much of this literature has focused on somewhat older children. These interventions can be carried out through integrated peer groups, classwide interventions, adult social groups, and videotapes to help the clients perceive themselves as they try to gain new interactional skills.

Complementary and Alternative Treatments

The National Center for Complementary and Alternative Medicine organizes its therapies into four domains: mind–body medicine, biologically based practices, manipulative and body-based practices, and energy medicine. Approximately half of families of children with ASD use a biologically based therapy (e.g., dietary supplements), 30% use a mind–body therapy (e.g., music therapy), and 25% use a manipulation or body-based method (e.g., auditory integration) (Hanson et al., 2007). Hanson et al., 2007. Reported that 41% of respondents endorsed the benefits of dietary and nutritional treatments, whereas Wong and Smith (2006) reported that 75% of respondents found their complementary and alternative treatments were helpful.

Engage, Assess, Intervene, Evaluate

Practice Behavior Example: Critically analyze, monitor, and evaluate interventions.

Critical Thinking Question: Single-subject designs are well suited for behavioral interventions. Which of Emmanuel's behaviors could be tracked through this method? Would some of those behaviors be better indicators of overall client progress than others?

Interventions for Adolescents and Adults

For adolescents, intervention emphasis should be placed on adaptive and vocational skills to prepare for independent living. Sexual development in adolescence brings some additional behavioral problems, which may be addressed using education and behavioral techniques. Such techniques include teaching basic social skills through operant conditioning (introducing oneself, responding to requests, not touching other persons inappropriately) (Holter, 2004). Among adults, the identification of community resources and supports for long-term care planning is critical. Such resources may include foster homes, semi-independent living situations, living with parents who may qualify for income supplements and insurance, and supervised group living (NIMH, 2007).

Directions Part III, Goal Setting and Treatment Planning   Given your risk and protective factors assessments of the individual, your knowledge of the disorder, and evidence-based practice guidelines, formulate goals and a possible treatment plan for this individual.

CRITICAL PERSPECTIVE

Autistic disorder may be better conceptualized as a continuum of disorders, with varying degrees of impairment that imply different interventions (Volkmar, Lord, et al., 2004). The DSM-IV does not distinguish between these levels of impairment, and it is often difficult to establish a diagnosis of autistic disorder that is clearly distinct from the other ASDs, which include Asperger's disorder, and PDD-NOS. Due to the symptom overlap between the various PDD disorders, it is debated whether autistic disorder is truly distinct from the others. Further debate ensues over the significant distinctions between high-functioning autism and Asperger's syndrome, and few studies find clear support for separate classifications (Kasari & Rotheram-Fuller, 2005).

As a result of the diagnostic difficulties described earlier, there is some disagreement as to whether autism should be assessed using a categorical (as in DSM-IV) or a dimensional classification system (Volkmar, Lord, et al., 2004). In DSM-IV a client either does or does not qualify for a diagnosis. A dimensional system would allow professionals to identify levels of disability more clearly in each of the core areas of autism and thus consider ASDs along a single spectrum of ability and disability. For this reason the DSM-V work group is considering conceptualizing all of the spectrum disorders as variants of "autistic disorder" (APA, 2010).

Directions Part IV, Critical Perspective   Formulate a critique of the diagnosis as it relates to this case example. Questions to consider include the following: Does this diagnosis represent a valid mental disorder from the social work perspective? Is this diagnosis significantly different from other possible diagnoses? Your critique should be based on the values of the social work profession (which are incongruent in some ways with the medical model) and the validity of the specific diagnostic criteria applied to this case.

Case 2   The Chung Family

Hao, a five-year-old child whose parents emigrated from Vietnam many years ago, was recently expelled from his parochial school kindergarten class and advised to seek placement at the public school. The reason for the expulsion was his inability to relate to other children in class, incessant hand washing, and inability to follow instructions. Hao could not follow the classroom routine and would stay only for activities in which he was interested, such as those focusing on math or science topics. At times he would grow so frustrated with what he saw as disruption to his favored activities that he had temper tantrums at school. His parents, Lang and An, are extremely disappointed and upset over Hao's expulsion and are not sure what the future holds for him.

Lang and An had no previous thoughts of seeking out services for their son until now. It was only when Hao faced the structure of the kindergarten day that problems emerged. Lang, a 43-year-old Vietnamese woman and primary informant during this assessment, enrolled Hao in preschool at the age of four and did notice at that time that Hao was not connecting personally with other children. She said, "Hao only wanted to play alone. He ran around the yard while other children played together." But when Lang asked the teachers about this, they said that Hao was a sweet little boy who displayed no unusual behaviors and that all children mature at different rates. Lang believes that the preschool teachers' patience served to elicit positive behavior from Hao. Hao thrived in preschool and responded well to the staff's consistent positive reinforcement. Hao never had a tantrum in preschool.

Lang tried for years to conceive before having Hao. She was able to access quality prenatal care and experienced a good pregnancy and vaginal delivery with no complications. Hao was a healthy infant, who weighed 7 pounds, 4 ounces, at birth. Hao walked at 11 months of age, had a vocabulary of about 20 words when he was 18 months (which is considered normal), and was toilet trained at 24 months of age. He also began to read at 24 months of age and learned how to use a computer before he was 36 months old. Hao now dedicates a significant portion of time to figuring out how to operate minute functions on the computer, fixing computer parts, and playing math and science games on the computer.

Hao is also gifted musically. He can play a song on his electric keyboard after hearing it only once. Hao was recently tested and found to have an IQ of 130. Hao was extremely interested in the testing process, asking questions about the instruments and questions. Sometimes he would ask the psychologist questions in response to her questions.

Lang appreciates the importance of Hao's gifts and nurtures his curiosity with books, musical instruments, and computer games. At the same time, she and An are both concerned about these attributes in terms of their impact on Hao's relationships with others. They believe Hao functions at such a high level that he would alienate peers by obsessing about his computer and academic pursuits and not just playing like a normal five-year-old.

Lang encourages Hao to dress himself, select his own breakfast (he is able to pour his own cereal and milk), and care for his books and toys. Hao needs help buttoning his clothing and tying his shoes because of a slight delay in fine-motor skills.

Lang notices a difference between her more compliant nieces and nephews and Hao, who would prefer to follow his own set of rules rather than those set forth by his family. Lang states that mealtimes are especially difficult for their family, because Hao refuses to sit for longer than two minutes and ignores them when they speak to him. Lang and An value order, not unlike most Vietnamese parents, according to Lang; Hao's frequent disruptions during meals are difficult to bear. Hao sits for two minutes at a time and then gets up to draw or write in his notebook. When he does sit at the table, Hao takes over an hour to finish a meal that should take 30 minutes to eat.

Hao tends to ignore his parents when they try to discipline him. When Hao does not follow instructions, he is responsive to time-outs, strong verbal communication, and direct eye contact from Lang. Time-outs have proved a deterrent to disruptive behavior, as Hao hates receiving time-outs. Lang and An try to be consistent in their approach to discipline. When asked how she has managed to be patient and firm with Hao in the face of his erratic behavior, Lang stated that it is very difficult but she has to do it in order to be a good mother for Hao. She stated that Hao needs extra attention and patience and that her faith helps her through tough times.

Hao has suffered from severe allergies since he began eating solid foods. Hao is allergic to peanuts, eggs, and milk and breaks out in eczema as a result. Lang and An are closely involved with Hao's pediatrician, and Lang constantly monitors his food intake. As a result, Hao has suffered few outbreaks of eczema in recent years.

Every Saturday and Sunday An brings Hao to the park, where they enjoy playing basketball, soccer, and other sports. An becomes frustrated with Hao's excessive laughter during these activities. At times An loses his patience and threatens to leave the park. Lang indicated that Hao's loss of control is unacceptable in the Vietnamese culture; children are expected to be more in control of their emotions by the time they are Hao's age.

Lang and An are healthy and report no chronic physical or mental illness in themselves or their own families. Lang is a high school graduate who is a trained hairdresser, and An is a college graduate currently working as an information technologist. They enjoy a financially secure life and comfortable existence. Lang has been able to stay home and care for Hao because of this financial security but is excited about getting back into hairdressing. She knows that she will be much happier when she is cutting hair again, in that she will have a personal and professional outlet.

As An works long hours, Lang bears the brunt of the responsibility for Hao. She complains of feeling exhausted and helpless. This difficulty has placed an occasional strain on Lang's marriage with An. Lang feels relieved when her husband is available to help.

An cooks dinner on weekends and will sometimes use his flex-leave to take Friday off, which allows Lang to have time to herself.

On weekends, Lang and An spend time with An's family. Lang enjoys this time, as she has a positive relationship with them. They eat meals and enjoy birthday parties together, and sometimes Lang will go shopping with her sister-in-law.

Hao has 11 first cousins. Hao sees them almost every weekend for birthdays, at church, and during dinner get-togethers. Hao and his first cousin, six-year-old Thanh, get along well, although Hao tends to focus too much on academics with Thanh. This irritates Lang, who picks up on Thanh's lack of interest, but Hao is unable to see it. Lang will at times firmly instruct Thanh to ignore Hao's questions about math, science, and reading, suggesting other toys and games they might enjoy instead. Hao's aunts and uncles don't always understand why his parents encourage his "different" personality and express distaste over what they perceive as his unusual habits.

Lang summed up her feelings about Hao's most pressing issue. Lang emphasized that while Hao is gifted intellectually, he is not developing socially. Lang stated, "I don't care if he is smart. How is he going to have friends and someday find a wife if he is this way?"

Lang explained that both she and her husband were "boat people." She escaped from Communist Vietnam 25 years ago and spent three years in Cambodia until she was able to locate a family member in the United States who was able to sponsor her. An had arrived in the United States five years before Lang arrived. The couple met in the United States and married 15 years ago. Lang stated that her faith in God and her determination helped her to persevere through many difficult obstacles when trying to come to the United States.

For Lang, An, and Hao, English is their second language. Vietnamese is spoken in the home, and the family holds traditional Vietnamese values. For example, Lang explained that family cohesiveness, spirituality, and work are important to them.

Lang reported that in Vietnam, Hao's behavior would be considered completely unacceptable and totally outside the norm. She stated that she was able to think "less Vietnamese and more American" about Hao when she observed the patience of American teachers in managing Hao. She is hopeful about the future and recognizes that she and An would not be receiving the support for Hao in Vietnam that they receive here. In Vietnam children are warned against bad behavior by being threatened with a wooden spoon. Often, children are hit with the spoon if they continue to misbehave. Lang reports that she has threatened Hao with the spoon only occasionally. Lang stated that when Hao misbehaves she gets down on her knees, uses direct visual contact, and speaks firmly. Lang has used time-outs successfully in the past and will continue to use them.

Lang, An, and Hao are devout Catholics and rely heavily on the guidance of their faith. Lang indicates that she prays often and speaks to her priest when she feels overwhelmed. Lang indicated that her priest has helped her to understand Hao better and told her that God made Hao and he should be accepted and loved. Lang gets a great deal of support from her priest and is able to find strength and patience through prayer. Lang sometimes prays at the dinner table when Hao is not cooperating and reports that it helps her not lose her patience with him. Lang often engages Hao in prayer to remedy his inattentiveness. This approach generally works, and Lang reports that Hao will sit and pray with her for periods of up to a minute or two.

Observations of Hao in his kindergarten classroom revealed that he speaks very loudly and in close proximity to other people's faces. The teacher says that he is unable to retain her instructions about standing back or speaking more quietly. Typically, Hao flatly looks off into space while the teacher speaks. His face displays little emotion. He does not react to questions or comments made by the teacher.

Please go to the Appendix for directions to this case.

Case 3   The Kindergartener

DeShon Johnson is a five-year-old African American male kindergarten student who has been referred to his school's Child Study Team. He is distant and aloof, does not relate to classmates and his teacher, and rarely makes eye contact. He does not play imaginatively like the other children in his class, although his mother says he entertains himself well, usually playing with small household items such as kitchen utensils, pencils, or small toys such as matchbox-style cars, for hours on end. He also likes being outside.

His mother reports that at times DeShon easily becomes frustrated, upset, and defiant—crying, screaming, and throwing himself to the floor—especially when having to transition from one activity to another. These tantrums last from 5 to 30 minutes and occur once or twice per day. DeShon's mother and her boyfriend react to these tantrums by either ignoring, yelling, or spanking him. Nothing, according to his mother, changes the nature of his tantrums.

At most times, his affect is flat. He is sensitive to tactile experiences, particularly with regard to food texture. For example, DeShon refuses to eat any food items that are crunchy or hard in consistency. He likes soft foods, such as yogurt, bananas, and soggy cereal. Although DeShon does talk, he displays echolalia, often repeating what others say to him. He also rocks back and forth and waves his hands in front of his face.

According to his mother, Ms. Turner, DeShon's birth history was normal, and he was healthy upon delivery. His mother stated that she became somewhat concerned about her son when he was between 18 and 24 months of age. She noted that DeShon's speech, which had apparently been developing relatively normally, stopped progressing. The little eye contact that DeShon had previously made became even less frequent. She also noted that DeShon seemed increasingly uninterested in social interaction, even with her, his older siblings, and others with whom he was quite familiar. Toilet training was reportedly an extensive, time-consuming, and difficult process for DeShon. Despite these concerns, DeShon did not receive consistent medical care and follow-up on referrals to specialists because of the family's frequent moves, lack of financial resources, and temporary homelessness. Consequently, DeShon entered kindergarten with no formal diagnosis or treatment plan.

DeShon Johnson resides with his mother, her male partner, and two older teenage siblings. Ms. Turner is 30 years old and attended school until the eighth grade, when she became pregnant with DeShon's 15-year-old brother. Each of her children has a different biological father. She is currently unemployed but has occasionally worked in the food services field. DeShon's biological father (Torrence Brown) is 39 years old and has been intermittently incarcerated since the age of 15 for drug charges. He has sporadic contact with DeShon and provides no financial support.

The family has Medicaid health coverage. However, DeShon's mother tends to let coverage lapse for a few months each year because she does not complete the required renewal paperwork in a timely manner. At the same time, DeShon's mother is fairly familiar with social services agencies and how to get assistance and financial help when she is in a tight spot.

Ms. Turner's boyfriend is 38 years old and has a tenth-grade education. At times he is employed as a painter. He has lived with the family off and on for approximately three years but has two children in other households living with their respective mothers.

DeShon's mother is able to meet the basic needs of her children: food, clothing, bathing, and shelter. While she obviously loves her children, she is inconsistent in disciplining them. She and her boyfriend often become frustrated with DeShon's challenging behaviors and communication difficulties and tend to rely on yelling and spanking for discipline.

Ms. Turner's stepmother and her aunt and uncle offer emotional support to the family; in addition, she sees other extended family members on occasion, perhaps several times per month. However, most members of her family are also struggling financially, so they are not able to offer financial aid.

The family lives in an apartment complex near DeShon's school. Although some parents in this area are reluctant to allow their children to play outside due to potential danger, DeShon's mother perceives the neighborhood as being much safer than some of her past neighborhoods.

DeShon attended no preschool or day care prior to entering public kindergarten as a five-year-old. During the first few days of school, DeShon's teacher recognized that not only had DeShon lacked exposure to any form of structure in his young life, but he seemed unusually detached from social interactions. This veteran teacher realized that DeShon was likely developmentally delayed, and she immediately referred him to the Child Study Team for an evaluation.

Upon learning of his behavioral characteristics and history, the Child Study Team recommended that DeShon undergo full assessments—psychological, educational, and sociological evaluations. This school system provides comprehensive services to children with special needs, and the special education teachers are experienced and dedicated. DeShon's mother is willing to seek and accept whatever assistance the school can offer.

Testing showed that DeShon has an IQ of 60 and that his strongest learning style is through visual means. His receptive listening skills are very poor. A medical exam indicated no known physical conditions that could have caused his current symptoms.

Please go to the Appendix for directions to this case.

PRACTICE TEST The following questions will test your knowledge of the content found within this chapter. For additional assessment, including licensing-exam type questions on applying chapter content to practice behaviors, visit **MySocialWorkLab.com**

1. The defining feature of the pervasive developmental disorders is:
   a. Odd repetitive behaviors
   b. Restricted interests
   c. Social impairments
   d. Communication problems

2. Current research on the development of pervasive developmental disorders holds that:
   a. Biological mechanisms responsible have been clearly identified
   b. A range of possible biological mechanisms have been put forward
   c. They are due to parenting style
   d. Vaccines are a primary cause

3. Wesley, a 15-year-old Asian male, was diagnosed with autism at age three. He did not babble as a baby, did not talk as a toddler, and had always had long, violent tantrums. He often engaged in out-of-control behavior when he was denied access to a desired item or wanted attention from others. Both his parents and teachers reported that he had never been capable of basic interaction with peers. Wesley was diagnosed with autistic disorder rather than Asperger's disorder because:
   a. His symptoms had an early onset
   b. He had restricted interests
   c. His intellectual functioning and speech development were significantly impaired
   d. He experienced severe social impairment for a boy his age

4. Wesley was identified as a good candidate for applied behavioral analysis. This intervention philosophy is best represented by:
   a. Family intervention to make sure that Wesley's parents were acting in a consistent manner toward him
   b. Surrounding Wesley with higher functioning peers who could model appropriate behavior for him
   c. Initiating a token economy system to increase Wesley's communication and decrease his harmful behaviors
   d. Introducing medications to reduce Wesley's level of agitation

5. Consider the three clients described in this chapter. Speculate on their potentials for eventual successful community living (supervised or not, but away from the family of origin). Describe the supports and agency services that would be needed to arrange this.

6. Design an appropriate weekly, 10-week, time-limited support group intervention for family members of persons with autism. Include a week-to-week schedule of topics and provide a justification for their selection.

SUCCEED WITH

Visit **MySocialWorkLab** for more licensing-exam test questions, and to access case studies, videos, and much more.

4

Attention-Deficit Hyperactivity Disorder

Competencies Applied with Practice Behaviors — in this Chapter				
☐ Professional Identity	☐ Ethical Practice	☒ Critical Thinking	☐ Diversity in Practice	☐ Human Rights & Justice
☒ Research-Based Practice	☒ Human Behavior	☐ Policy Practice	☐ Practice Contexts	☐ Engage, Assess, Intervene, Evaluate

Mrs. Bronsky, a 32-year-old Caucasian woman, brought her two children—Pauline, age 10, and Billy, age 8—to the agency because her new husband's 15-year-old nephew had sexually abused them.

Mrs. Bronsky says that Billy has always been a difficult child, independent of the sexual abuse. When asked to do chores or homework or given any instruction, he argues and refuses point blank. If he is doing something annoying to his mother, such as banging a toy against the wall and creating scuff marks, he keeps doing it, almost as if he enjoys getting on everyone's nerves.

His teachers report that Billy argues about teacher commands and refuses to do schoolwork. When teachers correct him on misbehavior, he blames classmates. Not surprisingly, he has always received poor conduct grades in school. He has also just barely passed each grade and is currently scraping by. His math and science grades are now at the failing level. Mrs. Bronsky says that he has not undergone any testing at the school; nor does he have an Individualized Education Plan (IEP). However, his teacher has suggested that Billy take Ritalin. Mrs. Bronsky states that she doesn't want her son on medication and has heard that some herbal remedies might help him. She admits that Billy does seem to have some difficulty keeping his attention on tasks. He is easily distracted (looking out the window at school and getting involved with what is happening out there rather than what the teacher is saying), doesn't seem to be listening when someone tells him something (but Mrs. Bronsky suspects that he's purposely being difficult), and loses and forgets things (his math book, his homework, or what the teacher has told him). Again,

Mrs. Bronsky thinks that these are purposeful behaviors to avoid the work rather than actual forgetfulness.

Attention-deficit hyperactivity disorder (ADHD), one of the disruptive behavior disorders, is characterized by a chronic pattern of *inattention* or *hyperactive/impulsive behavior* (or both) that is more severe than what is typically observed in peers (American Psychiatric Association [APA], 2000). Persons with the "inattention" subtype of the disorder manifest a failure to attend to details and make many careless mistakes, whereas those with the "hyperactive" subtype are characterized by restlessness and impulsivity. The ADHD diagnosis was once largely restricted to children and adolescents, but it is know known that the condition can persist into adulthood.

PREVALENCE AND COMORBIDITY

The Centers for Disease Control and Prevention (2005) reports an ADHD prevalence of 7.8% among children aged 4 to 17. About a third of children with ADHD also have a comorbid disorder (Jensen, Arnold, Swanson, et al., 2007). Most common concurrent disorders are either oppositional defiant disorder (ODD) or conduct disorder (CD), which puts a child at risk for poor outcomes, including the development of substance use disorders (Barkley, 2004) and mood disorders (Biederman et al., 2008) in adolescence and young adulthood. About 50% of youths with ADHD may have ODD or CD; this comorbidity pattern is more common in the combined than in the inattentive type (Connor, Steeber, & McBurnett, 2010).

ASSESSING ADHD

The way in which ADHD assessments are conducted depends on the age of the client. The diagnosis is particularly difficult in preschool children because of the lack of valid measurement tools and the difficulty of sorting out the possible psychological or environmental contributors to the child's symptoms (Shepard, Carter, & Cohen, 2000). As a result, most comprehensive assessments do not occur until elementary school. The social worker can assume primary responsibility for certain aspects of this assessment (clinical interviews with the child and parent, assessment of parent-child interactions, interviews with teachers, and implementation of standardized behavior rating scales). Other aspects of the assessment require referrals for medical and psychological evaluation. In summary, assessment at the school-age stage should comprise the following (American Academy of Pediatrics, 2000):

- A physical examination and a review of health records.
- Interviews with the child, parents, teachers, and any other significant persons. It must be noted that children tend to underreport their symptoms (Pelham, Fabiano, & Massetti, 2005). In addition, teachers are usually the first people (followed by parents) to suggest that a child be evaluated for ADHD (Sax & Kautz, 2003), and their judgment of a child's symptoms tends to be valid (Mannuzza, Klein, & Moulton, 2002).
- Rating scales completed by parents and teachers can also provide useful information. The Swanson, Nolan, and Pelham-IV Questionnaire (SNAP-IV) (Swanson, 1992; Swanson et al., 2001) has both parent and teacher versions for children aged 5 to 11 and is available online.
- A review of school records (report cards, achievement tests, and attendance).
- Behavioral observations of the child and of parent-child interaction.

Making a differential diagnosis between ADHD and other disorders is also important. Children with ODD behave in a way that purposely annoys and antagonizes others, whereas ADHD symptoms are displayed without regard to others. However, as noted, both disorders often co-occur. The practitioner must also explore any trauma history. Common traumas include abandonment, physical or sexual abuse, or observation of family or community violence. Some of the symptoms of posttraumatic stress disorder (PTSD) may mimic those of ADHD (Perrin, Smith, & Yule, 2000). Chronic hyperarousal and physiological reactivity to cues from the traumatic event can appear as hyperactivity and impulsivity. Intrusive thoughts of a trauma can interfere with attention and concentration.

In addition to the above steps, a clinical interview with adults should include a discussion of ADHD symptoms present in childhood and current symptoms. As will be discussed, many of the *Diagnostic and Statistical Manual of Mental Disorders* (DSM) criteria for ADHD are geared toward children, so adult variants of hyperactive symptoms may include workaholism, difficulty sitting through meetings at work, unwillingness to wait, and speeding (Weiss & Weiss, 2004). The clinician should further inquire about a history of drug and alcohol use (because ADHD can be comorbid with substance abuse). If possible, a collateral (a spouse, partner, parent) should be interviewed to provide a more objective appraisal of the client's symptoms (Murphy & Adler, 2004).

The health care system is where most children with ADHD are diagnosed and treated and so attempts have been made to educate primary care providers on appropriate practices (Wolraich, Bard, Stein, Rushton, & O'Connor, 2010). As a result, improvements have been made, in that the majority of physicians report using the DSM criteria (81%) and teacher rating scales (67%) to arrive at a diagnosis.

Although teacher reports are said to be important in making a diagnosis of ADHD, elsewhere in the chapter it is argued that teacher perceptions may be skewed, and you may have observed this phenomenon in your own experiences with clients. Given these facts, how will you decide whether a teacher's strong endorsement of a child having symptoms of ADHD is contrary to the child's caregivers' reports.

The following describes how Mrs. Bronsky should be considered:

Mrs. Bronsky says she has not talked to her children about the sexual abuse, both because they have been interviewed so many times and because they do not bring it up. She would prefer that they just all forget about it, but the women at the children's advocacy center emphasized that her children will need counseling. She reports, though, that the professionals attribute all of Billy's problems, such as his lack of following through with rules and his bed-wetting, to the abuse. As long as she can remember, however, Billy has had these problems. Mrs. Bronsky denies that he has had nightmares, changes in sleep or eating patterns, or any other specific fears since the abuse occurred. She reports that both Pauline and Billy liked their cousin who abused them and now ask when they can play with him again. When asked how she responds to those requests, Mrs. Bronsky says she tells them, "Now you know after what you said that you can't play with him ever again." When you explore with her what this could mean to the children, she says that she makes it clear that the abuse was the older cousin's fault, that he has a problem and needs a lot of counseling, and that they did the right thing in telling about it.

When asked about the bed-wetting, Mrs. Bronsky said that that is another long-standing problem, that Billy wets his bed almost every night and has done so ever since he was little. She says he rarely wets himself during the daytime. When asked how she has tried to address the problem, she says that she tries to limit his liquid intake after a certain time of day and makes sure he uses the bathroom before he goes to bed. She says that for the past year, Billy has occasionally (once a month) passed feces into his clothing during the daytime. She has had him checked medically, and no problem has been found. She says that she sees neither the bowel movements nor his urination as oppositional behaviors, because he is extremely embarrassed about these "accidents." When asked, she claimed that the doctor has given her no advice on how to handle these problems, other than to have Billy be responsible for washing his own sheets and clothing. She notes that he sometimes hides the sheets and clothes because he is embarrassed.

Mrs. Bronsky reports that she was married to Pauline and Billy's father for nine years and that he was physically abusive to her, but not the children. She admits that they witnessed some of the violence and would cry, but she denies that it had any lasting impact on them in terms of nightmares, flashbacks, or other fears. She says her husband hung out with a motorcycle gang and had a problem with "taking speed" in their early marriage, but now merely drinks heavily. She states that he eventually left her two years ago to be with another woman.

Mrs. Bronsky reports that her children have regular visitation with her ex-husband and have consistently denied to all who have asked that he is abusive to them. The children tell the therapist that they like his girlfriend, and that he is not drunk when they are over there, although he does sometimes drink beer. They enjoy their visits to his house. When asked the reason their parents are not together any-more, they say that he went to live with his girlfriend and do not mention the family violence.

Mrs. Bronsky says she has been married to her new husband, Don, for one year, and that she is happy because he is so much better than her ex-husband. He is not violent to her and holds a regular job. When asked how her new husband reacted to the report of Pauline and Billy's sexual abuse by his sister's son, she said that he believes it happened but doesn't want any part of the whole problem. He has played as minimal a role as possible in the police and the child protective services investigations. For example, Mrs. Bronsky has gone alone to the child advocacy center with her children to be interviewed and to have their medical examinations. When asked if the sexual abuse in the family has put any stress on her relationship with her husband, Mrs. Bronsky denies it. She says her husband is very good with her children, although when the children were alone together with the therapist in the second session, they reported, "Don yells a lot" at them and at their mother.

When the therapist was alone with Billy for the first session, he did not talk at all and just looked down as the therapist made various validating remarks ("It's hard talking to someone you don't know," "You're not in here for anything you've done wrong," etc.) or asked questions related to his expectations about counseling (e.g., "What did your mom tell you you were coming for?") or told him about her role ("My job is to talk to kids about things that have happened to them that have been hard to deal with," etc.). No matter what the therapist tried, Billy refused to answer. In the second session, Billy and his sister were together in the session and were more forthcoming, as indicated by the information they provided about their father, his girlfriend, and their stepfather. Billy was guarded when the therapist brought up the recent sexual abuse and avoided answering any questions, whereas his sister was willing to discuss it. He denied having bad dreams.

The social worker obtained a release from Mrs. Bronsky to talk to Billy's teacher, who says that in her mind, there is no doubt that Billy has ADHD. "He's classic. He can't sit still. He gets out of his seat if any item attracts his attention. He always has to be fiddling with something. He talks when I'm talking." When asked about oppositional symptoms, she says, "He talks back if I tell him to stop disrupting the class and makes excuses. He glowers at me and folds his arms, refusing to do his work at all at times. The little work he finishes is a mess and full of mistakes. Everyone else is always to blame. He's not accountable, at all."

Directions Part I, Multiaxial Diagnosis   Given the case information, prepare the following: a multiaxial diagnosis, the rationale for the diagnosis and global assessment of functioning score, and additional information you would like to know in order to make a more accurate diagnosis.

BIOPSYCHOSOCIAL RISK AND RESILIENCE INFLUENCES

Onset

Many researchers assert that ADHD represents a pattern of cognitive or neuropsychological impairment that is manifested in the person's deficits regarding self-regulation, behavior inhibition, and self-control (Barkley, 2006; Johnson, Wiersema, & Kuntsi, 2009). Although this conceptualization has not been proved, there is broad support for the fact that child factors, rather than family, neighborhood, and other influences related to socioeconomic status (SES), are responsible for ADHD (Ford, Goodman, & Meltzer, 2004). Risks for socially diverse populations are summarized in Box 4.1.

Biological Influences

ADHD is assumed to be an inherited genetic disorder with heritability estimates at over 70% (Faraone & Khan, 2006; Polderman et al., 2007). The precise genetic mechanisms that contribute to the onset of ADHD are not known (Neale et al., 2010), but dopamine

---

Box 4.1 • Risks for ADHD in Socially Diverse Populations

Females

- While ADHD is more prominent among boys by a ratio of 2.5:1,[1] girls may be underdiagnosed because they are not as disruptive as boys.[2]

- Impairment for girls with ADHD can cross many life domains and persist over time[3] and by young adulthood many suffer from antisocial, addictive, mood, anxiety, and eating disorders (Biederman et al., 2010, p. 409).

Ethnic Minority Groups

- Although African American children save more ADHD symptoms, they are diagnosed two thirds less frequently than Caucasian children. This pattern is not explained by teacher rating bias or SES, rather, it may be influenced by parent beliefs about ADHD, lack of treatment access and utilization, and the fact that existing assessment tools may not adequately capture ADHD manifestation in African Americans.[4]

- Lower treatment rates in African American children may be related to high rates of classroom behavior problems among African American youths.[5]

- In the Multimodal Treatment Study of ADHD, boys from ethnic minority backgrounds improved with a combination of behavioral therapy and medication compared to only medication.[6] In general, African American and Latino parents prefer psychosocial treatment to medication for ADHD.[7]

- Prevalence rates for Hispanic children are estimated at 3.3%, compared with 6.5% for Caucasian children; however, the condition may go unrecognized in Hispanics given the lack of population-based studies performed,[8] language barriers, underreporting by mothers due to lack of knowledge of symptoms, cultural differences in developmental expectations by Hispanic mothers, physician bias against taking concerns of parents seriously, and lack of access to treatment resources.[9]

Low SES

- Lead exposure increases the risk of ADHD.[10]

- Children living in low-SES homes are more likely to have an ADHD diagnosis than those in higher SES groups.[11]

---

[1]Centers for Disease Control, 2005.
[2]Ohan & Johnston, 2005.
[3]Hinshaw, Owens, Sami, & Fargeon, 2006.
[4]Miller, Nigg, & Miller, 2008.
[5]Miller et al., 2008.
[6]Jensen et al., 2007.
[7]Pham, Carlson, & Kosciuiek, 2009.
[8]Bloom & Dey, 2006.
[9]Rothe, 2005.
[10]Braum, Kahn, Froehlich, Auginger, & Lamphear, 2006.
[11]Merikangas et al., 2010.

transmitter and receptor genes, as well as several serotonin transporter and receptor genes, have been linked to the disorder (Faraone & Khan, 2006; Gizer, Ficks, & Waldman, 2009; Levy, Hay, & Bennett, 2006). There are also neurobiological factors, such as the capacity to inhibit impulsive behaviors, that protect youngsters from developing ADHD in the presence of environmental risk (Nigg, Nikolas, Friderici, Park, & Zucker, 2007).

Aside from genetics, other biological influences may influence the development of ADHD. Children who are born prematurely are at twice the risk for ADHD as full-term children (Bhutta, Cleves, Casey, Cradock, & Anand, 2002). Maternal smoking and drinking during pregnancy may independently act as predisposing influences (Kahn, Khoury, Nichols, & Lanphear, 2003). Lead exposure is also thought to have increased the number of U.S. ADHD cases by 290,000 (Braum et al., 2006). Other environmental toxins, including organophosphate pesticides, at levels common among U.S. children, may contribute to a diagnosis of ADHD (Bouchard, Bellinger, Wright, & Weisskopf, 2010).

Interestingly, an Australian study tracking maternal anxiety and attention problems in children found that anxiety during or after pregnancy was associated with attention problems in children at both 5 and 15 years (Clavarino et al., 2010). The effect of maternal anxiety was cumulative; that is, the more chronic the anxiety, the more likely the child was reported (by both mother and child) as being attention impaired. This relationship could be biological: Genetics may be responsible for both maternal anxiety and child ADHD. Alternatively, the child's inherited anxiety potential could influence his or her responsiveness to the environment through an alteration of the hormonal and autonomic nervous systems. The association found in this study could also be due to the parenting abilities and responsiveness of anxious mothers to their children's needs and behaviors.

Social Influences

Although many experts vigorously assert that ADHD is a neuropsychological disorder, others suggest that family and social risk influences may play a causal role (Counts, Nigg, Stawicki, Rappley, & Eye, 2005). Family dynamics in one longitudinal study, namely hostility in family interactions at age two was predictive of child ADHD at age seven (Jacobvitz, Hazen, Curran, & Hitchens, 2004). For boys, enmeshed relationships with their mother also predicted ADHD. It is unknown whether the symptoms of ADHD were already present in those toddlers, contributing to the family dynamics.

It is likely that adversity may affect children with a genetic vulnerability to develop ADHD (Laucht et al., 2007). For example, being reared in an institutional setting may also be associated with ADHD symptoms years after the child has been adopted (Stevens et al., 2008). Additionally, a U.S. survey of child and adolescent mental health disorders showed that those living in low SES were more likely to have an ADHD diagnosis than those in higher SES groups (Merikangas et al., 2010). Similarly, a Swedish study showed that a family's receipt of welfare benefits increased the risk of a child being prescribed ADHD medication by 135% when compared with households not claiming benefits (Hjern, Weitoft, & Lindblad, 2010). Moreover, mothers who did not have university degrees were 130% more likely to have a child on ADHD medication than women with university degrees. Finally, children were 54% more likely to be on ADHD medication if they came from a single-parent family rather than having both parents at home.

Critically evaluate empirically based research materials related to social work practice and understand the differences and appropriate applications of empirical and nonempirical professional literature.

Human Behavior

Practice Behavior Example: *Critique and apply knowledge to understand person and environment.*

Critical Thinking Question: Given the contradictory positions on the origins of ADHD, how will you reconcile these positions and their evidence when facing children who display symptoms of ADHD?

Course and Recovery

Continuance rates from childhood to adulthood ADHD are estimated to be 36% in the U.S. population (Breslau, Miller, Chung, & Schweitzer, 2011), with 8.1% of adults meeting diagnostic criteria (Kessler, Adler, Barkley, et al., 2005, 2006), although estimates vary (Simon, Czobor, Balint, et al., 2009). A recent study following youth diagnosed with ADHD in childhood found them more likely to be depressed and to attempt suicide in adolescence. Students with the combined type of ADHD, the most common type, have a higher likelihood of dropping out than students with disciplinary problems. Furthermore, even with treatment, youths with ADHD still had significantly more academic, social, and conduct problems than their non-ADHD counterparts (Molina et al., 2009).

In a study following hyperactive children into young adulthood, a third (32%) had failed to complete high school, and far fewer were enrolled in college compared with the control group (without hyperactivity) (Barkley, 2006). In addition, the young adults with hyperactivity had fewer friends and had more difficulty keeping friends. Sexual risk taking, in terms of both number of partners and unprotected sex, was also indicated. Moreover, adults with ADHD showed impaired work performance, and this effect was particularly evident among blue-collar workers (Kessler, Adler, Barkley, et al., 2005). People with ADHD have more car accidents, citations, and speeding tickets than people without ADHD, although they do not perceive themselves as poor drivers (Knouse, Bagwell, Barkley, & Murphy, 2005).

Long-term outcomes for persons with ADHD are influenced by the severity of the disorder; more severe ADHD is more persistent (Kessler, Adler, Barkley, et al., 2005) and is associated with worse outcomes (Barkley, Fischer, & Smallish, 2006). Any parental or family difficulties that contribute to inconsistent, coercive, or decreased efforts at managing the child's behavior may increase problem behaviors in the child with ADHD (Weiss & Hechtman, 1993) and may eventually lead to the development of ODD or CD, which presents further risk (Biederman et al., 2008). As noted earlier, family adversity, particularly marital conflict, is associated with ADHD (Counts et al., 2005). It is unclear whether these factors contribute to or are a consequence of child ADHD. Another factor identified in families involves household composition. A two-parent home may be a protective influence, because two parents are more likely to manage successfully the stress related to having a child with ADHD (Cuffe et al., 2001). A final factor associated with better adjustment is treatment response (Molina et al., 2009). Those who had responded well to treatment and had maintained gains for at least two years tended to be functioning the best at eight-year follow-up.

> **Directions Part II, Biopsychosocial Risk and Resilience Assessment**   Formulate a risk and resilience assessment, both for the onset of the disorder and for the course of the disorder, including the strengths that you see for this individual. What techniques could you use to elicit additional strengths in this client?

INTERVENTION

ADHD is a chronic developmental condition that requires ongoing management and monitoring. Intervention should focus on helping clients learn to cope with, compensate for, and accommodate to symptoms, as well as on reducing additional problems that may arise as a result of these symptoms (Barkley, 2004). Goals formed usually include improved school functioning, peer relationships, and family relationships (Pelham et al., 2005).

Controversy exists about the optimal treatment methods for ADHD—whether interventions should involve medication, psychosocial treatment, or a combination of both. Each is discussed here. It must be noted, however, that when youths treated for 12 months were followed up after eight years, there were no differences in symptoms or functioning among the youths assigned to medication, behavioral treatment, or the combined treatment (Molina et al., 2009). This result suggests that the type or intensity of a one-year treatment for ADHD in childhood does not predict future functioning.

Psychosocial Intervention

Psychosocial interventions may be targeted toward parents, children, and the school system and typically include behavioral and cognitive-behavioral strategies. Family and classroom interventions have been shown to be more effective than individual interventions aimed at children. The school system is a primary location for services for children with ADHD. These services rest on a foundation provided by several federal laws (DuPaul & Power, 2000; Root & Resnick, 2003; Tannock & Brown, 2000). These laws prohibit schools from discriminating against people with handicaps; mandate free and appropriate public education for children with ADHD; ensure a multidisciplinary evaluation process toward the development of an IEP; and guarantee reasonable accommodations for persons with a substantial limitation of a major life activity, of which learning is part.

Behavioral Treatment

The empirical literature on psychosocial intervention for ADHD mainly involves parent training (Barkley & Murphy, 2006). This is a brief treatment model involving about 12 sessions in either individual or group formats. Parents receive information about ADHD, medications used to treat ADHD, effective parenting practices, how to reinforce children's coping strategies, and how to manage parental stress. Through positive reinforcements children learn prosocial behavior such as following directions, completing homework, doing household chores, and getting along with siblings. Parents are taught to respond to children's negative behaviors by ignoring or punishing the child so that he or she will suffer negative consequences for engaging in the behavior. Parents are taught these principles through didactic instruction, behavioral rehearsal, modeling, and role playing. Because children with ADHD have problems with schoolwork, other interventions for parents include structuring the home environment so that the child has a place to work relatively free of distractions, regular teacher verification of satisfactory homework completion, and a home-based reinforcement system featuring regular school–home note exchanges (DuPaul & Power, 2000).

A meta-analysis of 16 studies in which parents were involved with their child's treatment was conducted (Corcoran & Dattalo, 2006). Compared to control conditions, parent-involved treatment had from a low to moderate effect on ADHD and externalizing symptoms. Given that some of the control conditions themselves involved viable treatments, such as medication and child treatment, it is noteworthy that parent-involved treatment produced overall gains above and beyond these control treatments. Parent-involved treatment had an even higher effect on internalizing symptoms and family functioning. The few studies to date assessing academic performance showed that family treatment may positively benefit academic performance. Children's social skills, on the other hand, were not affected by family treatment, despite the thrust of many programs to improve such skills.

For adults, cognitive-behavioral therapy includes psycho-education about ADHD, training in organizing and planning, learning skills to reduce distractibility, cognitive restructuring (learning to think more adaptively in situations that cause distress), and relapse prevention (Safren et al., 2010).

Medication

The psychostimulants have a long history of being prescribed for ADHD. The primary psychostimulant drugs used include methylphenidate (71% of cases), amphetamines, and pemoline (Bentley & Walsh, 2006). When these stimulants are compared with one another, few differences have been found in their relative effectiveness (Brown et al., 2005).

Although the randomized, controlled trials of methylphenidate (Ritalin) for youth have shown large treatment improvements compared to placebo, the trials conducted have been surprisingly short in duration (an average of three weeks) (Schachter, Pham, King, Langford, & Moher, 2001). In addition, decreased appetite as a side effect was common. Other researchers (Gould et al. 2009; Vitiello & Towbin, 2009) have discussed some of the controversies involved in medication for children, including the possibility of sudden death in rare cases. Finally, a majority of those children taking medication had stopped when followed up at 8 years (Molina et al., 2009). This trend indicates that medication may lose its appeal over time.

If a child does not respond to an alternative stimulant after the first stimulants are ineffective at therapeutic doses, then the recommendation is to try atomoxetine, a noradrenergic reuptake inhibitor (Pliszka et al., 2006). Antidepressants such as bupropion and the tricyclics (but not desipramine, which has been associated with child deaths) are a third option if the above have not been helpful.

Similar to the research with children, the shorter acting stimulants (namely methylphenate) were found to produce benefits over other medications for adults (Peterson, McDonagh, & Fu, 2008). Higher doses showed more benefits. An implication is that if adults do not experience adverse events, then they should receive a full therapeutic dose of methylphenidate. For those who experience lack of effectiveness or intolerable side effects, antidepressants are also used (Verbeeck, Tuinier, & Beckkering, 2009. Of all the antidepressants, only bupropion (Wellbutrin) has been shown to be helpful.

Critical Thinking

Practice Behavior Example: *Distinguish, appraise, and integrate multiple sources of knowledge, including research-based knowledge, and practice wisdom.*

Critical Thinking Question: Given the controversies about the most effective treatment for children with ADHD, how will you decide what to recommend to families when you face a child diagnosed with ADHD?

Research-Based Practice

Practice Behavior Example: *Use practice experience to inform research, employ evidence-based interventions, evaluate one's own practice, and use research findings to improve practice, policy, and social service delivery.*

Critical Thinking Question: Given the information about evidence-based treatment, how will you decide whether and how such treatment needs to be adapted for children who have suffered from stressful life events?

> **Directions Part III, Goal Setting and Treatment Planning** Given your risk and protective factors assessments of the individual, your knowledge of the disorder, and evidence-based practice guidelines, formulate goals and a possible treatment plan for the individual.

CRITIQUE

ADHD is considered an inherited neuropsychological disorder, but substantive supporting evidence about its specific nature is lacking (DeGrandpre, 1999). Social influences—for example, attachment patterns, parental stress, and poverty—and other biological contributing factors—for example, maternal smoking—may be underrecognized as risk mechanisms.

As mentioned, primary care physicians are primarily responsible for diagnosing and treating ADHD. However, due to time constraints and lack of training, they are often ill-equipped to manage and treat a mental health disorder such as ADHD. Although physicians may not always rely on diagnostic criteria in order to make the diagnosis, there is also ambiguity about how hyperactive, inattentive, or impulsive a child has to be to warrant the diagnosis, because the benchmark of normal age-group comparisons is unclear. That is, the diagnostic criteria are neither normed nor quantified (Mayes, Bagwell, & Erkulwater, 2009). These factors mean that much variation exists among clinicians. As a result, ADHD is both overdiagnosed (given to those who meet few symptoms of the criteria) and underdiagnosed (not given to those who meet full criteria) (Purdie, Hattie, & Carroll, 2002).

A further problem of misdiagnosis of ADHD involves the age of children relative to their classmates. Children who are the youngest in their classes are identified by their teachers as having more ADHD symptoms (Elder, 2010). The youngest kindergartners were 60% more likely to be diagnosed with ADHD than the oldest children in the same grade. Similarly, when that group of classmates reached the fifth and eighth grades, the youngest were more than twice as likely to be prescribed stimulants. Overall, this misdiagnosis likely accounts for about 20%—or 900,000—of the 4.5 million children currently identified as having ADHD.

Finally, although the prevalence of ADHD is often considered to be stable across countries, rates of diagnosis and prescription stimulant use are significantly higher in the United States. In fact, the United States consumes the majority of the world's production of stimulants, and its school-age children use as much as three times more psychiatric medication than children in the rest of the world combined . . . This enormous variation in stimulant use suggests that the boundaries between "normal" and "abnormal" are strongly influenced by social, cultural, and policy variations across countries (Mayes et al., 2009, p. 206).

A further problem with the diagnosis of ADHD involves the validity of the criteria for females and for adults. Fewer girls tend to be diagnosed with the disorder even controlling for referral bias. Females have a lower base level of inattentiveness and hyperactivity than their male counterparts and must therefore deviate much further from girls without symptoms in order to be diagnosed (Arnold, 1996).

Another phenomenon is the increasing number of adults that are now being diagnosed with ADHD. Symptoms, such as "procrastination, overreacting to frustration, poor motivation, insomnia, and difficulty with time management" (Weiss & Weiss, 2004, p. 27) are considered part of the ADHD pattern in adults. However, these symptoms are not listed in the DSM, where the diagnostic criteria centers on the behaviors of children. Efforts are now under way to institute criteria more relevant for adults. For instance, a note for the symptom of "often runs about or climbs excessively in situations in which it is inappropriate" may state that, for adolescents or adults, this may be translated into subjective feelings of restlessness (APA, 2000, p. 92). Still, criteria for adults must be made uniformly relevant and be empirically validated (Ramtekkar, Reierson, Todorov, & Todd, 2010).

The age-of-onset criterion has been widely debated (Cuffe et al., 2001; Loeber, Green, Lahey, Frick, & McBurnett, 2002; Willoughby, Curran, Costello, & Angold, 2000), especially for adults (Faraone et al., 2006). Given the lack of empirical evidence supporting the age-at-onset criterion, as well as difficulties in demonstrating impairment before the age of seven in older adolescents and adults, some have argued that the criterion should be revised to include a broader period of childhood, up to age 12 (Ohan & Johnston, 2005).

Human Behavior

Practice Behavior Example: *Utilize conceptual frameworks to guide the processes of assessment, intervention, and evaluation.*

Critical Thinking Question: Given the critiques of the diagnosis, how will you decide whether a child has a valid diagnosis of ADHD?

CRITICAL PERSPECTIVE

Directions Part IV, Critical Perspective   Formulate a critique of the diagnosis as it relates to this case example. Questions to consider include the following: Does this diagnosis represent a valid mental disorder from the social work perspective? Is this diagnosis significantly different from other possible diagnoses? Your critique should be based on the values of the social work profession (which are incongruent in some ways with the medical model) and the validity of the specific diagnostic criteria applied to this case.

Case 2   The Repairman

Wayne, a 40-year-old Caucasian male, came to see a social worker for counseling after Wendy, his girlfriend of nine months, broke up with him. He described feeling devastated by the breakup (a week ago) and said that he had pleaded with her to take him back. He admitted to calling her constantly since the breakup, to the point where she had changed her phone number. He said he felt nauseated and sick, had problems sleeping, thought about her "all the time," and didn't know what he was going to do without her. He also said he was thinking that he was a "fuck-up" for losing her.

Wayne admitted that he was the reason for the breakup. He said that he couldn't control his temper and that "one little thing" might set him off. He described a recent incident in which he and his girlfriend went rollerblading in a local park. He kept stopping because he felt his shoelaces weren't tight enough. As the more experienced skater, she started to feel frustrated and told him that she would skate on and that they could meet up in half an hour. He flew into a rage, started shouting at her in public, and then stomped off. An hour and a half later, when he had gotten over being mad, he returned to the car, where she was waiting for him. They argued about this incident for the rest of the day. He said, "Why does she have to get so upset? She knows I have a temper and that I'll eventually get over it."

Wayne, who worked as a repairman, also described himself as being very forgetful. For example, he would often leave tools in various apartments where he was working and then waste a lot of time trying to find them. He also left taps running in his own apartment because something else would catch his interest.

He became easily frustrated if he had to deal with too many things at once, such as a lot of work orders. He said Wendy had helped him to get more organized. She had bought a dry-erase board and a calendar to remind him of things that needed to be done. Wayne admitted to having a hard time concentrating on anything other than watching television. That's what had made it hard for him to do well in high school and why he didn't consider college.

In the second session Wayne was accompanied by his ex-girlfriend Wendy, who is college educated and works as a human resources manager. She maintained that they were still apart but that she would consider getting back with him if he made some changes, such as managing his frustration and acting maturely, with the help of counseling. She described Wayne as "like a child." She said it was part of his appeal when she first met him; he seemed so innocent and cute and just blurted out his thoughts. She said her initial attraction to him had been physical. She had been unemployed for a short period and lived in the apartment complex where he was working at the time. She had a lot of work done on her apartment, and he agreed to get her marijuana. After "partying" together, they became sexually involved. She said she was no longer smoking, because she had taken a job at a company that does random drug testing.

She said Wayne would lose his temper over anything, even "stuff that hadn't happened." She described one incident in which she went out with her coworkers for a good-bye dinner for an executive in her company. With the speeches and the various courses, the dinner went on longer than she had expected. By the time she got home, there were 10 messages on her answering machine from Wayne. On the final message, he broke up with her. She said it took an hour to convince him that she had been at the work dinner the whole time. Wendy said another problem was his driving. She refused to let him drive with her anymore, because he would drive too fast, switch in and out of lanes, and yell at other drivers. Wayne said he "hates traffic" and feels unbearable frustration when he is stuck behind other drivers.

Wendy realized she had her own "issues" and is working on them in her own therapy. She said that she didn't foresee marrying Wayne. He said that was fine because he never wanted to get married, but he would eventually like to live with her. He also said he never wanted children, and Wendy revealed that he had physically abused his previous girlfriend's child. He said, "I feel bad about that. He didn't deserve it. I know I'm too much of a kid myself to have kids."

Wendy said she had met Wayne's mother and was surprised she was so nice. Wayne's mother was sympathetic to Wendy's difficulties with him, commenting that, "He's always been like that." She said that he was an exhausting child, and from the time he could walk she ran after him constantly. Wayne didn't mind her, not so much because he was contrary but because he was so distracted; he went with whatever caught his fancy at the moment. Wendy said his mother had told her that Wayne had had some problems after his birth and he had had to stay in the hospital for a week. Wendy didn't know more specifics than that. She said Wayne's mother has never smoked cigarettes or used drugs and drinks alcohol minimally, although Wayne's father reportedly had a problem with alcohol. In the session, Wayne announced that he was thirsty and got up and left the office to use the drinking fountain down the hall. Wendy commented that this was a good example of how he was; if he felt a sensation or had a thought, he would act on it immediately, rather than delaying gratification or thinking things through.

Wayne graduated from high school but got poor grades throughout school. He denied being in any specialized classes ("I'm not a retard." Then he laughed. "At least I don't think I am."). He said he wasn't diagnosed with any learning disorders that he knew of or anything else as a child. He joined the army after high school, served for four years, and was honorably discharged. He said that he was in the army during peacetime, so he saw no combat.

After that he worked as a maintenance man for apartment complexes. He liked the work—moving around all day and figuring out how to fix things rather than being "stuck in an office." He also got a free apartment as part of his job. But he said the pay was "crap" and he didn't have health insurance. He admitted to having a hard time keeping a job for more than a year. It wasn't so much because he would forget instructions that were given to him; his work was usually good enough for management to overlook that. But he would usually end up talking back to management because he wouldn't "take any shit." He said that he had walked away from one job in the past for something that made him mad.

Wayne said he generally got along well with his coworkers and enjoyed talking to people who lived at the apartment complex. He said he had some good friends from the military that he still sees occasionally, although they don't live in the same town.

Wayne said he did not have a history of trouble with the law, except for traffic and speeding tickets, for which he was jailed once. Then he added that he had been arrested on one occasion for family violence charges against his previous girlfriend (the one before Wendy). He pointed out that in all his other serious relationships (four in all), he had behaved violently only with that one person and said that she was "stupid," "a bitch," and "knew how to get me." He said that his previous girlfriend was also violent with him, and the charges were eventually reduced to a class C misdemeanor for both of them. He said his previous girlfriend also had a drinking problem and would steal his belongings and pawn them in order to buy beer. She eventually left him after two years for another man.

Wayne said he liked to drink and occasionally smoked marijuana, but not like his past girlfriend and other friends who "couldn't stop." He said that he tended to lose interest after a few beers, and he never missed drinking if he didn't have money to buy beer. He denied any other drug use, said he "hated coke" because of the way people acted when on it, and commented that he was too "hyper" to take something like that.

As for Wayne's childhood, he didn't remember much. He didn't know his father at all. According to his mother, his father physically abused her, but she didn't leave him until he started physically abusing Wayne and his younger (by two years) brother. Wayne repeated that he did poorly in school and would run around the classroom when he was young. He said he still considered himself a slow reader.

Wayne was seeing the counselor as one of the agency's sliding-scale clients and said that as a result of having to pay the $5 fee, he would be eating macaroni and cheese, potatoes, and peanut butter and jelly sandwiches until the end of the month (a week away) when he got his check. He attributed this problem to the fact that he didn't get paid much, but also admitted to mismanaging his money. He would spend money on something that caught his eye and later not have money for food or bills.

Please go to the Appendix for directions to this case.

PRACTICE TEST

The following questions will test your knowledge of the content found within this chapter. For additional assessment, including licensing-exam type questions on applying chapter content to practice behaviors, visit **MySocialWorkLab.com**

1. Pertaining to the causation and diagnosis of ADHD, which statement is true?
   a. Biological tests can assess for the presence of ADHD
   b. Being born preterm may play a role in the development of ADHD
   c. ADHD is underdiagnosed
   d. Most theorists agree that ADHD is a result of early-life social deprivation

2. Which of the following is a risk influence specific to the course of ADHD:
   a. Being an only child
   b. Coercive parenting
   c. Single parenting
   d. Comorbid depression

3. Robbie's wife was threatening to leave him because he was irritable with her, blaming his moods on work stress, and drinking more than usual. Twenty-seven-year-old Robbie had been an energetic child who loved outdoor activities. He had never been a good student, complaining of being bored in the classroom. One year ago he was hired as the youth director of his church. Robbie loved working with the kids although serious problems surfaced on the job. He was extremely disorganized in tending to his administrative demands, and if he was interrupted from completing a task he could not remember later what he had been doing. Which of Robbie's behaviors seem to provide evidence of ADHD?
   a. Difficulty with the administrative tasks of his job
   b. Persistent irritability with his wife
   c. Increasing tendency to drink alcohol when frustrated
   d. His great enjoyment of outdoor activities with adolescents

4. Psychosocial interventions for children with ADHD usually involve parents and the school system. In Robbie's case, the social worker will want to enlist which of the following for ongoing consultation?
   a. His parents
   b. His minister/employer
   c. His wife
   d. Because Robbie is an adult he can address the problem adequately on his own

5. Now that you have critically examined the available treatments for ADHD, with what kinds of children and circumstances do you believe a medication-only treatment would suffice, when would a psychosocial-only approach suffice, and when would it be necessary to combine both medication and psychosocial treatment?

6. Given the critiques of ADHD as a diagnosis and your experiences with clients, what is your position on the existence of ADHD as a valid disorder? When are clients wrongfully given the diagnosis and what may be the repercussions of this practice?

SUCCEED WITH

Visit **MySocialWorkLab** for more licensing-exam test questions, and to access case studies, videos, and much more.

5

Oppositional Defiant Disorder and Conduct Disorder

Competencies Applied with Practice Behaviors — in this Chapter				
Professional Identity	Ethical Practice	✖ Critical Thinking	✖ Diversity in Practice	Human Rights & Justice
Research-Based Practice	Human Behavior	Policy Practice	✖ Practice Contexts	Engage, Assess, Intervene, Evaluate

> Josie is a 19-year-old Romanian female currently placed at a specialized school for children with developmental disabilities and emotional and behavioral problems. She has attended the program for the past year. Her teacher reports that she often disrupts class, becomes verbally aggressive, has attacked other students, and has difficulty transitioning from one activity to the next. The trigger for these behaviors is typically frustration due to her inability to complete or understand school assignments. She will make disparaging comments about herself ("I'm stupid") before erupting in anger.

Oppositional defiant disorder (ODD) and conduct disorder (CD), both categorized as disruptive behavior disorders of childhood and adolescence, are discussed together in this chapter because they feature anger, defiance, rebellion, lying, and school problems (Loeber, Burke, Lagey, Winters, & Zera, 2000). The major distinction between them is that youths with CD also violate societal norms through aggression, theft or deceit, and/or destruction of property (American Psychiatric Association [APA], 2000).

PREVALENCE AND COMORBIDITY

ODD is more common than CD, with a lifetime prevalence of 10.2% of the U.S. population (Nock, Kazdin, Hiripi, & Kessler, 2006). The median age of onset of CD is 11.6 years. For preschoolers, estimates for the rates of ODD range between 4 and 16.8%, and for

CD between 0 and 4.6% (Egger & Angold, 2006). Males have a higher rate of CD than females (12 versus 7.1%) (APA, 2000). CD increases the risk of many other mental, emotional, and behavioral disorders, such as substance use and mood disorders (Nock et al., 2006). Attention-deficit hyperactivity disorder (ADHD) is common in children with ODD and CD.

ASSESSMENT OF ODD AND CD

Social workers should always engage in a multifaceted approach to ODD and CD, using many informants—the child, parents, and school personnel—to obtain reports and different methods—interview, rating scales, and observations of the child—to formulate their assessments (Alvarez & Ollendick, 2003; Fonagy & Kurtz, 2002; McMahon & Frick, 2005). The *Diagnostic and Statistical Manual of Mental Disorders* (DSM) criteria require behavior problems in more than one setting. Children also tend to downplay their own symptoms (Loeber, Green, Lahey, Frick, & McBurnett, 2002). Symptom reports from parents and teachers are preferable, although even these sources have their biases. Teachers are more accurate than mothers at identifying a child's ADHD symptoms, whereas parents are more aware of their children's oppositional behavior. For different assessment tools for conduct problems, see McMahon and Frick (2005). Box 5.1 includes additional guidelines for making DSM diagnoses.

Box 5.1 • Guidelines for Assessing ODD and CD

- Transient oppositional behavior is common in children and adolescents.
- Consider a less severe diagnosis, such as adjustment disorder with disturbance of conduct (when there is a recent stressful life event) or the V-code "child or adolescent antisocial behavior."
- Oppositional behaviors should be distinguished from disruptive behaviors associated with ADHD, which occur in response to frustrations associated with inattention and hyperactivity.
- A diagnosis of ODD or CD should not be made when the symptomatic behavior is protective for a child (e.g., one living in an impoverished, high-crime community).
- Symptoms should not occur only in the context of a mood disturbance or symptoms of psychosis.
- Consider whether the oppositional and angry behaviors are part of a symptom pattern indicative of PTSD;

irritability and outbursts of anger are listed as symptoms under the hyperarousal criterion for PTSD.
- In cases where the client meets criteria for both ODD and CD, only CD should be diagnosed.
- When ODD or CD is diagnosed, a separate child and family relational problem (V-code) should not be included.
- CD should be diagnosed in adults older than 18 only if the criteria for antisocial personality disorder are not met.
- See suggested modifications to the DSM criteria for ODD and CD for preschoolers from the Research Diagnostic Criteria-Preschool Age (Task Force on Research Diagnostic Criteria: Infancy and Preschool, 2003) at http://www.infantinstitute.org.

Sources: APA, 2000; Carlson, Tamm, & Gaub, 1997.

Josie was born in Romania and placed in an orphanage at the age of six weeks, and she was finally adopted by an American couple at the age of eight. Her half sister (one year younger) was also adopted. Three years ago, Josie took the Wechsler Intelligence Scale for Children and was shown to have a verbal IQ of 57, a performance IQ of 65, and an overall IQ of 57. Severe deficits in expressive and receptive language were noted.

Results of the Vineland Adaptive Behavior Scales—Interview Edition indicated that her overall functioning fell into the low, mild-deficit range—a level comparable to that of an eight-year-old. Her communication skills fell at the 10.2 age equivalent, her daily living skills were at a nine-year-old equivalent, and her socialization skills were at 7.11 age equivalent. According to the Ekwall/Shanker Reading Inventory, she was reading at a first-grade level. Overall, results of individually administered, standardized testing in math, reading, and written expression placed her in the first percentile for her age, significantly lower than was expected for her IQ.

During the time of testing, Josie was attending a specialized school for students with learning disabilities, where she did well for a while but then began exhibiting aggressive and threatening behaviors toward students and staff. She was then referred to another specialized school that offered self-contained classrooms and a more restrictive program with a clinical team. Her behavior improved at this placement until her grandmother died two years ago, at which time the school also moved to a different building. School reports indicate that she was absent 23 days that year. In the file, school personnel remark on Josie's poor self-esteem, poor coping skills, difficulty transitioning to new environments and dealing with new people and experiences, tendency to be easily distracted, disruptiveness in class, defiance toward staff, and attention-seeking behaviors. A year and a half ago, Josie carried a pocketknife that was subsequently confiscated. She said she didn't intend to use it but only wanted to show it to her friends. From that point she had to be searched daily.

After that placement Josie was transferred to her current school, where she continues to display disruptive and angry behaviors, to the point of attacking other students on occasion. The teacher completed an ADHD rating scale, but neither the score on this test nor the teacher's remarks indicated that Josie had the disorder. However, her reactions when frustrated do tend to have an impulsive and explosive quality.

During the last semester Josie was absent 25 days, with six of those due to school suspension. At that time she had been in detention 66 times for a total of 38 hours for various reasons, including being out of location, throwing objects, disruption, and physical aggression toward staff. In addition to the pocketknife incident, Josie brought matches to the school on two occasions. She again mentioned that she had no intention of hurting anyone; she just wanted to show off. Staff have often had to restrain her while transporting her to locked support. In the hallways, she yells profanities, tears down bulletin boards, pushes other students, and runs away from staff.

In the school environment, Josie is said to have positive relationships with one of the assistant teachers and a counselor. One teacher described Josie as helpful in the classroom and showing pride in her accomplishments. Josie has a small group of friends and is particularly close to one other female student in the classroom. They spend a lot of time talking with each other, sometimes disrupting class with their chatter.

Her adoptive mother says that her relationship with Josie is good (which Josie confirms) and that Josie is able to confide in her. According to her mother, Josie also gets along well with her sister. However, her mother reports that Josie has become verbally threatening and abusive to her, although not physically. She says that Josie's temper rises when Josie faces tasks or chores she doesn't want to do. Josie's mother says that she finds herself giving in to Josie "more than I should" because she just wants to end the conflict.

The family lives in a middle socioeconomic neighborhood, where most of the residents know each other. Josie's father works long hours and travels frequently for business. He is not as involved with his children as his wife is and on weekends typically plays golf. Most of the parenting responsibility falls on Josie's mother, although she claims not to mind this. "All I've ever wanted to do was be a mother." Josie's mother says that she has a circle of friends that she relies on for support, although some of the parents are wary of Josie being around their children. The family regularly attends a Protestant church, and many of her own friends are from her church.

Josie's mother says that when Josie was adopted, she made a good transition, but they soon had her tested, not knowing if some of her difficulties in learning and delays in language were due to cognitive deficits.

Josie denied feelings of depression or sadness at this time with the social work intern, although she did say, "I'm stupid." There has been no change in her eating or sleeping habits. There is also no evidence of manic episodes.

Josie's most recent physical examination was conducted two months ago. No abnormal physical findings were noted. She had successful open-heart surgery while in Romania.

Directions Part I, Multiaxial Diagnosis   Given the case information, prepare the following: a multiaxial diagnosis, the rationale for the diagnosis and global assessment of functioning score, and additional information you would have wanted to know in order to make a more accurate diagnosis.

BIOPSYCHOSOCIAL RISK AND RESILIENCE INFLUENCES

Onset

The current understanding of ODD and CD is that they arise from an interaction of genetic risk and environmental adversity (Hicks, South, DiRago et al., 2009). The biological, psychosocial, and social risk and protective influences—and how they interact together—are discussed here. Additional risks in socially diverse populations are summarized in Box 5.2.

Box 5.2 • Oppositional Defiant Disorder and Conduct Disorder and Social Diversity

Females

- The disorders are less prevalent in females than males before puberty, but rates are more equal after puberty,[1] mainly due to girls' involvement with antisocial boyfriends.[2]
- CD may go unrecognized in females because of relational or indirect aggressiveness—for example, exclusion of others; threats of withdrawal from relationships; rumor spreading; and efforts to alienate, ostracize, or defame others.[3]
- Inadequate information exists for treatment for girls because of the lack of gender-specific treatment research.[4]

Ethnicity

- Hispanics are at lower risk for ODD.[5]
- When controlling for SES and neighborhood influences, there is little difference in the prevalence of most conduct problems among African American, Hispanic, and non-Hispanic white youths. Ethnic minority youths, however, are more likely to join gangs.[6]
- Physical discipline may not be associated with child aggression among African American children.[7]
- Insufficient data exist on effective interventions for children who are from minority groups,[8] although minority youths benefit from juvenile offender programs as well as Caucasian youths.[9]

Low SES

- Living in poor and disadvantaged communities poses substantial risks for antisocial behavior in children in terms of unemployment, community disorganization, availability of drugs, the presence of adults involved in crime, community violence, and racial prejudice.[10]
- Lead exposure elevates risk for conduct problems.[11]
- Other indirect influences are that parents living in poverty are overwhelmed by stressors, hindering their parenting ability.

---

[1]APA, 2000.
[2]Burke, Loeber, & Birmaher, 2002; Moffit, Caspi, Rutter, & Silva, 2001.
[3]Ledingham, 1999; Loeber et al., 2000.
[4]Brestan & Eyberg, 2008; Ehrensaft, 2005.
[5]Nock et al., 2006.
[6]Lahey & Waldman, 2003.
[7]Deater-Deckard, Dodge, & Sorbring, 2005.
[8]Brestan & Eyberg, 1998.
[9]Wilson, Lipsey, & Soydan, 2003.
[10]Hill, 2002; Loeber et al., 2000; McGee & Williams, 1999.
[11]Marcus, Fulton, & Clarke, 2009.

Biological Influences

About 50% of the variance in the inheritance of CD may be accounted for by genetics (Gelhorn et al., 2006). Children with a biological predisposition toward ODD or CD may demonstrate as newborns a difficult temperament (defined as negative emotionality, intense and reactive responses to stress and frustration, and inflexibility), which predicts conduct problems (Nigg & Huang-Pollock, 2003). In contrast, an inhibited or approach-withdrawal temperament is protective against antisocial behaviors (Burke et al., 2002; Lahey & Waldman, 2003).

Children with a greater genetic predisposition to conduct problems are, unfortunately, more likely to encounter environments that foster antisocial behavior (Loeber et al., 2002). Children predisposed to CD are likely to be raised by ineffective (and sometimes abusive) parents with histories of antisocial behavior, substance abuse problems, and other psychopathology. With regard to mating, the likelihood of persons with particular characteristics selectively partnering and producing children is substantial for antisocial behavior (Ehrensaft, 2005).

Low IQ, especially verbal deficits, may give rise to the development of antisocial behaviors (Hill, 2002; Nigg & Huang-Pollack, 2003; Wachs, 2000). Children who are unable to identify emotions in themselves and others and cannot reason well verbally may react aggressively rather than by talking about their feelings, seeking comfort, or problem solving.

Male gender is a risk influence for the development of conduct problems. Females may demonstrate more empathy and distress over breaking rules and hurting others at a younger age than boys do (Alvarez & Ollendick, 2003). Girls' communication skills are also more developed at a younger age, as are their social skills. Other reasons for differences in rates of conduct problems may include gender-specific hormone levels, especially testosterone.

A large-scale British study of 16,000 children showed that among a variety of pregnancy and birth factors examined, only prenatal maternal smoking was highly associated with conduct problems in youths (Murray, Irving, Farrington, Colman, & Bloxsom, 2010).

Psychological Influences

More severe and chronic conduct problems and poorer treatment outcomes are associated with a number of personality traits, such as lack of guilt, empathy, emotional expression, low harm avoidance; and a preference for novel, exciting, and dangerous activities. These traits are found in about a third of treatment-referred children with early-onset conduct problems (Frick, 2006). However, the dominant personality profile for this type of CD features impulsivity, low verbal IQ, and a lack of emotional regulation, coupled with higher rates of family problems. Problems with emotional regulation result in impulsive and reactively aggressive behaviors.

Social Influences

Children who live in poor and disadvantaged communities experience a variety of risks. These include poverty, unemployment, community disorganization, availability of drugs, the presence of adults involved in crime, community violence, racial prejudice, overcrowding, poor and unresponsive schools, and lack of access to services—for example, day care, after-school programs, and health and mental health services (Hankin, Abela, Auberbach, McWhinnie, & Skitch, 2005; Hill, 2002; Loeber et al., 2000). These stressors may overwhelm parenting abilities.

Any parental psychopathology, such as depression (Siolberg, Maes, & Eaves, 2010), substance use problems, antisocial personality disorder, and criminal offending, are risk influences (Steinberg, 2000). Further, parental rejection of the child, lack of supervision, and lack of involvement in the child's activities are risk influences for the disruptive disorders. Girls with conduct problems are more likely to come from homes characterized by intense emotional conflict and unstable interpersonal relationships (Ehrensaft, 2005). Conversely, family stability, stable parental relationships, and parental social support are protective. Moreover, child physical abuse and sexual abuse, which often occur in the context of the family, are associated with conduct problems but only in the presence of genetic risk (Jaffee, Caspi, & Moffitt, 2005).

Peer relationships can act as either a risk or a protective mechanism for the onset of and recovery from conduct problems. In particular, deviant peer relationships are a major pathway for adolescent-onset CD (Frick, 2006). Youths with conduct problems display several distortions in the way they perceive and code their social experiences (Dodge, 2003; Kazdin, 2001). These distortions include an inability to produce a variety of strategies to manage interpersonal problems, difficulty figuring out ways to achieve a particular desired outcome, problems identifying the consequences of a particular action and its effects on others, a tendency to attribute hostile motivations to the actions of others, and failure to understand how others feel. The combination of perceived threat and limited options for managing social situations makes antisocial youths more likely to respond with aggression rather than with prosocial problem-solving strategies. In general, children diagnosed with conduct problems often experience rejection by peers for their aggression and lack of social skills (Miller-Johnson, Coie, Maumary-Gremaud, & Bierman, 2002). As a result, delinquent youths often consort together, further reinforcing their conduct problems.

Course and Recovery

Approximately 40% of youths with ODD later develop CD (Egger & Angold, 2006) while antisocial personality disorder in adulthood is a possibility for 25% (Lemery & Doelger, 2005) of males who had conduct problems as youths, whereas borderline personality disorder may be a risk for girls with antisocial behavior (Ehrensaft, 2005). Of all the child and adolescent mental disorders, ODD is singular in being associated with a wide variety of mental disorders manifesting in young adulthood (Copeland, Shanahan, Costello, & Angold, 2009). Outcomes may partially result from the number of risk influences. In one study, only 2% of youths who had no childhood risk influences showed persistent delinquency in adolescence, compared with 71% of youths who had risk influences in five different areas of life (Frick, 2006).

Many of the risk and protective mechanisms for recovering from ODD or CD and subsequent adjustment are the same as those involved with the onset of these disorders. One other major factor relates to age of onset; compared with the adolescent-onset types, the childhood-onset type results in more severe and chronic problems that may persist into adulthood (Moffit, Caspi, Harrington, & Milne, 2002).

Directions Part II, Strengths-Based Assessment   Formulate a risk and resilience assessment, both for the onset of the disorder and for the course of the disorder. What additional techniques could you use to elicit strengths in this client and how would you use them?

INTERVENTIONS FOR ODD AND CD

Psychosocial Interventions

Individual treatment with the most research attention involves cognitive-behavioral therapy (CBT) intervention, often provided in the school setting. Many of these interventions focus on social information processing (Baker & Scarth, 2002), which is described in Table 5.1. Although effective, CBT interventions for children with conduct problems tend to show only small effect sizes over control conditions (Wilson & Lipsey, 2007).

For adolescents, Lipsey, Landenberger, and Wilson (2007) conducted a review of 58 studies of adolescent and adult offenders who received treatment while they were on probation. They found a 25% reduction in re-offending as a result of treatment. They also looked at commercial packages of CBT, such as aggression replacement training (Goldstein, Glick, & Gibbs, 1998), which involves social skills training, feeling management, stress management, learning alternatives to aggressions and how to plan ahead, anger control, and moral education. There were no statistically significant benefits in using these types of commercial packages, however. Instead, implementation of the program was a key moderator. When programs were implemented as they had been designed, better outcomes were produced. Crucial elements of CBT were also identified.

Table 5.1 **Interventions for ODD/CD**

Intervention	Description	Empirically validated manuals/programs
Social information processing	Involves the following steps: (1) encoding and then interpreting situational and internal cues (2) setting goals (3) determining possible responses (4) role playing responses	Anger control training (Lochman, Barry, & Pardini, 2003).
Parent training	Parents are taught to specify goals for behavioral change; track target behaviors; positively reinforce prosocial conduct through the use of attention, praise, and point systems; and employ alternative discipline methods.	Helping the Noncompliant Child (ages 3–8) (Forehand & McMahon, 1981), Living with Children (ages 3–12) (Patterson & Gullion, 1968), and The Incredible Years (ages 2–8) (Webster-Stratton, 2001).
Multisystemic therapy (MST)	A manualized, ecologically based family preservation program targeted at juvenile offending.	Henggeler, Schoenwald, Borduin, Rowland, and Cunningham (1998) and Henggeler, Schoenwald, Rowland, and Cunningham (2001).
Functional family therapy (FFT)	A behavioral-systems family therapy targeted at juvenile offending.	Alexander and Parsons (1982) and Gordon, Arbuthnot, Gustafson, and McGreen (1988).

Practice Contexts

Practice Behavior Example: *Provide leadership in promoting sustainable changes in service delivery and practice to improve the quality of social services.*

Critical Thinking Question: Given that cognitive-behavioral treatment has been the most researched intervention for ODD and CD, what will you do if you work at a school system, residential facility, or other treatment setting with a significant numbers of youths with ODD and CD, and these approaches are not used?

Critical Thinking

Practice Behavior Example: *Distinguish, appraise, and integrate multiple sources of knowledge, including research-based knowledge, and practice wisdom.*

Critical Thinking Question: Given the information provided about medication for this population and your knowledge of the risks of these medications, how will you advise families about the use of medication?

Anger control and interpersonal problem solving were important elements, whereas victim impact and behavior modification were not.

Family interventions have been tested for the treatment of conduct problems (Eyberg, Nelson, & Boggs, 2008). Of these, the most extensively investigated and demonstrably effective model is parent training (Table 5.1) (Dretzke, Davenport, Frew, et al., 2009; McCart et al., 2006). Other family interventions are described in Table 6.1. For more information on the empirical evidence of these models, see Corcoran (2011).

Medication

As discussed, many youths with ODD or CD will have comorbid ADHD. Stimulants are effective for reducing aggression with this population (Pappadopulos et al., 2006). In addition, risperidone reduces aggression substantially in youths with CD and below average IQ. Other classes of medication have either not been studied sufficiently or show little evidence of effectiveness. Aggression uncomplicated by ADHD should first be treated with a psychosocial approach, and such an approach should continue even when medications are used.

> **Directions Part III, Goal Setting and Treatment Planning** Given your risk and resilience assessments of the individual, your knowledge of the disorder, and evidence-based practice guidelines, formulate goals and a possible treatment plan for this individual.

CRITICAL PERSPECTIVE

The DSM criteria for CD include overt aggression, and as a result of this focus, females with this disorder may be underrecognized. The female presentation of CD tends to be less noticeable, because it involved indirect or relational aggressive behaviors such as the exclusion of others; threats of withdrawal from relationships; efforts to alienate, ostracize, or defame others; and rumor spreading (Ledingham, 1999; Loeber et al., 2000). Some experts have suggested that the diagnostic criteria for CD should be modified for females to include these variables (Loeber et al., 2000; Ohan & Johnston, 2005), although others have argued that there are no gender differences in symptom patterns (Moffit et al., 2001).

In their critique of the DSM-IV, Kutchins and Kirk (1997) emphasize the importance of distinguishing between behavior as a dysfunction within a person and as a reaction to life stressors. Although it is possible that a client's behaviors signify internal dysfunction as postulated by the DSM, it is possible that he or she is reacting negatively

Critical Thinking

Practice Behavior Example: *Distinguish, appraise, and integrate multiple sources of knowledge, including research-based knowledge, and practice wisdom.*

Critical Thinking Question: When there have been significant life stressors in a child's life that have played a role in the child's problems, how can suggested evidence-based approaches be adapted to take into account these stressors?

to environmental circumstances, or more likely, that a combination of these forces is working together. Indeed, the literature on ODD and CD identifies coercive family factors and other social environment variables as key to the development of these disorders. The DSM view of internal dysfunction is therefore not in line with what has been empirically validated as contributing to these disorders.

Directions Part IV, Critical Perspective   Formulate a critique of the diagnosis as it relates to this case example. Questions to consider include the following: Does this diagnosis represent a valid mental disorder from the social work perspective? Is this diagnosis significantly different from other possible diagnoses? Your critique should be based on the values of the social work profession (which are incongruent in some ways with the medical model) and the validity of the specific diagnostic criteria applied to this case.

Case 2   The Boy With No Restraint

Sam is a nine-year-old African American male who is new to a school that offers educational services for children who can no longer perform in an ordinary school setting. He came from an elementary school where he attended a special education program. He was referred to the specialized school because he continued to exhibit significant behavioral, social, emotional, and academic difficulties.

The prior public elementary school's psychological report stated that Sam spent a majority of his time out of the classroom, either on suspension or in counseling sessions because of his behavior. The report also stated that he required physical restraint on a number of occasions and was recently so aggressive and dangerous that the school filed a complaint with the court asserting that he was out of control both at home and in school. No further information was available about the outcome of this referral to the courts, nor about the specifics of the behavior that warranted such a referral.

Sam lives with his mother, his three-year-old brother, paternal great-grandmother, and uncle in his great-grandmother's home. The family recently moved from the home of Sam's grandmother after a heated argument between Sam's mother and her own mother. This is the third move and Sam's fourth school in just three years. Sam's father was shot to death a year ago (his mother was no longer with him at the time), and he has no contact with his father's family except for his paternal great-grandmother. Sam did have a relationship with his paternal grandmother, but she passed away six months ago.

Sam's mother completed the 11th grade, is currently unemployed, and collects Supplemental Security Income. It is unclear why Sam's mother receives such assistance. Sam also has a 12-year-old half brother and a 10-year-old half sister. All the children have the same mother but different fathers, and the older children live with their paternal relatives.

Sam's family had home-based services to assist with the difficulties they were experiencing, but the services were terminated several months ago because the agency lost all contact with Sam's mother. The home-based worker stated her belief that Sam's mother may have started a new relationship, and that in the past she has allowed her relationships with men to take away from her time with her children. The worker also stated that the unstable living situation and Sam's mother's mental state (which she believes may be dysthymic disorder) make it difficult to work with the family on a consistent basis. Through the home-based services agency, Sam was connected with mental health counseling, but his attendance and participation were sporadic.

About a year ago Sam took the Woodcock Johnson tests, which indicated that his reading, writing, and math skills were significantly delayed for his age, IQ, and educational level. His academic achievement is poor because of these delays. Because of his refusal to participate in a number of the tests, his IQ score could not be accurately identified, but the examiner estimated it to be in the range of 74 to 87.

Since the beginning of the school year Sam has continued to exhibit aggressive and dangerous behaviors. In a meeting with the behavior staff director of the school, the social work intern learned that Sam will have to be searched daily because of his many threats of bringing a knife or gun to school to kill staff. Sam has had to be physically restrained by staff at least a dozen times. The director stated that she would never restrain Sam alone and that it takes two to three staff to do so safely. In this same meeting, the director stated that Sam has attempted to stab staff with pencils and thumbtacks grabbed from hallway bulletin boards.

In locked restraint, Sam will kick the door and scream out obscenities. According to incident reports, Sam has spit at, lunged at, and attacked staff and has even tried biting. He tends to blame others for his behavior ("I'm in support because [staff member] said a bad word to me."). He neither shows remorse for his behavior nor empathy toward people he has been angry with.

Sam's teacher reports that he often has difficulty transitioning from one location to another or from one assignment to another. Sam refuses to complete his school assignments and will not accept redirection from his teacher. He often becomes verbally disrespectful toward her, but she reports he has not yet been physically aggressive. She does report that he often destroys property (ripping papers, breaking pencils, turning over chairs and desks) when upset and is known for tearing up his school worksheets when he does not want to work on them.

Sam currently spends a significant amount of time out of class because of his behaviors. He is falling behind in class work because of his absence from lessons and his refusal to participate. Not surprisingly, Sam doesn't have friends because other children are scared of his out-of-control behaviors.

Sam's mother is difficult to contact, and she doesn't return telephone calls in a timely manner. She is guarded about sharing personal information. She attended the most recent individualized educational plan (IEP) meeting and reports that since Sam was a young child, she has seen similar behaviors at home. When Sam gets frustrated, he becomes verbally and physically abusive toward her.

Sam's mother states that she has sought outside help to control Sam's behavior. She attempted mental health counseling, but discontinued services because he refused to speak. Sam's mother says that she is overwhelmed and has tried every punishment—spanking, sending him to his room, taking away privileges—but that none of her efforts has been successful in changing his behavior. She says that he does not seem depressed to her, just angry. Sam's mother states that she has also called Juvenile Court to relinquish Sam. She was told to come in to complete the intake process but did not do so.

ㅅ🕇ㅅ
Diversity in Practice

Practice Behavior Example: *Recognize the extent to which a culture's structures and values may oppress, marginalize, alienate, or create or enhance privilege and power.*

Critical Thinking Question: When considering children who are of ethnic minority and living in poverty, determine how oppression, discrimination, and trauma may have played a role in the development of an ODD or CD disorder?

Sam presents as a well-dressed and well-groomed young boy. When he is not upset, he is engaging and very polite. He states that he enjoys coming to the sessions with the social work intern, and he plays games cooperatively, though with high energy, during these times. He shows particular interest in sports, especially basketball. He doesn't bring up his deceased father or other aspects of his family life and shies away from questions about them, although he admits to feeling "sad" about his father's and his grandmother's deaths. He denies, however, that he is sad in general. He says he has not been sexually or physically abused, but says that in the past his mother and a couple of her boyfriends have "whipped" him but not left marks. Sam's most recent physical examination, performed a year ago, confirms that he is in good health and particularly noted that he has a good appetite.

Please go to the Appendix for directions to this case.

Case 3 Nell's Family Conflicts

Nell is a 13-year-old Hispanic-Caucasian female. She is currently detained at the county juvenile detention center for violating the conditions of probation by continuing to run away from home.

Nell previously resided with her mother, stepfather, 15-year-old brother, and 14-year-old sister in a single-family rental in a suburban, working-class neighborhood. Nell also has two older brothers who no longer live at home. The family just moved two months ago after being evicted from their last residence. The landlord told them that the neighbors complained about the police constantly being called to the house for family arguments and Nell's runaway behavior. Nell also admitted that she stole money from a neighbor's home on several occasions. The neighbors eventually confronted her, but the incident was not reported to the police.

Nell stated that she does not get along with her stepfather (he has been in her life for two years) and has a conflicted relationship with her mother. She says that she has a close relationship with her sister. Nell's parents agree that her stepfather is strict and inflexible about rules, whereas her mother gets in the middle of conflicts between her husband and her daughters. Nell's mother admits that her children take advantage of her. Nell's mother and stepfather claim that their relationship is "all right," but that the arguments over discipline and Nell's behavior in particular exact a toll. Despite Nell's negative behaviors, both her mother and stepfather actively participate in meetings involving treatment planning, academic issues, and court dates. They both stated that they love and care for Nell a great deal but are unsure what they can do to help her.

The family's socioeconomic status is low. Nell's stepfather works in retail, and Nell's mother said that she quit her job as a secretary when she was diagnosed with breast cancer. Her mother stated that she worries that her children do not always have the same clothing and "things" that their peers have. The family does have health insurance.

Nell is in seventh grade and is currently being schooled through the county school system at the juvenile detention center. She does enough, she says, "to get by." According to her parents, Nell was an honor roll student and a member of the safety patrol and the school choir until her behavior changed drastically about a year ago.

In the past year Nell has refused to obey her parents' rules and has run away from home over a dozen times. She often stays out late at night and refuses to tell her parents where she is going or with whom. She often misses school when on the run, and her grades have suffered significantly. Nell has admitted to hanging out with males who are in their 20s, including known gang members, but denies personal membership in any gang.

Nell's parents report that any time she does not get her way, she throws temper tantrums and threatens to run away. They state that she went from being a sweet, loving child to being disrespectful and unmanageable. Nell's acting out seemed to start when Nell's older sister disclosed to her mother that their biological father sexually molested her. Nell denies that she witnessed the sexual abuse or that she was sexually abused herself. After the sexual abuse disclosure, Nell's mother was diagnosed with breast cancer. Nell has shared some concern about this, stating, "I don't want my mom to die."

Nell admitted to engaging in sexual activity with at least ten male partners in the past several months. On at least two occasions she had sex with male strangers in laundromats for $5 because she was trying to save up enough money to move to another state. Nell stated that she almost always initiates the sex and cannot seem to control this behavior. She thought she was pregnant on more than one occasion, but stated that tests she took while in shelter care confirmed that she was not pregnant and did not have any sexually transmitted diseases. Nell has previously accused male staff at the shelter and the juvenile detention center of touching her in a sexually inappropriate manner, but all cases have been investigated and deemed unfounded.

Nell stated that she started using various substances about a year ago. Marijuana is her drug of choice, and at the height of her use (four months ago) she smoked every other day. Nell reported last using marijuana one month ago. Additionally, around this time she smoked marijuana laced with cocaine "once or twice" and reported snorting several lines of cocaine on one occasion.

Nell reported that she has also used alcohol, and four months ago her use increased to several times a week. She stated that she can consume five to seven 12-ounce beers before she is intoxicated. Nell reported vomiting on several occasions and experiencing three or four blackouts. She stated that she last consumed alcohol one month ago before she was admitted to the juvenile county detention center.

Nell admitted to dextromethorphan (DXM) use beginning this past year. DXM, the active ingredient found in many over-the-counter cough and cold medications, produces hallucinogenic and stimulant effects in high doses. Seven months ago, because of her running away and substance use, Nell was placed in a county shelter care residential facility. While there, staff reportedly took her to the hospital after she ingested 10 tablets of DXM. She stated that she last used DXM four months ago when she ingested 15 pills.

Nell denied experiencing withdrawal symptoms from any substance. She said that she does not see anything wrong with "smoking a little weed and having a few drinks" and was unable to articulate any negative consequences associated with substance use. She admitted that her incidents of sexual activity have been when she is under the influence of one substance or another, even when she has been with adult males unknown to her. She acknowledged that it is illegal for her to drink alcohol and use drugs and knows that it upsets her mother, but she has no intention of stopping. Nell reported that the majority of her friends also use alcohol and drugs. Access is no problem, she claims, because her friends are older and able to obtain marijuana and alcohol.

Nell's mother and stepfather state that they have witnessed her under the influence of substances and believe that a problem exists. Nell's mother says she herself rarely drinks, but Nell's stepfather says he has a "couple of beers" each night when he gets home from work. Both parents deny that he has a problem with alcohol. However, Nell's mother said that Nell's biological father was an alcoholic, and it was one of the reasons she left him, along with his sporadic employment. Nell has not had contact with her father since the divorce three years ago.

Nell has hypothyroidism, a medical condition in which the thyroid is underactive and does not produce a sufficient amount of thyroid hormones. She reported no other health or medical issues. Nell takes a thyroid hormone medication, Levothyroxine.

Nell ran away from shelter care but was returned there until five months ago, when she used a paper clip to cut her nickname into her forearm. At that point Nell was referred to a psychiatric hospital. Nell denied suicidality in the past or at present.

Diversity in Practice

Practice Behavior Example: _Recognize and communicate their understanding of the importance of difference in shaping life experiences._

Critical Thinking Question: For girls displaying a CD diagnosis, how may gender play a role in the development and presentation of the symptoms?

After her stay at the psychiatric hospital, Nell went home. Soon after, she had a fight with her mother and drank kitchen cleaner. Nell insisted that she drank it to make her mother feel bad and had no desire actually to harm herself. She was then placed in a non-profit home for at-risk adolescents but ran away on three occasions. She was put on probation for her runaway behaviors.

When reporting on her current mood, Nell states that although at times she feels sad and worried, she believes it is because of her circumstances—being locked up at the juvenile detention center. She is convinced she will feel better once she returns home with her family. While being interviewed, Nell showed little remorse for her actions and their effect on her family or her personal well-being.

Nell has several strengths. She has an engaging personality, is smart, and has an excellent singing voice. She used to be in the school choir, and her goal is to become a professional singer. Nell believes that her problems will be solved when she and her sister are able to get along with their mother and stepfather. Nell does not wish to return home until her relationship with her parents improves and they no longer see the need to criticize her and yell at her.

Please go to the Appendix for directions to this case.

PRACTICE TEST The following questions will test your knowledge of the content found within this chapter. For additional assessment, including licensing-exam type questions on applying chapter content to practice behaviors, visit **MySocialWorkLab.com**

1. A major difference between ODD and CD is:
   a. CD does not occur until age 12
   b. ODD is not characterized by violations of the rights of others
   c. CD is not characterized by defiant behavior
   d. ODD is not characterized by runaway behavior

2. Which of the following is true about the development of these disorders?
   a. They are due to deficits in social development
   b. They probably involve gene–environment interactions
   c. Strict parenting is implicated in their development
   d. Neighborhood factors play a primary role in their development

3. Fifteen-year-old Carolyn was referred to the mental health center after a series of runaway behaviors and recently setting fires to dry brush along the side of a highway. In the past, Carolyn had been in legal trouble for a series of petty theft incidents, and she had been in trouble with authority figures since the first grade. She was argumentative, moody, oppositional, and inconsistent in tending to her responsibilities. Carolyn did poorly in school, with no evident motivation to study. Although she appears to meet the criteria for both ODD and CD, this diagnostic decision would be based on:
   a. The predominance of CD symptoms
   b. The predominance of ODD symptoms
   c. The fire setting behavior
   d. The fact that when a client qualifies for both diagnoses, CD should be selected

4. Carolyn's social worker was intent on selecting the most appropriate intervention for Carolyn, based on evidence of effectiveness. This would be:
   a. Aggression replacement training
   b. Interpersonal problem solving
   c. Parent training
   d. Cognitive therapy

5. What ethical issues arise when treating youths with disruptive behavior disorders in terms of managing personal reactions, responding to harm and safety of others and the child, and respecting the dignity and worth of the individual?

6. What factors will help you decide the type of treatment approach that will be appropriate for a child with ODD or CD? Who will you involve in treatment?

SUCCEED WITH

Visit **MySocialWorkLab** for more licensing-exam test questions, and to access case studies, videos, and much more.

6

Alzheimer's Disease

Competencies Applied with Practice Behaviors — in this Chapter				
☒ Professional Identity	☒ Ethical Practice	▪ Critical Thinking	▪ Diversity in Practice	▪ Human Rights & Justice
▪ Research-Based Practice	▪ Human Behavior	▪ Policy Practice	▪ Practice Contexts	☒ Engage, Assess, Intervene, Evaluate

Mrs. Shirley Washington is an 89-year-old African American female who was admitted to the hospital with a diagnosis of lumbago (the medical term used for general lower back pain) and urinary retention (failure to empty the bladder completely). Mrs. Washington appeared confused and disoriented when the social work intern attempted to assess her. The social work intern then made an appointment with Mrs. Washington's son, who was listed in her chart as the emergency contact.

Mr. Washington appeared relieved when contacted by the social work intern. He reported that he was the primary caretaker of his elderly mother, whom a physician had diagnosed with dementia about one year ago after performing a series of tests. Mr. Washington said that the symptoms were initially not serious. Mrs. Washington would occasionally forget things, but she was able to take care of herself. The son stated, however, that during the last three or four months his mother was becoming more forgetful. She would pick up various personal items and then put them down, becoming frustrated when she was unable to find them. Mr. Washington reported that he kept finding these items in random places in and around the house. In addition, Mr. Washington reported that his mother is no longer able to perform certain activities, such as knitting, that she had done throughout her life. Mrs. Washington, he went on to say, often did not recognize her own children or other relatives and friends. She became panicky at such times and would yell at people to leave her alone. These episodes became worse around sunset.

Cognitive disorders are characterized by deficits in a person's thought processes that are due to brain dysfunction and account for a significant decline from the previous level of functioning (American Psychiatric Association [APA], 2000). The major classifications of cognitive disorders include *delirium* (a time-limited cognitive disturbance), the *amnestic disorders* (with memory impairment as the only symptom), and the *dementias* (which feature multiple cognitive deficits including memory impairment). This chapter focuses on Alzheimer's disease (AD), a debilitating cognitive disorder classified as a dementia. AD involves a progressive decline in the number of functioning neurons in the person's central nervous system (He et al., 2010). About 50 to 60% of persons with dementia have AD, the most common form of dementia worldwide (Dartingues, 2009). There are many other dementias that, unlike AD, stem from identifiable medical conditions; for example, vascular dementia is produced by a series of small strokes.

PREVALENCE AND COMORBIDITY

Old age is often falsely stereotyped as a stage of life that includes high rates of AD. Still, the disease affects as many as 5 million Americans (Mosconi et al., 2010). More than half of them receive care at home, whereas the others reside in health care institutions. The prevalence of AD doubles for every age group five years beyond age 65. Some studies indicate that nearly half of all people aged 85 and older have symptoms of AD (Boise, Neal, & Kaye, 2004). Prevalence estimates range from 1.4 to 1.6% for persons aged 65 to 69 years, rising to between 16 and 25% for persons over 85 years old. A study sponsored by the National Institute on Aging indicated that the annual number of cases in the United States is expected to double by the middle of the 21st century (Brookmeyer et al., 2011). The proportion of new cases identified after age 85 will increase from 40% (in 1995) to 62% in 2050, when the youngest baby boomers reach that age.

The most common observable symptoms of AD are apathy (found in 72% of persons), agitation and aggression (60%), anxiety (48%), and depression (48%) (Waldemar et al., 2007). It must be emphasized, however, that recent research has shown that persons with AD retain more of their emotional responsiveness to external stimuli than was once assumed (Henry, Rendell, Scicluna, Jackson, & Phillips, 2009). Ten to twenty percent of such persons qualify for a diagnosis of major depressive disorder, which presents somewhat differently than "typical" depression. In AD depression features the symptoms of poor motivation, delusions, anxiety, and agitation, but not suicidal ideation, guilt, or low self-esteem (Rosenberg et al., 2005).

ASSESSMENT GUIDELINES

Social workers who are involved with clients who have dementia are likely to function as members of interdisciplinary health care teams. They can provide comprehensive psychosocial assessments of client and family functioning, but AD must be diagnosed by a physician. The major symptoms of AD (listed in the order in which they develop) include loss of recent memory, loss of judgment, problems with abstract thinking, loss of higher order functions (planning), and personality changes (exaggerations of normal traits). There are no medical tests that can positively identify the presence of the disorder; instead, it is diagnosed when other possibilities are ruled out (Mungas et al., 2010). The following guidelines, however, can help differentiate possible AD from other cognitive and *Diagnostic and Statistical Manual of Mental Disorders* (DSM) disorders:

- Dementia is not diagnosed if the cognitive deficits occur exclusively during a period of delirium.
- Memory impairment alone is not sufficient to diagnose dementia (it may indicate the presence of an amnestic disorder).
- Some dementias are due to identifiable medical causes such as strokes, anemia, brain tumors, hypothyroidism, infections, and metabolic deficiencies.
- Cognitive impairments may occur due to the effects of substance intoxication or withdrawal, so these possible etiologies must be ruled out.
- Dementia differs from the cognitive disorder of schizophrenia, in that the latter diagnosis has an earlier age of onset, less severe cognitive impairment, and symptoms that usually include hallucinations and delusions.
- Memory deficits may be present in major depression; these deficits tend to remit with the depression.
- Most older adults experience age-related cognitive impairments, but these are not as severe as the symptoms of dementia; still, it is often difficult to distinguish "normal" cognitive decline from the early stages of dementia.

Engage, Assess, Intervene, Evaluate

Practice Behavior Example: Assess client strengths and limitations.

Critical Thinking Question: In what areas can social workers look for strengths in the person with AD? In the family system? What are some techniques that the social worker might use, or what kinds of questions might the social worker ask, toward these ends?

Mr. Washington stated that he locked the house at night and took the key to his bedroom because Mrs. Washington would sometimes wander through the house. On several occasions when the key was in the lock, she wandered into the streets and got lost. Fortunately, Mrs. Washington was never injured and was returned home by either neighbors or the police. Mr. Washington mentioned that his mother took medication for dementia, but the medication caused constipation. She ate prunes every morning and drank milk of magnesia.

When the social work intern asked Mr. Washington about his mother's substance use, he said that she used to smoke cigarettes. She didn't smoke on a regular basis anymore, but sometimes people would give her cigarettes that she would save and smoke later. Unfortunately, she would often put a lit cigarette down and then forget about it, leading to several small fires in the home. Mrs. Washington also used to drink two bottles of beer every night with dinner until about two months ago, when Mr. Washington started to give his mother nonalcoholic beer as recommended by her primary care physician.

Mr. Washington reported that his mother was still able to take care of most of her activities of daily living (ADLs). However, she did require help with washing and bathing. Because she had difficulty getting in and out of the bathtub, Mr. Washington remodeled the bathroom and installed a tub with a seat and a door on the side. When helping his mother undress for the bath during the past few weeks, Mr. Washington noticed some occasional incontinence.

Mr. Washington reported that the house in which he and his mother live has two levels, with 12 steps between levels. Mrs. Washington had no difficulty climbing the stairs prior to her recent hospitalization. She also did not use a cane, wheelchair, or any other durable medical equipment.

Mr. Washington stated that until recently one of his brothers lived in town and helped with the care of his mother; however, this brother moved out of state several months ago for a work-related reason. Mrs. Washington has two more sons, both of whom live out of state, and grandchildren scattered throughout the country. Mrs. Washington also has an elderly brother and sister who live in the area. In addition, Mr. Washington has many friends and a few other relatives who live locally and occasionally help out with the care of his mother.

Mr. Washington mentioned that his mother's symptoms of dementia have worsened over the past few months, and it has become increasingly difficult for him to take care of her. He expressed frustration that his mother had recently failed to recognize him on several occasions and had started shouting, believing him to be an intruder. Mr. Washington requested that the social work intern help him place his mother in long-term care because of his inability to continue providing adequate care. At 70 years of age, he is becoming an elderly person himself and is experiencing some health problems, including back pain, which make it difficult to help with his mother's ADLs such as washing and bathing. He has never married and said he needs to concentrate on looking after himself.

As for Mrs. Washington's previous life history, she received a high school diploma and spent most of her adult years taking care of her children. She worked for the Census Bureau for about 10 years.

Mr. Washington indicated that to his knowledge the family had no history of dementia or any other mental health disorders. He admitted that Mrs. Washington followed a high-fat diet for most of her life, eating a lot of fried foods.

Mrs. Washington lacks financial assets; she has no savings and does not own a home. Mr. Washington owns the house they are living in and has the financial means to take care of her. Mrs. Washington has health care access through Medicare and a private insurance company from her deceased husband's employment.

Professional Identity

Practice Behavior Example: *Attend to professional roles and boundaries.*

Critical Thinking Question: How much do social workers need to learn about the roles and activities of the various other health professionals working with Alzheimer's patients in order to clearly understand their own roles? What are the appropriate professional boundaries between social workers and physicians, and social workers and nurses? In Mrs. Washington's case, what role activities might be appropriate for the social worker?

Directions Part I, Multiaxial Diagnosis Given the case information prepare the following: a multiaxial diagnosis, the rationale for the diagnosis and global assessment of functioning score, and additional information you would have wanted to know in order to make a more accurate diagnosis.

Multiaxial Diagnosis

Axis I:
Axis II:
Axis III:
Axis IV:
Axis V:

Rationale and Differential Diagnosis

Additional Information Needed

BIOPSYCHOSOCIAL RISK AND RESILIENCE INFLUENCES

Onset

AD may be recorded as *with early onset* (before age 65) or *with late onset*. A minority of AD patients develop the disorder between the ages of 40 and 50, and an earlier onset implies a more rapid course. This form of AD often runs in families (McMurtray, Ringman, & Chao, 2006). In general, AD has a gradual onset and produces a slow, steady decline in the person's cognitive functioning. Risks for AD are heavily weighted toward biological mechanisms, but there are also some psychological and social influences on its development.

Biological Risk Influences

The role of genetics and biology is universally accepted as critical in the etiology and course of AD. An analysis of the Swedish Twin Registry reported a 58 to 79% biological heritability for AD for both men and women (Gatz et al., 2006). Age of onset is significantly more similar for monozygotic than for dizygotic twin pairs, however, indicating an important role for environmental influences.

In people with AD, brain cells in the cortex and hippocampus (areas that are responsible for learning, reasoning, and memory) die after they become clogged with two abnormal structures: *neurofibrillary tangles* (twisted masses of protein fibers) and *plaques* (deposits of a protein called amyloid) (Meeks, Ropacki, & Jeste, 2006). Symptoms begin with changes to the amyloid, which is part of a larger molecule, the amyloid-precursor protein (APP), which extends from a neuron's outer membrane (Ziabreva, Perry, & Perry, 2006). Normally APP is "chopped up" by other enzymes and dissolves after its use. In AD, however, a pair of enzymes (beta and gamma secretase) cleaves APP in the wrong places, leaving behind insoluble amyloid fragments, which then become prone to bind to each other and to other proteins, forming fibrils that make them even less soluble and harder for the body to clear (He et al., 2010). These fibrils in turn bind with one another to form plaques. When these substances reach a certain threshold, the brain can no longer function efficiently. Brain neurons slowly die and lower levels of essential neurotransmitters are produced, creating signaling problems among cells.

Specific information about genetic processes in AD is lacking, but mutations in any of four genes (located on chromosomes 1, 14, 19, and 21) are associated with its development (Glodzik-Sobanska et al., 2009). The APOE-2 and APOE-3 proteins appear to protect against AD by strengthening structures vital to nerve cell functioning.

For many years amyloid-beta plaques could be observed only in autopsied brains, but methods have recently emerged that allow the plaques to be seen in living brains (Mosconi et al., 2010). Researchers have discovered a greater number of protein clumps among the healthy adult children of persons with AD, especially among those whose mothers had been diagnosed, although the presence of these plaques does not necessarily mean that a person will develop the disease.

Some biological risk influences for AD are associated with gender and race. There is a gender difference in AD incidence, but it is not significant until the age of 90, after which it is higher among women (Musicco, 2010). One study of thousands of persons with AD and healthy volunteers revealed that the APOE-4 gene appears to increase the risk of AD for persons in many ethnic groups, but perhaps more consistently for Caucasians (Bachman, Green, Benke, Cupples, & Farrer, 2003). Persons with Down syndrome, which is related to an extra copy of chromosome 21, have an increased risk of AD. Mothers who deliver such children prior to age 35 also have an increased risk, because they may carry the marker gene. It must be emphasized that AD is a genetically heterogeneous disorder, and advances in the knowledge of the human genome may contribute to more accurate profiles of its development and course (Papassotiropoulos, Fountoulakis, Dunckley, Stephan, & Reiman, 2006).

Several biological protective influences have been identified for AD (Jedrziewski, Lee, & Trojanowski, 2005). These include regular exercise (Middleton, Barnes, Lui, & Yaffe, 2010), the maintenance of low cholesterol, the use of statins (medications that work to lower cholesterol), and the absence of head trauma.

Psychological Risk Influences

There are no known psychological causes of AD. One meta-analysis has, however, identified depression as a small but significant risk influence (Ownby, Crocco, Acevedo, John, & Loewenstein, 2006). Another five-year study of older adults found that although a history of depression did not predict an onset of AD, depressive symptoms are often an early symptom of the disease (Gatz, Tyas, St. John, & Montgomery, 2005). Higher rates of depression are found among first- and second-degree relatives of persons with AD, perhaps because the characteristic neurofibrillary tangles are higher in cerebral areas where the pathogenesis of depression takes place; thus the two disorders may share a biological association (Saczynski et al., 2010). When people begin to experience the symptoms of AD, however, depression and anxiety are common. People may exhibit mood swings, become distrustful of others, and show increased stubbornness. Those emotional states and behaviors may be in response to frustration and changes in self-image.

Social Risk Influences

Lifestyle factors may contribute to negative health conditions that put some people at greater risk for AD, although the role of these influences is somewhat speculative (Steinberg et al., 2006). The prevalence of possible contributing factors, such as infections, nutritional deficiencies, brain injury, endocrine conditions, cerebrovascular diseases, seizure disorders, substance abuse, and brain tumors, varies across cultural groups. Persons with higher risks of these types may have relatively low educational backgrounds and occupational status. They may consume high-fat foods, have low blood levels of folic acid and vitamin B-12, and have elevated levels of homocysteine, an amino acid that has been linked to circulatory problems. Their lifestyles may include poor exercise habits, cigarette smoking (Cataldo, Prochaska, & Glantz, 2010), and the ingestion of environmental toxins such as water pollutants.

Protective risk influences for AD have been identified in one literature review as including high educational level (Rolstad et al., 2010), continued employment, regular engagement in activities that use cognitive functions, and the pursuit of leisure activities (Jedrziewski et al., 2005).

Course and Recovery

AD cannot be cured or stabilized indefinitely; its downward course is unfortunately unremitting. The duration of its course is unpredictable, but 5 to 10 years is most common (Steeman, Decasterle, Godderis, & Grypdonck, 2006). Some mechanisms can either hasten or slow the progression of the disease, as outlined in Table 6.1. This section centers on family caregiving, as there are positive associations between caregiver coping and patient survival time (McClendon, Smyth, & Neundorfer, 2004), and between dysfunctional coping strategies and caregiver depression and anxiety (Cooper, Katone, Orrell, & Livingston, 2004). Research consistently shows that there is a sensitive psychological balance between patients with AD and their caregivers, and that the patient's agitation is related to caregiver behaviors and attitudes (Zarit & Femia, 2008).

Only one third of persons with dementia in the United States live in nursing homes (Boise et al., 2004), which means that families are the primary caregivers for the majority of these individuals. Although the symptoms of AD are distressing for the affected person, the situation may be equally stressful for the caregivers (Phillipe, Lalloue, & Preux, 2006). Behavior problems—perceptual disturbances, mood disturbances, wandering, agitation, sleep disturbances, incontinence, and refusal to eat—are the leading reason family members seek professional intervention on behalf of a person with apparent dementia (Lott & Klein, 2003). Predictors of caregiver burden are the older adult's behavioral disturbances (especially at night) and the presence of hallucinations (Allegri et al., 2006).

The caregiver faces ongoing challenges in balancing his or her own limits on time, energy, and patience. The stresses experienced by family caregivers may be heightened by their fears of loss, guilt over not being an adequate caregiver, ambivalence about the caregiver role, conflicts with each other, and fears about their own mortality. Caregivers with preexisting symptoms of depression experience these stresses more severely (Lu & Austrom, 2005). Support availability is significantly associated with less stress (Morano, 2003). Many caregivers also develop some degree of resentment toward the client because of the relentless responsibilities associated with client care (Martin-Cook, Remakel-Davis, Svetlick, Hynan, & Weiner, 2003).

There are some differences among caregivers of older adults (not limited to AD) from different ethnic groups with regard to stress, resource availability, and psychological outcomes. A meta-analysis of empirical studies found that minority caregivers were younger, less likely to be a spouse, and more likely to receive informal support (Pinquant & Sorensen, 2006). They provided more care than Caucasian caregivers and felt stronger obligations to do so. Asian American caregivers used less formal support than Caucasian caregivers and, like Hispanic caregivers, were more depressed than their Caucasian counterparts. One focus group study found that in each of these cultures, families were slower to seek out professional interventions than were their counterparts in Western cultures, being more likely to rely on cultural traditions of family caregiving (Jones, Chow, & Getz, 2005).

Engage, Assess, Intervene, Evaluate

Practice Behavior Example: *Implement prevention interventions that enhance client capacities.*

Critical Thinking Question: Now that you are aware of the risk and protective influences for AD, what kinds of preventive activities would you suggest to a family that experiences significant biological risks? How might your suggestions affect a family dealing with biological risks associated with AD?

Directions Part II, Biopsychosocial Risk and Resilience Assessment   Formulate a risk and resilience assessment, both for the onset of the disorder and for the course of the disorder, including the strengths that you see for this individual and the techniques you would use to elicit them.

Table 6.1   Biopsychosocial Risk and Resilience Assessment for the Course (or Quality of Life) of AD

Risk Influences	Protective Influences
Biological	
Early onset (before age 60)	Later onset (after age 60)
Cerebrovascular disease	Good physical health
Poor diet (fatty foods, low blood levels of folic acid and vitamin B-12)	Low-fat diet, high in folic acid and vitamin B-12, high fish diet
Psychological	
High levels of stress	Lower levels of stress
Depression	Stable mood
Social	
Later diagnosis	Early detection and intervention
Lack of resource availability	Resource availability
Absence of psychosocial interventions	Interpersonal supports
	Psychosocial interventions

INTERVENTION

Goals

Interventions for persons with AD are focused on promoting the client's safety, comfort, and productivity for as long as possible and helping the family or other caregivers be more competent and capable of managing the stresses that accompany their role. Early assessment and diagnosis can reveal the range of potential problems in need of intervention, help individuals prepare for the future, align them with support groups and other community resources, provide financial and legal referrals for persons and their families (such as information about disability benefits and power of attorney), and initiate ongoing counseling and monitoring.

Psychosocial Interventions

A literature review of evidence-based psychosocial interventions for AD patients found support for group activities, physical activities, activity planning based on an evaluation of behavior patterns, and sensory interventions such as music (Vernooij-Dassen, Vasse, Zuidema, Cohen-Mansfield, & Moyle, 2010). The psychosocial interventions described later provide examples of these kinds of interventions and are widely accepted by professionals as effective, but it should be kept in mind that there is not yet extensive evidence-based research to support some of them.

Traditional "talk" psychotherapies are not helpful to persons with AD except for their adjustment in the early stages of the disease, when cognitive functioning is largely intact. Both, interpersonal and cognitive therapies have been used with clients in the early stages. In one study, brief psychodynamic or interpersonal therapy (six sessions) helped clients to experience less subjective stress but had no effects on cognitive functions (Burns et al., 2005). In another study the use of cognitive interventions (focused on education and problem solving) helped the client and family to become proactive in managing the disease (Claire, Wilson, Carter, Roth, & Hodges, 2004). Cognitive rehabilitation and training, however, are not effective for improving the client's cognitive functioning (Clare, Woods, Moniz-Cook, Orrel, & Spector, 2007).

Many studies suggest that psychosocial interventions are helpful in improving the patient's quality of life (feelings of well-being and comfort). In one study of 201 persons with AD, perceived quality of life improved with regular cognitive stimulation (being encouraged to engage in regular physical activity and discussion), although this did not affect the course of the disorder (Lu et al., 2006). Another study of residents in a Florida nursing home found that when nursing staff were trained to communicate more often and more substantively with residents, those residents' self-reports of depression diminished (Bourgeois, Dijkstra, & Hickey, 2005). Further, staff gained a greater awareness of the residents' personal lives and cognitive abilities.

There is wide agreement among researchers and practitioners that *behavioral* interventions can be modestly effective in reducing or abolishing certain problem behaviors of clients with AD, including aggression, screaming, poor hygiene, and incontinence (Conn & Seitz, 2010). For behavioral interventions to be effective, the social worker needs first to clarify the target behavior and break it down into steps. The social worker next identifies the relevant antecedent and consequent reinforcers of the target behavior as clearly as possible, including the roles of significant others, and then enlists the caregivers to develop environmental conditions that will make the client more likely to exhibit the desired behavior.

Lichtenberg and his colleagues have developed a "well-being" intervention for persons with dementia residing in special care units in nursing homes (Lichtenberg, Kemp-Havican,

MacNeill, & Johnson, 2005). This intervention, which emphasizes the empirically validated strategy of increasing clients' activity levels, involves training nursing staff to implement a well-being treatment for individual clients three times weekly for 20 to 30 minutes. Following a brainstorming session with the resident's primary caregivers, the staff implement a series of structured pleasurable activities for the residents on the unit, such as bird watching, walking, and small-group interactions. The staff member assesses the client's mood and then engages in the activity, which is followed by rating the client's mood again. After a 13-week experimental study involving 20 residents with dementia, members of the experimental group had significantly fewer behavioral problems, even though their levels of depression were unchanged.

Three other types of cognitive and behavioral interventions are commonly associated with older adults, including those with AD: reminiscence, validation, and reality orientation therapies. The reminiscence and validation therapies attempt to improve or maintain the patient's quality of life and self-esteem, and prevent depression, anxiety, and behavior problems, by stimulating the client's memory (Pot et al., 2010). There is evidence to support the usefulness of reminiscence therapy, as some participants experience cognition and mood improvement, and caregivers may experience lower strain. Validation therapy represents a similar intervention, except that the client's erroneous statements and observations are not challenged. The point of the intervention is to relieve the client's negative moods by facilitating emotional expression and conveying empathy (Zeltzer & Cohn, 2006). Reality orientation, which is used to increase the client's awareness of the present and ability to focus on self-care, also seems to have modest benefits, although these tend not to persist beyond the situation in which they are applied (O'Connell et al., 2007). These two interventions include some possible adverse effects, however, such as increased agitation and frustration in clients and stress in caregivers who apply them.

Other therapies have been adapted for use with persons who have AD. The recreational therapies provide stimulation and enrichment for persons with dementia, mobilizing their cognitive processes. These interventions also seem to produce short-term improvements in mood and decreases in behavioral problems (Fitzsimmons & Buettner, 2003; Heyn, 2003). Art interventions focus on the patient's self-expression through the visual arts, which may help persons with AD tap into memories (Abraham, 2005). One study of persons in the early and middle stages of dementia found that participants demonstrated significantly more interest, sustained pleasure, attention, self-esteem, and normalcy during a creative arts program (Kinney & Rentz, 2005). Still, these persons showed no differences in negative affect. Studies of music therapy as a means of diminishing behavior and cognitive problems, and improving social and emotional functioning, are also inconclusive (Vink, Birks, Bruinsma, & Scholten, 2007).

Nutritional Interventions

Many persons with AD gradually lose their interest in eating, which contributes to their health problems. Several studies have considered the effects of interventions on nutritional outcomes. In one study, behavioral interventions by nursing staff were successful in keeping residents with AD at their meal tables longer and eating more food (Beattie, Algase, & Song, 2004). The use of nutritional supplements improved weight gain in another experimental study of 91 patients, although their weight gain was not associated with changes in mood or cognitive function (Lauque et al., 2004). Still, nutritional supplements are least likely to enhance energy intake in persons with low body weight (Young, Greenwood, Van Reekum, & Binns, 2004). Diets high in carbohydrates are more favored by persons in the late stage of the disease and thus should be provided for those persons (Young et al., 2004).

Medications

The ideal remedy for AD would slow the production of amyloid by disabling the enzymes that fabricate it. Current drug research is focused on the development of *beta secretase* (a type of enzyme that affects the speed of molecular processes in the body), because the earlier gamma blockers (which moderate the activity of a certain brain neurotransmitter) seemed to interfere with normal brain function (He et al., 2010). Other drugs are being targeted to prevent the binding of amyloid fragments and to bolster the immune system to ward off development of amyloid. New drugs under investigation may mimic the protective actions of APOE-2 or APOE-3, or block the effects of APP-4. Drug therapy may be able to decrease blood levels of APOE-4 and support growth factors that keep brains healthy (Lavretsky, Nguyen, & Goldstein, 2006).

With the above in mind, no known medical treatment exists at the present time to cure AD or stop its progression. At present, drug interventions are limited to those that modify its symptoms and slow its progression (López & Birks, 2007; McShane, Areosa-Sastre, & Minakaran, 2007). The most prominent of these are the cholinesterase inhibitors. The FDA has approved four such drugs since 1994: tactrine, donepezil, rivastigmine, and galantamine. These medications work by inhibiting the breakdown of a key brain chemical, acetylcholine. A meta-analysis reveals that these medications may improve cognitive function and global level of functioning in persons with mild to moderate AD, but that no solid evidence for drug therapy in severe dementia exists (Birks, Grimley-Evans, Iakovidou, & Tsolaki, 2007; Olsen, Poulsen, & Lubline, 2005). Adverse effects are significant and account for high rates of medication withdrawal. There is little evidence that any one of the specific drugs is superior to the others in producing these modest effects.

Several claims have been made that the cholinesterase inhibitors (donepezil in particular) can improve the person's responsiveness to psychosocial interventions. One experimental study found that the use of donepezil in combination with a cognitive stimulation program (12 hours of participatory activities involving homework and life-story discussions provided over eight weeks) had greater effects on conversational and functional abilities than the medication alone (Zientz, Rackley, & Chapman, 2007). Another randomized, controlled trial found that reality-orientation interventions by caregivers (engaging the patient in reality-based communication for 30 minutes three times a week) enhanced the effects of donepezil (Onder, Orazio, & Ezio, 2005).

Antipsychotic drugs are the only class of medications effective in reducing or eliminating symptoms of psychosis and agitation (Lonergan, Luxenberg, Colford, & Birks, 2007). No differences in effectiveness have been found between the older ("conventional") and newer ("atypical") medications. Still, because of the increased incidence of cerebrovascular events in dementia patients treated with these medications, caution is advised in their use (Ballard & Waite, 2006).

Formal evaluations of the efficacy of antidepressants with dementia clients are lacking. One meta-analysis of controlled studies found very weak support for the contention that antidepressants are an effective intervention for persons with depression and dementia (Bains, Birks, & Dening, 2005). Another review of double-blind, placebo-controlled, randomized trials found that antidepressant drugs improved depression but did not reduce agitation (Franco & Messinger-Rapport, 2005). The newer selective serotonin reuptake inhibitors, which have not yet been studied for this purpose, are generally the first choice of physicians because of their relatively mild side effects.

Ethical Practice

Practice Behavior Example: *Make ethical decisions by applying standards of the National Association of Social Workers Code of Ethics and, as applicable, of the International Federation of Social Workers/International Association of Schools of Social Work Ethics in Social Work, Statement of Principles.*

Critical Thinking Question: How would you respond to those who say that intervention resources should be limited for persons with AD, given its downward course and the client's loss of orientation toward the end? Can you see any merit to this perspective? Which social work values does this issue touch on?

Interventions for Caregivers

Interventions for caregivers should include both skill-building and coping components. As summarized by Walsh (2010), psychoeducational interventions have been found to be effective for alleviating the stress of caregivers and improving their coping skills. Even "lay" community consultants may be successfully trained to provide caregivers with support and education, to an extent that caregivers experience less depression, less sense of burden, and diminished reactivity to client behavior (Teri, McCurry, Logsdon, & Gibbons, 2005).

Media-based psychoeducational interventions show promise as well. Caregivers who participated in a 12-month computer-mediated, voice-interactive intervention designed to assist with responding to patient problem behaviors through counseling, access to stress experts, and a voice-mail telephone support group resulted in significantly lower anxiety, depression, and sense of bother about caregiving (Mahoney, Tarlow, & Jones, 2003). A related study demonstrated the utility of a telephone-based intervention for rural caregivers providing information, education, and support on an as-needed basis (Glueckauf et al., 2005).

> **Directions Part III, Goal Setting and Treatment Planning**   Given your risk and resilience assessments of the individual, your knowledge of the disorder, and evidence-based practice guidelines, formulate goals and a possible treatment plan for this individual.

CRITICAL PERSPECTIVE

Research on AD overwhelmingly concludes that the disorder results from degenerative biological processes in the brain. There appear to be no significant psychological or social factors that directly affect its onset, although its course may be exacerbated or slowed in the context of certain emotional and social factors. For these reasons AD is universally accepted as a medical disorder. It does not generate much debate within the social work profession about negative labeling, stigma, subjectivity, and the effects of values on diagnosis. In fact, one may wonder why AD is included in the DSM at all, although cognitive disorders related to aging, substance abuse, and injury have been included in the manual since its first edition in 1952. In spite of these points, the specific causes and range of biological characteristics of AD have not been clearly identified, which points to the need for further research before its etiology, symptoms, and course can be specified.

> **Directions Part IV, Critical Perspective**   Formulate a critique of the diagnosis as it relates to this case example. Questions to consider include the following: Does this diagnosis represent a valid mental disorder from the social work perspective? Is this diagnosis significantly different from other possible diagnoses? Your critique should be based on the values of the social work profession (which are incongruent in some ways with the medical model) and the validity of the specific diagnostic criteria applied to this case.

Case 2   From the Group Home to the Nursing Facility

Paul is a 56-year-old Caucasian male. He was raised by both parents and has one brother, but little is known about his early years or his family's medical history. He was diagnosed with Down syndrome and moderate mental retardation sometime during his youth. He attended a special education program in the public school system until his 18th birthday. Afterward he remained at home with his parents and did not participate in any day programs for his cognitive impairment. When Paul was 20 years old, his mother died from complications due to diabetes. Paul took her death very hard, secluding himself and rarely leaving his home. His father had a serious stroke when Paul was 33, and they both moved to another state to live with his brother. Paul started working in a sheltered workshop shortly after arriving there. He had a hard time coping with these adjustments and began experiencing depressive symptoms as well as significant anxiety. He also gained almost 50 pounds. He began seeing a therapist and was put on medication for depression and anxiety. Three years later the family moved to yet another state; soon afterward, Paul entered the County Mental Retardation Residential Program and moved into a group home.

Paul thrived in this program. Within two years he lost all of the weight he had gained after his mother's death and no longer needed psychotropic medication. Initially Paul was living in a home with 24-hour supports, but he was so successful there that he was given the opportunity to move into a more independent placement, a town home for four adult males. Daytime supports were in place to help the residents with budgeting, shopping, home maintenance, transportation to medical appointments, and medication administration. Paul was able to perform most other daily living tasks on his own, including showering, dressing himself, cooking simple meals, doing his laundry, and using public transportation. Paul also had no problems communicating with others; he spoke clearly and had a fairly diverse vocabulary. He was never able to read, but he was able to comprehend most of what was read to him and always asked questions about things he didn't understand.

For about the past 15 years, Paul worked in a variety of jobs for an employment company that helps find jobs for people with cognitive disabilities. His most recent job was in a hotel, where he worked in the kitchen polishing all of the dinner and banquet ware for the catering department. He enjoyed this job and took pride in bringing home his paychecks. His supervisor said he was an excellent employee, always on task and pleasant.

Paul is a friendly, helpful, and compassionate person. He is always open to new learning experiences and enjoys spending time in the community. He particularly likes live music and theater, dancing, bowling, and movies. He is well liked by all who know him.

After Paul's father died 20 years ago, he and his brother eventually lost contact. Preceding this, his brother would routinely cancel plans to spend time with him, usually without any notice. Paul also reported that his brother treated him poorly when they did spend time together, calling him stupid, yelling at him, and pushing him around physically. As a result, Paul decided that he no longer wanted to spend any time with his brother. They had no contact for over 10 years, until his brother wrote an e-mail to the County Mental Health and Mental Retardation system earlier this year, inquiring about him. Paul received the message and wrote back, but there was no response. His brother visited Paul once when he was in the hospital for 10 minutes, but there has been no contact since.

Paul does have some close friends. He has a very close bond with the three men with whom he lived for 15 years, as well as with one housemate's family whom he routinely visits. He also befriended some of the program staff members, maintaining relationships with them long after they worked with him. He often spent the holidays and weekends with these friends.

Over the years Paul has developed a number of health problems. He has alopecia, a disease that caused him to lose all of the hair on his body, and he also has diverticulosis, a growth in the intestinal wall. Until recently he exercised at the local gym several days a week and has been eating healthy foods, so he has suffered few negative effects from these disorders.

About four years ago Paul's residential program underwent some changes. The level of staff support increased as the needs of Paul and his housemates also grew. They now had overnight support to ensure that the men got up and went to work on time during the week. They also had staff for extended hours on the weekends to help transport them to community and recreational activities, as navigating public transportation became harder. Paul was still able to communicate and perform his daily living skills with little assistance until fairly recently.

Two years ago the staff at Paul's group home began noticing changes in his behavior. He was beginning to struggle with signing his name. He also began repeating questions multiple times, for example, "What are we doing today?" When reminded, he would say, "Oh, that's right." Over the next year the staff noticed additional changes, such as Paul's increased apprehension of the unknown and greater fearfulness of walking on grass or any unpaved surfaces due to fear of falling. His repetition of questions also became more frequent. Due to the emergence of these behaviors, and his Down syndrome, his neurologist put him on Aricept, a medication designed to stabilize the symptoms of early cognitive deterioration, one year ago.

Around this time Paul began having a harder time remembering the names of people he knows, but with prompting he was able to recall them. He also began developing behavioral problems, such as incontinence during the night and smearing feces in the bathroom. His emotions became much more intense, and he cried easily whether he was happy, sad, or upset. During the past year Paul began to struggle with tasks such as cooking and laundry that he was previously able to complete. He lost his desire to go outside the home as well. His "lifeline" also appeared to be blurring. He had always talked fondly of his years growing up, but he began talking as if those memories were recent, and to speak about his parents as if they were still alive. He was taken off Aricept six months ago because of concern that it was exacerbating his symptoms. While the smearing ceased, no other changes were noted.

Six months ago there was a marked decline in Paul's appetite and an increase in lethargic behavior. Initially, staff thought this was due to a virus but after two weeks he was unable to overcome it. His doctor did some tests and determined that he was dehydrated. A few days later his energy appeared to be returning, but he then had a seizure at home and was taken to the hospital by ambulance. Because Paul had no history of seizure activity, doctors ordered a CAT scan and an MRI. There was no evidence of stroke, but the doctor said that small strokes are rarely evident in such tests, and he suspected that Paul had had several.

After Paul returned from the hospital, his condition deteriorated further. He was no longer able to dress or shower without full assistance. He had frequent accidents with incontinence and began wearing special undergarments. He was unable to complete his duties at work and had to quit his job. After a few weeks he began to sit slumped over and was no longer able to eat solid food, or even feed himself. His communication skills suffered, he had trouble focusing on what people were saying, and he answered questions with only one word. Soon he could walk only with support.

Because his decline during the past month had been so rapid, Paul was re-admitted to the hospital. The doctors thought that some of his behaviors could be due to a too-strong dose of antiseizure medications, so these were discontinued. After a few days Paul began to regain some of his faculties. He was able to converse with others, sit up straight, eat on his own (although still only pureed foods), and walk with support. He was introduced to a new antiseizure medication while still in the hospital, and upon release was referred to a rehabilitation facility for physical and occupational therapy.

Paul did well in his physical and occupational therapy sessions. He became strong enough to walk on his own, and some remnants of his "old self" returned. Still, he was unable to return to the group home, because he required more daily support than the facility was able to provide. He applied for Medicaid and became a resident in another long-term nursing facility.

At the present time Paul's condition fluctuates day by day. He is still able to walk but sometimes has difficulty eating without assistance, often forgetting how to use utensils properly. He recognizes his friends when they visit but is unable to recall their names. Paul is still affectionate and enjoys company, but he generally speaks in one-word phrases, and his responses to questions often seem nonsensical. He can often be found staring into space with a blank expression or playing intently with a small object, such as a straw or piece of paper.

Paul has been hospitalized twice since moving into his present nursing facility. Once he was found lying on the floor of his room with a dangerously low amount of oxygen in his system, and the other time he had another seizure. A friend of his has been appointed his legal guardian to make medical and monetary decisions for him. The guardian is currently trying to transfer him into a group home that offers more intensive support, or to a different nursing home, due to concerns that have arisen in his current placement. His current roommate has pretty much taken control of all extra space and has been heard calling him "stupid" and other similar terms. Paul is also not generally encouraged to use the skills he does have in this facility. For example, staff were transporting him everywhere in a wheelchair, unaware that he could still walk. A similar scenario occurred in regard to his feeding himself.

Please go to the Appendix for directions to this case.

Case 3　The Former Volunteer

Mr. Grahm is an 88-year-old Caucasian widower and father of 11 children. After his wife died 21 years ago, Mr. Grahm retired and moved into his daughter's urban home. For 11 years following the move, Mr. Grahm volunteered by coaching at a local high school, filing at one local hospital, and transporting patients around the buildings at another hospital. In addition, Mr. Grahm stayed active by attending church on a daily basis, attending his grandchildren's sports activities, and visiting with family members whenever possible. Mr. Grahm also walked two miles every day to stay healthy.

Beginning 10 years ago, Mr. Grahm's daughter and family noticed that he frequently misplaced his keys, hats, wallet, and other items. Mr. Grahm also started to forget that he had eaten less than an hour after he had had a meal. In addition, his volunteer supervisors reported that Mr. Grahm was found wandering the parking lot, confused about where he was. He made filing errors and asked for assistance at least once a week regarding the filing system that he had initially developed and with which he had been quite conversant. Eight years ago, Mr. Grahm began getting lost driving to his volunteer jobs.

Over the next few years, Mr. Grahm cut back on his volunteer work because of increasing trouble with the tasks, getting lost, and displaying general confusion. Mr. Grahm's confusion increased at home as well. He lost items more regularly and frequently forgot his daily schedule, whether or not he had eaten, and whether he had turned off the stove. These problems caused Mr. Grahm to become frustrated, agitated, and confrontational with his daughter.

Six years ago Mr. Grahm suffered an atrial fibrillation, a heart rhythm disturbance that caused him to experience a series of minor strokes. He was admitted to the hospital for several days. Upon returning home, Mr. Grahm's family noticed a marked decline in his functioning. Mr. Grahm could not remember card games he had played his whole life. He called family members by the wrong name. He occasionally forgot how to get to church and back.

Shortly after his hospital stay, Mr. Grahm retired from all volunteer activities because his family members took his car away from him. Mr. Grahm also began to worry about intruders at night. He would get up to check the doors, the hallways, and the kitchen. He looked for robbers, and he accused neighbors and family members of spying on him and stealing his money. He hid his personal items and could not find them. Following this, Mr. Grahm could no longer balance his checkbook, remember how to fill out a check, or pay bills.

As the years passed, Mr. Grahm's mental functioning continued to deteriorate, and he became more stubborn and agitated. The family reports that as of four months ago Mr. Grahm rarely remembered where his personal items were, people's names, recent events, what he was doing, or what day it was. He forgot people and would become upset or anxious because he did not know who the people in the house were. Mr. Grahm accused family members of stealing from him daily. He awoke at night wandering around. When asked, he could not remember where he was. At night, Mr. Grahm often believed he was a college student or young husband again; he would deny having children and would insist upon completing his homework or whatever task he needed to complete. He would often think he was in one of his past houses. He slept later into the morning and took naps during the day. He was unable to prepare toast in the morning because he couldn't remember what he was doing long enough to put the bread in the toaster. Mr. Grahm's memory of the past was starting to fade, with the most recent memories vanishing first.

Several months ago, Mr. Grahm was found unconscious in his room and was taken to the hospital, where he remained for one week. The social worker did not have access to the medical reports from this hospital stay. Upon Mr. Grahm's return to the home, he began having auditory hallucinations and became delusional several times a day. He thought that bugs were attacking him. He could not remember most people, even his caregivers, and was suspicious of everyone. Mr. Grahm also began to wet himself. He could no longer follow two-step instructions, because he could not remember each step nor which one came first. Mr. Grahm remains in this state currently.

Regarding his developmental and social history, Mr. Grahm experienced a normal birth. He had three older brothers, one younger brother, and an older sister, and reports having close relationships with his parents and siblings. His younger brother is his only living relative, and this brother suffers from AD. His sister was diagnosed with schizophrenia and lived her adult life in supervised residential facilities. Two of his brothers had alcohol use problems. Mr. Grahm denies any substance abuse or having ever seen a psychologist or psychiatrist.

Mr. Grahm grew up on a farm and his family had lower-middle socioeconomic standing. He completed two years of college and then worked two blue-collar jobs most of his adult life to support his family. Mr. Grahm retired at age 67.

Mr. Grahm had kidney stones removed at age 66. Since then he has undergone two hip replacement surgeries and cataract surgery. He was diagnosed with diabetes mellitus, type II, at age 82, although he made only minor dietary changes to manage this. That same year Mr. Grahm was diagnosed with hypertension and severe rheumatoid arthritis in his neck, shoulder, hands, and hips. Mr. Grahm currently takes eight medications for his various health problems.

Mr. Grahm lives with his youngest and middle daughter and her husband. These three family members provide Mr. Grahm with his basic care. All family members work, so Mr. Grahm is left alone during the day. Three of his other children visit him weekly, and all others visit him twice a month and call him each week. Mr. Grahm reportedly had close relationships with his children and grandchildren.

Mr. Grahm's primary caregivers report being exhausted and on edge. Because of his nightly wandering and hallucinations, at least one of the caregivers stays up with him each night. At the same time, his agitation and suspicion cause him to reject their care, and he lashes out at them. The family is concerned about Mr. Grahm's safety during the day and the caregivers' ability to provide him with proper care.

Mr. Grahm is a practicing Catholic and his faith is a strong support for him. Until this year he attended Mass each morning and had a core group of friends from the church. He still attends Mass and sees his friends on Sundays. Mr. Grahm occasionally speaks with his former coworkers and volunteers, and they have provided him with additional support and conversation when needed.

The family reports that Mr. Grahm functions best at home during the day and when there are a lot of people around. He suffers most at night after a long day of visitors. Mr. Grahm enjoys reminiscing and watching live sports outside. The middle daughter, with whom he lives, most easily calms him. Mr. Grahm is also more alert when he eats regular meals that are low in sugar. He denies suicidal thoughts, although he says that he is lonely and sleeps when he is alone.

Please go to the Appendix for directions to this case.

PRACTICE TEST The following questions will test your knowledge of the content found within this chapter. For additional assessment, including licensing-exam type questions on applying chapter content to practice behaviors, visit **MySocialWorkLab.com**

1. Which of the following is required to make a diagnosis of dementia?
   a. Memory impairment
   b. Loss of ability to use common objects
   c. Loss of ability to use words appropriately
   d. Behavioral symptoms

2. Which of the following is not an appropriate social work role when working with persons who have dementia?
   a. Psychosocial assessments of client and family functioning
   b. Diagnosis
   c. Psychosocial interventions to clients with dementia
   d. Emotional support to family members and caregivers

3. Forrest McDonald, age 83, had become increasingly forgetful. His doctors suspected that he may be experiencing dementia, but initially could not be sure. "We'll just have to see how this progresses" was a typical response. "He's in excellent physical condition." Forrest became even more forgetful, prone to periods of agitation, and at times paranoid. Finally, he was not able to recognize his wife and demonstrated dangerous wandering behavior. The physician then confirmed a diagnosis of dementia. Mr. McDonald received a diagnosis of AD rather than vascular dementia because:
   a. His cognitive problems followed a downward course during the past five years
   b. His wandering behavior was a relatively late symptom
   c. He did not appear to experience depression
   d. He was in good physical health

4. Like all persons with dementia, Forrest was becoming increasingly forgetful over the years. Which of the following interventions might help stimulate Mr. McDonald's memory capacity?
   a. Validation therapy
   b. Reality orientation
   c. Nutritional intervention
   d. Cognitive therapy

5. Some psychosocial interventions for persons with AD are supported by research evidence, whereas others are not, even though they may make "practical" sense to the provider. Given the interventions described in this chapter, to what extent should a social worker rely on evidence-based strategies when helping to formulate a treatment plan?

6. Many families of persons with AD feel guilty about placing their older loved ones in supportive care facilities. What range of supports would be required to allow such an individual to live comfortably and safely with his or her family members?

SUCCEED WITH

Visit **MySocialWorkLab** for more licensing-exam test questions, and to access case studies, videos, and much more.

7

Substance Use Disorders

Competencies Applied with Practice Behaviors — in this Chapter				
Professional Identity	Ethical Practice	Critical Thinking	Diversity in Practice	Human Rights & Justice
Research-Based Practice	Human Behavior	Policy Practice	Practice Contexts	Engage, Assess, Intervene, Evaluate

Vlad is a 17-year-old Caucasian male court-mandated to attend a six-month residential treatment program at a local juvenile detention center for breaking and entering and unauthorized possession of a firearm. Vlad has unsuccessfully participated in several residential placements in the past few years and has repeatedly had positive urine screens for marijuana use.

Substance use and abuse are both highly prevalent in American society. Social workers often work with clients who have substance-related problems, regardless of their agency settings. This situation arises partly because of the high comorbidity found between substance-related and other disorders, as well as problems such as domestic violence and child abuse. Social workers thus need to be able to assess for substance use disorders and become familiar with their empirically validated treatments. Alcohol-related disorders in adolescence and adulthood are the primary focus of this chapter, although other substances will be incorporated into the presentation.

The *Diagnostic and Statistical Manual of Mental Disorders* (DSM) provides general criteria for *substance abuse* and *substance dependence* rather than separate criteria for each substance, of which there are 11 classes (American Psychiatric Association [APA], 2000). The defining characteristic of *abuse* involves negative consequences of use, whereas *dependence* indicates compulsive use despite serious consequences, often accompanied by tolerance and withdrawal. The DSM also describes *substance-induced disorders*, among them intoxication, withdrawal, dementia, amnesia, and psychosis as well as mood, anxiety, sexual dysfunction, and sleep problems.

PREVALENCE AND COMORBIDITY

Substance abuse disorders are the fourth most diagnosed group of disorders in the United States (Kessler, Chiu, Demler, & Walters, 2005). The National Epidemiologic Survey on Alcohol and Related Conditions reported a 17.8% lifetime prevalence of alcohol abuse and a 4.7% prevalence during the past year (Hasin, Stinson, Ogburn, & Grant, 2007). The lifetime prevalence for alcohol dependence was 12.5% and past year dependence was 3.8%. The lifetime and 12-month prevalences of drug abuse were 1.4 and 7.7%, respectively, and for drug dependence they was 0.6 and 2.6%, respectively (Compton, Thomas, Stinson, & Grant, 2007).

In older adults, one-month prevalence rates for alcohol use disorders ranged from 0.9 to 2.2% (Office of the Surgeon General, 1999). According to the National Surveys on Drug Use and Health, drug abuse or dependence in those over age 50 is very low (0.33%) (Blazer & Wu, 2009). In 2004 the rate of substance dependence or abuse was 8.8% for youths aged 12 to 17 (Substance Abuse and Mental Health Services Administration [SAMHSA], 2006).

There is a high degree of psychological comorbidity with substance use disorders (Stinson et al., 2005). The National Comorbidity Survey reported that more than half (51.4%) of adults with substance use disorders at some point in their lives also had another mental disorder (Kessler, 2004). The co-occurrence of substance use and personality disorders, for example, is 39% for those with alcohol dependence and 69% for those with drug dependence (Jané-Llopis & Matytsina, 2006). Antisocial personality disorder is particularly common in men who abuse substances.

Adolescent abusers have a 60% likelihood of being diagnosed with another psychiatric disorder, most frequently the disruptive disorders (conduct disorder [CD], oppositional defiant disorder [ODD], and attention-deficit hyperactivity disorder [ADHD]), depression, and posttraumatic stress disorder (PTSD) (Armstrong & Costello, 2002; Chung & Maisto, 2006).

Not surprisingly, alcohol and drug use disorders are highly comorbid with each other. Among individuals with an alcohol use disorder, over half (55.17%) also had a drug use disorder (Stinson et al., 2005).

Various theories have been postulated to explain the high comorbidity between substance use and other mental disorders. Buckley (2006) suggests the following three:

1. People use substances to medicate symptoms of other mental disorders.

2. Substance use may precipitate mental illness.

3. There may be genetic vulnerability to both substance use and mental disorders involving certain neurotransmitter systems.

Unfortunately, substance use by people with mental disorders may lead to destabilization and exacerbation of mental illness symptoms, medication noncompliance, health consequences, and risky behavior such as increased suicidal ideation (Buckley, 2006).

Substance use disorders also have significant medical consequences. Substance dependence (excluding nicotine) in the United States annually accounts for 40% of all hospital admissions and 25% of mortality rates (500,000 deaths) (SAMHSA, 2006). Medical problems related to drinking include gastrointestinal (gastritis, ulcers, liver problems, and pancreatitis) and cardiovascular (hypertension and cholesterol and subsequent heart disease) conditions (Corrao, Bagnardi, Zambon, & Arico, 1999).

ASSESSMENT

Social workers should routinely screen both their clients and clients' family members for alcohol and drug problems (McCrady, 2005).

Box 7.1 summarizes assessment guidelines for use with clients of all age groups.

Box 7.1 • Assessment of Substance Abuse

1. Examine patterns of use, including onset, frequency, quantity, drugs of choice, tolerance, or withdrawal symptoms.

2. Examine "triggers" and contexts of use.

3. Review consequences of substance abuse in the physical (might include physical examination), psychological, legal, financial, occupational, and educational realms.

4. Assess motivation for treatment, including the perceived advantages and disadvantages of use.

5. Review major life events that may contribute to substance abuse.

6. Assess the possible coexistence of other disorders, including the relationship between the onset and progression of the other symptoms and their relationship to substance use. Optimally, the assessment of comorbid disorders should take place about three to four weeks after the person has stopped using substances.

7. Consider the client's strengths and coping skills, and inquire about periods of abstinence or reduced use.

8. Assess the client's social support networks.

9. Assess for suicide risk (see chapter 10 for guidelines on how to conduct such an assessment).

For Adolescents

Interview the adolescent and parent(s) separately. The interview with the parent should be done to gather information about the child but should also address the extent of parental substance use, attitudes toward their child's use, the amount of monitoring and supervision the youth receives, and the level of cohesion in the family (Bukstein et al., 1997).

Sources: Bradizza, Stasiewicz, & Paas, 2006; Bukstein, Cornelius, Trunzo, Kelly, & Wood, 2005; Graybeal, 2001; Miller & Rollnick, 2002; Riggs & Whitmore, 1999.

Vlad is on probation for breaking and entering until his 18th birthday. He entered a neighbor's house through the window and stole money and electronics. Upon searching his bedroom, police discovered a gun, which resulted in a second charge of unauthorized possession of a firearm. Vlad states that after being threatened, he bought the gun from a friend but had no intention of using it. After he was arrested and charged, his mother paid his restitution, and he has yet to repay her. He also underwent urine screens as a condition of his probation, which were repeatedly positive for marijuana use.

Vlad has attended but failed to complete several residential placements in the past several years, including a military school, a private alternative school, and a wilderness program. His disregard of regulations has contributed to his termination from several previous placements. Despite reports of his prior disrespect toward authority figures, Vlad presents as cooperative, bright, and approachable. His posture and eye contact are appropriate, but he displays a somewhat flat affect. He expresses a desire to improve his relationship with his family and to stay out of trouble. He says that the burglary occurred four months prior and admits that until he was placed at the residential program he continued to flout the rules his parents had set for him. He recognizes that once he turns 18, the legal repercussions for any crimes he commits will become more severe.

Vlad was adopted at age seven from an orphanage in Russia. His biological parents were alcoholics, and his father was physically abusive toward his mother. It is unknown whether Vlad was abused, but his father literally threw him out on the street when he was five years old. He was discovered by the Russian police wandering the streets with frozen nasal passages and frostbite due to the extreme cold. Parental custody was rescinded, and Vlad was placed in an orphanage.

Vlad's two younger biological brothers were adopted by a family in the United States. When this family discovered that the two boys had an older brother still in Russia, Vlad was adopted by a relative of this family. Prior to his incarceration, Vlad lived with his adoptive parents, Mr. and Mrs. Meyers, and two younger adopted sisters. Vlad also has three much older stepbrothers from Mr. Meyers's first marriage. Mr. and Mrs. Meyers are officers in the U.S. military. Mr. Meyer is now retired and lives with the two girls; Mrs. Meyers is currently stationed overseas. Despite the physical distance between them, Mr. Meyers claims that he and his wife are close. The family is well off financially, and the parents appear to be invested in their children's well-being. Mr. Meyers says the family's main support is their extended family out of state.

Vlad states that his most important relationships are with his adoptive sisters and his biological brothers, all of whom live out of state. However, Mrs. Meyers says that even when given the opportunity to visit with his biological brothers, he has chosen to stay at home. Vlad's relationship with his adoptive father is beginning to improve, but he expresses an immense amount of anger and resentment toward his adoptive mother. Both his adoptive mother and father state that Vlad does not have close attachments to other people. According to his adoptive parents, Vlad has always preferred to be alone in his room and shies away from physical affection.

Of his early childhood in Russia, Vlad recalls little, unsure whether his memories are "real or dreams." Mr. Meyers attends the bi-weekly family therapy sessions and reports that Vlad was a "wonderful, happy little boy." Both Vlad and Mr. Meyers deny a history of significant illnesses or injuries and state that Vlad is in excellent physical health. He does have some residual sinus problems and is susceptible to allergies as a result of his early childhood experience. It is unknown whether there is a history of mental illness in Vlad's biological family other than his parents' alcoholism.

Vlad has a history of unsuccessfully treated mental health issues. He has received psychological evaluations and counseling at most of his past placements. He says that at age 11, he took Adderall to treat his ADHD, but he is not currently taking any medications. Vlad adamantly denies a history of cruelty toward animals or fire setting. He states that he gets into fights only when antagonized by others.

Vlad has a history of frequent and persistent alcohol and marijuana use beginning at age 11 or 12. Vlad admits to smoking daily "as long as me or my friends had some." He reports evidence of tolerance to marijuana, both increasing the amount to achieve the desired effect and reduced feelings of intoxication with continued use. Despite a history of negative consequences—criminal involvement, academic problems, and interpersonal conflicts—he has not been successful in controlling or limiting his marijuana use. He says he experiences cravings for marijuana every day and admits that he would still be using if he had access. He says that he used alcohol less frequently ("a few times a week, mostly beer"), but more often when marijuana wasn't available. He said he was able to control or stop his alcohol consumption "when I tried, although I didn't usually want to." He said he doesn't miss alcohol as much as he does marijuana. He admits that he tried PCP on two occasions but found the effects dysphoric and unpleasant. He denies using any other substances.

Vlad does not display empathy for the victims of his crime nor express guilt for the stress he has caused his family. He is aware, however, that the majority of his problems stem from his substance use and involvement with undesirable peers. He admits that he has a problem with substances and that he would probably be using if he had access to drugs and alcohol.

Vlad has had two heterosexual relationships. He reports that he felt a strong attachment to his first girlfriend but believes that his parents sabotaged the relationship. He admits that on two occasions he hit his last girlfriend during arguments while he was under the influence of alcohol and marijuana. He claims that she sustained no injuries as a result of his abuse.

Beginning around age 11, Vlad began to associate with a group of undesirable peers. Even after the family relocated to a new neighborhood at age 14, Vlad continued to select unsuitable friends, and his behavior worsened. He repeatedly stayed out past his curfew and on several occasions ran away overnight when his parents attempted to ground him. He started skipping classes at school, and his academic performance began to suffer, although he had received good grades before this time. He was also unable to play basketball, a sport at which he excelled, given the school policy requiring a minimum grade point average to play sports.

Vlad attended school at the detention center and was able to earn his GED with minimal preparation. His father reports that Vlad has always been a talented artist. He initially had some difficulty processing his feelings verbally and was given the option of using a therapeutic journal and mandala circle drawings as an outlet for his emotions. Vlad used both outlets effectively and produced some creative works depicting both positive and negative feelings he experienced over the course of therapy. Vlad can be stubborn at times, but because of this trait he tends to work hard at an assignment or project until it is satisfactorily completed. For example, he was given an art assignment when he was first placed in the detention center and spent a month working on the drawing. He created a beautiful final product of which he was extremely proud.

Vlad expresses interest in attending a trade school or community college where he can study to become a car mechanic or electrician, as he is "good at fixing things." Mr. Meyers says he will support Vlad in whatever educational and occupational decisions he makes. Vlad is athletic and hopes to resume playing basketball in the future. The Meyers family regularly attends a Catholic church, and Mr. Meyers has a close relationship with the priest. Vlad identifies as Catholic and previously attended a church youth group.

While in the program Vlad has been sharing living quarters with up to 14 other adolescents and is well liked by his peers. His peers describe him as funny, athletic, competitive, and helpful on the unit. Vlad denies any feelings of depression, sadness, or suicidal intent. He also denies experiencing any manic symptoms or episodes when these were described to him. He says the main feeling he struggles with is anger. He admits that he has difficulty controlling himself when he is mad, and he typically yells and throws things.

Vlad views his biggest problems as his negative relationship with his parents and his marijuana use. He states that he would know his problems were solved when he could communicate with his parents about any problems involving work, friends, or school. Vlad would like to be able to ask his parents questions about his birth family and adoption and hopes to feel close enough to them to have a conversation about his early life. Once he gets out of the residential treatment program, he would like to start eating dinner with his family on a regular basis and playing basketball with his dad and his sisters.

Vlad hopes that one day he will no longer feel the urge to get high and thinks this will happen when he does not feel so angry all of the time. He recognizes that for his situation to change he would have to stop feeling so angry toward his parents, become more capable of effectively managing his anger, and feel more connected to his family and peers. Rather than reacting to angry feelings by yelling or throwing something, Vlad hopes to be able to walk away from a situation and address whatever made him angry when he calms down. Vlad said that he would know his situation has changed for the better when his parents stop criticizing him for his friends and choices. When asked what he would be doing when his parents accept him, Vlad admitted that he would have to be making better choices. Vlad says that if he is busy with school, work, and other positive activities, he will no longer struggle with boredom, which he identified as a trigger for his drug use.

When asked the miracle question ("What would you experience if you woke up one day and your life was the way you want it to be?"), Vlad states that he would be enrolled in college and getting good grades, working at a part-time job that pays well, have a girlfriend who does not use drugs, and enjoy a close relationship with his family.

Human Behavior

Practice Behavior Example: *Utilize conceptual frameworks to guide the processes of assessment, intervention, and evaluation.*

Critical Thinking Question: Given the prevalence of substance use disorders and the high correlation between substance use disorders and other mental health disorders, how will you ensure that you appropriately identify this problem in individuals and families with whom you work when substance use is not the presenting problem?

Directions Part I, Multiaxial Diagnosis Given the case information, prepare the following: a multiaxial diagnosis, the rationale for the diagnosis and global assessment of functioning score, and additional information you would have wanted to know in order to make a more accurate diagnosis.

BIOPSYCHOSOCIAL RISK AND RESILIENCE INFLUENCES

Onset

Substance use disorders usually begin in late adolescence or early adulthood, with a median age of 20 years (Kessler et al., 2005). The various risk and protective processes for the onset of adolescent substance use disorders are listed in Table 7.1. Note that although these are listed separately, there are typically interactional effects among them. For example, family stress and parental heavy substance use can amplify the negative influence of teen peers on alcohol misuse (Ennett et al., 2008).

Genetic mechanisms have received much attention with regard to the onset of substance use disorders in adults, but one meta-analysis established that heritability is actually quite low, though stronger for males (Walters, 2002). One factor that protects against the development of substance use disorders is not having a mental disorder (Armstrong & Costello, 2002). Disorders that often precede substance use are depression in females and antisocial personality disorder in males (Lynch, Roth, & Carrol, 2002). Many females with substance use problems have a history of physical or sexual abuse, both as children and as adults (Orwin, Maranda, & Brady, 2001). At the social level, peers who use substances place an individual at risk, whereas friends who do not support such use are protective against the development of alcohol and drug problems. Even for older

Table 7.1 **Biopsychosocial Risk and Resilience Assessment for the Onset of Substance Use Disorder**

Risk influences	Protective influences
Biological	
Problem alcohol use seems to be moderately heritable[1]	
Psychological	
Early onset of drinking (defined as before age 14)[2]	
Early externalizing problems[3]	
Social	
Child abuse and neglect[4]	Parental warnings about alcohol
Lack of parental monitoring[5]	Parents who were both warm and required that their children were accountable
A parenting style which is either warm without holding children accountable or strict without warmth[6]	Having abstinent friends
Alcohol availability in terms of alcohol retailers in the neighborhood	

[1]Young, Rhee, Stallings, Corley, & Hewitt, 2006.
[2]Hingson, Hereen, & Winter, 2006.
[3]Siebenbruner, Englund, Egeland, & Hudson, 2006.
[4]Shin, Edwards, & Heeren, 2009.
[5]Siebenbruner, Englund, Egeland, & Hudson, 2006.
[6]Bahr & Hoffmann, 2010.

adults, the social context plays a role. Results of one study showed that older adults who have more money, engage in more social activities, and whose friends approve of drinking are more likely to engage in what is considered high-risk drinking, defined as more than three drinks per day or more than 14 drinks per week (Holahan et al., 2010). Finally, the availability of drugs in a particular neighborhood confers risk for those residents. At a policy level, increasing the tax on alcohol can also reduce drinking overall as well as heavy drinking and death rates from alcohol-associated diseases (Maldonado-Molina & Wagenaar, 2010).

Course and Recovery

Despite the severe consequences to health and well-being, only a minority of those with drug and alcohol disorders seeks treatment (Compton et al., 2007; Hasin et al., 2007). For drug use disorders, lifetime help-seeking behavior is uncommon (8.1% for abuse and 37.9% for dependence) (Compton et al., 2007). Only 24.1% of those with alcohol dependence ever receive treatment (Hasin et al., 2007). For adolescents, only 10% of those that have substance use disorders receive treatment (Kraft, Schubert, Pond, & Augirre-Molina, 2006).

Several characteristics of clients, their substance use patterns, and their environments influence the course of recovery (Bond, Kaskutas, & Weisner, 2003; Chung & Maisto, 2006; Conner, Sorenson, & Leonard, 2005; Karageorge & Wisdom, 2001; McKay, 1999; Orwin et al., 2001; SAMHSA, 2006) and many of these involve socially diverse groups (see Box 7.2).

Patterns of use that present risk include high levels of pretreatment use, substance use during treatment, and substance use the year after treatment. Abstinence lasting two years is a protective influence. Protective client characteristics include client motivation and the absence of a comorbid mental health problem. PTSD may put a client at risk for worse outcomes (Bradizza et al., 2006). For this reason, clients with PTSD should receive treatment for this disorder soon after receiving substance use treatment. Social workers should also be aware that people with depression may be slower to benefit from treatment (Conner et al., 2005) and that depression may impede recovery (Kodl et al., 2008). For adolescents, conduct problems, depression, and ADHD present risk for relapse (Chung & Maisto, 2006).

The coping strategy of avoidance rather than that of problem solving leads to more cravings when a user is confronted with stress (Cleveland & Harris, 2010).

Socially, a lack of family support for sobriety, substance-abusing family members, socializing with substance-abusing peers (especially for teenagers), low socioeconomic status, and life events featuring physical or sexual victimization are risk influences. Protective mechanisms include family support for sobriety, nonsubstance-using peers, the ability to develop new relationships, Alcoholics Anonymous (AA) attendance, and interventions that attend to culturally relevant beliefs.

There are some gender differences in relapse propensity. In general, women tend to benefit more than men in treatment for alcohol use disorders (though not necessarily for drug disorders) despite greater pretreatment risks (Walitzer & Dearing, 2006). Negative mood states and depression, overall, play a greater role for adults than teenagers, whose main risks typically involve the social context (Chung & Maisto, 2006). Negative mood is a particular risk for women, whereas positive mood is associated with relapse for men.

Diversity in Practice

Practice Behavior Example: *Recognize the extent to which a culture's structures and values may oppress, marginalize, alienate, or create or enhance privilege and power.*

Critical Thinking Question: If there are many risk influences present for both the onset and course of substance use disorders in women presenting for treatment, how will you counteract these risks?

Box 7.2 • Substance Use Disorders and Social Diversity

Youths

- Children born to addicted mothers are at risk for health problems, including fetal alcohol syndrome, low birth weight, complications of postnatal withdrawal, and HIV infection.[1]

Racial and Ethnic Minorities

- The rate of substance dependence or abuse is similar among African Americans and Caucasians (9.5 and 9.3%, respectively) but lower for Latinos.[2]
- The rate of substance abuse or dependence is highest among Native Americans and Alaska Natives.[3]
- The second highest rate of substance abuse or dependence (13%) is among biracial persons.[4]
- Being Asian offers protection against substance use disorders—the annual prevalence rate among Asians is 4.2%[5]—possibly because of the negative physiological response ("flushing") found in many Asian groups (Japanese, Chinese, and Koreans).
- Ethnic minorities are less likely to have access to services.[6]
- While it is recommended that intervention should integrate culturally relevant beliefs and healing practices, such guidelines have tended to be nonspecific and have not yet been subjected to empirical testing.[7]

Socioeconomic Status (SES)

- People with lower education and low SES are at higher risk for drug abuse and dependence.[8]
- People of low SES have limited access to affordable treatment.[9]

Gay and Lesbian Persons

- Homosexuals are at increased risk for substance abuse[10] for the following possible reasons: limited social venues where alcohol is not a feature of the environment; limited access to societal institutions that provide protection against substance abuse (i.e., marriage); lack of social support; coping with grief over loss of gay peers through disease and death; coping with discrimination.
- Only (6%) substance abuse treatment facilities surveyed across the nation offer special programs for gay and lesbian clients.[11]

Women

- Males have a higher risk of having substance use disorders, except for younger cohorts. In 2004, males aged 12 or older were twice as likely as females to be classified with substance dependence or abuse problems (12.7 versus 6.2%), but among youths aged 12 to 17, the rate of substance dependence or abuse was similar (8.7 to 9.0%).[12]
- Women are more susceptible than men to rapid onset of addiction and health problems once they begin drinking[13]; this disparity may be partly due to women's higher fat and lower water ratios, which may impair their ability to metabolize alcohol.
- In treatment, females have more health problems than males, including respiratory, gynecological, heart, and digestive conditions.[14]
- Depression often precedes substance use in females, so use seems to be a coping response.
- Many females with substance use problems have a history of physical or sexual abuse (both as children and as adults),[15] and a history of victimization is associated with a worse outcome.
- Financial barriers such as lack of money, health insurance, child care, and transportation, as well as the fear of social stigma associated with substance abuse, may contribute to women's underrepresentation in treatment.[16]
- Women often develop substance use problems in the context of relationships with substance-abusing male partners.[17]

Older Adults

- Age bias among health care providers may present obstacles to assessment of substance use disorders in the elderly,[18] as providers may not believe that elders can benefit from intervention or that their quality of life would improve as a result.

[1]Finnegan & Kandall, 2008.
[2]Breslau, Kendler, Su, Gaxiola-Aguilar, & Kessler, 2005.
[3]Huang et al., 2006; Surgeon General, 1999.
[4]Surgeon General, 1999.
[5]Mirin et al., 2002.
[6]Wells, Klap, Koike, & Sherbourne, 2001.
[7]Castro, Proescholdbell, Abeita, & Rodriquez, 1999.
[8]Huang et al., 2006; Stinson et al., 2005.
[9]SAMHSA, 2006.
[10]Beatty, Geckle, Huggins, et al., 1999.
[11]SAMHSA, 2007.
[12]SAMHSA, 2006.
[13]Brady & Back, 2008.
[14]Wechsberg, Craddock, & Hubbard, 1998.
[15]Orwin et al., 2001.
[16]Nelson-Zlupko, Kauffman, & Dore, 1995.
[17]Ashley, Marsden, & Brady, 2003.
[18]Vinton & Wambach, 2005.

Other gender differences in relapse risk involve marital and interpersonal conflicts (for women) and being unmarried or alone (for men) (Walitzer & Dearing, 2006). Being married may not be protective for women because they are often partnered with men who have substance use problems.

For adolescents, among pretreatment, treatment, and posttreatment factors, it was the third of these, including participation in aftercare and AA meetings, a lack of substance-using peers, involvement in a variety of nonsubstance-related activities, use of coping strategies learned in treatment, and motivation to continue sobriety, that had the most influence on outcomes (Chung & Maisto, 2006).

> **Directions Part II, Biopsychosocial Risk and Resilience Assessment**   Formulate a risk and resilience assessment, both for the onset of the disorder and for the course of the disorder, including the strengths that you see for this individual and the techniques you would use to elicit them.

INTERVENTION

Intervention goals for clients who abuse substances are summarized in Box 7.3. Generally speaking, permanent abstinence is the major goal of intervention. Whether adult clients can manage controlled drinking is a controversial topic. Controlled drinking may also be an interim goal for some people or may be appropriate in the early stages of alcohol abuse (Mirin et al., 2002).

About half of those with a substance use disorder will eventually make treatment contact (Wang et al., 2005), although past-year treatment seeking is low: 6% for people with alcohol use disorders, 16% for people with drug use disorders, and 22% for people with both alcohol and drug use disorders (Stinson et al., 2005). Commonly available treatment settings include (in order of usage) outpatient rehabilitation facilities, inpatient rehabilitation facilities, inpatient hospitals, and outpatient mental health centers (SAMHSA, 2006). Some programs are specifically designed for adolescents, pregnant or

---

Box 7.3 • Intervention Goals

1. Reduce or eliminate substance use.
2. Improve psychological and social functioning by mending disrupted relationships, reducing impulsivity, building social and vocational skills, and maintaining employment.
3. Prevent relapse by discussing the client's ambivalence about sobriety, identifying the emotional and environmental triggers of craving, developing coping strategies to deal with internal or external stressors, exploring the chain of decisions leading to the resumption of substance use, and learning from brief relapse episodes (slips) about triggers leading to relapse so as to develop effective techniques for early intervention.

For Adolescents

1. Improve family communication.
2. Train parents to provide proper guidance and limit setting for the youths.
3. Recognize and, if possible, treat addiction patterns in the parents.
4. Help adolescents and their families to develop alcohol- and drug-free lifestyles.

Sources: Bukstein et al., 2005; Larimer, Palmer, & Marlatt, 1999.

postpartum women, and women with young children. Many people receive intervention from locations that are not specialized for the treatment of these disorders, including self-help groups, private doctors' offices, emergency rooms, and prisons or jails (SAMHSA). For further guidance on appropriate placement, social workers should be aware of the Patient Placement Criteria for the Treatment of Substance-Related Disorders of the American Society of Addiction Medicine (Mee-Lee, Shulman, Fishman, Gastfriend, & Griffith, 2001).

Adolescents who access care for substance abuse are often clients in other intervention systems, such as child welfare, juvenile justice, and mental health. The needs of each young person may consequently be managed by multiple agencies, and providing quality treatment often requires the social worker's navigation across these systems (Kraft et al., 2006).

Client characteristics that influence decision making about the most appropriate treatment setting include the perceived potential harm of withdrawal, the severity of comorbid health and mental health concerns, the level of previous treatment response, and the extent of environmental support for the client's sobriety (Mirin et al., 2002). These risks need to be addressed in treatment with either a high degree of community support or temporary removal from those circumstances through residential treatment. Regardless of the treatment site or modalities utilized, positive outcomes are associated with the frequency, intensity, and duration of treatment participation (Mirin et al., 2002; Prendergast, Podus, & Change, 2000).

Psychosocial Treatments

Although AA models of recovery have tended to dominate the substance abuse field (Fuller & Hiller-Sturmhofel, 1999; Kelly, Myers, & Brown, 2002; Sheehan & Owen, 1999), social workers should be aware of alternatives for people who need help with substance use disorders. Here, we will talk about AA, alternative self-help groups, motivational interviewing, cognitive-behavioral treatment, and family interventions. In AA self-help groups, the participant reaches and maintains abstinence by moving through a series of 12 steps with the assistance of a support group and sponsor. AA and NA (Narcotics Anonymous) self-help groups have been shown to increase abstinence, self-efficacy, and social functioning for those who attend, especially when they engage in outside activities with people they meet at AA (Humphreys et al., 2004). Attendance at AA meetings may also stave off the depression that often accompanies heavy drinking (Kelly, Stout, Magill, Tonigan, & Pagano, 2010). However, self-help groups should probably not act as a substitute for professional intervention, especially for those who are mandated to attend treatment, as nonvoluntary clients typically do not stop drinking when attending AA (Kownacki & Shadish, 1999).

AA treatment models have also been developed as a treatment modality. In one large-scale study called Project MATCH, the AA model was effective as other treatments, especially for those who initially showed severe dependence and for those whose social networks supported drinking (Longabaugh, Wirtz, Zweben, & Stout, 1998; Project MATCH Research Group, 1997).

The reader should be aware that, in addition to 12-step groups, there are alternative self-help groups available to clients. These include Secular Organization for Sobriety, SMART Recovery, Women for Sobriety, and Moderation Management (Humphreys et al., 2004).

Of course, many people who present to treatment are not willing to change and maintain that they do not have a problem. One treatment approach, known as motivational interviewing, has been designed for such nonvoluntary clients (Miller & Rollnick, 2002).

See Table 7.2. Another individually oriented approach that is typically used when the client is more motivated to change is cognitive behavioral therapy. These interventions focus on certain aspects of the substance use behavior and can be utilized in a variety of comprehensive approaches (Kaminer & Waldron, 2006). Other cognitive-behavioral treatments that are part of family intervention are described here.

Table 7.2   Psychosocial Treatment for Substance Use Disorders

Theoretical orientation	Description	Indications and contraindications
Individual		
Motivational interviewing	A brief model (1–4 sessions) exploring and resolving the ambivalence people have about changing.	Can be effective with clients who demonstrate high levels of anger[1].
Cognitive-behavioral	Techniques include self-monitoring, the avoidance of stimulus cues, changing reinforcement patterns, and developing coping skills to manage and resist urges to use. Other skills that can be incorporated include substance refusal skills, communication skills, problem-solving skills, assertiveness, relaxation training, anger management, modifying cognitive distortions, and relapse prevention.	The person should be motivated to change his or her behaviors because cognitive-behavioral therapy (CBT) is an action-oriented approach.
Family		
Behavioral training for family member (i.e., CRAFT)[2]	The family member removes conditions in the environment supportive of drinking, reinforces appropriate behavior of the addict, gives feedback about inappropriate behavior while drinking, and provides consequences if behavior exceeds agreed-upon limits.	Although results are mixed for whether adjustment improves for the family member,[3,4] the research shows that these approaches have resulted in the person with substance use entering treatment at a significantly higher rate and with reduced drinking than in the comparison conditions.
Behavioral couples therapy	A brief (10 to 15 sessions) CBT approach delivered in either individual or couples' group modalities that entails building communication skills, planning family activities, initiating caring behaviors, and expressing feelings.	A meta-analysis found that couples therapy was superior to individual treatment at posttest on relationship satisfaction, but not until the follow-up period were substance use outcomes superior to the control conditions.[5] Most of the research has been done with men, but recently women with substance use disorders have been a focus, and couples therapy especially has been found helpful for women with Axis I and II disorders.[6]

[1]Longabaugh et al., 1998; Project MATCH Research Group, 1997.
[2]Miller, Meyers, & Tonigan, 1999.
[3]Miller et al., 1999.
[4]Thomas & Corcoran, 2001.
[5]Powers, Vedel, & Emmelkamp, 2008.
[6]Fals-Stewart, Birchler, & Kelley, 2006; McCrady, Epstein, Cook, Jensen, & Hildebrandt, 2009; Winters, Fals-Stewart, O'Farrell, Birchler, & Kelley, 2002.

Families have tremendous potential impact on either perpetuating or ameliorating the substance abuse problems of a family member, including the abuser's ability and willingness to comply with intervention (Mirin et al., 2002). For the partners of people with addictions, Al-Anon has been a widely used intervention approach. Al-Anon is a 12-step model derived from AA and cultivates detachment from the person with the addiction and the well-being of the family member. A lesser known family of interventions, called by various names, such as CRAFT (Miller et al., 1999) essentially trains family members in behavioral techniques to exert influence on the "drinker" so that he or she may develop motivation to change. Behavioral couples therapy is another research-focused approach for use when there is both a substance use problem (either alcohol or drug use) and a conflict issue within the couple. The main objective of couples therapy is to alter patterns of interaction that maintain chemical abuse and build a relationship that more effectively supports sobriety (O'Farrell & Fals-Stewart, 2006).

Family therapy approaches have received the most research attention for adolescent substance abuse disorders (Bukstein et al., 2005), along with CBT (Waldron & Turner, 2008). Because of the multidimensional nature of substance use problems in adolescence, most family therapy approaches integrate several theoretical frameworks. For instance, *brief strategic family therapy* (Szapocznik & Williams, 2000) incorporates both structural and strategic techniques. *Functional family therapy* possesses elements of structural and strategic family systems approaches, as well as behavioral family therapy, with a particular emphasis on the functions of symptoms (Alexander & Parsons, 1982). Both *multidimensional family therapy* (Liddle, 1999) and *multisystemic therapy* (Henggeler, Schoenwald, Borduin, Rowland, & Cunningham, 1998) are presented as "ecologically integrative approaches" (Mirin et al., 2002), because they go beyond family therapy to modify multiple domains of functioning affecting the youth's behavior, including other key supports and systems in the youth's life.

As discussed, other mental health problems often coexist with substance use disorders. Some guidelines have been developed for the treatment of people with co-occurring psychiatric and substance use disorders (Petrakis, Gonzalez, Rosenheck, & Krystal, 2002), and these are summarized in Box 7.4.

Practice Contexts

Practice Behavior Example: *Continuously discover, appraise, and attend to changing locales, populations, scientific and technological developments, and emerging societal trends to provide relevant services.*

Critical Thinking Question: Given the variety of evidence-based treatments available, how would you go about influencing the system of a facility of which you were an employer if they soley used an AA approach?

Box 7.4 • Guidelines for the Treatment of Co-Occurring Mental Health and Substance Use Disorders

1. Concrete needs, such as shelter and physical health, must be a priority.
2. The mental disorder should first be stabilized.
3. Motivational interviewing may help people comply with mental health treatment and substance use treatment.
4. Confrontation, a common approach in many substance abuse treatment settings, may not be effective for clients who are psychotic or potentially suicidal, and a supportive approach is suggested instead.
5. For clients with depression and anxiety, CBT can address both the psychiatric and substance use concerns.
6. The initial phase of substance abuse treatment may be crucial to successful engagement and retention, so developing interventions that focus on improving early success in clients who are depressed may be beneficial.

Sources: Conner et al., 2005; Martino, Carroll, Kostas, Perkins, & Rounsaville, 2002; Petrakis et al., 2002; Rosenthal & Westreich, 1999.

Pharmacologic Interventions

Three types of medications are currently used in substance abuse treatment: (1) aversive medications (such as Antabuse), designed to deter client drinking; (2) anticraving medications (known as the antidipsotropics); and (3) substitution therapy. Details about these medications are provided in Table 7.3. As aversive medications have lost popularity, anticraving medications have become more widely used. Evidence indicates more support for Naltrexone than Acamprosate (Anton et al., 2006). It has recently been found that a prescription of Naltrexone for those with drinking problems substantially reduced health care costs compared to those without a prescription (Kranzler, Montejano, Stephenson, Wang, & Gastfriend, 2010). The use of Naltrexone may thus be a cost-effective method of treatment.

Table 7.3 Pharmacological Treatment of Substance Use Disorders

Type	Description	Indications and contraindications
Aversive		
Antabuse	Inhibits the activity of aldehyde dehydrogenase, the enzyme that metabolizes acetaldehyde, the first metabolic breakdown product of alcohol. In the presence of disulfram, alcohol use results in an accumulation of toxic levels of acetaldehyde, which is accompanied by a variety of unpleasant and potentially dangerous (but rarely lethal) symptoms[1]	Compliance with this medication is difficult and physicians may be reluctant to prescribe because of common adverse reactions[2]
Anticraving		
Naltrexone	An opioid receptor antagonist, a substance that blocks opioid receptors in the brain, so that the individual fails to experience positive effects from opiates or alcohol.	Meta-analysis[3]: better at preventing a "lapse" from becoming a relapse COMBINE study[4]: performed as well as behavioral treatment on drinking outcomes
Acamprosate	May block glutamine receptors while activating gamma-aminobutyric acid	Meta-analysis[5]: better at preventing a relapse COMBINE study[6]: showed no evidence of efficacy
Substitution (for opioid addiction)		
Methadone	Works on opioid receptors	Substitution medication for opioid (heroin) addiction
Buprenorphine	Works on opioid receptors	Can be prescribed on an outpatient basis

Sources: Ross & Peselow, 2009.
[1]Mirin et al., 2002.
[2]McLellan, 2008.
[3]Rosner, Leucht, Lehert, & Soyka, 2008.
[4]Anton et al., 2006.
[5]Rosner et al., 2008.
[6]Anton et al., 2006.

Substitution medications, such as methadone and buprenorphine, are used for heroin dependence specifically. The goals of such medications are the prevention of withdrawal, the elimination of cravings, and the blockage of euphoric effects obtained by illegal opiate use (Bukstein & Cornelius, 2006). The addition of psychosocial intervention to methadone or buprenorphine seems to produce benefits in terms of compliance with treatment, reduced use of opiates, and abstinence from drugs at follow-up over medication alone (Amato et al., 2009).

> **Directions Part III, Goal Setting and Treatment Planning**   Given your risk and resilience assessments of the individual, your knowledge of the disorder, and evidence-based practice guidelines, formulate goals and a possible treatment plan for this individual.

CRITICAL PERSPECTIVE

A difficulty with applying diagnostic criteria to substance use disorders is that so often comorbid disorders are present—about 50% of such persons will have a co-occurring mental health disorder. The symptoms of substance abuse or dependence, and the effects of certain substances and withdrawal from substances, are often difficult to disentangle from symptoms of other mental disorders, such as depression, anxiety, and ADHD. Substance abuse can be a stand-alone disorder or it may mask the presence of other disorders in which it is comorbid to those disorders. A conservative position is to wait until after six weeks of sobriety to determine the presence of comorbid disorders, although this practice is typically not implemented in treatment settings.

Another critique, regarding treatment services, is that many facilities are still oriented around the "disease model of recovery." Although this has been useful for many people, our position is that substance use disorders, as well as other mental health problems, are a biopsychosocial manifestation and that other research-based treatments should be readily available and disseminated in addiction treatment settings. This is not so much a critique of the validity of the disorder as much as the way in which addiction is perceived by the substance abuse treatment field, and even among some social work professionals.

> **Directions Part IV, Critical Perspective**   Formulate a critique of the diagnosis as it relates to this case example. Questions to consider include the following: Does this diagnosis represent a valid mental disorder from the social work perspective? Is this diagnosis significantly different from other possible diagnoses? Your critique should be based on the values of the social work profession (which are incongruent in some ways with the medical model) and the validity of the specific diagnostic criteria applied to this case.

Case 2   The Coffee Shop Waitress

Janelle is a 53-year-old widowed Caucasian female who began individual therapy three months ago in a women's outpatient substance abuse program as a self-referral. She wants to quit drinking once and for all and also to get help for a deepening depression. She reports having been "depressed" since the death of her second husband four years ago (of a heart attack), but this has gotten worse in the past six months as she has tried to stop drinking.

Janelle has abused alcohol on and off since she was 15. She takes no other drugs. Janelle's father and one of her uncles were alcohol abusers, and her adult daughter (age 29) drinks heavily.

When Janelle began individual therapy, she reported having drunk approximately 10 beers a day during a previous nine-month time span, which ended six months ago (after which her depression began to worsen). During that time, she drank in larger and larger amounts to achieve the desired effect, despite the fact that she was aware of the possible negative effects on her health. Janelle states that her impulse to drink was strong whenever she tried to stop and that she experienced spells of shaking when she went without alcohol. Janelle reports having abused alcohol for many years before that, but not on a daily basis. She was more of a "binge drinker," drinking mixed drinks in bars and at home to the point of passing out, alone or with friends, once every week or two. Janelle currently reports having abstained from alcohol for the past six months, except for two episodes of binge drinking since she began treatment one month ago. These episodes were related to being alone and feeling lonely.

Janelle admits that she feels "terrible" about herself, because she continues to drink so much at times. "I must be a real weakling to have to rely on alcohol and not be able to quit. I'm certainly not very attractive in this condition." In addition to the issues related to her drinking, Janelle reports experiencing intense feelings of loneliness that she attributes to a long-term sadness due to the loss of her second husband.

Janelle also has a serious physical condition. She was diagnosed with type II diabetes eight years ago and currently adheres to a special diet to control that illness. She reports several past hospitalizations due to dehydration, which frequently occurs in persons with type II diabetes. Janelle reports that she must be sure to drink enough liquids and watch out for symptoms such as dizziness and feeling weak. Janelle has also experienced episodes of nausea and vomiting since undergoing stomach surgery for an ulcer four months ago. Her doctor had told her to expect periods of nausea related to her stomach condition. Janelle reports that she used to "love food," but since the stomach surgery she has experienced a decreased appetite and general lack of interest in food. She finds this very frustrating and admits that "now and then" she "forgets" about her diet and just eats what she wants, even though she may feel ill afterward. She has been warned by physicians that drinking alcohol is hard on her stomach, and although this serves as a motivator for her to stop, she still can't "just do it." She sees her medical doctor regularly but cannot sustain the treatment plans he initiates with her.

Janelle is currently working as a waitress at a coffee shop. She seems to have a strong work ethic and has had a variety of jobs throughout her adolescent and adult life. They are all unskilled jobs, as Janelle has only a high school diploma and never "sets out to work in one place for too long, because my kids have always needed me." Her three children are adults now, but she is highly involved in the lives of her two grandchildren, often caring for them. Janelle misses work occasionally due to oversleeping or being hung over, but she has never lost a job due to this behavior. She states that she is considered to be "likable" and a "good worker." She adds that "working has been especially helpful since my husband died," because it keeps her mind off her sadness. She admits that if she doesn't have to go to work in the morning, she tends to lie in bed alone for many hours, feeling preoccupied with her sadness and crying about her lack of "purpose" in life.

Janelle currently lives alone in an apartment. She is in regular contact with her children. Although her family relationships provide her with support, they are also sources of stress in Janelle's life. Her children make frequent and last-minute demands on her time for child care and financial assistance. Janelle currently has a romantic partner, who is separated but still involved with his wife. She views this relationship as shallow and temporary, and she wonders if she will ever again be close to a man. In addition to still grieving the loss of her second husband, she is also mourning the recent death of a good friend. Janelle currently has few friends, and although her church community is a possible source of support, she is not currently very involved with it. Janelle does not have regular transportation and must rely on friends and family in order to meet this need.

Despite her current stresses she enjoys some activities, most notably fishing and cooking. She greatly values her role as a grandmother. Janelle also maintains a sense of humor about her physical health, her often stressful relationships with her children, and her overall life situation.

Janelle grew up in a rural community in the mountains of Virginia. She was raised and continues to identify as Baptist. She considers herself a religious person, and she attended church regularly in the past.

Janelle also grew up in a household that featured emotional and physical family violence. Her father was alcohol-dependent and physically and emotionally abusive toward Janelle, her two brothers, and her mother. Janelle identifies using alcohol as one way she learned to cope with the trauma and stress of her family situation. Alcohol was easily obtained in her community, even by adolescents, and Janelle states that she began to enjoy the "buzz" from whisky and wine very quickly after she began drinking. She and her friends often drank in each other's homes and in the nearby woods and were rarely caught or confronted about their activity.

Shortly after graduating from high school, Janelle married a man she believed would be a "good provider." She states that her attraction to the man, whom she never knew "too well," abated after a year or so, but she stayed in that emotionally abusive marriage for the next 20 years, because "I had kids then." He berated her as a wife, parent, and person. Janelle worked a series of unskilled part-time jobs during those years and says she was never happy. She saw her life as "all stress and all work." She was prone to spells of extreme hopelessness in which she stayed in bed, wished that she could die, and wondered why there was nothing "pleasurable" in her life. Janelle reports that in the past six months, and at several other times in her life, she experienced symptoms such as low mood, fatigue, feelings of worthlessness, excessive guilt, and trouble falling asleep.

Please go to the Appendix for directions to this case.

Case 3   The Restless Realtor

Larry is a 27-year-old Caucasian male who lost his driver's license six months ago after his third DUI offense; he is required to complete a substance abuse program in order to have the license reinstated. He kept drinking on the first two occasions he was placed in the program and refused to attend the required weekly AA meetings. This is the last opportunity the agency will give him to comply with the program requirements before they close his case. Larry came to the interview at the treatment facility well dressed and spoke articulately. He was somewhat fidgety, constantly wringing his hands and shifting in his seat. He also had some difficulty keeping his train of thought as he spoke about his situation, stating that he felt "distracted."

Larry started using marijuana when he was 14 and drinking when he was 16. He was arrested for several drug- and alcohol-related offenses in his youth and spent time in a juvenile justice facility as a result. He was diagnosed with ADHD when he was in elementary school and struggled with all academic subjects, especially math. He was on Ritalin for several years but is no longer taking it. He dropped out of school during his senior year because he was making so much money dealing drugs that he did not see the need to continue struggling in school. He later completed his GED while serving a jail sentence for dealing.

Larry is now working as a realtor, but his business is suffering because he cannot drive. Although he seems motivated to complete the program so that he can get his license back, he believes he has learned to "control" his drinking and sees no problem with his regular marijuana use. When asked what he means by "controlling" his drinking, he said that the three DUIs got his attention and he doesn't want to get into further legal trouble. He now drinks only "a couple of beers" on weekdays; on weekends, he consumes a six pack each night. He no longer drinks at bars because he can't drive and can't afford to buy drinks. He says he is not seeing much of his friends lately because of his transportation problems. Another reason he views his alcohol use as not being a problem is that his friends tend to drink more than he does. In contrast, he sees himself as only a social drinker.

In sum, Larry does not think he should be in a substance abuse program. He also thinks he should be given credit for the few weeks he attended the program in the past, so that his current requirements could be shortened. Larry is disgusted that he is required to attend AA, stating that he is "not like those people" and asking, "How am I supposed to attend all these meetings and groups if I can't drive?"

Larry is the older of two boys. His parents divorced when he was 11, leaving his family to struggle financially. He is close to his mother. Larry considers his mother his strongest support and often turns to her for help. He says she is sympathetic to his driving prohibition, and she sometimes takes him places he needs to go. She supports his need to seek treatment so that he can get his license back, but according to Larry, "she doesn't think I have a problem either." Larry has not kept in touch with his father, and his relationship with his brother is somewhat strained. Larry claims that his brother is the source of much of his stress and that he has a lot of resentment toward him. It seems that Larry and his brother started a business together that is not working out, and Larry feels his brother is to blame. Members of Larry's paternal family (an uncle and grandfather) have a history of alcohol use disorders.

Larry is currently living with his girlfriend of 18 months and their three-month-old daughter in an apartment. His relationship with his girlfriend has been a major source of stress for the last six months. They were engaged to be married but have broken the engagement, as Larry wants to "move on." Though they still live together, they are not getting along, and Larry is having a hard time dealing with the tension. He says they argue about his inadequate earnings, his drinking and marijuana use, and his children from a previous marriage. Larry admits he gets so frustrated with the situation that he has been violent with his girlfriend, usually when drinking. She has called the police, and Larry has been arrested twice for family violence. When questioned about these episodes, Larry says, "I've never hit her." He does, however, admit to once pinning her against the wall and "getting in her face." He also shoved her out of the way when she blocked his way out of a room, which on at least one occasion resulted in her being knocked to the floor.

Larry has three children from a previous marriage whom he cares for every other weekend. His relationship with his ex-wife is acrimonious, according to his description. His oldest child, who is six, was diagnosed with leukemia three years ago. During that time, Larry was taking antidepressants to help him deal with "that gut-wrenching situation." The child's cancer is now in remission, and Larry is no longer taking the medication. When asked, he said that he did not notice if his distractibility and fidgeting were any better on antidepressants as "I had other things on my mind." He says that he does not feel depressed currently but is "stressed out."

Larry says he smokes marijuana to help him relax, and that it is the only thing that helps him in this way. He has used it at least twice a week for several years in the evening. He finds using marijuana preferable to being on medication. He does not report tolerance, saying that he has always smoked one joint "to get high" and this amount has not changed in years.

Larry considers himself in excellent health and reports that "everything checked out fine" at a physical examination about a year ago. He suffers from asthma, but keeps it under control by using an inhaler before he exercises. He is not currently taking any other medications. He tries to work out every day and notices that he is having an easier time working out since he quit smoking last month.

Larry states that he has problems sleeping. It is not hard for him to fall asleep, but he wakes frequently and has trouble getting back to sleep. He feels that he does not get enough "deep sleep" to feel refreshed in the morning. Larry also complains that he feels anxious all the time and cannot remember when he has not felt that way. He worries about his children, his relationship with his girlfriend, his job, and his need to complete

Ethical Practice

Practice Behavior Example: *Recognize and manage personal values in a way that allows professional values to guide practice.*

Critical Thinking Question: When you have a client who continues substance use despite obvious adverse consequences, how do you recognize and manage your personal values and reactions to the problematic use so that you can help him or her?

this program. He feels this anxiety in his stomach and in his head and neck.

Given his visible symptoms of distractibility and hyperactivity and the fact that Larry was diagnosed with ADHD as a child, the social work intern asked about other symptoms of inattention, hyperactivity, and impulsivity. In regard to inattention, Larry admitted to avoiding tasks that take a lot of mental energy and having difficulty keeping his attention on paperwork. He says that he would probably make more money if he were better organized. He says that his girlfriend complains about his forgetfulness and inattentiveness to her, even when she speaks to him directly. With regard to hyperactivity, Larry fidgets, but he denies any of the other symptoms when asked about them. However, he admits to "feeling restless" if he does not drink or smoke marijuana in the evenings.

Please go to the Appendix for directions to this case.

PRACTICE TEST The following questions will test your knowledge of the content found within this chapter. For additional assessment, including licensing-exam type questions on applying chapter content to practice behaviors, visit **MySocialWorkLab.com**

1. Which of the following can distinguish substance abuse from dependence?

   a. There are negative social consequences to dependence, but not to abuse

   b. For dependence, physiological dependence is required, but for abuse it is not

   c. Tolerance is a characteristic of abuse, and withdrawal is a characteristic of dependence

   d. For dependence, the person has made at least one temporarily successful attempt to cut down on substance use, and for abuse the person has not necessarily done so

2. In considering the causes of substance use disorders, which of the following is true?

   a. It is determined by genetics

   b. It is determined by family dysfunction

   c. It is a biopsychosocial disorder

   d. It is a disease

3. Marguerite is a 29-year-old single female hospital nurse who lives with three friends. They lead active social lives, hosting parties where alcohol is consumed in large quantities and they go out together to taverns most nights of the week. Marguerite becomes intoxicated most evenings and admits that she has been "blacking out" and losing track of time. Given that Marguerite is not sure whether she wants to quit drinking, an appropriate intervention would be:

   a. Motivational interviewing

   b. AA

   c. Cognitive behavior therapy

   d. Self-monitoring of attempts to reduce, but not stop, drinking

4. Marguerite says that although she has never missed work, she is routinely hung over, and her work performance is beginning to suffer. She often sets limits on her plans for drinking before going out, but she invariably exceeds these limits. Marguerite has never experienced withdrawal symptoms, but she still qualifies for the diagnosis of substance dependence because:

   a. She needs increasing amounts of alcohol to become intoxicated

   b. She often drinks more than she plans to

   c. She experiences diminished effects when using her "baseline" amount of alcohol

   d. She is unable to manage her job effectively

5. Given the information provided on comorbid disorders with substance use disorders and the cases presented in this chapter, what is your conclusion about the presence of comorbid disorders? How will you determine how to go about treating both the substance use disorder and the comorbid disorder? How will you address the sequence of such treatments?

6. Given the information about substance use disorders presented in this chapter and the available treatments of substance use disorders, what is your position to those who argue that alcoholism is a "disease" and requires a spiritual approach?

SUCCEED WITH

Visit **MySocialWorkLab** for more licensing-exam test questions, and to access case studies, videos, and much more.

8

Schizophrenia

Case 1

Anna Yannucci is a 26-year-old single Caucasian female who was referred to the out-patient mental health facility following a two-week stay at a psychiatric unit of a local hospital. A report from the hospital indicated that her father, Thomas Yannucci, took Anna to the hospital from an apartment where she had been staying for two weeks with a 45-year-old man. Her father believed that this man was a drug user and barely knew his daughter. Mr. Yannucci had learned where Anna was staying when she called him one day to ask for money. He came to the apartment immediately and found that his daughter was apparently not eating well, not changing or washing her clothes, not going outside, and not communicating coherently. When her father arrived, Anna was sitting still and remained quiet, watching television absently. When spoken to, she replied in polite but short phrases and did not initiate conversation. She seemed "lost in her own little world." Mr. Yannucci brought Anna home from the apartment and later that day drove her to the emergency services unit of the hospital. Mr. Yannucci stated that his daughter "behaves like this much of the time" but he thought that she had lately become even more difficult to communicate with. He added that she always "sat around, spaced out" when she was in her own apartment.

Schizophrenia is a mental disorder characterized by a person's abnormal patterns of thought and perception. It is a *psychotic* disorder, that is, a mental state in which the person's thoughts and perceptions are severely impaired. Schizophrenia includes two types of symptoms (American Psychiatric Association, 2000). *Positive* symptoms represent exaggerations of normal behavior and include hallucinations, delusions, disorganized thinking, and tendencies toward agitation. *Negative* symptoms represent the absence of what would be considered normal behavior and include flat affect (the absence of expression), social withdrawal, noncommunication, passivity, and ambivalence in decision making. There are five subtypes of schizophrenia based on its particular symptom presentation (paranoid, disorganized, catatonic, undifferentiated, and residual), but these have been proposed for removal in the next edition of the *Diagnostic and Statistical Manual of Mental Disorders* (DSM) (American Psychiatric Association, 2010).

PREVALENCE AND COMORBIDITY

Schizophrenia has a worldwide prevalence of approximately 1% (Murray, Jones, & Susser, 2003). Data from the National Institute of Mental Health-sponsored Epidemiological Catchment Area research project noted the lifetime prevalence of schizophrenia to be 1.3% in the United States (Kessler, Berglund, et al., 2005). Schizophrenia tends to be diagnosed among African American persons more frequently than among Caucasians. This imbalance may result because practitioners attribute and weigh particular symptoms differently for clients of different races (Luhrmann, 2010). Clinicians of Caucasian origin tend to interpret the suspicious attitudes of African Americans as symptomatic of schizophrenia, representing delusions or negative symptoms, when these attitudes may in fact be protective in situations of perceived discrimination.

Persons with schizophrenia have a high rate of comorbidity for other DSM disorders. The national comorbidity study noted earlier found that 79.4% of persons with lifetime nonaffective psychosis (most often schizophrenia) meet the criteria for one or more other disorders (Kessler, Birnbaum, et al., 2005). These include a mood disorder (most often major depression) (52.6%), anxiety disorders (especially the phobias, posttraumatic stress disorder, and panic disorder) (62.9%), and substance abuse (26.8%). A recent meta-analysis found that persons with schizophrenia who abuse substances experience fewer negative symptoms than those who are abstinent (Potvin, Sepehry, & Strip, 2006). This suggests either that substance abuse relieves negative symptoms or that persons with fewer negative symptoms are more prone to substance use. Along these same lines, several studies have found that nicotine use helps alleviate psychotic symptoms in some persons with schizophrenia (Punnoose & Belgamwar, 2006). Finally, schizophrenia is often comorbid with the schizotypal, schizoid, and paranoid personality disorders (Newton-Howes, Tyrer, North, & Young, 2008).

ASSESSMENT

The clinical assessment of schizophrenia is done through client interviews, interviews with significant others, and history gathering. There are no tests currently available that conclusively determine when schizophrenia is present. See Box 8.1 for assessment guidelines.

The admission report stated that Anna had been living with her younger sister in a condominium owned by her father for the past six months. Anna met the man with whom she was most recently staying at a fast-food restaurant. He had bought her lunch and then invited her to his apartment, where he lived alone. Mr. Yannucci did not know why Anna would accept the invitation, but he added that "she does crazy things sometimes." He thought that the man wanted to take advantage of his daughter financially.

Box 8.1 • Assessment of Schizophrenia

Adults

- Criterion A for schizophrenia requires two of the following symptoms: delusions, hallucinations, disorganized speech, grossly disorganized or catatonic behavior, and negative symptoms for a period of one month.
- Assess for the duration of active symptoms, which may rule out brief reactive psychosis or schizophreniform disorder.
- Refer client for medical evaluation to rule out any medical conditions that may be contributing to symptom development.
- Assess whether the client abuses substances or is currently under the influence of a drug that may be causing symptoms.
- Assess for psychosocial stressors that may be contributing to symptom development.
- Assess for psychotic or mood disorders among relatives.
- Assess the family system for the possibility of stresses that may precipitate an onset of psychotic symptoms.

- Assess for mood swings at present or in the client's history that may indicate a schizoaffective, major depressive, or bipolar disorder.
- Assess for premorbid functioning to determine the presence of a possible schizotypal, schizoid, or paranoid personality disorder.
- The practitioner must be careful to rule out the possibility of organic, major affective, pervasive developmental, obsessive-compulsive, and substance use disorders.

Childhood

- In cases of childhood psychosis, rule out the presence or influence of developmental, anxiety, and mood disorders.
- Visual hallucinations and disorganized speech may be more common than delusions and hallucinations.

Adapted from Volk et al., 2008.

Doctors at the hospital ordered a variety of neurological tests to rule out physical causes of Anna's symptoms. A toxicology screen found no traces of drugs in her system. While at the hospital Anna was cooperative, except that she refused to consider taking medications. When asked for her reasons, she replied simply, "I just don't want to." Staff efforts to help the client elaborate on any of her thoughts and feelings were not successful. In fact, Anna seemed to become mildly irritable when asked questions, always saying, rather politely but in a monotone, "I just don't have a lot to talk about right now." She rarely made direct eye contact with staff but tended to stare blankly. Anna did seem to enjoy walking about the unit, and the nursing staff reported that she often appeared to be talking to herself. Her mood was quite consistent, but as one nurse wrote, "the patient doesn't seem to be feeling anything."

Anna's condominium was located one mile from the mental health agency. She walked to her first appointment alone, arriving on time and with the card in her hand. Her father met her there, coming from his job at a bakery. Anna was dressed appropriately but appeared not to have changed her clothes or bathed in the recent past. She exuded such a strong, disagreeable odor that support staff at the agency complained to the director about her presence in the waiting room. Anna seemed oblivious to this condition. Upon questioning, she denied hearing voices but seemed highly distracted at times, as if her attention were focused on somewhere far away. She minimized the issues of her personal hygiene, saying that she eats "something good every day" and bathes "when I need to." Her answers to all questions were brief. She seemed preoccupied but not upset about being at the agency.

Anna stated that she spent most of her time at home but added, "I like to take walks for exercise." When asked to elaborate, she said that she took walks every day to nearby fast-food restaurants or the bank to deposit and withdraw money. She did not have a job, did not attend school, and was not involved in any recreational activities. When asked about her goals in these areas, she said, "I'd like to have a job someday when I'm ready." When asked about any friends, she said, "I'd like to have friends someday," but about the present, she said, "People can't be trusted." Anna stated that she got along with her sister, but that "we don't really talk much." Thirty minutes into the interview Anna said, "It's nice meeting you, but I should go now." The social worker asked if she would mind waiting in the room or outside on the porch while he talked with her father. She agreed, and walked outside. Throughout this interview Anna had maintained the same blank look on her face, revealing no affect.

Mr. Yannucci remained for another half hour and provided much background information. He is a 50-year-old Italian American who came to the United States when he was 10 years old. He has worked successfully in the restaurant business for the past 30 years, always maintaining strong ties to the Italian community in his city. The welfare of his family is paramount to him. He clearly does not understand what might be "wrong" with his daughter, and he tends to see her behavior as "willful misbehaving." Yet he tried hard to understand her as he told the story of her background.

"I have to be responsible for my daughter. It is a father's responsibility to care for his family. But I do not understand why she does not try harder. Anna's mother and I never got along. I was the breadwinner and she was the mother, and she became very strange not long after we married. She stayed home all the time and sometimes did not come out of her room. She cried often for no good reason and did not do enough to take care of Anna, her sister, and me. She talked about crazy things and never made sense. Sometimes she walked away from home and did not return for days. Sometimes the hospital would call me—or the police would. She was always wandering around looking for Lord knows what, finally getting into trouble when she stole food and objects out of people's yards. I did my best to help her get more rest and get outside more with good people, but it did not work. Her behavior became worse as the years went on. Finally, she left me for good. I don't know where she is, but she lives here in town. A few times she comes to get money from me, but that's all."

"Anna was a good girl growing up. She wanted to be a nurse, and she got good grades in school. Every day she came home from school and went to her room and studied. But she was not a sociable girl. She never had a boyfriend. That was good, because I didn't want her with dangerous boys. She stayed home and studied and helped take care of me and her sister Beth. She never talked much, but she behaved well and was respectful."

When asked for details about Anna's functioning as a child and adolescent, Mr. Yannucci stated, "She did not ever seem to be happy, but that's only because she was serious, which is a good thing. She didn't have friends, but that was fine, too, because she was busy at home. She never wanted to go out and play in the neighborhood, even as a young girl. Like I said, she kept to herself and studied. She didn't need much help from her mother or me. She was independent."

"I didn't want her going to college, but Anna was determined. She lived at home and went to the university, but she did not do well. She stopped going to school and started staying in her room more. She was still helping out around the house, but not as much, and it got worse. After about a year she started to loaf all the time and sat in the television room alone. She started having bad dreams, because I could hear her screaming many nights in her bedroom. Many times I would notice her talking to herself, but when I asked what she was doing she got quiet and said, 'Nothing.' "

"Two years ago I met my current wife, Margaret, and she did not care for Anna's behavior at all. Margaret thought that Anna was 'crazy,' which is a terrible thing to say about someone. She thought that Anna should be forced to move away or go to school again, and leave us to our new life. But my wife is a good person. She thought that I was babying Anna, and that I should make her live on her own. But I can't do that. So as a compromise I got a condominium for Anna and her sister. Margaret told me that she would not marry me unless I did that. I go and see them every day! I plead with Anna to get a job and to get busy, but she will not do it. She stays home and does nothing. She is a nice girl, so why would she not want to

Engage, Assess, Intervene, Evaluate

Practice Behavior Example: *Negotiate, mediate, and advocate for clients.*

Critical Thinking Question: Suppose the agency support staff met with the director about refusing Anna's admittance into the agency because of her disagreeable personal hygiene, which did indeed offend other clients in the waiting room. What might the social worker's appropriate role be as a negotiator, mediator, or client advocate? Which of the social worker's roles, if any, might come into conflict during this process?

Ethical Practice

Practice Behavior Example: *Apply strategies of ethical reasoning to arrive at principled decisions.*

Critical Thinking Question: If Anna was to prohibit the social worker from further conversations with her father, what kind of ethical dilemma might this present to the social worker who wants to provide comprehensive services to the client? How might such a dilemma be resolved? What would be the possible positive and negative outcomes of any decision the social worker makes?

be busy and have friends? I don't understand her. And lately she has started wandering off, just like her mother."

At this point, the interview ended. Anna returned to the room for a few minutes and politely declined an offer to see a physician for a medication evaluation. She did agree to come back to the agency in two days to meet with the social worker again. "It wouldn't hurt anything" was her response to the invitation.

Directions Part I, Multiaxial Diagnosis   Given the case information, prepare the following: a multiaxial diagnosis, the rationale for the diagnosis and global assessment of functioning score, and additional information you would have wanted to know in order to make a more accurate diagnosis.

Multiaxial Diagnosis

Axis I:
Axis II:
Axis III:
Axis IV:
Axis V:

Rationale and Differential Diagnosis

Additional Information Needed

BIOPSYCHOSOCIAL RISK AND RESILIENCE INFLUENCES

Onset

The specific causes of schizophrenia are not known. Its onset and course are likely due to a mix of biological, psychological, and perhaps some social influences (Cardno & Murray, 2003). Many persons who develop schizophrenia display what is called *premorbid* or "early warning" signs. These include social withdrawal, a loss of interest in life activities, deterioration in self-care, and a variety of "odd" behaviors. The signs can exist for many years, but even when present they do *not* guarantee the eventual onset of schizophrenia. The *stress/diathesis theory* holds that schizophrenia results from a mix of heritability and biological influences (perhaps 70%) and environmental and stress factors (approximately 30%) (Cardno & Murray, 2003), which may include insults to the brain, threatening physical environments, emotionally intrusive or demanding experiences, and emotional deprivation.

See Box 8.2 for a summary of issues related to the diagnosis of schizophrenia in special populations.

Box 8.2 • Schizophrenia in Vulnerable and Oppressed Populations

Children

- Schizophrenia is rare prior to adolescence, with only 10% of persons experiencing its onset by that time.[1]

Women

- Men have an earlier onset (ages 18 to 26) compared with women (26 to 40 years).[2]
- Women tend to have higher levels of premorbid (prepsychotic) functioning and more positive symptoms than men do; women also have a better prognosis with regard to their social functioning potential and response to intervention.[3]

Minorities

- African Americans are more frequently diagnosed with schizophrenia than are Caucasians, possibly due to clinician interpretation of culturally appropriate suspicion within the African American community as a negative symptom, rather than a learned attitude.[4]

Low SES

- The prevalence of schizophrenia is twice as high in lower than in higher socioeconomic classes for the following three reasons:[5] increased stressors due to living in low SES may contribute to the onset of schizophrenia; persons who develop schizophrenia lose occupational and social skills and fall into the lower classes; and others never develop skills to establish themselves in stable social roles.

Older Adults

- Older adults have not been studied as extensively with regard to antipsychotic medications effects, so at present there is little data to guide decisions about which medications to prescribe for them.[6]
- There is no clear evidence that any particular psychosocial interventions are suited to older adult clients.[7]

---

[1]Fonagy, Target, Cottrell, Phillips, & Kurtz, 2002.
[2]Seeman, 2003.
[3]Seeman, 2003.
[4]Trierweiler et al., 2000.
[5]Mulvany, O'Callaghan, Takei, Byrne, & Fearon, 2001.
[6]Marriott, Neil, & Waddingham, 2006.
[7]Van Citters, Pratt, Barters, & Jeste, 2005.

Biological Influences

Biological theories of schizophrenia implicate the brain's limbic system (center of emotional activity), frontal cortex (governing personality, emotion, and reasoning), and basal ganglia (regulating muscle and skeletal movement) as primary sites of malfunction (Conklin & Iacono, 2003). People with schizophrenia are believed to have a relatively high concentration of the neurotransmitter dopamine in nerve cell pathways extending into the cortex and limbic system. Dopamine levels are not considered causal for the disorder, however, and other neurotransmitters, including serotonin and norepinephrine, have also been proposed as risk influences (van Os, Rutten, Bart, & Poulton, 2008). Whether symptoms result from abnormal development or deterioration of function is not clear.

Some researchers are beginning to study the influences of certain chromosomes on molecular pathways in the brain as causal mechanisms for schizophrenia (e.g., Detera-Wadleigh & McMahon, 2006), but this work remains speculative. Still, its genetic transmission is supported by the higher-than-average risk mechanisms among family members of persons with the disorder (Ivleva, Thaker, & Tamminga, 2008). An identical twin of a person with schizophrenia has a 47% chance of developing the disorder. A nonidentical twin has only a 12% likelihood, which is the same probability as for a child with one parent who has schizophrenia. Other risk factors include a maternal history of schizophrenia and affective disorder (Byrne, Agerbo, & Mortensen, 2002). The age of onset for a child tends to be earlier when the mother has schizophrenia. Further, negative symptoms are frequently seen among nonpsychotic first-degree relatives of people with schizophrenia.

It has also been hypothesized that a variety of neurodevelopmental phenomena account for the onset of schizophrenia (Fatjó-Vilas et al., 2008). These include central nervous system development, the quality of nerve cell connections, the manner in which nerve cell activity influences the formation of circuits underlying brain functions, and the development of the dopamine system. The brain volumes of persons with schizophrenia appear to be lesser than those of persons without the disorder. A recent literature review found that the whole-brain and hippocampus volumes of most study participants were reduced, while ventricular volume was increased (Steen, Mull, McClure, Hamer, & Lieberman, 2006). In genetically predisposed subjects, the change from vulnerability to developing psychosis may be marked by a reduced size and impaired function of the temporal lobe (Crow, Honea, Passingham, & Mackay, 2005), although some researchers do not agree that a reduction in size of the temporal lobe or amygdala is inevitable (Vita, Silenzi, & Dieci, 2006). Traumatic brain injury, often cited as a contributing cause of the disorder, increases the chances of schizophrenia in families, but only when there is already a genetic loading (Kim, 2008).

Brain trauma from birth complications has been postulated as one of the pathways to the disorder (Prasad, Shirts, Yolken, Keshavan, & Nimgaonkar, 2007), and obstetrical complications are related to earlier age of onset (Mittal, Ellman, & Cannon, 2008). Postmortem studies show brain abnormalities indicative of developmental problems in the second or third trimester of pregnancy, such as altered cell migration in the hippocampus and prefrontal cortex. Other postulated (but debated) causes of these abnormalities are related to the higher-than-expected frequencies of prenatal exposure to influenza viruses and infections (urinary and respiratory) in persons who later develop schizophrenia (Keshavan, Gilbert, & Diwadkar, 2006). People with schizophrenia tend to be born in winter or early spring, which means that their mothers were pregnant during a time of year when viruses are more prevalent (Reid & Zborowski, 2006). Also, older men are more likely than younger men to father sons with schizophrenia (Torrey et al., 2009). Although the risk influence is not clear, it could be due to a mild biological degeneration in the father's reproductive system.

Biological characteristics that are protective of a person's developing schizophrenia include the absence of a family history of the disorder, normal prenatal development, and a normally developed central nervous system. Protective environmental influences include being born during the late spring, summer, or fall and an absence of physically traumatic events during childhood and adolescence (Geanellos, 2005; Jobe & Harrow, 2005).

Psychosocial Influences

There are no known psychological influences of specific stress events, on the development of schizophrenia, although many years ago they were considered the likely dominant causes (Phillips, Francey, Edwards, & McMurray, 2007). There are, however, some possible social risk influences for schizophrenia. These include living in an urban versus a rural environment, being born into a relatively low socioeconomic status (SES), and having migrated into a new culture (Selten, Cantor-Graae, & Kahn, 2007). Conversely, living in a rural environment, being of middle- or upper-class SES, and geographic stability would be protective.

COURSE AND RECOVERY

Schizophrenia tends to be a chronic disorder and complete remission is uncommon (Perkins, Miller-Anderson, & Lieberman, 2006). Its course, however, is variable. Suicide is unfortunately the leading cause of premature death in schizophrenia, as 20 to 40% of persons attempt suicide at some point in their lives and 9 to 13% succeed (Pinikahana, Happell, & Keks, 2003). Persons most at risk for suicidal ideation during the early stages of the disorder are young white males who are depressed, unmarried, unemployed, socially isolated, functionally impaired, and lacking external support (Pinikahana et al., 2003). The average life span of persons with schizophrenia is approximately 15 years less than the national average in the United States, although this reduced life expectancy is largely due to lifestyle factors such as high rates of smoking, medication use, side effects of medication, substance use, diet, poor access to health care, and other risks related to poverty (Wildgust, Hodgson, & Beary, 2010).

Although the causes of schizophrenia are uncertain, clues are available to differentiate a better or worse prognosis. These are listed in Table 8.1.

> **Directions Part II, Biopsychosocial Risk and Resilience Assessment** Formulate a risk and resilience assessment, both for the onset of the disorder and for the course of the disorder, including the strengths that you see for this individual.

Table 8.1 Risk and Resilience Assessment

Risk mechanisms	Protective mechanisms
Biological	**Biological**
Gradual symptom onset	Later age of onset
Prominence of negative symptoms	Brief duration of active phases
Repeated relapses of active symptoms	Good interepisode functioning (with minimal residual symptoms)
Medication absence or noncompliance	Absence of brain structure abnormalities
	Family history of mood disorder
Psychological	**Psychological**
Poor insight into the disorder	Insight into the disorder
Delay in intervention	Early and ongoing intervention
Social	**Social**
Significant family expressed emotion	Development of social skills prior to onset of the disorder
Poor social adjustment prior to the onset of schizophrenia	Family participation in intervention
Noncompliance with, or absence of, psychosocial interventions	Interest in independent living
Absence of a support system	Participation in a range of psychosocial interventions
Living in an urban area	Presence of support systems
	Living in a nonurban area

Sources: Andreasen et al., 2005; Lenoir, Dingemans, Schene, Hart, & Linszen, 2002; Pharoah, Rathbone, Mari, & Streiner, 2003; Zammit, Lewis, Dalman, & Allbeck, 2010.

INTERVENTION

Although strong empirical research support for many interventions is lacking, there is a consensus that the treatment of schizophrenia should be multimodal and include interventions targeted at specific symptoms as well as the social and educational needs of the client and family (Spaulding & Nolting, 2006). In this section we will review medication, individual therapy, group intervention, family intervention, assertive community treatment (ACT), case management interventions, hospitalization, vocational rehabilitation, and early intervention. One literature review established that client satisfaction with interventions for schizophrenia and other psychotic disorders is influenced by multiple factors, including an absence of significant drug side effects, participation in treatment planning and decision making, and involving family members in the intervention plan (Chue, 2006).

Medications

Medication is the primary intervention modality for persons with schizophrenia. It cannot "cure" a person of the disorder but can be effective in eliminating or reducing some of the symptoms. The first-generation antipsychotic drugs, most popular from the 1950s through the 1980s, act primarily by binding to dopamine receptors and blocking their transmission (Leonard, 2003). These medications act on all dopamine sites in the brain, although only those in the forebrain contribute to the symptoms of schizophrenia. A reduction in dopamine in other areas (extending from the midbrain to basal ganglia) causes adverse effects of akathisia (restlessness and agitation), dystonia (muscle spasms), parkinsonism (muscle stiffness and tremor), and tardive dyskinesia (involuntary muscle movements of the face and limbs). Anticholinergic medications are often prescribed to combat these effects, although they in turn have their own adverse effects of blurred vision, dry mouth, and constipation.

The "second-generation" antipsychotic medications, available in the United States since the late 1980s, act differently from those developed earlier. Clozapine, the first of these, acts selectively on dopamine receptors (Faron-Gorecka et al., 2008). Their sites of action are the limbic forebrain and the frontal cortex, and thus they do not carry the risk of adverse effects for the muscular system. The fact that they block receptors for serotonin suggests that this neurotransmitter also has a role in the production of symptoms. Risperidone, introduced in 1994, has fewer adverse effects than the first-generation drugs and is at present the most widely prescribed antipsychotic drug (Yu et al., 2006). Olanzapine, sertindole, ziprasidone, quetiapine, aripiprazole, and amisulpride are other newer medications on the market (Schatzberg & Nemeroff, 2001). Their somewhat greater alleviation of negative symptoms suggests that serotonin antagonist activity is significant in this regard.

Both the first- and second-generation medications continue to be used to treat persons with schizophrenia. Prescribing practices depend on the physician's preferences and the client's family history and financial status (the older medications are less expensive). The effects of antipsychotic medications on older adults have not been studied as extensively, so at present there is little data to guide decisions about which medications to prescribe for them (Marriott et al., 2006). There is some evidence that the newer atypical antipsychotic medications are more effective for older adults than the first-generation drugs (Van Citters, Pratt, Barters, & Jeste, 2005).

Although almost all physicians recommend antipsychotic medication for persons with schizophrenia, their relative risks and benefits with regard to the patient's physical and emotional well-being are subject to debate (Cohen, 2002). Studies of drug effectiveness for schizophrenia symptoms consistently show that many clients discontinue their medication for a variety of reasons, such as perceived ineffectiveness and adverse side effects. One large-scale study found that the first-generation medications were as effective as the newer medications, but discontinuation rates over an 18-month period for all medications were alarmingly high, at 74% (Lieberman et al., 2005). Up until this study, it was assumed that the lesser adverse side effects of the newer medications would be associated with increased compliance.

Nonadherence is best predicted by recent illicit drug or alcohol use and medication-related cognitive impairment (Ascher-Svanum et al., 2006). Fortunately, clinical practices such as counseling, written information, and occasional phone calls can increase medication adherence, at least in the short term (Hanes et al., 2005). Despite the issues of adverse effects and limited effectiveness, medication nonadherence is significantly associated with poorer outcomes in schizophrenia. A multisite study of 1,900 consumers found that client nonadherence was associated with greater risks of hospitalization, use of emergency services, arrests, violence, victimization, poorer mental functioning, greater substance abuse, and alcohol-related problems (Ascher-Svanum et al., 2006).

Other types of medication are occasionally prescribed for persons who have schizophrenia, usually along with the antipsychotic drugs. These include the antidepressants, benzodiazepines, and mood stabilizers (Wolff-Menzler, Hasan, Malchow, Failki, & Wobrock, 2010). There is no clear evidence that these medications help alleviate symptoms of depression or control psychotic symptoms, however.

Electroconvulsive therapy (the induction of a seizure by administering an electrical shock to the scalp) is an intervention that has been used for more than 50 years with persons who have schizophrenia. Although controversial, several dozen studies have shown that it can be an effective short-term option for alleviating symptoms, especially when the client has not responded to medication or rapid improvement is sought (Tharyan & Adams, 2005).

Human Rights & Justice

Practice Behavior Example: *Incorporate social justice practices in organizations, institutions, and society to insure that these basic human rights are distributed equally and without prejudice.*

Critical Thinking Question: Are there policies in your field agency, or another agency with which you may be familiar, regarding medication accessibility for clients with low incomes? Although the older antipsychotic medications are less expensive, the newer drugs have fewer adverse effects. How can a social worker advocate for clients with schizophrenia so that his or her clients might be able to receive the newer medications?

Psychosocial Interventions

Individual Psychotherapy

Research on psychodynamic intervention with schizophrenia has limited empirical support. Malmberg and Fenton (2005) concluded that individual psychodynamic treatment is not effective in symptom reduction, reduced hospitalizations, and improved community adjustment. One positive aspect of this type of intervention, however, is that it alerts the practitioner to the importance of the worker–client relationship. Persons with schizophrenia are often initially distrustful of service providers, so no matter what type of intervention is provided, the practitioner must take care to develop a positive working alliance with the client over time.

Cognitive-behavioral therapy (CBT) is increasingly being used to treat persons with schizophrenia (Kuipers, Garety, & Fowler, 2006). This is based on the premise that current beliefs and attitudes mediate much of the person's affect and behavior. CBT focuses first on a review of the client's core beliefs regarding self-worth, the ability to create changes in his or her life, and realistic short- and long-term goals. If the client appears to be thinking "irrationally" in any of these core areas (i.e., drawing conclusions that are insufficiently based on external evidence), the social worker can work toward the client's acquisition of more "rational" thinking. Clients are helped to (1) modify their assumptions about the self, the world, and the future; (2) improve coping responses to stressful events and life challenges; (3) relabel some psychotic experiences as symptoms rather than external reality; and (4) improve their social skills. It is important to emphasize that although clients with schizophrenia engage in psychotic thinking about some or many issues in their lives, some aspects of their thinking are either "rational" or amenable to change.

A meta-analysis of research on the efficacy of CBT for schizophrenia indicates that it is an effective adjunct to medication (Pfammatter, Junghan, & Brenner, 2006). Despite these encouraging findings, it is not yet clear what the specific ingredients of effective psychosocial intervention are or which interventions are most effective in particular settings. Further, CBT does not affect social behavior and overall cognitive functioning (Rathod, Phiri, & Kingdon, 2010). Another group of researchers reviewed clinical trials and concluded that although CBT showed promise, more research was needed to demonstrate its effectiveness relative to "supportive" therapies (Jones, Cormac, da Mota Neto, & Campbell, 2004).

Social skills training (SST) is a type of CBT that addresses deficits in interpersonal relations, which are common among persons with schizophrenia. SST promotes the client's acquisition of social skills and leads to short-term improvements in cognitive and social functioning (Pfammatter et al., 2006). In a meta-analysis of 22 randomized, control group studies, Kurtz and Mueser (2008) concluded that such training was effective, with certain caveats. Clients perform best on tests of the content of the training interventions but less well on their transfer of that training to activities of daily living. SST also seems to have a mild positive effect on general measures of pathology.

Group Interventions

Group interventions include insight-oriented, supportive, and behavioral modalities. They are often used in conjunction with other interventions such as medication and CBT. There are few controlled studies of group therapy. In his review of the descriptive literature on both inpatient and outpatient groups, Kanas (2005) concluded that for persons with schizophrenia, groups focused on increased social interaction, learning about and managing symptoms, were often effective. Group interventions are widely used in inpatient settings, but there is little evidence of their effectiveness in helping stabilize persons who are recently highly symptomatic. A systematic review of five controlled trials of group CBT for schizophrenia indicated, however, that benefits were evident with regard to some symptoms, most prominently anxiety and depression (Lawrence, Bradshaw, & Mairs, 2006).

Family Interventions

Family participation in the client's intervention is a protective influence (Pharoah, Mari, Rathbone, & Wong, 2010). When a person has schizophrenia, a chronic emotional burden develops, which is shared by all family members. Their common reactions include stress, anxiety, resentment of the impaired member, grief, and depression (McFarlane, 2002). The concept of family (or caregiver) expressed emotion (EE) has been prominent in the schizophrenia literature for the past 30 years (Kymalainen & Weisman de Mamani, 2008). EE can be defined as the negative behaviors of close relatives toward a family member with schizophrenia, including emotional over-involvement and expressions of criticism and hostility. The concept is not used to blame family members for the course of a relative's illness, but to affirm that families need support in coping with it. In a meta-analysis of 27 studies by Sutcliff and Hooley (1998), EE was consistently shown to correlate with symptom relapse, especially for clients with a more chronic disorder. Family environments with low EE are associated with fewer symptom relapses and rehospitalizations than those with high EE environments are.

Family interventions in schizophrenia usually focus in part on producing a more positive atmosphere for all members, which in turn contributes to the ill relative's adjustment. Pilling et al. (2002) conducted a meta-analysis of all randomized clinical studies done on single- and multiple-family intervention (conducted in groups) and found that these interventions were more effective at 12 months than the comparison conditions, which usually included some form of "standard care" (such as medication alone). Single-family interventions reduced readmission rates in the first year. After two years all 18 family interventions lowered the relapse and readmission rates of the ill relative and increased medication compliance. Another review of the literature on EE showed that family interventions designed to reduce expressed levels of criticism, hostility, or over-involvement tend to decrease relapse and increase medication compliance, although families are still left with a significant burden (Pharoah, Rathbone, Mari, & Streiner, 2005).

Family psychoeducation refers to interventions that are focused on educating participants about the ill relative's schizophrenia, helping them develop resource supports in managing the disorder, and developing coping skills to deal with related challenges (Griffiths, 2006). A review of 40 randomized controlled studies indicated that (1) education improved members' knowledge of mental illness, (2) behavioral instruction helped members ensure that their ill relative take medications as prescribed, (3) relapse prevention skills development reduced the ill relative's relapses and rehospitalizations, and (4) new coping skills development reduced the distress associated with caregiving (Mueser et al., 2002).

Assertive Community Treatment and Case Management Interventions

Case management is a term used to describe a variety of community-based intervention modalities designed to help clients receive a full range of support and rehabilitation services in a timely, appropriate fashion (Northway, 2005). Case management interventions are usually carried out in the context of large, community-based programs. The most famous of these, ACT, was developed by Stein and Test (1980) in Wisconsin and has since been replicated in many other sites around the world. By 1996 there were 397 such programs in the United States (Mueser, Bond, Drake, & Resnick, 1998). The core characteristics of the ACT model of service delivery are assertive engagement, service delivery in the client's natural environment, a multidisciplinary team approach, staff continuity over time, low staff-to-client ratios, and frequent client contacts. Services are provided in the client's home or wherever the client feels comfortable and focus on everyday needs. Frequency of contact is variable, depending on assessed client need. Other kinds of case management programs share some, but not all, characteristics of the ACT model.

A number of comprehensive reviews of ACT have been conducted. A recent systematic literature review of 38 studies by Dieterich, Irving, Park, and Marshall (2010) concluded that clients receiving ACT services were significantly more likely to remain in treatment, experience improved general functioning, find employment, not be homeless, and experience shorter hospital stays. There was also a suggestion that such clients had a lesser risk of death and suicide. In an earlier review of 75 studies, Marshall and Lockwood (2003) found that both ACT and case management were more effective than other forms of intervention in helping clients stay in contact with services, spend fewer days in the hospital, secure employment, and experience life satisfaction. There were no clear differences, however, in measures of mental status and social functioning. ACT was superior to case management in client use of hospitalization, but differences on the other measures were not clear. Although ACT does promote greater client acceptance of interventions (Tyrer, 1999), another comprehensive review indicated that the programs vary considerably with regard to staffing, types of clients, and resources; comparisons are thus difficult to make (Mueser et al., 1998). Further, efforts to make interventions compulsory are not effective in engaging clients (Kisely & Campbell, & 2007). That being said, the reviewers found that client gains persist only as long as comprehensive services are continued.

Hospitalization

It is widely believed that inpatient hospitalization is an expensive, ineffective, and socially undesirable treatment setting for persons with schizophrenia. Hospitalization is primarily used now to stabilize persons who are a danger to themselves and others, rather than providing active and ongoing interventions. Five randomized controlled trials showed that a planned short-term stay does not encourage a revolving door pattern of admission for people with serious mental illnesses (Johnstone & Zolese, 2005). Still, the use of clubhouses and other partial or day hospitalization programs is effective in reducing inpatient admission and improving outcomes (Marshall et al., 2006). Partial or day hospital programs are staff-run, structured, psychosocial rehabilitation programs for persons with schizophrenia who have the capacity to live in the community. Clubhouses are vocational rehabilitation programs in which members work side by side with staff to complete the work of the facility (e.g., cooking lunch, keeping records, managing a member bank, and answering phones). Members are not paid for their participation, but an employment specialist helps place members in community jobs.

Vocational Rehabilitation

Vocational rehabilitation is work-related activity that provides clients with pay and the experience of participating in productive social activity. The goals of vocational programs may be full-time competitive employment, any paid or volunteer job, the development of job-related skills, and job satisfaction. Twamley, Jeste, and Lehman (2003) conducted a meta-analysis of randomized controlled trials of vocational rehabilitation that focused on both client placement and support (with training, placement, and occasional contact) or supported employment (more intensive participation by the case manager in the client's job functions). Programs have a positive influence on promoting work-related activities such as paid employment, job starts, duration of employment, and earnings. Supportive employment programs tend to be more effective than pre-vocational training (Zito, Grieg, Wexler, & Bell, 2007). Unfortunately, a diagnosis of schizophrenia is negatively related to the attainment and maintenance of employment when compared with other diagnoses.

Bond (2004) conducted another meta-analysis of the effectiveness of supported employment for people with severe mental illness. He found that in 13 studies, 40 to 60% of clients obtain competitive employment, versus 20% of those not enrolled. Interestingly, although clients who hold jobs for an extended period of time show benefits such as improved self-esteem and symptom control, their employment does not correlate with outcomes such as prevention of hospitalization and quality of life. Another recent systematic review suggests that ACT intervention models produce vocational outcomes that are superior to usual treatment (Kirsh & Cockburn, 2007). The authors emphasize that ACT teams who designated a vocational specialist were most successful in this regard.

Early Intervention

Early intervention refers to efforts to detect schizophrenia in its early stages and then provide those persons with phase-specific treatment. Several such programs have been initiated in the United States,

Engage, Assess, Intervene, Evaluate

Practice Behavior Example: *Develop mutually agreed-on intervention goals and objectives.*

Critical Thinking Question: Many clients with schizophrenia, because of the effects of the symptoms on their thinking, want to set goals that seem clearly unrealistic to the social worker. Consider Anna's goals (or lack thereof). In this case, how might the social worker try to develop mutually agreed-on goals and objectives?

Europe, and Australia (Marshall & Rathbone, 2006). Data regarding the risks and benefits of early detection and intervention remain sparse, and the evidence is not sufficient to justify pre-onset treatment as a standard practice (McGlashan, Miller, & Woods, 2001). There are also ethical issues involved in primary prevention efforts, including clinical priorities, screening ethics, stigma, confidentiality, and informed consent.

> **Directions Part III, Goal Setting and Treatment Planning**   Given your risk and protective factors assessments of the individual, your knowledge of the disorder, and evidence-based practice guidelines, formulate goals and a possible treatment plan for this individual.

CRITICAL PERSPECTIVE

Schizophrenia remains an enigma. Although it is among the most disabling of all mental disorders, researchers and clinical practitioners are not able to describe exactly what it is, how it is caused, or how it can be effectively prevented or treated. There is a consensus, however, that its primary causes are biological or hereditary (although the extent of those influences is debated), and that family and social environments are more significant to its course than to its onset. There is also a general worldwide agreement on its basic symptom profile. Schizophrenia thus appears to be recognized as a valid mental disorder. Some theorists debate, however, whether the symptoms of schizophrenia represent a single or several disorders, and refer to the *schizophrenia spectrum* disorders as also including schizo-affective disorder and the paranoid, schizoid, and schizotypal personality disorders (Keefe & Fenton, 2007).

A major problem with the diagnosis of schizophrenia is that its causal influences are inferred from the hypothesized actions of antipsychotic medications (Conklin & Iacono, 2003). As more information about the condition's neurobiology is developed, professionals may become able to articulate its core features. As described earlier, the limited effectiveness of these medications casts some doubt on the validity of the presumed "nature" of schizophrenia. Still, because the pharmaceutical industry and psychiatric profession are so heavily invested in drug marketing (Moncrieff, Hopker, & Thomas, 2005), relatively little research currently focuses on the psychosocial influences of the disorder.

> **Directions Part IV, Critical Perspective**   Formulate a critique of the diagnosis as it relates to this case example. Questions to consider include the following: Does this diagnosis represent a valid mental disorder from the social work perspective? Is this diagnosis significantly different from other possible diagnoses? Your critique should be based on the values of the social work profession (which are incongruent in some way with the medical model) and the validity of the specific diagnostic criteria applied to this case.

Case 2 The Reluctant Day Treatment Member

Donald is a 23-year-old Caucasian male who presents as quiet and polite, with a flat affect. At age 20, he was in church with his family when he started spinning his body around, feeling that something was pushing him. After returning home, he felt restless and randomly moved items and furniture around the house. Over a short period of time, his parents noticed that his speech was becoming disorganized and his behavior more erratic. He would sit outside in cold weather with light clothing, sleep in the backyard, and live in his car. At one point, Donald felt he was possessed by demons and needed to purify his body by not eating. He thought that if he lost weight, the demons would have to leave. From the initial onset of his symptoms until early last year, Donald was hospitalized 14 times as a result of aggressive behavior toward his family. His aggression was usually characterized by shouting and shoving his parents. Once he punched his father in the face. At times Donald is bothered by his aggressive thoughts and has sufficient insight to recognize that his illness impacts his life.

Donald is currently receiving treatment from a county mental health agency as an outpatient. He is seen regularly by a social worker and by the psychiatrist who monitors Donald's medication and coordinates treatment with his primary care physician. Donald is also attempting to become more involved with a day treatment program, but is finding it difficult. Initially, he liked the idea of participating in group activities and having the chance to develop social relationships. Over time it became stressful for him, and at one point he said he felt the program was "evil" so he stopped attending. He is trying to attend again, but initially he would go out on the grounds and stay behind the trees. Donald has progressed to being able to come out from behind the trees and sometimes enter the building, but he is still not able to engage in any kind of social interaction. He has been known to wear earplugs during his entire time at the day program to protect himself from perceived ridicule.

When at home, Donald spends the vast majority of his time in his room. He no longer watches television or listens to music, activities he previously enjoyed doing. His parents encourage Donald to eat dinner with the family several times a week to foster the social interaction he otherwise lacks. He is notably distracted by his internal stimuli and often talks and laughs to himself. He paces, goes in and out of the house, and picks up and examines items that are not there. His speech is often tangential.

Donald is currently obsessed with children and their safety. He mistrusts his father and fathers in general, although abuse by his father has been ruled out. He mistrusts the Catholic church because of reports of child abuse by priests. He often misinterprets parental behavior as child abuse. On a recent visit to a fast-food restaurant, Donald saw a father holding a fussy child. He thought the child was crying because the father was holding the child "in a perverted way," and he demanded that the father put the child down.

At his intake for the day treatment program, Donald told the doctor that his parents and siblings had murdered his friend. In truth, the friend had died of a heroin overdose. He also reported that he hears a voice that is "nasty" in tone. He stated that the voices "do cruel jokes" on him, and he laughs or talks back to them. He tries to control the voices by praying. Donald also talks about "a presence touching me." He described it as a sharp jolt of terror, as if someone was in the room with him, touching him. This presence comes and goes, and Donald thinks it may be Satan. He also thinks that people are reading his mind and making fun of him.

Recently, Donald has had problems sleeping and is becoming increasingly agitated over the need to organize protests against abortion. His father contacted Donald's social worker and requested that both the social worker and the doctor see Donald to reevaluate his medication. When Donald was informed of this appointment, he became extremely annoyed and threatened to cut the doctor's throat. He left the house on foot, returning several hours later at 2:00 A.M., cold, tired, and wet from the rain. He agreed to be hospitalized the next day.

Over the course of his illness Donald has continued to experience periods of depression. During these periods, which last for several weeks, he will sleep at least 12 to 14 hours a day and has a great deal of difficulty waking. By his parents' report, he eats less, is more withdrawn, more isolated, and less active than at other times. His depressed moods are noted by his mother, his social worker, and the psychiatrist. He has described other moods in which he feels like "doing a lot of things," but these episodes were short lived and do not meet the criteria for manic or hypomanic states. According to both Donald and his family members, he does not smoke or use drugs or alcohol.

Despite his psychotic and depressive symptoms, there are times (at most a few days at a time) when he is oriented to reality and does exhibit some insight regarding his illness. However, he continues to experience "voices" (although understanding that these are not real) and flat affect and withdrawal, even during these periods.

Donald is the youngest of three children. His mother reported that she had a normal pregnancy and delivery with Donald. He was born in February. Donald's older brother is 34 and his sister is 26. His mother works as a nurse, and his father is an engineer. There is a family history of mental and mood disorders. Donald's mother is taking antidepressants, and her brother has bipolar disorder with manic episodes marked by psychosis and a substance use disorder. There is also a history of attempted suicides in Donald's mother's family, and a paternal great-uncle had "a breakdown."

Donald's parents describe him as a shy child who did well in school. He was diagnosed with depression at age 13 and took antidepressants until he was 20. At age 15 he had his first suicidal ideation but made no attempt to take his life. He also reported thoughts of suicide when he was 19 and 20, but never made any attempts.

Donald graduated from high school with a 3.6 GPA. He attended college for three semesters, earning a 3.1 GPA in his studies. During high school and college Donald held several jobs. He worked in a veterinarian's office for nine months. He was also employed in retail and as a waiter in several eating establishments, but was unable to stay employed at any of these places more than a few weeks.

The medications Donald currently takes are a cause for concern. His illness has not responded well to medications, even though he is taking many of them. These include Depakote, Zyprexa, Abilify, Geodon, and Risperdal. He is experiencing several undesirable side effects, most notably tremors of his hands, arms, and feet. The health care providers treating Donald would like to have him try clozapine, described by his social worker as a drug of last resort. This is an unlikely possibility, however, as transitioning medications requires a person to be hospitalized. The patient is then monitored twice weekly during the first six months and weekly for the following six months. Donald has not been particularly compliant with medication and treatment but is especially reluctant to be hospitalized, feeling that hospitals are "evil."

Please go to the Appendix for directions to this case.

Case 3 Emma's Private World

Emma is a 59-year-old African American woman, born in July, who presents with a well-groomed appearance but flat affect. Her medical chart shows that her weight is in the normal range for her height, and she has a medical diagnosis of hypertension. Emma is an inpatient resident at a mental health facility, where she has resided since her admission one year ago.

Emma believes that she still owns a house in another city, in spite of having been shown the deed of sale from 13 years ago. She says her son has been replaced by an impostor who came from a seedpod. Emma also states that she was shot while at work but went home because she didn't bleed. She denies that she has siblings, saying they were just people who were put in her parents' house to be raised. She says she doesn't want contact with them, and they don't attempt to contact her. When questioned about some of these beliefs, Emma states that she was instructed by a secret group, of which she is part, not to give out further information. When staff challenge her beliefs, she says it hurts her feelings and responds to them in anger.

Emma has been observed responding to internal stimuli. She also reported in rounds that while in her room, she heard her psychiatrist's voice telling her she was released. Emma does not believe herself to have a mental illness or hypertension and states that she takes her medication only because the nurses give it to her. She is currently being treated with Haldol (a first-generation antipsychotic), the dosage of which was recently increased due to persistent delusions. A previous medication, Zyprexa (a second-generation antipsychotic), was recently discontinued due to lack of efficacy.

This is Emma's third admission to an inpatient mental health facility. Emma is pleasant when approached. She attends scheduled treatment groups independently. Her records show her to be Protestant, but she does not attend any spiritual services at this time. She participates in occasional outings if prompted.

Prior to admission, Emma was living with her son in a large urban area where she was noncompliant with medication and reportedly caused problems at home. She was originally placed with her son 14 years ago after becoming unable to care for herself in her home, which was located in another city where she had lived for 10 years. At the time she was removed, she had no electricity and no running water. Her son was appointed legal guardian and payee at that time. At his house, her son stated that Emma would sit in front of the television with no sound and get up only to go outside to smoke. She was reported as being aggressive toward her grandchild and attempted to return to the home she no longer owns. On one occasion she had to be removed from her son's house by the police for aggressive behavior toward him. On another occasion she had to be removed by the police from a bank, where she erroneously insisted that she had an account. Emma is now estranged from her son. He says he is "worn out from dealing with her."

Emma has a history of noncompliance with outpatient treatment. She has no history of drug or alcohol abuse but does smoke about half a pack of cigarettes per day. Neither does she have a history of depressive or manic episodes. Her son said there was no family history of schizophrenia that he knew of, and he didn't think that his mother had suffered from traumatic events as a child. He said that his mother's parents were strict and would give out "whippings" for misbehavior. Emma came from a poor background, and when she married, the family could have been classified as "working poor."

When Emma was going through a divorce in her 40s, she told her son that she'd bought him a car and that he should go to the dealer and pick it up. When he spoke with the car dealer, he discovered that his mother had had a number of confused conversations with the dealer, telling him the bank would provide the necessary money. She had not, in fact, bought a car. He soon found out that his mother had also not paid his college tuition bill, which she denied.

Emma was recently evaluated by the occupational therapy department using the Kohlman Evaluation of Living Skills (KELS) and the Allen Cognitive Level Screen (ACLS). Emma was reported to be friendly and cooperative during this 90-minute evaluation. Emma's KELS score showed her as able to accomplish some tasks independently but having poor judgment in other areas. She was unable to identify her current source of income but stated that the bank gives money to people who need it. She has not been employed for over 20 years but states that after her release from the mental health facility, her prior employer will find her and send her to France to a government school. Emma's ACLS results showed weakness in the areas of problem solving, insight, and judgment. Overall, her scores, KELS/fair and ACLS/4.4, demonstrate her need to live in a 24-hour supervised environment.

Please go to the Appendix for directions to this case.

PRACTICE TEST The following questions will test your knowledge of the content found within this chapter. For additional assessment, including licensing-exam type questions on applying chapter content to practice behaviors, visit **MySocialWorkLab.com**

1. Which of the following is true of hallucinations?
   a. They can be experienced as the faces of devils in the wallpaper
   b. They can be experienced as the idea that one's thoughts are being broadcast
   c. They can be experienced as a belief of supreme power
   d. They can be experienced as a belief that the government is in secret pursuit

2. What psychosocial interventions have the most evidence supporting their use for people with schizophrenia?
   a. CBT
   b. Family psychoeducation
   c. Traditional case management
   d. Personal therapy

3. Barry was a 25-year-old unemployed male with schizophrenia who lived with his mother. He had been extremely withdrawn from family and peers throughout his adolescence and early adulthood. In late adolescence

Barry began to experience hallucinations, including two voices. His limited abilities to function socially were in decline. Barry had become extremely withdrawn during his psychotic episode, which provides evidence of the existence of:
   a. Delusions
   b. Ideas of reference
   c. Disorganized thinking
   d. Negative symptoms

4. Barry identified three goals for his intervention: getting a job, finding his own apartment, and making a few friends. The social worker linked Barry with a psychiatrist and eventually enrolled him in a computer-training program, psychosocial clubhouse, and a volunteer position to test his work readiness. These services were primarily intended to:
   a. Stabilize his thought processes
   b. Address his personal goals
   c. Work counter to his isolative tendencies
   d. Lift his overall mood

5. Review the cases in this chapter and note the strengths possessed by each client. Based on this assessment, which of the clients demonstrates the highest potential at present for independent living? How would his or her strengths be utilized to achieve this end?

6. Select any of the clients described in this chapter (but not the one you may have chosen for responding to question 5) and describe what might be an "ideal" lifestyle, including a living environment and neighborhood that would be most conducive to their well-being.

SUCCEED WITH

Visit **MySocialWorkLab** for more licensing-exam test questions, and to access case studies, videos, and much more.

9

Depressive Disorders

Tammy is a 44-year-old African American female who was diagnosed with multiple sclerosis (MS), a degenerative autoimmune disease, nearly 15 years ago. The disease has progressed to the point where she walks with two canes, one in each hand, when she leaves her house, although she is able to use only one cane around the house. Tammy is unable to hold a job because of her disability and receives about $500 in Supplemental Security Income each month. In addition, she receives food stamps and Medicaid.

Tammy first sought assistance from the social work department a month ago because of her housing situation. She has lived with a friend in her basement bedroom for the past 18 months. The friend's grown son, who does not live with them, owns the house. The friend also has two other sons who live in the house. Tammy pays them $200 in rent each month and uses her food stamps to buy food for the entire household. The situation is causing her great stress, as the two young men make her feel unwanted. They are loud and harass her (they "get on me") and make it difficult to sleep. She is unable to use the shower because it is not big enough for her safety seat, and she has fallen a few times while using it. She takes sponge baths in her room instead.

The stress of her living situation is worrying her, and she is afraid that she'll have another attack of MS and require hospitalization. She has been hospitalized once since moving in with this friend. In addition, she has checked herself into a psychiatric hospital twice since living with her friend. Now, for the past several weeks, she has found herself crying every day, feeling hopeless, and wanting to hurt herself. She has never actually attempted self-harm, however. She stays in her bed, either sleeping or watching television, most days, except for the times she has her physical therapy appointments. She describes feeling "incredibly tired" and also says that she wants to stay out of the way of her roommates so that they won't bother her.

PREVALENCE AND COMORBIDITY OF DEPRESSION

Of all disorders that may be experienced in one's lifetime, depression is the most common. Indeed, 16.6% of people in the United States will experience a major depressive disorder in their lifetime (Kessler, Berglund, et al., 2005). A *major depression* is a period of two weeks or longer during which a person experiences a depressed mood or loss of interest in nearly all life activities. *Dysthymic disorder* represents a general personality style featuring symptoms that are similar to, but less intense than, those of major depression. In a given year, 1.5% of the adult population will suffer from dysthymic disorder (Kessler, Chiu, Demler, & Walters, 2005). The prevalence rates for youth depression are 2.8% in children and 5.7% in adolescents (Costello, Erkanli, & Angold, 2006). The rate of past year major depressive disorder was lower among persons aged 50 or older (5.8%) than among younger adults (Substance Abuse and Mental Health Services Administration, 2009).

The lifetime rate of comorbidity for adults with major depressive disorder is nearly three fourths (72.1%) (Kessler, Berglund, et al., 2005). The most common comorbid disorders by far are the anxiety disorders (59.2%), followed by impulse control and substance use disorders. In the Treatment for Adolescents with Depression Study (TADS) (TADS, 2006, 2007), the most common concurrent diagnoses were anxiety disorders, attention-deficit hyperactivity disorder, oppositional defiant disorder, and dysthymia.

ASSESSMENT

General practitioners are often responsible for diagnosing depression because people initially seek help from the medical system. Unfortunately, general practitioners are able to detect the presence of depression less than 50% of the time (Mitchell, Rao, & Vaze, 2010). This is partly because the majority of physicians fail to use *Diagnostic and Statistical Manual of Mental Disorders* (DSM) criteria to diagnose depression (Zimmerman & Galione, 2010). Box 9.1 provides general assessment guidelines for clients who may have depression, and Box 9.2 lists risks for depression among vulnerable and oppressed populations.

Box 9.1 • Assessment Guidelines for Depression

- Assess the recent occurrence of any stressors that may account for the client's symptoms of depression, to consider the possibility of an adjustment disorder.

- Determine whether the client is under the influence of any substances that may account for the depressive symptoms.

- Assess the client for symptoms of mania, to rule out bipolar disorder.

- With children and adolescents, seek collateral reports from parents and teachers, given many adolescents' reluctance to disclose their feelings. When they do communicate, adolescents tend to be accurate reporters of their emotions. Count a symptom as present if *either* the parent or the child reports it.

- Older adults do not typically complain of sadness, anxiety, or hopelessness but speak instead of physical (weight loss, insomnia, and fatigue) and cognitive (such as memory and concentration impairment) signs of depression.

- For all clients, especially older adults, symptoms of depression are common to many medical conditions and can be brought on by medications taken for physical disorders.

- For resources on standardized assessment instruments for depression, see Joiner, Walker, Pettit, Perez, and Cukrowicz (2005) for adults and Klein, Dougherty, and Olino (2005) for children and adolescents.

Sources: Alexopoulos et al., 2001; Bird & Parslow, 2002; Kotlyar, Dysken, & Adson, 2005; Waslick, Kandel, & Kakouros, 2002.

Box 9.2 • Depression and Social Diversity

Youths

- Teens, especially girls, are at increased vulnerability for depression,[1] which may place an individual at risk for future episodes and other mental disorders into adulthood.[2] Adolescence is a period of risk because it is when people develop formal operational thinking; they can reflect upon causality for events in their lives and assume a future orientation in which they may experience hopelessness about the future.[3]

Older Adults

- Many people, particularly older adults, do not see depression as a health problem that can be treated but rather as a character weakness or a sign of being "crazy" (Laidlow, Thompson, Gallagher, & Dick-Siskin, 2003). Other older adults may view depression as a normal event in older age.

- Depressive symptoms can be precipitated by common ailments at this stage of life, such as Alzheimer's disease, stroke, Parkinson's disease, heart disease, cancer, and arthritis;[4] however, prolonged and unresolved grief, dependence upon others, and the accumulation of negative life events[5] may also contribute to depression.

- Older adults who live in low-SES neighborhoods and receive treatment for depression tend to respond less well to treatment than their counterparts residing in middle-income tracts.[6]

- Older adults may not participate in psychotherapy because of out-of-pocket payments required, lack of referrals from health care providers, or the lack of availability of local psychotherapy providers.[7]

Women

- Rates of depression for women are twice that of men,[8] beginning by age 14, and persisting through the life span.[9] A number of reasons may account for the disparity: female hormonal changes,[10] rumination as a coping strategy,[11] higher rates of sexual abuse,[12] greater interpersonal stress,[13] lower appreciation and pay for women's work, and role overload.[14]

- For teenage girls, interpersonal stress may contribute to the onset of depression as they typically invest more than boys in relationships.[15]

People with Disabilities

- Medical conditions and disabilities increase the risk of depression[16] and its continuance.[17]

Ethnic Minorities

- The prevalence of major depression in adults is equivalent among different ethnic groups (Caucasians, Mexican Americans, Puerto Ricans, Caribbean Blacks, and African Americans). Although ethnic disparities in the diagnosis and treatment of depression have been reduced in the psychiatric care system in the last 10 years, these gains are not reflected in the primary care system, where many people from ethnic minority groups are served for their mental health needs.[18]

- Mexican American teens have a significantly higher rate of mood disorders than Caucasians or African Americans.[19]

- Latino teens may not receive adequate mental health care compared to Caucasians, but having Medicaid or State Children's Health Insurance increases the odds of receiving appropriate intervention.[20]

- African American women have the lowest rates of suicide.[21]

- American Indian and Alaskan Natives have the highest rate of suicide among those aged 15 to 24.[22]

- Labor migrants have a 20% prevalence rate for depression.[23]

- Refugees have a 44% prevalence rate.[24]

- Hispanics have a higher risk of discontinuing prescribed medication prematurely compared to people from other ethnic groups.[25]

Low SES

- A significant proportion (17.4%) of single women facing the termination of welfare benefits suffered from depression in the last 12 months, which is more than twice the rate of women in the general population.[26]

- Individuals who are of low SES are at particular risk for stopping the use of medication prematurely.[27]

---

[1]Kovacs, 2001.
[2]Fergusson, Horwood, & Lynskey, 1996.
[3]Abela, Brozina, & Haigh, 2002.
[4]Alexopoulos et al., 2001; Shanmugham, Karp, Drayer, Reynolds, & Alexopoulos, 2005.
[5]Cole, 2005.
[6]Cohen et al., 2006.
[7]Wei, Sambamoorthi, Olfson, Walkup, & Crystal, 2005.
[8]Kovacs, 2001.
[9]Kessler, 2003.
[10]Desai & Jann, 2000.
[11]Nolen-Hoeksema, 2002.
[12]Bolen & Scannapieco, 1999.
[13]Girgus & Nolen-Hoeksema, 2006.
[14]Le, Munoz, Ippen, & Stoddard, 2003.
[15]Girgus & Nolen-Hoeksema, 2006; Hammen, Brennan, & Keenan-Miller, 2008; Rudolph, 2002.
[16]Ciesla & Roberts, 2001; Karasu, Gelenberg, Merriam, & Wang, 2002.
[17]Huijbregts et al., 2010.
[18]Stockdale, Lagomasino, Siddique, et al., 2008.
[19]Merikangas et al., 2010.
[20]Alexandre, Martins, & Richard, 2009.
[21]Tondo, Albert, & Baldessarini, 2006.
[22]Centers for Disease Control and Prevention, 2004.
[23]Lindert, Ehrenstein, Priebe, Mielck, & Brähler, 2009.
[24]Lindert et al., 2009.
[25]Olfson, Marcus, Tedeschi, & Wan, 2006.
[26]Cook, Mock, Jonikas, et al., 2009.
[27]Olfson et al., 2006.

Tammy has been a patient at the rehabilitation hospital for most of the course of her disease. She sometimes has what she calls "attacks" in which her MS symptoms worsen and she needs to be hospitalized. She recognizes that this usually happens when she is under great stress. Currently she is seen in the outpatient clinic and attends physical therapy twice a week. She hopes to become strong enough to need only one cane while out in public, and none at home. Her therapist believes that she is making good progress and that her goal is attainable.

Tammy's family situation is marked by conflict and estrangement. Tammy is divorced and has two daughters and a son, all grown. Her son is in jail. Her younger daughter is pregnant, and her older daughter just moved into a subsidized apartment. She says her relationship with her older daughter is strained, but they do speak. Her ex-husband died a few years ago while in prison. She has a sister who lives in a shelter in a neighboring county, but they also are not on speaking terms. Tammy says this is because while she was still married, her sister had an affair with her ex-husband. All her brothers are in jail, and she is not close to any other relatives.

Tammy is not eligible for public housing. She used to live in a Section 8 apartment, but was evicted. Her children were responsible for paying her bills, and she did not realize that they were not paying her rent until she learned that she owed over $2,000. She is ineligible to get back on the public housing list until she has paid this money. She has worked with the Center for Independent Living to try to find alternatives, but the cheapest apartments they have found have rents higher than her monthly income.

Tammy says she does not take beta interferon, a medication used to treat MS symptoms that has a suspected connection to the development of depression (Arnett & Randolph, 2006). On her most recent admission, eight months ago, the psychiatrist prescribed an antidepressant medication and recommended psychotherapy when she left the hospital. Tammy said she went to only one psychotherapy appointment and stopped taking the antidepressants when she began feeling better. She now reports that she is starting to wonder if she should go back to the psychiatric hospital, but she is afraid that if she leaves her friend's house this time, the friend will not let her move back in. She would rather work on easing the stress in her life.

One method Tammy uses to cope with her feelings is smoking marijuana. She started smoking it to relieve the symptoms of her MS, but in the past few months, she admits she has been using it more to cope with psychological stresses. She said she smokes approximately every other day and gets marijuana from the young men with whom she lives.

Tammy does not have many outside social activities. She used to belong to a church, but when she was evicted and moved in with her friend it was too far to walk, so she stopped attending. She does have a strong faith in God and believes that despite all the troubles she is having, things could be much worse. She is grateful that she has housing for the moment and is able to receive her medical care.

Tammy has a tenth-grade education. She said she used to smoke crack cocaine in her "younger days," but after her then husband went to prison for drugs 20 years ago, she stopped. She said that it wasn't that difficult when she "made up her mind to do it." She said that both her parents drank too much and fought with each other verbally and physically when she was growing up. She said both her parents died when she was a young adult—her father from emphysema and her mother from cancer.

Human Behavior

Practice Behavior Example: *Critique and apply knowledge to understand person and environment.*

Critical Thinking Question: When clients have chronic medical problems, how do you determine the effects of the medical condition and any medication a client takes from depressive symptoms?

Directions Part I, Multiaxial Diagnosis   Given the case information, prepare the following: a multiaxial diagnosis, the rationale for the diagnosis and global assessment of functioning score, and additional information you would have wanted to know in order to make a more accurate diagnosis.

BIOPSYCHOSOCIAL RISK AND RESILIENCE INFLUENCES

Onset

Biological Influences

The fact that major depression tends to run in families partially supports the notion of genetic transmission. The extent of variance that heritability explains for major depression ranges from 31 to 42% (Sullivan, Neale, & Kendler, 2000). Many types of depression are thought to be associated with deficiencies of certain neurotransmitters in the limbic area of the brain, which controls emotions. Although no genes linked to depression have been found to have more than small effects (Ebmeier, Donaghey, & Steele, 2006), studies have centered on the serotonin transporter gene (Kumsta, Stevens, Brookes, et al., 2010) and its interaction with stressful life events, such as childhood maltreatment (Caspi et al., 2003).

Other biological processes implicated in depression include the secretion of the cortical enzyme in response to stress (Sher, 2003) and impairment in the hypothalamic–pituitary–adrenal axis of the brain (Vreeburg, Hoogendijk, van Pelt et al., 2009).

More recently, cigarette smoking, obesity, and sleep problems demonstrate risk for depression. When tracked over a 10-year period, smoking doubled the odds of women developing major depression (Pasco et al., 2008). Although this study seems to indicate that smoking increases risk for depression, a bi-directional relationship appears to exist between depression and obesity. People with obesity had a 55% increased risk of developing depression over time. Additionally, people with depression had a 58% likelihood of becoming obese (Luppino et al., 2010). Certain mechanisms have been proposed to account for this association. Because thinness is considered a beauty ideal in both the United States and Europe, being overweight may contribute to body dissatisfaction and low self-esteem, placing individuals at risk for depression. Additionally, depression may increase weight over time through interference with the endocrine system. A self-medication basis may also operate, in that people may eat in order to improve mood.

Sleep also seems to play a critical role in depression. For example, teenagers reporting five or fewer hours per night were 71% more likely to suffer from depression and 48% more likely to think about committing suicide than those who reported getting eight hours of nightly sleep (Gangwisch et al., 2010).

Finally, a major contributor to depression is poor physical health. Medical conditions such as heart attack, cancer, stroke, MS, HIV, and diabetes increase one's risk of depression (Ciesla & Roberts, 2001; Karasu et al., 2002; Shanmugham et al., 2005). People who were unhappy with their health had high rates of past year major depressive disorder (14.2%) compared to those who stated their health as excellent (4.3%) (Substance Abuse and Mental Health Services Administration, 2009). Further, depression can be detrimental to physical health, involving activity restriction, illnesses, increased health care use, and mortality (Rugulies, 2002; Shanmugham et al., 2005).

Psychological Influences

At the psychological level, depression is related to distorted and rigid beliefs and thoughts. These typically involve the "cognitive triad" of depression (thoughts about the self as worthless, the world as unfair, and the future as hopeless) (Beck, Rush, Shaw, & Emery, 1979). Coping style is another psychological variable associated with the onset of depression. Coping methods that are more active in nature, such as problem solving, have the potential to ward off depression. However, avoidant coping styles, such as evading situations and indulging in ruminative thinking (the tendency to focus on the symptoms of a distressed mood in an incessant and passive way (Nolen-Hoeksema, 2002), present risk.

Social Influences

Family factors can influence the development and maintenance of depression in youth. Hostility and a lack of parental warmth and availability have been particularly associated with depression (McLeod, Weisz, & Wood, 2007; Sander & McCarty, 2005). Depression in mothers is a particular risk mechanism for depression and other disorders (Hammen et al., 2008; Pilowsky et al., 2006; Weissman, Wickramaratne, & Yoko, 2006). The association of parental depression with increased rates of depression in children may be accounted for by genetics, biological impairment in utero transmitted from mother to developing fetus, dysfunctional parenting, modeling, and the link of depression with parental marital problems (Goodman, 2007).

A number of studies have indicated a significant relationship between depression and childhood physical abuse and sexual abuse (Penza, Heim, & Nemeroff, 2006). Of all types of maltreatment, sexual abuse poses the greatest risk for depression and suicide attempts (Fergusson, Boden, & Horwood, 2008). Adults who reported being maltreated as children appear to have an elevated inflammatory response to stress compared to adults who lacked child mistreatment in their histories; thus childhood maltreatment may create a possible biological vulnerability to depression (Carpenter et al., 2010).

Other family relationships may influence the development of depression. For adults, those who were divorced or separated were more likely to experience major depressive disorder in the past year (13.1%) than people in other relationship status categories (Substance Abuse and Mental Health Services Administration, 2009). Conversely, sibling affection and support may play a protective role (Padilla-Walker, Harper, & Jensen, 2010).

In general, social support may mitigate harsh early family circumstances and the stressful life events that people with depression are prone to experience (De Beurs et al., 2001; Kraaij, Arensman, & Spinhoven, 2002). Friends can provide support and enable people to self-disclose in a safe setting. Having positive peers is associated with less depression in adolescence (Gutman & Sameroff, 2004), whereas bullying (being either a perpetrator or a victim) was associated with depression, with higher frequencies of bullying (physical, verbal, or relational) having a linear relationship to levels of depression (Wang, Nansel, & Iannotti, 2011). For girls, relational victimization, when paired with genetic vulnerability, is also predictive of depression (Benjet, Thompson, & Gotib, 2010).

In terms of the wider social environment, neighborhood cohesiveness acts as a protective influence for adolescent females, whereas neighborhood problems pose risk (Gutman & Sameroff, 2004). Finally, socioeconomic status (SES), and its link to depression for youths aged 10 to 15 years, was studied in a systematic review (Lemstra, Neudorf, D'Arcy, et al., 2008) establishing a negative association between the two variables. That is, the lower the SES, the higher the rate of depression.

Course and Recovery

Depressive disorders are associated with high rates of relapse (Brodaty, Luscombe, Peisah, Anstey, & Andrews, 2001; Klein, Shankman, & Rose, 2006). About 50% of people with one episode of major depressive disorder go on to experience another (Hammen et al., 2008). However, the course of depression is variable, depending on the balance of risk and protective influences. Several studies have identified risk and protective factors that influence outcomes (Friedman et al., 2009; Klein et al., 2008; Korczak & Goldstein, 2009; McGrath et al., 2008).

At the biological level, a familial loading for chronic depression seems to carry risk, as well as a childhood onset (Crum et al., 2008). As with onset, medical problems continue to pose risk for relapse.

At the psychological level, personality disorders can confer risk and their very absence is protective (Korczak & Goldstein, 2009). Drug abuse and other comorbid Axis I disorders, including posttraumatic stress disorder, other anxiety disorders, and hypochondriasis, are also risk influences. Melancholic depression (characterized by the inability to find pleasure in positive things, weight loss, psychomotor agitation or retardation, insomnia with early morning awakenings, feelings of guilt, and a worsening of symptoms in the morning with improvement at night) is also believed to be a pernicious subtype.

Family risk influences include a poor relationship with the mother in childhood and a sexual abuse history, the latter which is also a contributor to the onset of depression. People who have less than a college education also tend to have poorer outcomes, likely owing to their lack of resources to obtain effective treatment.

> **Directions Part II, Risk and Resilience Assessment** Formulate a risk and protective mechanisms assessment both for the onset of the disorder and for the course of the disorder, including the techniques that you would use to elicit additional strengths in this client.

Policy Practice

Practice Behavior Example: Analyze, formulate, and advocate for policies that advance social well-being.

Critical Thinking Question: Given the fact that many people receive help for depression from the general health system, how can social workers intervene—and at what levels—in order to ensure that people receive appropriate care?

INTERVENTION

Almost two thirds (64.5%) of adults who experienced past year major depressive disorder received treatment (Substance Abuse and Mental Health Services Administration, 2009), which seems to represent a substantial increase in the number of people who receive timely intervention (Wang, Berglund, et al., 2005). However, many people seek help from the general health system. As a result, only about 19% of this group receive appropriate care, defined as using medication or counseling in ways that are consistent with empirically validated treatment guidelines (Young, Klap, Sherbourne, & Wells, 2001). Not surprisingly, there is more reliance on medication than psychotherapy in the health system (Olfson & Marcus, 2009).

The initial stage of intervention for persons who are depressed is to assess for suicidal risk, which is associated with the following factors (Borges, 2006; Fawcett, 2006):

- Presence of suicidal or homicidal ideation, with intent or plans
- History and seriousness of previous attempts (a key factor)
- Access to lethal means for suicide
- Presence of psychotic symptoms
- Presence of severe anxiety
- Presence of substance use
- Presence of conduct problems
- Family history of or recent exposure to suicide

Some social factors involved with suicide attempts include young age, low SES, divorce (Borges et al., 2006), and cultural and religious beliefs that promote suicide—for instance, that suicide is a noble way to handle difficulties (U.S. Department of Health and Human Services, 2001).

The social worker can also ask a number of strengths-based questions when doing a suicide risk assessment, such as the following (Bertolino & O'Hanlon, 2002):

- Have you had thoughts about hurting yourself in the past? What did you do to get past that point?
- Things sounded really hard then. How did you manage? How did you stop things from getting even worse?
- What needs to happen now so that you feel a bit better? What will that look like?

If the practitioner concludes that the risk of suicidal behavior is considerable, inpatient treatment should be considered. Inpatient intervention is especially indicated if the client is psychotic, severely hopeless, demonstrates suicidal or homicidal ideation with significant substance abuse, has strong impulses or plans to act on these ideas, has inadequate social supports for effective outpatient treatment, and has a complicating psychiatric or medical condition that makes outpatient medication treatment unsafe (Fawcett, 2006). Outpatient intervention is indicated if the client is free of psychosis, not abusing substances, and maintaining control over suicidal thoughts.

If a client with suicidal ideation is seen on an outpatient basis, the social worker should take certain precautions (Fawcett, 2006). He or she should provide education about the symptoms of depression and the effectiveness of treatment; develop a "no harm" contract; advise abstinence from substances, as these may increase symptoms and impulsive behaviors; see the client at least weekly to monitor suicidal ideation, hopelessness, and substance abuse; explain to family members how to respond to suicidal ideas; and remove any firearms from the house.

After suicide risk has been assessed, interventions for persons with depression may include psychotherapy and medication. A more recent trend has been for people to receive the latter than the former (Olfson & Marcus, 2009). Although medication is considered to act on the biological mechanisms of depression, it must be recognized that psychotherapy may also enact biological change. For example, Koch et al. (2009) describes the way in which psychotherapy for major depression alters the plasticity of the brain.

Psychotherapy

The benefits of psychotherapy are that many clients prefer it to medication; it is appropriate for clients who have mild, moderate, or chronic depression; and the person learns to cope with or avoid factors that precipitate the depressive episodes (Karasu et al., 2002). Psychotherapy is particularly indicated when the person's life is characterized by psychosocial stress, difficulty coping, and interpersonal problems. Sometimes psychotherapy is not indicated, however, at least not by itself—for example, if the person is at risk of not completing the course of treatment. Further, sessions may be time consuming, and it may not be easy to find high-quality treatment and practitioners.

Psychotherapies with a lot of research attention include cognitive-behavioral therapy (CBT) and interpersonal therapy (IPT). CBT involves *behavioral* models that focus on the development of coping skills, especially in the domains of social skills and pleasant daily activities, so that the person receives more reinforcement from his or her environment. *Cognitive* models include assessing and changing the distorted thinking that people with depression exhibit. Although typically delivered as a package of interventions, some of the techniques have been used as stand-alone treatment. These include behavioral activation treatment, which centers on activity scheduling and increasing pleasant activities, and problem-solving therapy, which focuses on behaviorally defining specific problems, brainstorming ideas to solve them, and deciding upon and implementing solutions.

IPT is a relatively brief psychodynamic intervention (approximately 12 sessions) focusing on how current interpersonal relationships have contributed to the person's depression. This perspective considers interpersonal conflicts to be a major source of depression. The social worker's goal is to help the client repair these conflicts (Weissman, Markowitz, & Klerman, 2000). Intervention focuses on significant role transitions, grief processes, and interpersonal disputes or deficits; it has also been adapted for use with adolescents (Mufson, Dorta, Moreau, & Weissman, 2005).

Various psychotherapies for depression in adults were compared in a meta-analysis (Cuijpers, van Straten, Andersson, & van Oppen, 2008). These included IPT, psychodynamic therapy, nondirective supportive treatment (any unstructured therapy without specific techniques such as offering empathy and helping people to ventilate their experiences and emotions), CBT, behavioral activation treatment, and problem-solving therapy. The authors found that none of the treatments were appreciably more efficacious than others, except for IPT (which was superior to others at a small effect size) and nondirective, supportive therapy (which was less effective than the others at a very small effect). One limitation of the Cuijpers et al. (2008) meta-analysis is that effect sizes calculated were nonindependent, which means that comparison groups were sometimes counted more than once. This may render the results less valid.

Although nearly all older adults in the United States have basic health coverage through Medicare, fee-for-service reimbursements currently cover only 50% of mental health care costs (Wei et al., 2005). Depressed older adults are often unwilling to seek treatment when they have to pay out of pocket. Further, primary care physicians may not refer older adults to psychotherapy because of a lack of awareness of its possible clinical efficacy. A national survey of community-dwelling Medicare beneficiaries aged 65 and older found that the use of psychotherapy was associated with relatively younger age, a college education, and the availability of psychotherapists (Wei et al., 2005). Even when psychotherapy was used, a minority (33%) included clients who remained in consistent treatment, defined as extending for at least two thirds of the episode of depression. The availability of local providers correlated positively with consistent psychotherapy use. One implication of this study is that for older adults with less formal education, social workers may need to provide education on how psychotherapy works and respond to an individual's concerns about therapy.

In addition to CBT, discussed earlier, reminiscence and life review therapies may be effective for older adults, according to a study of old-age well-being in long-term care facilities (Bishop, Martin, MacDonald, & Poon, 2010), a meta-analysis of 24 studies (Bohlmeijer, Smit, & Cuijpers, 2003), and a study of old-age well-being (Bishop et al., 2010). A strong effect was shown for these interventions, especially for persons with severe depression. Most of the studies were conducted in noninstitutionalized settings, however, so the results may not generalize to the older adults in nursing home and extended care facilities.

Medication

The use of antidepressants has increased drastically in recent years from 5.84% in 1996 to 10.12% in the United States in 2005 (Olfson & Marcus, 2009), and medication has also increased in relation to psychotherapy to treat depression (Olfson, Marcus, Druss, et al., 2002). At the same time, the use of antipsychotics to treat depression has increased for both adults (Olfson & Marcus, 2009) and children (Olfson, Blanco, Liu, Moreno, & Laje, 2006).

The latter is a concern because there are no controlled studies on the use of antipsychotics for the treatment of depression in youth. Most medications are prescribed by general practitioners rather than psychiatrists, and majority of general physicians fail to use DSM criteria to diagnose depression (Zimmerman & Galione, 2010). Because of these recent patterns, social workers should be prepared to educate clients and their families about the benefits and limitations of medication. The prescribing physician should see clients often (every one to two weeks) in the initial treatment phase. Close monitoring produces greater treatment adherence and more opportunities for education, and also enables clinicians (including social workers) to assess clients for potential worsening of symptoms, the emergence of suicidal thinking, and other complicating factors.

Policy Practice

Practice Behavior Example: *Analyze, formulate, and advocate for policies that advance social well-being.*

Critical Thinking Question: Given the fact that people are more likely to receive medication for depression than psychotherapy, how can social workers intervene—and at what levels—in order to ensure that people receive appropriate care?

Youths

Concerns have been raised about the use of medication with youngsters. For children, cardiac problems may be associated with the tricyclic medications (Silva, Gabbay, & Minami, 2005). Indeed, these older antidepressants are not recommended for children, given the lack of evidence to support their use (Hazell, O'Connell, Heathcote, & Henry, 2003). Newer antidepressants (developed since the late 1980s) are characterized by their actions on serotonin. The selective serotonin reuptake inhibitor (SSRI) drugs block the uptake of serotonin. An even newer class of medication, the dual serotonin and norepinephrine reuptake inhibitors (SNRIs), does not interfere with other chemicals that are affected by the cyclic antidepressants to cause adverse effects.

In this country SSRIs are used with adolescents and have shown greater therapeutic effectiveness and fewer adverse effects than the tricyclic drugs. A systematic review of SSRIs with youths aged 5 to 18 found that only fluoxetine (Prozac) showed favorable risk-to-benefit profiles (Whittington et al., 2004). A more recent meta-analysis indicated that Prozac, as well as other antidepressants, although having only a modest effect on depression, has benefits greater than the risks from suicidal ideation or attempts in teenagers (Bridge et al., 2007). Further, only Prozac outperformed placebo in children younger than 12. Therefore, social workers should be aware that other SSRIs are not indicated for the treatment of depression in children.

The Treatment of Adolescent Depression Study (TADS), a large-scale, multisite study, looked at combing medication and CBT, and comparing it to antidepressants and psychotherapy alone (TADS, 2006, 2007). The researchers found that a combined approach, offering both medication (in the study Prozac was given) and CBT over six to nine months, was the ideal treatment for adolescents who are moderately to severely depressed (March & Vitiello, 2009). CBT may protect against the suicidality that might develop with the use of medication. Brief treatment may therefore not be sufficient.

Adults

There is a common perception that the newer SSRIs are more effective than the older tricyclic antidepressants, but a meta-analysis of 102 randomized controlled trials found no overall difference in efficacy between the two classes of drugs (Anderson, 2000). The SSRI drugs are better tolerated, however, with significantly lower rates of treatment discontinuation. Further, studies have shown that the effects of antidepressants are not substantially greater than placebo effects, the latter which may account for 68% of the improvement for depression (Rief et al., 2009). Therefore, it seems that the major influence of antidepressants may be due to placebo or people's expectation that they will get better.

Indeed, a meta-analysis examining the severity of depression and response to medication showed that the benefit of antidepressant medication compared with placebo increases with severity of depression symptoms. In other words, medication benefits may be minimal or nonexistent, on average, in people with mild or moderate symptoms (Fournier et al., 2010). For people with severe depression, improvement due to antidepressants over placebo may be substantial.

The largest study on "real-life" community clients with depression showed that an initial trial of antidepressant medication produced remission rates (defined as the absence of symptoms) of 28% and response rates (a reduction of about half in symptom levels) of 47% (Trivedi, Rush, Wisniewski, et al., (2006)). As discussed in the risk and protective influences, remission is a desirable outcome because residual symptoms after treatment put people at risk for relapse. The study by Trivedi, Rush, Wisniewski, et al., 2006 demonstrates that a majority of people (over 70%) do not meet the desired goal of medication, and fewer than half show a response.

A common practice following the lack of response to one antidepressant is to try another. For instance, in a continuation of the study described earlier, remission rates were examined for those who initially lacked response to Celexa when another SSRI or SNRI was tried (Rush et al., 2006). Apparently, there was little difference in performance between the various SSRIs or SNRIs, with remission rates ranging between 17.6 and 24.8%. Another practice following the lack of response to one medication is to augment it with another antidepressant. Referring again to the earlier study, Trivedi, Fava, Wisniewski, et al. (2006) found that adding bupropion (Wellbutrin) to Celexa resulted in remission rates of nearly 30%.

As with younger adults, about 50% of older people will experience treatment response, defined as a reduction of half their symptoms, from a course of antidepressants. Because of physiological changes in older adults, clinicians should increase doses more slowly than in younger clients and monitor them closely for side effects and medication interactions, to which older adults tend to be more sensitive (Alexopoulos et al., 2001).

Many people fail to comply with prescribed medication. A nationally representative sample indicated that a significant proportion of clients (40%) discontinue taking medication during the first 30 days of treatment (Olfson et al., 2006). Side effects are common and are generally underreported to medical doctors (Zimmerman et al., 2010). Clients treated with SSRIs or SNRIs were more likely to continue medication than those treated with the older medications. The use of psychotherapy was positively related to drug adherence in this review.

To summarize, the use of medication to treat depression has both indications and contraindications (Agency for Health Care Policy and Research, 1993; Karusu et al., 2002). Medications may be indicated if the client has severe depression, prefers the option of medication, has a personal or a first-degree relative history of prior positive response, is likely to adhere to a medication regime, and can work with an experienced physician. Medication may also be indicated when psychotherapy alone has not been successful (Antonuccio, Thomas, & Danton, 1997). Medication may not be indicated if there are cost considerations or if the client has a medical illness or takes other medications that make its use risky. The benefits of medication are that it is easily administered and can produce a relatively rapid response (four to six weeks). Its limitations are the need for monitoring, the possibility of adverse effects, potential use in suicide attempts, and the possibility of nonadherence. Further, it is difficult to predict how a certain person will react to a particular medication. The process of finding a medication and appropriate dosage that helps improve mood is one of trial and error (Healy, 2002).

Diversity in Practice

Practice Behavior Example: *Recognize and communicate their understanding of the importance of difference in shaping life experiences.*

Critical Thinking Question: Based on your knowledge of culturally diverse groups, what are some of the fears about taking medication for depression that people may experience? How would you discover these concerns and address them?

CRITICAL PERSPECTIVE

As major depressive disorder criteria stemmed from clinical consensus, Zimmerman, McGlinchey, Young, and Chelminski (2006) conducted an empirical analysis and found that the weight change and indecisiveness criteria could be eliminated from the diagnosis. This modification would result in more streamlined criteria and would include subthreshold cases (those that currently do not meet all the necessary criteria), in which there is often significant impairment.

It must also be acknowledged that the criteria for depression, focusing on affective and cognitive symptoms, comprise a view that is particular to industrialized, Western nations (Maracek, 2006). Other cultures describe different ways of understanding depressive suffering. For example, in many Asian cultures, somatic complaints are foremost. The DSM criteria fail to capture these culture-bound experiences.

The chief limitation of the psychiatric view of depression is the assumption underlying the diagnosis, namely, that it is due to internal dysfunction. This assumption can be seen in the widespread acceptability of biological theories of depression and the use of medication as treatment. The focus on medication, which furthers the interest of the pharmaceutical companies, has also been criticized as a method aimed at providing only symptom relief rather than targeting broader social changes (Maracek, 2006).

Case 2   The Lonely Group Home Resident

Note: Although the following clinical illustration is intended to focus on Axis I disorders, the client in this case also experiences *mental retardation*, an Axis II disorder that is not covered in this book. Mental retardation is a developmental disability, presumed to be lifelong. It is characterized by an IQ below 70 that creates significant impairments in two or more of the following areas: self-care, communication, home living, social and interpersonal skills, use of community resources, self-direction, functional academic skills, work, leisure, health, and safety. It is important to emphasize that the diagnosis is made not on the basis of IQ alone but on the interaction of IQ with the person's environment, which together affect the client's ability to function. Mental retardation may be mild (IQ of 50–55 to 70), moderate (IQ of 30–35 to 50–55), severe (IQ of 20–25 to 35–40), or profound (IQ less than 20 to 25).

Indira is a 23-year-old female who, after a long waiting period, was accepted to live in a group home for people with mental retardation. Twelve individuals live in the group home, which is located in a middle-class neighborhood. The home is split up into three apartments, with four residents each.

Prior to her move to the group home, which occurred four months ago, Indira lived with her parents and younger brother in a private home. Her parents came to the United States from India before Indira and her brother were born. Her father is a computer analyst, and her mother never worked outside the home. Indira was the first child; she was born prematurely and with the umbilical cord wrapped around her neck. According to Indira's mother, the doctors did not believe that Indira would survive, and she spent many months in the hospital before her parents were allowed to take her home.

During her childhood Indira was tested and found to have an IQ of about 15; she is also blind and suffers from a seizure disorder. Indira cannot walk more than a few steps and only when she can hold onto someone with both hands. She is wheelchair-bound and overweight. Indira cannot communicate verbally but understands the English language. She conveys "yes" and "no" by nodding or shaking her head. She can follow simple commands. Indira can't complete any activities of daily living by herself. For example, she is incontinent. She can feed herself with a spoon, but only messily, and she has to wear a bib. She can drink with a straw but cannot lift a cup. She can rattle toys and put them in her mouth.

When she was a child, Indira attended a school for children with severe disabilities, autism, and mental retardation. After graduating from this school, Indira participated in a day program for adults with mental handicaps. At the day program, participants typically watch television, do puzzles, and color.

According to Indira's mother, there is no history of mental illness in either her or her husband's family, and she has never suffered from depression, although she is very sad about Indira's current plight. She denies that Indira has ever suffered from depression.

The relationship between her parents appears to be loving. Indira's brother enjoyed a healthy childhood and is now a senior in high school. Indira's primary caregiver has always been her mother. However, after 23 years of caring for her handicapped and overweight child, her mother started to experience health problems, especially backaches. The family decided that they could no longer adequately care for Indira and asked a social worker for help in finding a suitable placement.

After several visits to the group home, Indira was accepted and she was moved in. She had one staff member assigned to her in the morning and a different one in the evening, and she appeared to connect well with both of them. She smiled and responded to games and outings that were initiated by staff. Two weeks after Indira moved into the group home, however, management changed and several permanent staff quit their job. The result was that Indira now had relief staff caring for her, meaning different voices on a daily basis. Especially during the weekends, Indira did not have much to do. She got up late and then spent most of her day in the living room, where the television was on. Outings were rare due to the unstable staff situation, and relief staff did not want to take the responsibility of taking residents into the community.

Indira started to become less active; she did not smile anymore and was easily annoyed and distracted, making her feelings known through nonverbal sounds and body position. She refused to eat most meals except for desserts and started losing weight. Indira's refusal to eat might have been caused by the different food. Her mother usually cooked Indian food, with lots of rice, spiced vegetables, and fruits. Because the cow is sacred for Hindus, Indira had never eaten beef before. The cook in the group home was not able to reproduce these foods and prepared standard American meals, such as hamburger, macaroni and cheese, and tuna helper.

At night staff would often hear her crying for a long time until she fell asleep. Indira then had a difficult time getting up in the mornings. She used to be cooperative and help staff by moving her body into the right position for washing and dressing but refused to do so after a while. She appeared to become more withdrawn and closed her eyes more often during the day. When staff tried to engage her in an activity, Indira would bury her face in her hands and rock herself back and forth as if to comfort herself, while making noises that sounded as if she was crying—even though no tears streamed down her face.

Indira's parents became very concerned for their daughter; they visited her two to three times a week, but Indira did not change her behavior when they were around. She rejected the hands of her mother and did not hug her as she used to do.

Indira's behavior changed gradually at first and became more severe after several weeks. In the meantime, the staff situation in the group home did not stabilize; Indira continued to have different caregivers. Indira exhibited the same behavior in her day placement, and her counselor consistently reported that Indira was not eating her lunch and was not participating in group activities as she used to. The nurse at the group home eventually became concerned enough to schedule a complete physical exam and visit with the psychiatrist for Indira, even though when her doctors saw her just prior to her move into the group home, everything had seemed fine.

Please go to the Appendix for directions to this case.

Case 3   An Unsettling Transition

Mrs. Elizabeth Cuthbert is an 81-year-old Caucasian female. She has been diagnosed with syncope (fainting spells), hypertension, and chronic obstructive pulmonary disease. For the last four months she has resided in a nursing facility and receives skilled nursing services. Mrs. Cuthbert's move to the facility occurred as a result of repeated syncope and falls. Her condition has been exacerbated by the recent development of a foot drop, a weakening of the structures in her ankle that allows the foot to dangle when walking. This ailment has increased her risk of falling. Mrs. Cuthbert has been fitted with an ankle foot orthosis (AFO) and provided with a walker, but she claims these aids make her feel "weak." Mrs. Cuthbert receives physical therapy for her balance and occupational therapy for her tasks of daily living. Her discharge plan involves placement in an assisted living apartment once she has developed the safety and ambulation skills that will allow her to live without constant monitoring.

Mrs. Cuthbert's medications for the LAST six months include therapeutic aspirin, blood pressure medication, and Tylenol for pain relief from her fall and osteoarthritis. She is compliant with her medications.

Mrs. Cuthbert was widowed 20 years ago and has lived alone in her home of 35 years since that time. Her immediate family includes two adult children, who live in the area, and three grandchildren, who visit and send her letters. Family members visit frequently, at least twice a week.

Mrs. Cuthbert expresses a negative attitude toward the aged in comments during unrelated discussions. For instance, when the social work intern first met her, she cast aspersions on an "old dog" who lived in the unit, and then went on to make negative comments about her own appearance, saying she looked like "an old hag." She received the social worker's supportive comments positively, but the change in attitude appears transitory.

The results of a mini-mental status examination conducted on Mrs. Cuthbert indicated that she was aware of person, time, and place. Mrs. Cuthbert was also evaluated using a mood scale to determine her risk for depression. She scored 7 out of 15 (a score higher than 5 is indicative of depression). Her response to the mood-scale questions revealed feelings of worthlessness, low energy, insomnia, and diminished interest in pleasurable activities. Mrs. Cuthbert evidences no symptoms of mania.

Mrs. Cuthbert is undergoing significant change in her social support system as a result of her recent move to the nursing facility. She no longer has the neighbors whom she visited each day as she went about retrieving her newspaper, checking on her garden, and watering her outdoor plants. She has lost the use of her car and feels that she should give up driving permanently to prevent possible accidents. She also no longer has the option of walking to her place of worship because of her current condition.

An additional problem for Mrs. Cuthbert is her reluctance to make safety changes that will allow her to move to an assisted living apartment in a nearby community where several lifelong friends reside. She has been very reluctant to adopt the walker or the AFO and has been refusing the majority of her physical and occupational therapy treatments because she is "tired."

During her care plan meeting, Mrs. Cuthbert expressed surprise that the entire interdisciplinary team had gathered to discuss her case with her and her family. She asked, "Why are all of you interested in me?" She stated that she wanted to move to assisted living because she would be able to visit with her friends there once she did so. When told that she could not move until she addressed the safety and ambulation deficits she is experiencing, she expressed interest in cooperating with the various therapists and counselors.

According to Mrs. Cuthbert's daughter, Barbara, until her current health problems and the move to the nursing facility, Mrs. Cuthbert was a relatively contented person. She crocheted, enjoyed crossword puzzles, called on friends, assisted two shut-ins whom she has known for years, and had her grandchildren over for weekend visits. Since her admission to the nursing home, it has become difficult for Mrs. Cuthbert to accomplish several of her old activities, and simply not feasible to continue others. However, she has also discontinued the activities that were appropriate for her while at the nursing home, except for doing crossword puzzles. Barbara noted that her mother was not interested in going out for meals as she had been before her fall. Her daughter speculated that her mother might not want to be seen in public with the AFO and walker, but noted that she also refused take-out meals offered as well. When asked, Barbara was unaware of any history of mood disorders or other mental illness in her mother's background, but said that her mother wouldn't typically speak of such things anyway.

Mrs. Cuthbert's financial situation is sound. She owns her own house and collects pensions from both her own employment as a secretary and her husband's work.

Please go to the Appendix for directions to this case.

PRACTICE TEST The following questions will test your knowledge of the content found within this chapter. For additional assessment, including licensing-exam type questions on applying chapter content to practice behaviors, visit **MySocialWorkLab.com**.

1. What is likely true about the etiology of depression?
   a. It represents a chemical imbalance
   b. A genetic risk is activated in the presence of environmental adversity
   c. It is prompted by a lack of adequate serotonin in the nervous system
   d. Its onset is facilitated by a genetic marker

2. Depression in girls becomes more common in adolescence for which of the following reasons?
   a. Females become targets of harassment by boys
   b. Hormonal changes
   c. Girls use alcohol as a coping mechanism far less than boys
   d. Interpersonal stress is heightened due to relational aggression

3. Nora was a 40-year-old grocery store baker with two adult daughters, both of whom had recently moved out of the house, and an unemployed husband. She had been in depression for more than six months due to the stresses of managing work and domestic responsibilities, and a lack of personal support. Her symptoms included low moods for most of the day, undesired weight gain, insomnia, low energy, and thoughts of death. The distinguishing factor between Nora's diagnosis of major depression or dysthymic disorder would be:
   a. Her ability to concentrate well enough to manage her job
   b. The presence or absence of substance abuse as a coping mechanism
   c. The intensity of her depressive symptoms
   d. The quality of her self-esteem

4. Nora felt trapped in her "traditional" role of housewife. Getting an outside job was a partial solution for her, in that she enjoyed being with other people, but it added to her range of daily pressures. IPT might be helpful for Nora because:
   a. It may involve family work
   b. It includes a feminist perspective in helping clients change their social role assumptions
   c. It is a supportive approach, and Nora seems to lack interpersonal supports
   d. She has recently experienced a major role transition

5. Given the prevalence of depression and its potentially long-term course and dire consequences, what are your recommendations for how nonmental health settings, such as schools, child welfare agencies, welfare services, and health clinics, identify and appropriately treat or refer people with depression?

6. Given the information on risk and protective factors and evidence-based treatment and the case material provided in the chapter, what factors will you weigh to determine the appropriate theoretical orientation and modality of treatment for a particular individual?

SUCCEED WITH

PEARSON
mysocialworklab

Visit **MySocialWorkLab** for more licensing-exam test questions, and to access case studies, videos, and much more.

10

Bipolar Disorder

Catherine is a 38-year-old married Mexican American female with no children who lives in a rural county. She was court-ordered to attend an outpatient mental health clinic for individual and group anger management services. Two months ago she was charged with assault by her husband after stabbing him in the shoulder with a steak knife during an argument at a local restaurant. Catherine is also awaiting incarceration for an arrest in which she was recklessly driving a vehicle without a license. She has in fact been jailed on five occasions for offenses ranging from disturbing the peace to assault. The social worker met with Catherine on four occasions over five weeks. Catherine is separated from her husband but is open to possibly reuniting with him after she receives professional help.

Catherine is in generally good physical health and reports that she is in regular contact with her family physician. She broke her arm two years ago in a saloon fight, however, and has diminished strength in that arm. She also reports having ankle pain due to possible arthritis, which moderately decreases her mobility. Still, Catherine has kept a full-time job at the post office for the last 15 years, working primarily as a mail sorter but occasionally as a deliverer.

Catherine reports that she has had irritable and "up and down" moods for most of her adult life. She describes extended periods of time when she becomes "hyperactive" and easily annoyed by people around her. Catherine says she has "incredible energy" at those times and "gets a lot done." At those times she likes delivering the mail, working out at the local recreation center, eating out in restaurants, and going to bars. She rests primarily with "short naps" during her energy bursts. Catherine drinks alcohol (only beer) regularly and makes no apologies for it. "It's fun. Who says girls can't hold their liquor like the guys?"

Upon further questioning, she admits that she drinks only "enough to get drunk" when she is in a "high-energy" phase. Otherwise she limits herself to a few beers on the weekends.

Catherine admits that she "wears herself out" after about a month of this hyperactivity, becoming "shaky" and "disoriented" from the lack of sleep. When in a manic episode, she is apt to lose her temper and argue with "almost anyone" who gets in the way of her activities. She gets into physical fights frequently, often with strangers, but sees this as acceptable behavior. "I was raised to take care of myself. No one is going to push me around." Despite her erratic behaviors, Catherine is "accepted for who I am" in her small community. The culture of her Mexican American family of origin features high levels of emotional expressiveness and Catherine is comfortable behaving this way. She is usually released from jail a few days after her arrests to the custody of her husband, with the charges dropped.

Bipolar disorder is a mood disorder in which a person experiences one or more manic episodes that usually alternate with episodes of major depression (American Psychiatric Association [APA], 2000). Depressive episodes are described in chapter 9. A manic episode is a period in which a person's mood is elevated and expansive to such a degree that he or she experiences serious functional impairment in all areas of life. Manic episodes may be characterized by unrealistically inflated self-esteem, a decreased need for sleep, pressured speech, racing thoughts, distractibility, an increase in unrealistic goal-directed activity, and involvement in activities with a high potential for negative consequences. Manic episodes develop rapidly and may persist for a few days or up to several months. The average duration of bipolar I mood episodes is 13 weeks (Solomon et al., 2010).

Another feature associated with bipolar disorder is the *hypomanic* episode (APA, 2000), a gradual escalation over a period of days or weeks from a stable mood to a manic state. In this mild form of mania, the person experiences higher self-esteem, a decreased need for sleep, a higher energy level, an increase in overall productivity, and more intensive involvement in pleasurable activities. Its related behaviors may be socially acceptable, but the danger is that the bipolar person's decreased insight may lead him or her to believe that the disorder has permanently remitted and that there is no need for ongoing interventions. In fact, poor insight is a prominent characteristic of the active phases of bipolar disorder (Grant, Stinson, et al., 2005).

There are two types of bipolar disorder (APA, 2000): *Bipolar I* disorder is characterized by one or more manic episodes, usually accompanied by a major depressive episode. *Bipolar II* disorder is characterized by one or more major depressive episodes accompanied by at least one hypomanic episode. Although generally "milder" than bipolar I disorder, bipolar II disorder is characterized by a higher incidence of comorbidity, suicidal ideation, and rapid cycling (Vieta & Suppes, 2008). For both types of the disorder the duration between episodes tends to decrease as further cycles occur (Geller, Tillman, Bolhofner, & Zimmerman, 2008).

PREVALENCE AND COMORBIDITY

Prevalence estimates of bipolar disorder have increased in recent years and range from 0.5 to 5% (Matza, Rajagopalan, Thompson, & Lissovoy, 2005). The estimated prevalence in the most recent National Comorbidity Survey was 2.1% (Merikangas et al., 2007).

The lifetime prevalence of bipolar I disorder is equal in men and women (close to 1%), although bipolar II disorder is more common in women (up to 5%) (Barnes & Mitchell, 2005). In men the number of manic episodes equals or exceeds the number of depressive episodes, whereas in women depressive episodes predominate. Between 1994 and 2003 there was a 40-fold increase in child and adolescent diagnoses of the disorder, which may be due to changing diagnostic criteria (perhaps informally) or greater practitioner sensitivity to its symptoms (Moreno, Blanco, Jiung, Schmidt, & Olfson, 2007).

Bipolar I disorder is often comorbid with other disorders. Its highest rates of comorbidity are 71% for anxiety disorders, 56% for substance use disorders, 49% for alcohol abuse, 47% for social phobia, and 36% for a personality disorder (Marangell, Kupfer, Sachs, & Swann, 2006). One study of 500 clients in a bipolar disorder treatment program noted an earlier age of onset (15.6 versus 19.4 years) and an increased presence of suicidal ideation in persons with comorbid anxiety disorders (Simon et al., 2004). Another study concluded that bipolar disorder is more often accompanied by cluster B personality disorders (antisocial, borderline, narcissistic, and histrionic) than by major depressive disorder (Mantere et al., 2006). Further, a one-year prospective study of 539 outpatients revealed that persons with rapid-cycling bipolar disorder have higher rates of lifetime substance abuse (45.4 versus 36.4%) and anxiety disorders (50.2 versus 30.7%) (Kupka, Luckenbaugh, & Post, 2005). Bipolar disorder is also modestly associated with medical illnesses in adulthood, such as cardiovascular, cerebrovascular, and respiratory diseases (Krishnan, 2005).

Bipolar women are 2.7 times more likely than men to have a comorbid disorder. Women with bipolar disorder have a premature mortality rate, which may be related to metabolic changes that increase their risk of diabetes and vascular disease (Taylor & MacQueen, 2006). Women are also at greater risk for anxiety disorders and thyroid problems. Women have an increased risk of developing episodes of bipolar I disorder in the postpartum period. Bipolar men have a greater prevalence of alcoholism than women do (Barnes & Mitchell, 2005).

Given this information about comorbid disorders, it is important to note that substance abuse and the presence of another comorbid disorder are two major risk influences for suicidal ideation and behavior among persons with bipolar disorder (Hawton, Sutton, Haw, Sinclair, & Harris, 2005). Other risk influences identified in this meta-analysis include a family history of suicide, an early onset of bipolar disorder, high levels of depression, severity of the affective episodes, the "mixed" type of the disorder, and the presence of rapid cycling.

Catherine says that she doesn't know why her energy bursts come and go. "I don't know, it's all about biorhythms, isn't it?" She admits to getting "dark, really dark" for extended periods of time as well, sometimes for several months. She is barely able to get her work done when depressed and admits that her boss complains about her "laziness." When she is not in a "hyper" or "down" mood, Catherine's moods tend to change throughout any given day. She reports the following symptoms at those times: forgetfulness, shifting ideas, distractibility, cycling between not sleeping at all and sleeping too much, bursts of energy, feelings of elation, decreased interest in most of her daily activities, fatigue, feelings of sadness, and impulsivity.

When asked whether it has ever been suggested that she has a mental problem, Catherine sighs. "My doctor thinks I should take medicine for my moods, but I don't want to do that. I'm not a doper. I like to drink, but I'm not a doper." When pressed on this point, Catherine adds, "I'm usually pretty calm when I see my doctor. I don't go to him when I'm hyper." Surprisingly, Catherine does not recall that many people in her community have suggested professional intervention to her. "I can take care of myself. All of us had to learn to do that where I came from." Regarding her drinking, Catherine does not exhibit signs of tolerance or withdrawal. She experiences no physical symptoms when she does not drink for weeks at a time, and she has not increased her overall alcohol intake over the years.

Catherine was born and raised in the Midwest and moved to the mid-Atlantic region when she was six years old. Her mother was a homemaker who was considered "odd" by her siblings. "She stayed home most of the time and seemed sad. She never had any fun. She was pretty, though, but I think Dad married her because he got her pregnant." Catherine says her mother was nice but not very active and that she drank too much. Her father, a military veteran, was a "great man" whom she loved very much. He "worked all the time" but played with Catherine and her younger brother, to whom she has never been close.

When Catherine was 16 years old, her father died. She says her father was the most important person in her life and remembers becoming "out of control" at about this time. Her mother died of breast cancer when she was 29 years old, though she reports that her mother's passing was more manageable for her.

Catherine has been married for 15 years to a seemingly supportive husband. "We met at community college. He's a good man, a calm man, and he taught me to get more focused about my life." Carl, a manager at a local manufacturing plant, reports that he loves his wife and states, "She is my heart and my life." Catherine and her husband report having frequent financial difficulties, requiring her husband to work long hours and leaving Catherine at home alone many evenings.

Catherine says she has some friends but inconsistent contact with the people in the community. "I'm friendly with everyone, but nobody in particular." She stated that she is eager for her mandated treatment to end so that she can resume her work routines without interruption. When asked about her possible sentencing to more time in jail, she shrugged. "I'm sorry for acting up like I do. I hope the judge knows that. My husband is OK with me now. I'm a good person."

ASSESSMENT OF BIPOLAR DISORDER

Because of the presumed biological influences of bipolar disorder, social workers need to participate in a multidisciplinary assessment of persons with possible bipolar disorder. A meta-analysis of 17 studies revealed that most persons with bipolar disorder were able to identify symptoms in advance of their first episode, the most common of which is sleep disturbance (77% median prevalence) (Jackson, Cavanaugh, & Scott, 2003). Adults with bipolar disorder are sometimes misdiagnosed with borderline personality disorder, and as noted earlier, the two disorders are sometimes comorbid (Zanarini, Frankenburg, & Hennen, Reich, & Silk, 2004). There is much symptom overlap between them, as both types of clients may experience mood swings, alternating periods of depression and elation, and transient psychotic symptoms. With the personality disorder, however, the mood changes are related to environmental influences and chronic feelings of insecurity, whereas bipolar disorder features more biologically patterned mood changes (Stone, 2006). Further, the client with bipolar disorder may function very well when stable, whereas the client with a personality disorder tends to be continuously labile. Other general assessment guidelines are summarized in Box 10.1.

Social workers must be extremely cautious in their diagnoses of children, because there is controversy about appropriate criteria with that population (Stone, 2006). Most researchers agree that bipolar disorder can occur in childhood and adolescence, but that it presents differently

---

Box 10.1 • Assessment Guidelines for Bipolar Disorder

- Assess family history for the presence of bipolar disorder, other mood disorders, or substance use disorders.
- Assess the client's social history for evidence of any significant mood problems.
- Facilitate a medical examination to rule out any medical conditions that may be responsible for the symptoms.
- Make sure the symptoms are not the result of the direct physiological effects of substance abuse.
- Rule out major depression, which would be the diagnosis in the absence of any manic or hypomanic episodes.

- Rule out cyclothymic disorder, which is characterized by the presence of hypomanic episodes and episodes of depression that do not meet criteria for that disorder.
- Rule out psychotic disorders, which are characterized by psychotic symptoms in the absence of a mood disorder.
- Assess for suicidal ideation.
- Assess the quality of the client's social supports.
- Evaluate the client's insight into the disorder.

Source: First, Francis, & Pinkus, 2002.

in those age groups (Birmaher et al., 2006). Symptoms that are most specific to childhood bipolar disorder include elevated mood, pressured speech, racing thoughts, and hypersensitivity (Youngstrom, Findling, Youngstrom, & Calabrese, 2005). The child typically engages in reckless behavior, but this must be distinguished from either normal behavior or that which may also be associated with other disorders. In fact, a recent longitudinal study found that among children aged 6 to 12 who exhibited symptoms of mania only 11% had bipolar disorder (Findling et al., 2010). The valid diagnosis of bipolar disorder in children can be facilitated with the use of a screening instrument such as the Child Behavior Checklist (Youngstrom et al., 2005).

> **Directions Part I, Multiaxial Diagnosis**   Given the case information, prepare the following: a multiaxial diagnosis, the rationale for the diagnosis and global assessment of functioning score, and additional information you would have wanted to know in order to make a more accurate diagnosis.

Multiaxial Diagnosis

Axis I:
Axis II:
Axis III:
Axis IV:
Axis V:

Rationale and Differential Diagnosis

Additional Information Needed

BIOPSYCHOSOCIAL RISK AND RESILIENCE INFLUENCES

Onset

The etiology of bipolar disorder is primarily biological, although certain psychological and social stresses may contribute to the first episode of mania or depression (Leahy, 2007).

Genetic and Biological Influences

Family history studies indicate a higher-than-average aggregation of bipolar disorder in families. Children with a bipolar parent are at an increased risk for mental disorders in general (Birmaher et al., 2009), and their chances of developing bipolar disorder are between 2 and 10% (Youngstrom et al., 2005). Persons who have a first-degree relative with a mood disorder are more likely to have an earlier age of onset than persons without a familial pattern. Twin studies further support the heritability of the disorder. A study of identical and fraternal twins in which one member of the pair had bipolar disorder showed a concordance rate of 85% (McGuffin, et al., 2003).

Researchers once speculated that the potential for bipolar disorder emanated from a single gene, but studies are now focusing on polygenic models of transmission (Ryan,

Lockstone, & Huffaker, 2006). Although genetic research remains promising, the "core" of bipolar disorder remains elusive, because no brain-imaging techniques exist that might provide details about its causes.

The limbic system and its associated regions in the brain are thought to serve as the primary site of dysfunction for all the mood disorders. Four areas under study include the role of neurotransmitters, the endocrine system, physical biorhythms, and physical complications during the mother's pregnancy and childbirth (Swann, 2006). The amounts and activity of norepinephrine, serotonin, gamma-aminobutyric acid, and perhaps other nerve tract messengers are abnormal in persons with bipolar disorder, although the causes of these imbalances are unknown (Miklowitz, 2007). Some theories focus on the actions of the thyroid and other endocrine glands to account for nervous system changes that contribute to manic and depressive episodes. Biorhythms, or the body's natural sleep and wake cycles, are erratic in some bipolar persons and may account for, or result from, chemical imbalances that trigger manic episodes. Finally, a few studies have associated obstetrical complications with early-onset and severe bipolar disorder (Scott, McNeil, & Cavanaugh, 2006).

Psychosocial Influences

Stressful life events may play an activating role in early episodes of bipolar disorder, with subsequent episodes arising more in the absence of clear external precipitants (Newman, 2006). Many of these life events are associated with social rhythm disturbances (sleep, wake, and activity cycles) (Berk et al., 2007). Persons with bipolar disorder who have a history of extreme early-life adversity (such as physical or sexual abuse) show an earlier age of onset, faster and more frequent cycling, increased suicidality, and more comorbid conditions, including alcohol and substance abuse (Post, Leverich, King, & Weiss, 2001). Most clients can recognize that a depressive or manic episode is coming two to three weeks in advance (Marangell et al., 2006). Such symptoms include changes in motivation, sleep cycle disturbances, impulsive behavior (for mania), and changing interpersonal behavior. Although such insight may be fleeting, the client may avoid a full manic or depressive episode if he or she receives intervention during this time.

Course and Recovery

Bipolar I disorder is highly recurrent, with 90% of persons who have a manic episode developing future episodes (Sierra, Livianos, Arques, Castello, & Rojo, 2007). The number of episodes tends to average four in 10 years (APA, 2000). Approximately 50% of persons with bipolar disorder move through alternating manic and depressed cycles (Tyrer, 2006). About 10% experience rapid cycling (APA, 2000), which implies a poorer long-term outcome, because such persons are at a higher risk for both relapse and suicidal ideation (75% have contemplated suicide) (Mackinnon, Potash, McMahon, & Simpson, 2005). The probability of recovery is also decreased for persons with severe onset and greater cumulative comorbidity (Solomon et al., 2010). It is estimated that 40% have a "mixed" type of the disorder, in which a prolonged depressive episode features short bursts of mania. Women are at risk for an episode of bipolar disorder in the postpartum stage, and they experience rapid cycling more than men do, possibly because of hormonal differences and natural changes in thyroid function (Barnes & Mitchell, 2005). A majority of those affected (70 to 90%) return to a stable mood and functioning capacity between episodes. Between 5 and 15% of persons with bipolar II disorder develop a manic episode within five years, which means that their diagnosis must be changed to bipolar I disorder (APA, 2000). Studies of the natural course of the disorder over one decade indicate that persons with bipolar I disorder experience depression for 30.6% of weeks, compared with 9.8% of weeks for hypomanic or manic symptoms (Michalak, Murray, Young, & Lam, 2008).

A recent meta-analysis of the literature has summarized the predictors of relapse in bipolar disorder (Altman, Haeri, & Cohen, 2006). Major predictors include the number of previous manic or depressive episodes, a history of anxiety, a persistence of affective symptoms even when the mood is relatively stable, and the occurrence of stressful life events. Other predictors include poor occupational functioning, a lack of social support, high levels of expressed emotion in the family, and the personality characteristics of introversion and obsessionality. We will elaborate on many of these predictors later.

Persons with bipolar disorder tend to experience serious occupational and social problems (Marangell et al., 2006). One study indicated a stable working capacity in only 45% of clients, and 28% experienced a steady decline in job status and performance (Hirschfeld, Lewis, & Vornik, 2003). Missed work, poor work quality, and conflicts with coworkers all contribute to the downward trend for clients who cannot maintain mood stability. From 30 to 60% fail to regain full function between episodes with regard to vocational and social performance. A systematic review by Burdick, Braga, Goldberg, and Malhotra (2007) suggests that although general intellectual function is preserved in persons with bipolar disorder who have stabilized, there may be some negative effects related to verbal memory and attention capacity.

An adolescent who develops bipolar disorder may experience an arrest in psychological development, thus developing self-efficacy and dependency problems that endure into adulthood (Floersch, 2003). A study of 263 children and adolescents with the disorder highlighted some issues related to course (Birmaher et al., 2006). Approximately 70% of the subjects recovered from their first episodes and 50% showed at least one recurrence, most often with a depressive episode. Box 10.2 summarizes other risk influences for bipolar disorder among members of vulnerable populations.

Clients who experience high levels of life stress *after* the onset of bipolar disorder are four times more likely to have a relapse than clients with low levels of life stress (Tyrer, 2006). Events that can cause these episodes include disruptions in social and family supports and changes in daily routines or sleep–wake cycles, such as air travel and changes in work schedules.

Critical Thinking

Practice Behavior Example: Demonstrate effective oral and written communication in working with individuals, families, groups, organizations, communities, and colleagues.

Critical Thinking Question: How you would describe to Catherine and her husband, in "plain language," what bipolar disorder is, and why it is important for her to receive ongoing treatment? How might you, at the same time, address the likelihood of her feeling stigmatized as "mentally ill"?

Box 10.2 • Bipolar Disorder in Vulnerable and Oppressed Populations

Females
- Women are at greater risk of developing bipolar II disorder, which is characterized by symptoms of major depression.[1]
- Women have an increased risk of developing subsequent episodes of bipolar I disorder during the postpartum period.[2]
- Women are more likely to experience a first episode of depression in bipolar I disorder.
- Rapid-cycling bipolar disorder is more common.[3]
- Women with bipolar disorder are more likely than men to have a comorbid disorder.
- Women with bipolar disorder are more likely to die earlier than women without the disorder.
- Women are more at risk for anxiety disorders and thyroid problems.

Youths
- Extreme early-life adversity may place one at more risk of developing bipolar disorder. This experience may also predetermine an earlier age of onset, faster and more frequent cycling, increased suicidality, and more comorbid conditions (including alcohol and substance abuse).[4]

Race
- Prevalence of bipolar disorder is less among persons of Asian background, but similar among Caucasians, Latinos, and African Americans.

Sources: Ingram & Smith, 2008; Michalak et al., 2008; Muroff, Edelsohn, Joe, & Ford, 2008; Taylor & MacQueen, 2006.
[1]Hilty, Brady, & Hales, 1999.
[2]Hilty et al., 1999.
[3]Hilty et al., 1999.
[4]Post et al., 2001.

One study found that relapse risk was related to both the lingering presence of symptoms of mania and harsh comments from relatives (Schenkel, West, Harrel, Patel, & Pavluri, 2008). Clients from families that are high in expressed emotion (critical comments) were likely to suffer a relapse during a nine-month follow-up period. Another study of 360 persons with bipolar disorder indicated that family interactions had impact on the one-year course of the disorder (Miklowitz, Wisniewski, Otto, & Sachs, 2005). Clients who were more distressed by their relatives' criticisms had more severe depressive and manic symptoms than persons who were less distressed.

Directions Part II, Biopsychosocial Risk and Protective Factors Assessment   Using Tables 10.1 and 10.2 formulate a risk and protective factors assessment, both for the onset of the disorder and for the course of the disorder, including the strengths that you see for this individual. What techniques could you use to elicit additional strengths in this client?

Table 10.1   Risk and Protective Influences for the Onset of Bipolar Disorder

Risk influences	Protective influences
Biological	**Biological**
First-degree relative with bipolar disorder	Absence of mood disorders among first-degree relatives
Endocrine system imbalances	Asian race
Neurotransmitter imbalances	
Irregular circadian rhythms	
Obstetrical complications	
Postpartum hormone changes	
Psychological	**Psychological**
Poor sleep hygiene	Effective communication and problem-solving skills
Irregular daily living routines	Structured daily living routines
Traumatic experiences during childhood	Sense of self-direction, internal rewards
Hypersensitivity	
Self-criticism, low self-esteem	Positive self-esteem
Exaggerated use of denial	
Substance abuse disorders	Absence of substance abuse
Mood lability	
Transient psychotic episodes	
Social	**Social**
Ongoing conflict with family members	Positive family relationships

Sources: Berk et al., 2007; Lockstone & Huffaker, 2006; Newman, 2006; Scott et al., 2006; Swann, 2006; Youngstrom et al., 2005.

Table 10.2	**Risk and Protective Influences for the Course of Bipolar Disorder**	
Risk Influences	**Protective influences**	
Biological	**Biological**	
Childhood onset	Adolescent or adult onset	
Antidepressant drugs (for bipolar I type)		
Number of previous episodes		
Persistence of affective symptoms	Absence of interepisode mood symptoms and medication adherence	
Substance use		
Psychological	**Psychological**	
Irregular social rhythms	Regular social rhythms, sleep cycle	
Introversion/obsessiveness		
History of anxiety	Knowledge about the disorder	
Exaggerated use of denial	Willingness to assume responsibility for the disorder	
Social	**Social**	
Low levels of social support	Identification and use of social and community resources	
	Participation in support groups	
Absence of professional intervention	Ongoing positive alliance with family, mental health professionals	
Marital conflicts		
Work-related difficulties		
High family expressed emotion		

Sources: Miklowitz, 2007; Schenkel et al., 2008; Tyrer, 2006.

INTERVENTION

The National Comorbidity Study indicates that 80.1% of all persons with bipolar disorder have received any intervention (Merikangas et al., 2007). In another study, more than half (53.9%) of those who sought treatment attended a mental health facility, although 38.3% received services from general medical providers and 20.9% received treatment from non–health care providers (percentages are overlapping) (Wang, Berglund, et al., 2005). These statistics are significant, in that medication is always recommended as a primary intervention for bipolar disorder, so clients will likely benefit from seeing psychiatrists. Psychosocial interventions can be helpful for controlling the course of the disorder. A recent literature review found that service providers prefer first to stabilize the client's mental status and then introduce psychosocial interventions (Fava, Ruini, & Rafanelli, 2005).

Table 10.3	FDA-Approved Medications Used to Treat Bipolar Disorder
Symptoms	**Medication**
For acute mania	Lithium, carbamazepine, divalproex, risperidone, olanzapine, quetiapine, ziprasidone, and aripiprazole
For maintenance of stable mood following an acute phase	Lithium, olanzapine, lamotrigine, and aripiprazole
For long-term treatment of bipolar disorder	Lithium, lamotrigine, and olanzapine
For acute bipolar depression	The combination of olanzapine and fluoxetine

Medications

The Food and Drug Administration (FDA) has approved a number of medications for the treatment of bipolar disorder (Ketter & Wang, 2010). These are summarized in Table 10.3. Most physicians recommend that clients take medication even after their moods stabilize to reduce the risk of recurrence of another mood episode. Generally a single mood-stabilizing drug is not effective indefinitely, and a combination of medications is more often used (Hamrin & Pachler, 2007). It must be emphasized that although older adults may benefit from the same medications as younger populations, they are more susceptible to adverse effects (Young, 2005). Lithium, carbamazepine, valproate, and lamotrigine are all used with children who have bipolar disorder, although none has been subjected to randomized, controlled trials (Findling, 2009).

Lithium is the best studied of the mood-stabilizing drugs. It is effective for stabilizing both manic and depressive episodes in bipolar disorder, although it takes several weeks to take effect and is more effective for treating manic than mixed or rapid-cycling episodes (Huang, Lei, & El-Malach, 2007). As a maintenance drug, lithium has been shown in a meta-analysis to be effective in preventing all types of relapses, but it is most effective with manic relapses (Geddes, Burgess, Hawton, Jamison, & Goodwin, 2004). Lithium also has a positive effect on clients' suicidal ideation. A meta-analysis documented an 80% decrease in such episodes for consumers who have used the drug for 18 months (Baldessarini et al., 2006). Another meta-analysis demonstrated that lithium, compared to both placebo and other medications, is effective in the prevention of deliberate self-harm (with 80% fewer episodes) and death from all causes (55% fewer episodes) in persons with mood disorders (Cipriani, Pretty, Hawton, & Geddes, 2005). Still, lithium is less effective at preventing relapses after about five years of use (Scott, Colom, & Vieta, 2007).

The difference between therapeutic and toxic levels of lithium is not great, so monitoring blood levels is important. Most of the common side effects of lithium are transient and benign, but lithium toxicity is characterized by diarrhea, dizziness, nausea and fatigue, slurred speech, and spastic muscle movements. Lithium should not be prescribed for women during pregnancy, as it is associated with fetal heart problems (Bowden, 2000), and it should not be used by breast-feeding women because it is excreted in breast milk. Lithium seems to have an anti-aggression effect on children and adolescents (Carlson, 2002). It is not advised for children under age eight, as its effects on them have not been adequately studied. Adolescents appear to tolerate long-term lithium use well, but there are concerns about its accumulation in bone tissue and effects on thyroid and kidney function. The decreased kidney clearance rates of older adults put them at a higher risk for toxic blood levels (Schatzberg & Nemeroff, 2001).

Another class of medications, the anticonvulsants, is also effective for the treatment of bipolar disorder, although like lithium they are not effective in treating mania in its earliest stages. Three of these are FDA-approved: valproate, carbamazepine, and lamotrigine (Melvin et al., 2008). These medications offer an advantage over lithium in that they usually begin to stabilize a person's mood in two to five days. A recent systematic review, however, concluded that these drugs are not more effective than lithium overall in preventing relapses (Hirschowitz, Kolevzon, & Garakani, 2010).

Valproate is the most thoroughly tested of the anticonvulsants. Carbamazepine is a leading alternative to lithium and valproate, but its side effects tend to be more discomfiting than those of the other drugs, and only about 50% of clients who use the medication are still taking it one year later (Nemeroff, 2000). A third anticonvulsant drug, lamotrigine, is used less often to treat manic episodes, but according to a large randomized trial, it is the only drug that is effective for bipolar depression (Bowden, 2005).

The anticonvulsant drugs are all used in the treatment of children with bipolar disorder, but few studies have been done to establish long-term safety (McIntosh & Trotter, 2006). The same qualifications that apply to lithium for pregnant women, children, and older adults also apply to the anticonvulsant medications. Carbamazepine is used more cautiously with children, as it can precipitate aggression (Ginsberg, 2006), and it has also been associated with developmental and cranial defects in newborns (Swann & Ginsberg, 2004).

Antidepressant medications (usually the selective serotonin reuptake inhibitors) are not generally used for the treatment of bipolar I disorder. They have been shown to induce mania in as many as one third of all clients, and one fourth of consumers experience the activation of a rapid-cycling course (Vieta & Suppess, 2008). In bipolar II disorder, however, the antidepressants may be used along with an antimania drug for mood stabilization (Cipriani et al., 2006). After a first episode of bipolar depression, antidepressant therapy should be tapered in two to six months to minimize the possibility of the development of a manic episode.

Many clients are prescribed antipsychotic medications on a short-term basis to control the agitation and psychotic symptoms that may accompany their mood episodes. Approximately one third of persons with bipolar disorder use small doses of these drugs during the maintenance phase of treatment as well, because they tend to experience periods of intense agitation (Faravelli, Rosi, & Scarpato, 2006). Among the newer antipsychotic medications, aripriprazole, olanzapine, risperidone, quetiapine, and ziprasidone have been tested as treatment adjuncts. In a meta-analysis of 18 studies, all of these drugs were superior to placebo in treating bipolar mania, with no significant differences among them (Perlis, Welge, Vornik, Hirschfeld, & Keck, 2006). These medications may be effective for acute bipolar depression as well.

Two alternative methods of mood stabilization are available for persons with bipolar disorder who do not respond positively to medication. One is electroconvulsive therapy (ECT), in which electrical shocks are given to the client, usually in a series over several weeks. Although this form of treatment seems overly invasive to some professionals, it is a demonstrated safe and effective method of stabilizing a client's mood (Rush, Sackeim, & Marangell, 2005). Vagus nerve stimulation, provided far less often than ECT, relies on an implanted stimulator that sends electrical impulses to the left vagus nerve in the neck. Even more invasive than ECT, it has been shown to be effective in people who experience severe depression with bipolar disorder (Fink, 2006).

Diversity in Practice

Practice Behavior Example: *Understand the dimensions of diversity as the intersectionality of multiple factors including age, class, color, culture, disability, ethnicity, gender, gender identity and expression, immigration status, political ideology, race, religion, and sexual orientation.*

Critical Thinking Question: How would you help Catherine, or any other female client with bipolar disorder, manage her symptoms if she was pregnant and unable to safely take most medications? Might there be times when the potential benefits of medication would outweigh the risks?

Psychosocial Interventions

There is no evidence that psychotherapy without medication can eliminate the risk of bipolar disorder in persons with other predisposing factors. However, psychosocial interventions have an important role in educating the client about the illness and its repercussions so that it can be controlled (Miklowitz, Otto, & Frank, 2007). Teaching clients to identify early warning signs of a manic or depressive episode can significantly reduce their frequency of recurrence (Altman et al., 2006). Clients' feelings and beliefs about their illness greatly affect their medication adherence. In addition, many people with bipolar disorder continue to have problems in their work and social environments despite medication use, and psychosocial intervention can help improve functioning in these areas (Miklowitz & Otto, 2006). Further, psychosocial treatment can help people with bipolar disorder to develop a regular schedule for their daily living activities (sleep, meals, exercise, and work) to prevent disrupted rhythms or stressful life events from triggering a bipolar episode.

Although studies have been few, a review has indicated empirical support for four types of interventions incorporating the above elements (Miklowitz & Otto, 2006):

- Interpersonal and social rhythm therapy is based on the assumption that interpersonal conflicts are a major source of depression for clients, including those with bipolar disorder (Frank, 2007). It also targets the person's regular scheduling of daily activities. Two large studies have supported the efficacy of interpersonal therapy in combination with medication compliance to other forms of intensive case management, which focus only on symptom management (Miklowitz & Otto, 2006).

- Cognitive-behavioral therapy (CBT) interventions challenge a client's cognitions that may activate episodes of mania or depression (such as "I have no control over my moods"), and they can also target cognitions related to medication compliance (Basco & Rush, 2005). CBT further incorporates client education (to help the client overcome cognitive deficits) and systematic problem-solving strategies for clients (Zaretsky, Lancee, Miller, Harris, & Parikh, 2008). A recent systematic review concluded that CBT interventions have a moderately positive effect on symptoms and functioning, although these effects may diminish after several months (Szentagotai & David, 2010).

Engage, Assess, Intervene, Evaluate

Practice Behavior Example: *Critically analyze, monitor, and evaluate interventions.*

Critical Thinking Question: Beyond what is written in your treatment plan for Catherine, what specific tasks and lifestyle activities might you suggest to minimize her risks for a recurrence of the disorder? How could you help her recognize the importance of these activities?

- Family-focused therapy trains family members in communication and problem-solving skills. As discussed earlier, there is much evidence that expressed emotion is associated with poorer outcomes in bipolar disorder, and these therapies address those issues, among others (Miklowitz, Wisniewski, Otto, & Sachs, 2005). A recent systematic review found mixed results for these interventions, but the authors noted that they need to be studied more carefully (Justo, Soares, & Calil, 2009).

- Group psychoeducation may be a more cost-effective modality of treatment.

Engage, Assess, Intervene, Evaluate

Practice Behavior Example: *Critically analyze, monitor, and evaluate interventions.*

Critical Thinking Question: What short-term behavioral markers could you set with Catherine so that she (and you) could monitor the stability of her mental status? Who else in her support system might you consult with to assist in this monitoring process?

> **Directions Part III, Goal Setting and Treatment Planning**
> Given your risk and protective factors assessments of the individual, your knowledge of the disorder, and evidence-based practice guidelines, formulate goals and a possible treatment plan for this individual.

CRITICAL PERSPECTIVE

The onset of bipolar disorder appears to result from a complex set of genetic, biological, and psychosocial factors. Research overwhelmingly suggests that biological factors are predominant, whereas other factors may account more for the timing and course of the disorder. For this reason, bipolar disorder has legitimacy within the social work value system as a mental disorder. Still, there are several controversial aspects to the diagnosis of bipolar disorder. First, the disorder has been diagnosed more often in children and adolescents in the past 20 years, and there is much disagreement about the appropriate symptom profile in this age group, raising concerns about its validity. In fact, the DSM criteria for diagnosing bipolar disorder are essentially abandoned when diagnosing children (Birmaher, 2006). Among young people there is much symptom overlap with the disruptive behavior disorders. A new diagnosis for children, known as "Temper Dysregulation Disorder with Dysphoria" has been proposed for DSM-V in an effort to better clarify differences among these disorders (American Psychiatric Association, 2010).

Another issue related to diagnostic validity is the relationship among bipolar I disorder, bipolar II disorder, and major depression. These distinctions were not established until the publication of DSM-IV, and questions have been raised about whether the disorders are truly distinct from one another. One pair of researchers studied whether the mood disorders might exist on a continuum, based on the observation that manic-type symptoms are present to a variable degree in all mood disorders (Serretti & Olgiati, 2005). They found that when compared with bipolar II disorder, persons with bipolar I disorder had a higher prevalence of reckless activity, distractibility, psychomotor agitation, irritable mood, and increased self-esteem. Still, one or two manic symptoms were observed in more than 30% of persons with a major depressive disorder, with psychomotor agitation being the most frequent. Given that excitatory manic signs and symptoms are present to a decreasing degree in bipolar I, bipolar II, and major depressive disorders, the authors concluded that they can be proposed to lie along a dimensional model.

> **Directions Part IV, Critical Perspective**   Formulate a critique of the diagnosis as it relates to this case example. Questions to consider include the following: Does this diagnosis represent a valid mental disorder from the social work perspective? Is this diagnosis significantly different from other possible diagnoses? Your critique should be based on the values of the social work profession (which are incongruent in some ways with the medical model) and the validity of the specific diagnostic criteria applied to this case.

Case 2   The Pediatrician

Ms. Daniels is a 76-year-old Caucasian woman who has been residing in a publicly run assisted living facility (ALF) for the last seven months. For three years prior to moving into this facility she was a resident in another ALF. While there, Ms. Daniels suffered a myocardial infarction that required hospitalization. She subsequently lost her bed and was forced to find a new residence, bringing her to the new ALF. While at the previous facility Ms. Daniels was deemed incompetent to care for her financial affairs for reasons of mental illness and was granted a guardian, a former friend. Prior to her stay at the first ALF, she had lived alone in a rented townhouse for 18 years.

Ms. Daniels reports that she is a retired pediatrician, has never been married, and has no children. Ms. Daniels says that during college, she would have periods in which she thought she could accomplish anything and that everybody loved her. But then she would slide into a depression for several months at a time when a "blackness" would be upon her. Despite these mood swings, she functioned with some success and graduated with honors.

She next went to a prestigious university to undertake her premed coursework and attend medical school. Throughout these years Ms. Daniels felt at times, usually when depressed, that the "authorities" were watching her closely for instability. She kept herself in "close check" because they were always looking for reasons to throw her out. During medical school Ms. Daniels sought psychiatric help but was considered to be a "diagnostic puzzle" (in her words). She recalls being given medication for her "anxieties," but she does not recall what these were.

Ms. Daniels's depression and mood swings continued into her medical residency, immediately following which she took $5,000 from her father's savings account without permission and traveled to Europe, where she met "the most interesting people" of her life. Ms. Daniels remembers being "very talkative" at this time and sleeping little, usually on the beach or the street. She had sexual relations with a man the day after they met, and they became engaged two days later. During that time, she wrote a 200-page treatise on how to cure cancer. During her three-week stay she spent all the money before receiving a medical escort home at her father's expense. Ms. Daniels was briefly hospitalized upon her return. She was stabilized with anti-anxiety medication and shortly thereafter began her career in pediatric public health.

Her mood swings, which were primarily characterized by depressive episodes, continued until about 10 years ago. Her depressive episodes lasted between two weeks and six months. She states that her illness features impulsive and reckless acts, but she can give no examples of these. Ms. Daniels denies that she was ever hospitalized again, yet over the next 20 years she held 15 different medical positions, and she attributes the volatility of her career to her mental illness. She retired from medical practice about 15 years ago and complains about the lack of money she had accumulated at retirement.

It was not until 10 years ago that Ms. Daniels started receiving psychotropic medication (lithium) that helped control her symptoms. The social worker asked Ms. Daniels what that was like and she said, "It was as if the blinders had been taken off, the shades had been lifted, and my eyes had been dusted. Everything seemed so bright it hurt to look around. I felt a huge weight had been lifted from my back that I had been carrying for a long time and I could walk upright with a spring in my step. Even my chest felt clearer and I could take deep breaths again. I didn't know what to do with myself. I had spent so much of my time depressed; I no longer knew how to be happy." When asked how often she experienced these feelings, Ms. Daniels said, tearfully, "only a few times."

For the last three months Ms. Daniels has felt useless and that she is not accomplishing anything. She lacks the ability to concentrate, often thinks "black thoughts," and is unsure she wants to continue living. Ms. Daniels feels she cannot safely eat or sleep during her "dark" periods, because she wonders if she is "being watched."

Ms. Daniels's medical diagnoses include glaucoma, peripheral vascular disease, hypertension, osteoporosis, hypothyroidism, allergic rhinitis, gastroenteritis reflux disease, and osteoarthritis. Although these conditions are serious, they are being controlled with medical care and do not incapacitate her. Ms. Daniels ambulates throughout the ALF with the aid of a walker. Her sleep is within normal limits.

Although Ms. Daniels has no difficulty making friends currently, keeping them is more of a challenge to her. After a few weeks of friendship, Ms. Daniels suggests that her new friend has some incurable disease and needs a nursing home or hospice care. The same scenarios play out with her ALF roommates, and three of them have asked for transfers. Ms. Daniels has two outside friends. One is 45 years old, on dialysis, and calls Ms. Daniels every night. This friend has told the nursing staff that she is in acute renal failure and is not expected to live more than a couple of months. The second friend is 62 years old and in good health, and she seems to take Ms. Daniels's pronouncements in stride. When Ms. Daniels was asked how she could predict the ends of people's lives, she responded that it was because she is a doctor.

Ms. Daniels reports that she had a distant relationship with her parents because she was a girl and had older, high-achieving brothers. Her father died when she was 39, and her mother died when she was 50. Neither death triggered a worsening of her symptoms.

Her two brothers, aged 86 and 82, both live in the vicinity but are frail and have infrequent contact with her. When asked about her relationships with her brothers, Ms. Daniels stated, "They would be great if their money-grubbing wives would just die."

Four mini-mental status exams have been performed since Ms. Daniels has been at this ALF, and she has scored well on each of them. Prior to her latest depressive episode, she participated in activities at the ALF, including a book club, arts and crafts, walks, resident council, a political discussion group, and recreational outings. She now participates in only a few activities. At the end of the interview, she said, "I think there'll be a time when I'm going to feel desperate. I don't think I'm going to kill myself, but I just feel trapped. I don't have enough money to live anywhere else, and I don't want to live here. There's not enough for me here. I'm not being challenged or stimulated, and I don't know what to do."

Regarding strengths, Ms. Daniels is intelligent, well educated, and capable of interacting coherently with others; she maintains a high activity level some of the time, has several friends, does not have life-threatening health problems, can verbalize her needs, and adheres to her medication regimen.

Please go to the Appendix for directions to this case.

Case Study   The Postman

Gregory Jackson has just recently been released from an inpatient facility after a one-week stay. He is a 46-year-old, bisexual, African American veteran with asymptomatic HIV infection and asthma. Mr. Jackson has been employed at the post office since 1985. He was hospitalized recently after going to the hospital and reporting that he had been placed on administrative leave from his job after threatening bodily harm to a coworker. Mr. Jackson indicated that he felt as though he was going to "murder someone" unless he was seen by a psychiatrist and put back on psychotropic medication. He cannot stop talking, but can be understood. Mr. Jackson states, "I just need my cocaine and I need my medication. I'm going to New York City to get cocaine because they step on it too much in D.C." Throughout the hospital's initial assessment, Mr. Jackson did not stop talking for even a moment. He admits that he takes his psychotropic medications only when he is having problems like this at work, and that he last took medication about one year ago.

His partner indicates that Mr. Jackson was involved in an incident five years ago at the post office, where he became agitated and a security guard had to physically remove him from the building. While involved in an altercation with the security guard, Mr. Jackson fell down the stairs. Since this time he has felt great hostility toward the security guard and has mentioned several times that he plans on hurting or killing him. His partner indicates that since being placed on administrative leave two weeks ago, Mr. Jackson has been calling the post office and threatening to blow up the building. One day earlier, he paced in front of the post office yelling obscenities and threatening to sue. Mr. Jackson also demonstrated disruptive and threatening behavior toward the staff at the leasing office of his Section 8 apartment building, which resulted in the staff filing for a restraining order against him. When his partner had expressed concern to the client about his behavior, Mr. Jackson has threatened to kill his partner or his partner's brother if he were to ever leave him. His partner feels the client may follow through on his threats toward the post office, because Mr. Jackson mentioned to him yesterday that he has a friend who will sell him a gun for $300. His partner indicates that Mr. Jackson becomes agitated and restless, with a decreased need for sleep (taking only one short nap per day), every year around this time. He began to notice the client's mood shift approximately three weeks ago.

After agreeing to be admitted into the hospital, Mr. Jackson became frustrated and angry when he learned of the hospital's no smoking policy. At this point Mr. Jackson insisted on being discharged while pacing up and down the hall with his backpack slung over his shoulder. He then lit a cigarette in the middle of the inpatient hallway while stating that he would slit his wrists and "bathe his blood" along the unit unless he is allowed to leave. When Mr. Jackson is able to calm himself slightly, he indicates to the social worker that he does not have a psychiatric condition that requires medication or hospitalization. When asked why he believes he was committed to the hospital, Mr. Jackson says that it is because people are intimidated by him. When asked to talk more quietly he states, "I am a New Yorker and we talk loud. I'm fine. This is the way I am." Mr. Jackson occasionally shifts from anger to fear, stating that he often feels afraid that others might come after him because he is "suing the post office for 10.5 million dollars for throwing an HIV nigger down the stairs." At these times Mr. Jackson admits to feeling grateful for being in the hospital because he feels safe there. At one point during his stay he asked the social worker and other patients if they were "black Greeks," recounting all the black Greeks he had slept with. Mr. Jackson went on to tell the social worker that all the patients were asking for sexual favors from him. The next day, however, he indicated that he wanted to go home and be in a "homosexual environment" because he was tired of the other patients asking him disrespectful questions about his sexuality. Mr. Jackson denies experiencing hallucinations, although in the past he has admitted to "feeling" voices and said that he feels as if he has "four brothers" inside of him and fears what may happen if he becomes angry enough.

Mr. Jackson has been seen at the hospital on several occasions over the past 10 years. At one point he responded very well to medication and complied with treatment for six months, which is the longest that he has been compliant with treatment. During those six months Mr. Jackson appeared calm and had insight into his disability, stating that "I have mental issues and I am here to control my mind." He appeared less agitated and anxious and was able to remain focused and state his needs clearly. When asked about depression, Mr. Jackson stated that he currently felt as if he was beginning to be in a "low" and indicated feeling this way several times in the past, though he denies suicidal ideation at any point. When asked about how he felt during these "lows" in the past, Mr. Jackson indicated that he usually stays home in his apartment and watches TV all day or sleeps. He says that he feels tired and doesn't feel as if it is "worth it" to do anything else. He indicates that he eats more during these times and frequently notices an increase in his weight which bothers him at times. Mr. Jackson is generally fit, but notices his physique changing occasionally, which is alarming to him, yet he feels as if there is nothing he is able to do about it. He occasionally misses work when he feels like this, because he is "tired and lazy." Eventually, he will shift out of this mood and will gain more energy and motivation.

Mr. Jackson was raised by his parents in Brooklyn, New York. His parents report that as a child he frequently banged his head on objects and shook his crib. In high school Mr. Jackson experienced racism as the civil rights movement was taking place during this time. He has two older sisters and an older brother. Mr. Jackson completed high school before entering the military at the age of 19 where he served on active duty for three years. Immediately after his release, Mr. Jackson was hired at the post office where he has been employed ever since with the exception of a three-year period when he was called into active duty in order to serve as a sergeant in Desert Storm. Mr. Jackson indicates that he has been placed on administrative leave from the post office for angry and threatening behavior seven times. He makes approximately $4,000 per month at this job. Mr. Jackson was married for six years after his release from active duty in the military, during which time he had two daughters with whom he recently resumed contact. He is currently divorced and pays child support. Prior to the divorce Mr. Jackson went through a nasty custody battle during which his wife refused to let him see his children. He states that he is a "founding father" of a brotherhood organization in New York with 50 members that preaches against racial violence. When describing his current lifestyle, Mr. Jackson admits that he rents a new car every weekend and spends a lot of money for his New York trips, saying "every weekend I go to the best clubs in New York City. . . . Shirley Chisholm used to listen to me speak . . . I'm a leader in the African-American community. I want to live each day as if it is my last."

Mr. Jackson reports that he grew up in a "ghetto" and witnessed several murders in his neighborhood as a child. His father, who passed away two years ago, was an alcoholic whose interactions with his children were characterized by violence. His mother, who passed away seven years ago due to complications from AIDS, had untreated bipolar disorder. Mr. Jackson states that at times his mother was supportive and caring and that she usually fulfilled his basic needs. As a child, Mr. Jackson watched his grandfather almost kill his father, and his mother would often beat his father in front of the children. Additionally, Mr. Jackson's father knocked the client unconscious when he was six or seven years old after the father came home intoxicated and became angry that his wife was not home. Mr. Jackson indicates that he was regularly beaten with a cord or tied to the bed when he misbehaved. In addition to his physical abuse, Mr. Jackson says he was sexually abused at the age of nine by his father, brother, sister, and several older men. Mr. Jackson had several imaginary friends as a child and "could become anyone he wanted."

In addition to his father's alcoholism, Mr. Jackson admits that most of his family (siblings, aunts, uncles, cousins) abuse alcohol. His brother is addicted to crack and is currently in prison. His two sisters live in low-income housing in New York and Tidewater, Virginia. Mr. Jackson drinks approximately a 12-pack of malt liquor four to five times per week both socially and when he is alone. He admits to using powdered cocaine and crack cocaine "when I have the money." He states that he spends approximately $300 a weekend on cocaine but denies having used anything for approximately three weeks, due to not having any money. Mr. Jackson denies experiencing any symptoms of withdrawal, including shakes, seizures, and delirium tremens, when he stops using. His partner indicates that he has only infrequently known Mr. Jackson to use cocaine when he is not manic. When admitted to the hospital, Mr. Jackson tested negative for all substances. Mr. Jackson indicates that he began drinking when he was nine years old and started experimenting with various substances when he was 14 years old. His use has elevated since that time. He does not believe he has an alcohol problem and does not plan on stopping, although he admits that he should control his drinking in order not to further complicate his HIV infection. He was arrested for a DUI approximately 20 years ago. When he was 17, he was arrested for disorderly conduct and spent one night in jail.

Unfortunately, Mr. Jackson has been noncompliant with his HIV medications. Although he is able to receive his medications free of charge from the VA hospital, he has been inconsistent in doing so. His immune cell count is very low, although he has remained asymptomatic. While in the hospital, Mr. Jackson indicates that he does not feel he needs medication because he "is protected, because I walk with God and Jesus Christ." He offers his low CD4 count as proof that God is protecting him.

Mr. Jackson is a Baptist, and although he does not actively practice his religion he feels as though he is a "semi-good" religious man. When he is not hostile or upset, Mr. Jackson presents as an intelligent, funny, charming individual who is sometimes able to laugh at himself when confronted with his past behavior. When asked about his strengths, he indicates that he is a "good comedian, a good politician, a strong leader, and a good father." Mr. Jackson has worked as a DJ in the past and enjoys doing this. He believes that he has an excellent support system in his friends and family. At times, he has insight into his illnesses, stating that he "should stay on my HIV medication, reduce my alcohol consumption, and be nicer to people, especially my lover-boy." Although Mr. Jackson presents as having many problems with the post office, he generally enjoys his job and fears that, one day, he will be "kicked out for good."

Please go to the Appendix for directions to this case.

PRACTICE TEST The following questions will test your knowledge of the content found within this chapter. For additional assessment, including licensing-exam type questions on applying chapter content to practice behaviors, visit **MySocialWorkLab.com**

---

1. Which of the following is true about the diagnosis of bipolar disorder?

   a. Bipolar I disorder is less prevalent than bipolar II disorder

   b. The requirement for a diagnosis of bipolar II disorder is to have had only one manic episode in the past, in addition to depressive episodes

   c. Women are more often diagnosed with bipolar I disorder

   d. Bipolar disorders and depressive disorders can be considered on a continuum of mood disorders

2. Which of the following is true about the diagnosis and treatment of children with bipolar disorder?

   a. Children are prescribed mood stabilizers and antipsychotics

   b. There are many randomized, controlled studies on mood stabilizers and antipsychotics for use with children

   c. The DSM-IV describes symptoms that are appropriate for children

   d. Psychosocial interventions are always used as a first-line treatment for children

3. Sharon was a single, 23-year-old college student who had recently been hospitalized for the treatment of a manic episode. She had been psychotic during her mania, with sleeplessness, hyperactivity, racing thoughts, hypersexuality, paranoid delusions, and alcohol abuse. Sharon's mood disorder was exacerbated by environmental stresses. Sharon's diagnosis of bipolar I versus bipolar II disorder would be differentiated by considering:

   a. Her positive response to anti-manic medication

   b. Her experience of psychotic symptoms

   c. Her experience of hypomania prior to depression

   d. The effect of environmental factors on her symptoms

4. The social worker met with Sharon weekly to help her develop strengths for coping with various age-appropriate responsibilities. Sharon made steady progress although she suffered some setbacks, including two additional manic episodes during the next four years. The appropriate specifier for Sharon's diagnosis would be:

   a. Single manic episode

   b. Most recent episode mixed

   c. Most recent episode manic

   d. Most recent episode depressed

5. Some states are instituting legal "advance directives" so that persons with a recurrent disorder featuring psychotic features can, while stable, put plans in place for involuntary treatment if they are later deemed unable to care for themselves by a psychiatrist. What are the ethical issues, pros and cons, to be considered in this process?

6. Many persons with bipolar disorder face lifelong challenges in managing the stigma that comes with other people's awareness of their disorder. Construct an intervention that might effectively minimize the sense of stigma carried by such a client.

SUCCEED WITH

Visit **MySocialWorkLab** for more licensing-exam test questions, and to access case studies, videos, and much more.

11

Anxiety Disorders

Competencies Applied with Practice Behaviors — in this Chapter				
Professional Identity	Ethical Practice	✖ Critical Thinking	✖ Diversity in Practice	Human Rights & Justice
Research-Based Practice	✖ Human Behavior	✖ Policy Practice	Practice Contexts	Engage, Assess, Intervene, Evaluate

Andrew is a 15-year-old Argentinian male currently enrolled in the ninth grade. His mother contacted an outpatient mental health agency because of her son's extreme fears of going to school and stated that he has not been able to attend a single day of class since the academic year started two months ago.

At intake, Andrew said he was nervous and was also sweating profusely, but he came across as friendly and mature. He smiled a lot, even when discussing painful subjects. He sustained minimal eye contact, however, and focused instead on the floor.

Andrew explained that he tried to go to school at the beginning of the year but could not get out of his mother's car because he was "so scared." Specifically, he feared "the larger class sizes in high school and "the large crowds of people looking at me and laughing." He realized that "people are probably not saying anything," but he couldn't stop worrying about it. He described physical symptoms such as sweating and a racing heart. He said that he does not have friends at this school and does not know which students from his middle school are now in his high school classes. Andrew mentioned that he does have a small social network outside school. These friends are three years older and primarily his brother's friends. Andrew describes these individuals as "part of the Argentinian community," and "people who have known me for a long time." Andrew also reported difficulty in other areas such as sleeping and eating. He stated that he tries to go to sleep before midnight but sometimes cannot fall asleep until 3:00 A.M. Sometimes he will lie in bed and "just wait to sleep"; at other times he will go to the kitchen and consume large quantities of food because "I'm so hungry." He reported that he does not eat for the rest of the day because he does not feel hungry then. He maintained that his weight has not changed; he does not feel guilty or bad about his eating habits but does think they are "strange."

Anxiety disorders are characterized by intense, almost unbearable fears that disrupt a person's capacity for social functioning. The DSM chapter on anxiety disorders includes 11 such disorders, and separation anxiety disorder is included with the disorders of infancy and childhood. Brief descriptions of the anxiety disorders, which are differentiated by the nature of the anxious response or feared stimulus, are offered in Table 11.1, along with their prevalence and recurrence rates (when available). This chapter discusses anxiety disorders in general terms, although at times it will focus on specific anxiety disorders, most notably posttraumatic stress disorder (PTSD). Information about anxiety disorders among socially diverse populations is included in Box 11.1.

Table 11.1 Anxiety Disorders and Their Prevalence

Disorder and Description	Prevalence	Course (if available)
Separation anxiety disorder describes excessive anxiety about separating from a major attachment figure.	Lifetime prevalence in children is 4.1% and is 6.6% higher in children living in single-parent and low-income households.	One third (36%) of childhood cases persist into adulthood.
Panic disorders involve unpredictable anxiety attacks. In panic disorder with agoraphobia, the panic attacks arise from anxiety about being in places or circumstances where escape might be difficult or embarrassing.	Adult lifetime prevalence is 1.1%.	Panic disorder without agoraphobia has a 0.82 probability of recovery and a 0.56 recurrence rate. Panic disorder with agoraphobia has a 0.48 recovery rate and a 0.58 recurrence rate.
In panic disorder without agoraphobia, attacks are not associated with particular situations but are characterized by fears of losing self-control.	Adult lifetime prevalence is 3.7%.	
In agoraphobia without history of panic disorder, panic symptoms are experienced in places or situations from which escape might be difficult.	Adult lifetime prevalence is 0.8%.	
Phobia is anxiety triggered by a specific object or situation and impedes the person's functioning or results in considerable distress.	Lifetime prevalence rates range from 10 to 11.3%. 12-month prevalence is 8%. The majority of those diagnosed are female.	
Social phobia is anxiety related to social situations. Fear of negative evaluation from others is the overwhelming worry.	Both 12-month and lifetime prevalence are 5% in the United States. Risk influences include being Native American and of low income.	The probability of recovery is 0.37; mean duration is 16.3 years.
Generalized anxiety disorder is persistent, excessive worry that lasts for at least six months, occurring more days than not, and accompanied by at least three of the following symptoms: restlessness, fatigue, difficulty concentrating, irritability, muscle tension, and disturbed sleep.	A lifetime prevalence of 4.1%.	The recovery rate is 0.58 with the probability of recurrence 0.45.

(Continues)

Table 11.1   Anxiety Disorders and Their Prevalence (*Continued*)

Disorder and Description	Prevalence	Course (if available)
Obsessive–compulsive disorder (OCD) describes recurring thoughts that cause marked anxiety, and compulsive behaviors that temporarily serve to neutralize the anxiety.	Lifetime prevalence rates are approximately 2.5% in the community overall, and 1 to 3.6% for adolescents. Childhood rates are about 1%.	
PTSD is characterized by symptoms of anxiety that follow exposure to a traumatic stressor. Three major symptom categories include reexperiencing the trauma, avoidance and numbing, and increased arousal.	1 to 14%, lifetime prevalence rate of 6.8%, of youths exposed to traumatic events, 36% have PTSD.	Symptoms in 90% of individuals with PTSD persisted for more than three months; for over 70%, the disorder lasted for more than a year; more than one third of people never fully recovered.

Sources: American Psychiatric Association, 2000; Bruce et al., 2005; Cronk, Slutske, Madden, Bucholz, & Heath, 2004; Fletcher, 1996; Gorman et al., 2002; Grant, Hasin, Blanco, et al., 2005; Kessler, Berglund, Demler, et al., 2005; Kessler, Chiu, et al., 2006; Schnurr, Friedman, & Bernardy, 2002; Shear, Jin, & Ruscio, 2006.

Box 11.1 • Anxiety Disorders and Social Diversity

Women

- Girls present with more fears than boys and generally have higher rates of anxiety disorders, starting during adolescence and continuing through the life span; whether the gender difference is due to biological factors, social factors (such as increased rates of sexual abuse), or a combination of the two is unknown.[1]

Older Adults

- Clinical trials that track the effectiveness of standard medications or psychosocial treatments in older adults are lacking.[2]
- Prevalence rates for PTSD are unknown, although rates for anxiety disorders in general range from 3.5 to 10.2%.[3]

Ethnicity

- Although African Americans have lower rates of anxiety disorders than Caucasians,[4] their anxiety disorders are more likely to persist.[5]
- African Americans are more likely to report somatic symptoms and to seek medical attention rather than mental health care, which may result in misdiagnosis.[6]

- High rates of PTSD have been found among Asian Americans and Hispanic Americans who have been exposed to trauma prior to immigration.[7]
- Narrative exposure therapy, a method by which the survivor is asked to detail the trauma, but also put it into the larger context of social justice and political considerations, was found to have the best evidence for the treatment of PTSD in refugees and asylum seekers.[8]
- Labor migrants have a 21% prevalence rate for an anxiety disorder (including PTSD).[9]
- Refugees have a 40% prevalence rate.[10]

---

[1]Hagopian & Ollendick, 1997; Ozer, Best, Lipsey, & Weiss, 2003.
[2]Gorman et al., 2002.
[3]Wetherell, Lenze, & Stanley, 2005.
[4]Breslau, Kendler, Su, Gaxiola-Aguilar, & Kessler, 2005.
[5]Breslau et al., 2005.
[6]Gorman et al., 2002.
[7]U.S. Department of Health and Human Services, 1999.
[8]Crumlish & O'Rourke, 2010.
[9]Lindert, Ehrenstein, Priebe, Mielck, & Brähler, 2009.
[10]Lindert et al., 2009.

PREVALENCE AND COMORBIDITY

Anxiety disorders are the most common mental health disorders in the United States, with a lifetime prevalence of 28.8% (Kessler, Berglund, Demler, et al., 2005). Their prevalence among children and adolescents varies considerably among studies (Cartwright-Hatton, McNicol, & Doubleday, 2006; Velting et al., 2004), but in a recent national study, 8% of youths reported being severely impaired by at least one type of anxiety disorder (Merikangas et al., 2010).

Anxiety disorders in general are comorbid with one another and with depression. Substance use disorders are also highly co-morbid with anxiety disorders (Kolodziej, Griffin, & Najavits, 2005). Comorbid disorders are common with childhood anxiety and are often associated with less positive outcomes (Storch et al., 2008). Axis II disorders afflict about 50% of people with panic disorder (Gorman et al., 2002). The most common of these are the avoidant, dependent, and obsessive-compulsive types. Along with psychiatric comorbidity, poor physical health is associated with the anxiety disorders, although the direction of causality is unknown (Sareen, Cox, Clara, & Asmundson, 2005). Medical problems may also be a consequence of trauma (Schnurr et al., 2002), even for children and adolescents (Seng, Graham-Bermann, Clark, McCarthy, & Ronis, 2005).

Human Behavior

Practice Behavior Example: *Utilize conceptual frameworks to guide the processes of assessment, intervention, and evaluation.*

Critical Thinking Question: Given the prevalence of anxiety disorders, how can social workers employed in school settings ensure that they are correctly identifying those children who have anxiety disorder and that identified children are receiving appropriate treatment and/or referral?

ASSESSMENT OF THE ANXIETY DISORDERS

The clinical assessment of anxiety should include a variety of focus areas (Bernstein & Shaw, 1997; Gorman et al., 2002). Box 11.2 provides a summary of these.

When the client is a child, separate interviews with parents and child are recommended (Velting et al., 2004). Children frequently report fewer symptoms than their parents and tend to be less reliable than parents in reporting details about the onset and duration of anxiety symptoms. For standardized assessment instruments for anxiety disorders, see Martin, Orsillo, and Roemer (2001) for adults, and for children and adolescents, see Fonseca and Perrin (2001).

Box 11.2 • Areas of Assessment for the Anxiety Disorders

- History of the onset, development, frequency, and nature of the anxiety symptoms.
- Family history of anxiety.
- Any coexisting psychiatric disorders, including substance abuse.
- A general medical history and review of a person's medications, including a physical examination to search for a possible physical basis for the anxiety. This is especially critical for older adults. If there is a physical basis for the symptoms, the appropriate

diagnosis is anxiety disorder due to a general medical condition. For medication or substance-induced anxiety, the appropriate diagnosis is substance-induced anxiety disorder.

- The client's response to life transitions, major life events, and stressors.
- Social, school, and occupational history.
- An investigation of times when the anxiety symptoms are not present or are more manageable, and what is different about those times.

Assessment Concerns Specific to PTSD

Although parent reporting is critical for diagnosing PTSD in children, parents often have a tendency to minimize symptoms (Cohen, 1998; Scheeringa, Zeanah, Drell, & Larrieu, 1995). On the other hand, when parents have experienced trauma, they may be biased toward seeing more symptoms in their children. Of course, children whose parents have been traumatized may experience impairments in their own adjustment to trauma (Scheeringa, Peebles, Cook, & Zeanah, 2001). Also with children, the social worker must make a careful distinction between attention-deficit hyperactivity disorder (ADHD) and PTSD (Perrin, Smith, & Yule, 2000; Weinstein, Staffelbach, & Biaggo, 2000). Trauma may attenuate already existing ADHD symptoms. Further, chronic hyperarousal and other symptoms of trauma can look like hyperactivity and poor impulse control, and intrusive thoughts can interfere with attention and concentration.

Other differential diagnoses to consider when assessing for PTSD in children or adults include the following (Perrin et al., 2000):

- Acute stress disorder, which resolves within four weeks of the traumatic event.
- Adjustment disorder with anxiety, in which the number of symptoms is not sufficient for PTSD.
- Psychotic disorders, in which the illusions, hallucinations, and other perceptual disturbances are unrelated to exposure to an extreme stressor. When psychotic symptoms accompany PTSD, however, the disorder can be characterized as severe (Sareen, Cox, Goodwin, & Admundson, 2005).
- Bereavement, which involves the nontraumatic (anticipated) death of a loved one and is characterized by negative feelings and recollections of the loved one.
- Other diagnoses, such as a mood disorder or another anxiety disorder, should be considered if the trauma did not precede the PTSD symptoms (Cohen, 1998).

Andrew mentioned that he has felt sad and lonely for a long time. He described intermittent suicidal ideation, but has no intention or plan of hurting himself. He said that he does not talk to anyone about these feelings but occasionally cries and "stays under the covers." He added that his friends "don't even know the truth about why I don't go to school—they just think I'm being a slacker." When asked what he does during the day while he is not in school, Andrew said that he "does nothing except watch Argentinian soap operas on the dish and do homework," which a family friend brings to the home on a biweekly basis.

Andrew's inability to attend school is a great concern for both him and his mother. Andrew wants to become an architect, so he knows it's important to keep up with his schoolwork. Andrew and his mother, along with the family friend, have had numerous meetings with the school regarding this difficulty. The school has tried to make Andrew feel comfortable by showing him around the campus after school hours and introducing him to teachers. However, Andrew reported that he did not find this helpful. Currently, his family is looking for the county to provide him with home tutoring until he can return to class. Andrew maintains that his fear of school and other social situations began the previous year while he was in middle school. He denied any negative experiences at school or with his peers and could not identify possible causes of this change. He reported that he missed approximately two to three days per week for about seven months during eighth grade because he was so nervous about going to school. At that time he also began to avoid answering the door and the telephone because he worried about "saying something stupid or wrong." Additionally, he began to avoid social situations, such as going to the mall, going to concerts, and taking public transportation, because he didn't like people looking at him. He stated that he sometimes wishes that he were invisible.

Andrew said he believed that if people looked at him it was because of something negative, but described himself as "normal looking." He explained that he will occasionally go to small parties where he knows the people, but only after he asks the host to list everyone who is expected to attend. If he does not know the people, he will not go. Even when he knows the people, Andrew still feels "nervous" and drinks two to three beers to make himself feel better. He reported that he drinks only in social situations and denied ever using drugs or smoking.

Andrew's mother believes that her son started to change following her divorce from Andrew's father three years ago. The mother, who speaks Spanish, explained in broken English and through Andrew's translation that her son became more withdrawn after his father left the house. Andrew stated that he and his brother have infrequent contact with his father, who currently resides out of state with a girlfriend. Andrew didn't think his father could be helpful or supportive with his current struggles.

Andrew expressed anger with his father for moving the family to the United States and then "dumping us" to be with another woman. Andrew's mother explained that the family had moved to the United States to improve their economic situation five years ago. Currently, Andrew resides with his older brother and his mother in a rented house. Andrew stated that his older brother works at a shop and that his mother "is in business." When asked to describe the type of business, Andrew turned bright red, looked down, and answered that "she cleans houses." Andrew mentioned that his mother is currently dating someone but could not remember his name. He said that the family was better off financially when their father was around. He said that his father paints houses for a living and doesn't give his mother money now that they are divorced. The family does not have health insurance.

Andrew's mother indicated that she did not know a lot about her family's mental health history but stated that she cried a lot when she was pregnant with Andrew. She reported a normal family medical history. She mentioned that Andrew developed normally and has been fairly healthy except for strep throat approximately six months ago. Andrew's goals for therapy include going back to school and feeling like "the happy kid I used to be when I lived in Argentina." When asked to be more specific, Andrew said he used to enjoy drawing and going out with friends.

> **Directions Part I, Multiaxial Diagnosis**   Given the case information, prepare the following: a multiaxial diagnosis, the rationale for the diagnosis and global assessment of functioning score, and additional information you would have wanted to know in order to make a more accurate and comprehensive diagnosis.

BIOPSYCHOSOCIAL RISK AND RESILIENCE

Onset

Genetic and Biological Influences

A predisposition to anxiety is genetically based but modestly so, accounting for 30 to 40% of the variance of the etiology (Hettema, Neale, & Kendler, 2001). Genetic influences may account for the majority of variation in anxiety in young children, but as children grow older environmental influences assume a greater role (Boomsma, van Beijsterveldt, & Hudziak, 2005). For PTSD, having a shorter version of the serotonin transporter gene appears to increase one's risk for depression, as well as PTSD after exposure to extremely stressful situations (Bryan et al., 2010); this has been demonstrated in both Caucasian and African American samples (Xie et al., 2009). This same gene variant increases the activation of an emotion control center in the brain known as the amygdala (Bryant et al., 2010).

Other biological processes have been associated with the occurrence of PTSD, in particular (Knapp, 2006). People with PTSD tend to have abnormal levels of some key hormones that are involved in their response to stress. Their cortisol levels are lower than normal, and their norepinephrine and epinephrine levels are higher than average. Scientists have also found that people with PTSD experience alterations in the function of the thyroid gland and in neurotransmitter activity involving serotonin and the opiates (Yehuda, 2006). When people are in danger, they naturally produce high levels of opiates, which temporarily mask emotional pain, but people with PTSD continue to produce those higher levels even after the danger has passed. This may lead to the blunted emotions associated with the condition.

Brain-imaging studies show that the hippocampus (a part of the brain critical to emotion-laden memories) appears to be smaller in persons with PTSD (Jatzko, Rothenhofer, & Schmitt, 2006). Changes in the hippocampus are thought to be responsible for the intrusive memories and flashbacks that occur in people with the disorder, and scientists are investigating whether this symptom is related to short-term memory problems. The extent to which these processes are risk influences for PTSD or result from the person's experiencing certain types of traumatic events is unknown.

Another biological risk factor involves illness. Chronic illness may contribute to the development of anxiety in adolescence (Hayward et al., 2008), as well as anxiety being related to the onset of problematic physical health. Although most people who experience severe trauma exhibit a normal stress response, the stress response system becomes deregulated and chronically overactive in PTSD, causing compromised immune functioning. PTSD has long been linked to increased risk of numerous physical health problems, including diabetes and cardiovascular disease. The reason why PTSD is so strongly associated with physical health problems is that exposure causes epigenetic changes in immune system genes and thus compromises immune functioning (Uddin et al., 2010).

Finally, the development of anxiety may be associated with temperamental style, which, as discussed in chapter 2, might have a biological basis. Risk influences related to one's temperament involve *anxiety sensitivity* (the tendency to respond fearfully to anxiety symptoms), *temperamental sensitivity* (including a range of emotional reactions toward negativity, such as fear, sadness, self-dissatisfaction, hostility, and worry), and *behavioral inhibition* (timidity, shyness, emotional restraint, and withdrawal from unfamiliar situations) (Bosquet & Egeland, 2006; Essex, Klein, Statterly, Goldsmith, & Kalin, 2010). Conversely, an extroverted temperament exerts a protective influence (Bosquet & Egeland, 2006).

Psychological Influences

Psychological theories about the development of anxiety are dominated by the concept of *conditioning*, which is the process of developing patterns of behavior through responses to certain environmental stimuli or behavioral consequences (Kazdin, 2001). An initially neutral stimulus comes to produce a conditioned response after being paired repeatedly with a conditioned stimulus. For example, surviving a traffic accident may evoke overwhelming anxiety when the person passes by an intersection similar to the one where the accident occurred. Although a client's initial symptoms may be directly caused by the trauma, ongoing symptoms may result from avoiding contact with a feared situation (in this example, avoidance of driving), which paradoxically may reinforce the occurrence of the anxiety through negative reinforcement (Foa, Keane, & Friedman, 2000).

Along with avoidance as a poor coping method, the coping method of dissociation after a trauma puts a person at risk for the development of PTSD (Ozer et al., 2003). In general, problem-solving coping methods are protective against anxiety disorders (Hino, Takeuchi, & Yamanouchi, 2002).

Certain mental disorders put a person at risk for the development of anxiety disorders in adulthood. For example, a history of separation anxiety disorder could predispose a child to later anxiety problems (Hayward, Wilson, Lagle, Killen, & Taylor, 2004). In addition, major depression often precedes an anxiety disorder, and comorbid depression further increases the risk of the chronicity of anxiety disorders (Bruce et al., 2005). Substance use disorders are also a risk influence for the development of problems with anxiety.

An association between intelligence quotient (IQ) and PTSD has also been postulated. On the protective side for intelligence, Storr, Ialongo, Anthony, and Breslau (2007) followed children prospectively from first grade to young adulthood. Those in the lowest quartile on reading scores were more likely to be exposed to trauma and therefore to develop PTSD. If causal, it may be that children of lower intelligence are unable to cognitively process trauma or do not have the coping methods to deal with the event and their symptoms (Silva & Kessler, 2004). Alternatively, IQ could be a confounded variable, occurring with other events, such as brain damage and maternal deprivation, which could result in both lower IQ and PTSD (Silva & Kessler, 2004).

Finally, prior mental health problems, particularly internalizing problems, appear to place children at risk for developing PTSD. In the Storr et al. (2007) prospective study, children who were more anxious and depressed in first grade were more likely to suffer from PTSD when later exposed to trauma. Preexisting anxiety was also a risk factor in another study of trauma response (Copeland, Miller-Johnson, Keeler, & Angold, 2007).

Social Influences

Two meta-analyses conducted to determine predictors for the onset of PTSD found that social influences, involving trauma severity and lack of social support, posed the largest risks (Brewin, Andrews, & Valentine, 2000; Ozer et al., 2003). In addition to severity, other features of the traumatic experience linked to PTSD involve the degree of exposure to the trauma (intensity, duration, and frequency) and the person's subjective sense of danger (Ford, Stockton, & Kaltman, 2006). Certain types of traumatic events may also predispose to PTSD; these include war-related events (including refugee and immigration status), criminal victimization, and exposure to natural disasters (Mineka & Zinbarg, 2006). Additional social stressors after the traumatic experience, such as homelessness, may lead to PTSD (Creamer, McFarlane, & Burgess, 2005).

Family-related influences for the onset of anxiety disorders include stressful, negative, or traumatic life events, including disruptions of relationships (Bandelow et al., 2002; Phillips, Hammen, Brennan, Najman, & Bor, 2005). Anxious attachment patterns in children are another family-related risk factor. Anxious attachment is characterized by an infant's becoming distressed and frantically seeking comfort from the attachment figure through clinging and crying when faced with something the child fears (Hanklin, Kassel, & Abela, 2005). Subsequent contact with the caregiver, however, does not seem to help the child experience a sense of security or reduce the anxiety. In a study that tracked children from infancy to adolescence, youths with an anxious attachment pattern were more likely to suffer from an anxiety disorder as teenagers than those who were securely attached or showed avoidant attachment (Warren, Huston, Egeland, & Sroufe, 1997). The means by which insecure attachment history exerts its influence on adolescent anxiety appeared to be related to negative representations of the relationship that are internalized by the child (Bosquet & Egeland, 2006).

A number of other interpersonal patterns are seen in families of children with anxiety disorders, particularly parental over-control (McLeod, Weisz, & Wood, 2007), but also overprotection,

Diversity in Practice

Practice Behavior Example: *Appreciate that, as a consequence of difference, a person's life experiences may include oppression, poverty, marginalization, and alienation as well as privilege, power, and acclaim.*

Critical Thinking Question: Given risk and protective factors that influence the development of anxiety disorders, how does being a member of an ethnic minority group involve particular risk?

and criticism (Donovan & Spence, 2000). As well as having a genetic risk, children of anxious parents may be more likely to observe anxiety in their parents and to have fearful behavior reinforced by their parents (Bandelow et al., 2002; Hagopian & Ollendick, 1997). Despite the number of possible family factors involved, family factors explain only a modest amount (4%) of the variance in anxiety (McLeod et al., 2007).

Finally, socioeconomic status (SES) and its link to anxiety for youths aged 10 to 15 years, was studied in a systematic review (Lemstra et al., 2008). Findings established a negative association; that is, the lower the SES, the higher the rate of anxiety.

Course and Recovery

The specific anxiety disorders have different prognoses, but most moderate to severe cases are not likely to remit spontaneously. Indeed, the anxiety disorders tend to be chronic, with low rates of recovery and high probabilities of recurrence (Bruce et al., 2005). For example, the mean duration of social anxiety is 15.1 years (Grant, Hasin, Blanco, et al., 2005). When OCD in youths was followed up nine years later, it had continued in 41% of cases (Micali et al., 2010).

Anxiety disorders also increase the risk of suicidality. Having one anxiety disorder increases the odds of suicidal ideation by 7.96 times and the rate of attempts by 5.85 times (Boden, Fergusson, & Horwood, 2007). Risk unfortunately increases with the number of anxiety disorders present. The authors of this longitudinal study suggest that addressing anxiety disorders is an important part of suicide prevention.

As for risk and protective influences for recovery, genetic factors may play a role in response to treatment. In a recent study, people with PTSD who carried the short allele of the serotonin transporter gene promoter responded less well to cognitive-behavioral treatment than other individuals with PTSD (Bryant et al., 2010).

At the psychological level, the presence of residual symptoms has been identified as placing a person at risk for relapse or the development of another anxiety disorder (Connolly & Bernstein, 2007). This information should be shared with clients to motivate them to continue treatment until no symptoms remain. Increased severity of the anxiety disorder (Micali et al., 2010) and comorbidity are also implicated with poor outcome (Connolly & Bernstein, 2007).

As for social influences, family factors are associated with recovery. Parental anxiety is a risk factor for the child's recovery from an anxiety disorder. However, if a parent is anxiety free, the child may have more positive outcomes from treatment (Kendall, Hudson, Gosch, Flannery-Schroeder, & Suveg, 2008). For OCD, family dysfunction and accommodation to the disorder were predictors of poor outcome to CBT (Ginsburg, Kingery, Drake, & Grados, 2008; Keeley, Storch, Merlo, & Geffken, 2008.

Intervention is discussed in the next section, but it may be said here that seeking help from the general health system is associated with less effective care (Wang, Lane, Olfson, et al., 2005). Young, Klap, Sherbourne, and Wells (2001) found that lack of appropriate care for anxiety was associated with being male, African American, uneducated, younger than 30, or older than 59.

Directions Part II, Strengths-Based Assessment   Formulate a risk and protective influences assessment, both for the onset of the disorder and the course of the disorder, including the strengths that you see for this individual. What techniques could you use to elicit additional strengths in this client?

INTERVENTION

Psychosocial Interventions

People with anxiety disorders tend to delay seeking treatment, sometimes for up to 23 years after onset (Wang, Berglund, Olfson, et al., 2005), and they tend to seek help from the health system rather than the mental health system (Young et al., 2001). Perhaps as a result, only about one fourth of clients received appropriate medication, and few (8.5%) received referrals for intervention that fit the empirically validated treatment models described here (Stein et al., 2004).

CBT

The evidence-based approach to treating anxiety disorders is cognitive-behavioral treatment (CBT) featuring exposure, for both children (James, Soler, & Weatherall, 2005) and adults (Hoffman & Smits, 2008). See Box 11.3. Brief (i.e., 12-session) protocols have been described with individual, group, and family (for children) formats equally effective (James et al., 2005). Therapist competence in delivering cognitive therapy may be important for recovery (Strunk, Brotman, DeRubeis, & Hollon, 2010), and discussion has particularly centered on the lack of a properly trained workforce on child anxiety treatment (Connolly & Bernstein, 2007).

For PTSD, interventions with a direct focus on the trauma are most effective (Bisson & Andrew, 2005). Imaginal exposure, a process in which clients confront their memories of the traumatic event, is often used for treating PTSD (Johnson & Lubin, 2006). For example, an initial exposure exercise might consist of the client's writing a detailed account of the trauma and reading it in a therapy session and also at home.

Children who suffer from PTSD are encouraged through desensitization procedures to describe the traumatic event and its aftermath in a manner that diminishes arousal and distressing emotions (Cohen, 2005). Stress management techniques—for example, progressive muscle relaxation, thought stopping, positive imagery, and deep breathing—should be taught to the child prior to detailed discussions of the trauma.

Box 11.3 • Components of CBT for Anxiety Disorders

Psychoeducation: providing information about the nature of anxiety and how it can be controlled.

Monitoring anxiety symptoms: their frequency, duration, and triggers.

Cognitive restructuring: identifying, challenging, and replacing maladaptive belief systems that contribute to anxiety.

Breathing retraining: to distract clients from anxiety symptoms and provide a sense of control over them.

Progressive muscle relaxation: to reduce tension in anxiety-provoking situations by alternately tightening and relaxing certain muscle groups.

Problem solving: for generating a variety of practical solutions to life challenges, and exposure.

Exposure: a process in which the client learns to face the feared object until the anxiety dissipates. Typically conducted in a graduated fashion, the practitioner helps the client construct a hierarchy of situations from least to most feared and then work through these in order, conquering smaller fears before going on to bigger ones. There are several variants of exposure: symbolic (through the use of pictures or props), simulated (through role playing), imaginal (the client imagines the feared situation), and in vivo, the preferred method (contact with the real situation/stimulus).

Sources: Gorman et al., 2002; Velting et al., 2004.

The social worker should be aware that intervention for children with PTSD involves direct exploration of the trauma. Although nondirective play therapy is a popular treatment approach (Cohen, Mannarino, & Rogal, 2001), it has not stood up well to CBT in studies (e.g., Cohen & Mannarino, 1996).

Combat-related PTSD appears to fare least well in treatment. This may be due to the greater severity of pathology of veterans who seek treatment at Veterans Administration hospitals, their tendency to limit disclosure upon returning home (which limits opportunities for both exposure and social support), and the potential for secondary gain (disability-based income may depend on remaining symptomatic) (Bradley, Greene, Russ, Dutra, & Westen, 2005).

Eye movement desensitization and reprocessing

Eye movement desensitization and reprocessing (EMDR) may be as effective as CBT (Bisson & Andrew, 2007; Davidson & Parker, 2001). Shapiro (1995) has outlined the method and created a training program for clinicians. Some consider EMDR a form of exposure treatment, because clients are asked to keep a traumatic memory in their minds as the clinician elicits the eye movements. However, a meta-analysis found no evidence that the eye movements were necessary (Davidson & Parker, 2001). Further, there were no significant differences between studies in which the clinicians had participated in approved training and those in which they had not.

Self-Help Manuals

Some general practitioners encourage client use of self-help treatment manuals (Jorm & Griffiths, 2006). One review of self-help treatment manuals administered in general practitioner settings was conducted, and the approach proved promising; the more time a facilitator spent on guidance in the use of materials, the more helpful the intervention (van Boeijen et al., 2005). Social workers should be aware that self-help manuals might be a useful intervention for those who are motivated or do not have other resources.

Crisis Debriefing

Crisis debriefing is often used by social workers and other mental health professionals to forestall the development of PTSD when people have undergone trauma. It involves meeting with people individually but most often in groups, educating them about the nature of trauma and its reactions, and encouraging their exploration of feelings. Unfortunately there is no empirical evidence as of yet that crisis debriefing is helpful for either children or adults, and may cause additional distress (Rose, Bisson, Churchill, & Wessely, 2002; Wethington et al., 2008).

Medication

The advantages of medications include their ready availability and the fact that less effort is required of the client (Gorman et al., 2002). Of course, side effects are a potential disadvantage of medication. For many years the benzodiazepines were the first-line treatment for anxiety, but they are no longer the drug of choice because of the risk of physical addiction with continuous use (DeVane, Chiao, Franklin, & Kru, 2005). Benzodiazepines may be used preferentially in situations where rapid symptom control is critical (e.g., the client is about to quit school or lose a job) (Gorman et al., 2002).

The past 10 years have seen an increased use of medications initially developed as antidepressants to treat anxiety disorders. In a meta-analysis of 43 studies, the selective serotonin reuptake inhibitors (SSRIs) and tricyclics (TCAs) were found to be equally effective in reducing symptoms of panic, agoraphobic avoidance, depression, and general anxiety (Bakker, van Balkom, & Spinhoven, 2002). The number of dropouts, however, was significantly lower in the clients treated with SSRIs (18 versus 31%), which suggests that these are tolerated better with regard to adverse effects. The side effects of TCAs include dry mouth, constipation, and blurred vision. With PTSD in adults, several controlled trials have shown that SSRIs produce positive effects (Stein, Zungu-Dirwayi, Van der Linden, & Seedat, 2003).

If a medication has been used effectively, a trial of discontinuation may be attempted after 12 to 18 months. Many clients (between 30 and 45%) partially or fully relapse when medication is discontinued (Gorman et al., 2002). Clients who show no improvement within 6 to 8 weeks with a particular medication should be reevaluated with regard to the need for either a different medication or a combined drug and psychosocial treatment approach.

Because of the physical and psychological dangers of prescribing any psychotropic drugs for children and adolescents, psychosocial interventions should always be used in conjunction with medication, with the exception of OCD (Bernstein & Shaw, 1997). There is a dearth of studies evaluating the effectiveness of psychotropic medications for treating PTSD in children, although physicians prescribe a variety of medications for the disorder (Cohen, 2005).

Few clinical trials have documented the effectiveness of standard medications or psychosocial treatments for older adults (Gorman et al., 2002), although the available evidence suggests the value of pharmacological treatment (Wetherell et al., 2005). If medication is used, the required dose is generally lower than that for younger persons, and any increases should be more gradual than with younger adults.

Critical Thinking

Practice Behavior Example: *Distinguish, appraise, and integrate multiple sources of knowledge, including research-based knowledge, and practice wisdom.*

Critical Thinking Question: What type of adaptations might be needed to make the interventions that have empirical support relevant to clients, who face many life stressors?

Policy Practice

Practice Behavior Example: *Collaborate with colleagues and clients for effective policy action.*

Critical Thinking Question: Given the fact that African Americans are more likely to report somatic symptoms and to seek medical attention rather than mental health care, what can social workers do—and at what levels—to ensure that African Americans with anxiety disorders receive appropriate assessment and treatment?

Directions Part III, Goal Setting and Treatment Planning   Given your risk and protective factors assessments of the individual, your knowledge of the disorder, and evidence-based practice guidelines, formulate goals and a possible treatment plan for this individual.

CRITICAL PERSPECTIVE

Some have argued that the expanded classification of disorders in the DSM-IV has furthered the purposes of pharmaceutical companies (Angell, 2004). As more constellations of behaviors are considered mental disorders, they become reimbursable and treatable through medication. For instance, in a critique of the DSM, Kutchins and Kirk (1997) discuss social phobia as an example of what could be considered a normal behavior (shyness) now being construed as a mental disorder. The National Comorbidity Survey Replication indicates that 12.1% of the U.S. population suffers from social phobia in their lifetime (Kessler, Berglund, Demler, et al., 2005), and it is the second highest disorder reported in the last 12 months (Kessler, Chiu, Demler, & Walters, 2005). Paxil, one of the SSRI drugs, is now marketed specifically for the treatment of social phobia, even though its actions are no different from other antidepressants of its class.

Several other critiques pertain to PTSD specifically. PTSD is one of the disorders in the DSM that is conceptualized in terms of problematic functioning in the person-environment system because a traumatic event has occurred (Bradshaw & Thomlison, 1996). However, PTSD is not a unique outcome of trauma; depression is as common a response as other anxiety disorders, substance use disorders, and eating disorders (Romano, 2004). In addition, in a majority of cases PTSD is accompanied by another disorder. Symptom overlap among diagnostic categories helps explain the high likelihood of lifetime comorbid disorders seen in PTSD. These facts indicate that diagnostic clarity is lacking for the disorder. In addition, the validity of PTSD in children can be questioned. Some of the DSM criteria may not be relevant to young children—for example, visual flashbacks, dissociation, numbing, and traumatic amnesia (Cohen, 1998). Further, clinician observations and interactions with children may not be extensive enough to garner valid information about symptoms. The extent to which trauma may be experienced differently in children is also unknown. The diagnostic criteria permit a great deal of latitude in determining whether a particular stressor is "extreme" (Perrin et al., 2000), and whether a liberal or strict threshold is used to define "persistent" symptoms (McHugo, Mooney, Racusin, Ford, & Fleischer, 2000).

Directions Part IV, Critical Perspective   Formulate a critique of the diagnosis as it relates to this case example. Questions to consider include the following: Does this diagnosis represent a valid mental disorder from the social work perspective? Is this diagnosis significantly different from other possible diagnoses? Your critique should be based on the values of the social work profession (which are incongruent in some ways with the medical model) and the validity of the specific diagnostic criteria applied to this case.

Case 2   After the Hurricane

Tracy Lo is a 30-year-old married Asian American woman with two young children. Her parents were born in China but moved to the United States before Tracy was born. She was raised largely with Chinese cultural traditions but married a Caucasian man when she was 22 years old. She was very happy, although her parents were disappointed that she married a "Westerner." Tracy's family situation is stable and her parents, to whom she remained close, have lived nearby since she got married. Tracy and her family lived in apartments until two years ago, when they were finally able to afford their first house in the suburban neighborhood of their large city. Tracy works part-time at a nearby bank, and her husband is a chemist at a plant that develops petroleum products. Their two children are in primary school.

One September the remnants of a hurricane passed through her city. This storm had been predicted as dangerous, and the Lo family took every reasonable precaution to prepare for it. However, a large tree from their backyard was blown over into the house and cut a large hole in the roof. The damage would take several months to repair, and many other homes in the area were also damaged.

Tracy and her family were forced to move temporarily into her parents' three-bedroom apartment. The extended family did its best to accommodate the situation, but space was cramped. It was the first time the extended family had lived together, and the situation was one that understandably resulted in a lack of privacy, frequent shortages of food and clean clothes, and some disagreements about parenting responsibilities. Tracy left her children in the care of her parents, who tended to be stricter than Tracy and her husband had been. Her parents complained that Tracy's husband was not providing the children with strong traditional values.

From the time of the storm, Tracy began to feel increasingly stressed with regard to the tasks of working, caring for her husband, mediating household conflicts, raising her children, and managing the home repair process. She became anxious (experiencing heart palpitations and feelings of unease in her abdomen), began to be irritable with her children, and showed some signs of depression (inability to sleep and concentrate on her work, feelings of overwhelming sadness). Tracy had not experienced symptoms of this type in the past, and in fact she had always functioned effectively and assertively. Her new feelings of helplessness were unfamiliar, and they frightened her. At the suggestion of a coworker, Tracy came to the emergency services unit of a nearby mental health center to ask for help, so that she would not "lose her mind." She did not tell her husband or children about this visit, because she did not want to appear "weak" in their eyes. Her parents in particular would not have approved her going outside the family for help.

Please go to the Appendix for directions to this case.

Case 3 In the Hospital

Jay is an 18-year-old African American male who has been treated since birth for hemoglobin SS, a form of sickle cell disease. Over the course of Jay's life, he has been hospitalized multiple times with pain crises and acute chest syndrome, both common ailments of those with sickle cell disease. Jay presents upon this hospital admission with both a sickle cell pain crisis and acute chest syndrome. This social work intern was consulted by the attending hematologist after Jay threatened to commit suicide if the doctor entered the room. Upon arrival, Jay allowed this social work intern into the room, where he continued to appear distressed, revealing that he felt as though he was "having trouble breathing."

Jay lives with his mother and 10-year-old half brother in a poor, urban area. His biological father was murdered when he was four. His mother was recently diagnosed with breast cancer. She is currently single and employed as an administrative assistant at a federal government agency. Jay is currently enrolled in the 11th grade at a charter school for those who excel in the arts. He is actively involved in the dance team and expresses his desire to become either a professional dancer or a fashion designer after graduation. His recurrent hospitalizations have forced him to repeat one grade and are currently affecting his ability to finish coursework to graduate on time. His health insurance is covered through Medicaid, which provides him with a case manager who is actively involved in coordinating all of his services.

When asked by this social work intern if he was having thoughts of suicide, Jay denied actually wanting to act upon his thoughts, but knew that it would "get the doctor out of the room." Jay reports that over the past 8 months he has been having episodes where he feels like he is "out of control" and these affect his breathing, heart rate, and cause him to have diarrhea. He reports that he does "not like" the doctor on service who entered the room when he was actively having an episode and that he "said the first thing that [he] thought would make him leave." He says that he feels like he is going to go crazy if he cannot get himself "under control." He reports he has these episodes up to two times a week and is always on edge because of fear of having another one.

Jay reports that over the past 8 months he has started consuming a larger amount of opioids to control his pain and anxiety. He says he wants a different doctor to see him, because the current physician will not increase the amount of medicine he needs to get his pain under control and stop the anxiety. In a family meeting, his mother stated that she has recently started keeping his pain medication in a lock box to keep Jay from consuming more than he should. Despite her best efforts, she reports that he sometimes finds a way to break into the lock box and obtain pain medication.

During this admission, Jay told this social work intern that he is bisexual and has been in a relationship with a male student at his school for the past several months. He reports that he wants to reveal his sexuality to his mother, but fears she will have a negative reaction. He also reports that he has anxiety over his mother's recent cancer diagnosis and has been cutting his arms with a kitchen knife when his emotions become "too strong." This social work intern did not observe any visible signs of the reported cutting.

Jay reports a strong relationship with his maternal grandmother who provides some financial support to his family. He attends church weekly and often has the hospital chaplain come to pray with him during admissions. He reports having a strong social support network at school and says that he has a good relationship with his dance coach who is trying to help him get into a training program after graduation. Several of his classmates have visited him during this admission, which he reports cheers him up.

He states that he is not currently sexually active with his boyfriend and is aware of safe sexual practices. He reports that recently, he has started smoking marijuana occasionally with his boyfriend and other friends at school, although he denies regular usage. He says he has a good relationship with his mother, but blames her for his sickle cell disease because it is a genetic disorder, and he inherited it from her side of the family. His mother reports that he often becomes very angry and yells at her when he does not get his way, saying that she is responsible for giving him anything that he wants because she gave him "this disease." She dismisses Jay's current symptoms of anxiety and says that he was a nervous child who has always been sick.

Jay admits being comfortable with this social work intern, but often says he does not want to become too close because "you will leave me just like everyone else ever has." Jay believes that he is not responsible for most of his problems and associates much of his distress with his lifelong medical condition. He believes that his recent episodes of extreme anxiety are related to worrying too much about his mother's cancer diagnosis and the possibility of revealing his sexuality to his mother.

Jay believes if he is able to come out to his mother, much of his anxiety will be relieved and some of his symptoms will subside. He knows that his fear of "going crazy" is sometimes irrational, but he feels like he loses all control when the symptoms begin, which causes him to spiral further out of control. He says he is open to receiving treatment, but prefers pharmacological agents to control the symptoms because these have helped calm him down in the past. His mother is also committed to being actively involved in improving Jay's condition and hopes that treatment will improve his overall mental status.

Please go to the Appendix for directions to this case.

PRACTICE TEST The following questions will test your knowledge of the content found within this chapter. For additional assessment, including licensing-exam type questions on applying chapter content to practice behaviors, visit **MySocialWorkLab.com**

1. Deciding whether to diagnose a client with panic disorder either with or without agoraphobia is distinguished by:
   a. The recurrence of panic attacks
   b. The level of social impairment experienced by the client
   c. Avoidance of certain situations that may prompt panic
   d. The presence or absence of a medical condition that may be associated with the panic episodes

2. What is true about the status of evidence-based treatment for anxiety disorders?
   a. CBT has not received empirical support
   b. Play therapy for children has little empirical support
   c. Interpersonal therapy has received empirical support
   d. Benzodiazepines are the preferred medications

3. Lynne was an unemployed 43-year-old divorced white female with two adult children and a history of being "constantly worrisome." Several months after divorcing her husband of 20 years, she began experiencing anxiety and panic attacks. She also felt great sadness and hopelessness, and often withdrew to her bedroom and slept, even during the daytime. Lynne's anxiety disorder appears to be associated with:
   a. Conduct disorder
   b. Substance use disorders
   c. Generalized anxiety disorder
   d. Depression

4. Lynne agreed to participate in exposure therapy to help her leave the house during the day and complete her grocery shopping with more confidence. Which of the following would not be an element of Lynne's exposure therapy:
   a. Desensitization
   b. Flooding
   c. Allowing her to avoid certain stimuli so she can calm down
   d. Relaxation

5. In the cases presented in this chapter, what role do you believe stressful life events and other environmental risk factors played in relation to genetic influences? Do you see any opportunities in these cases for prevention before the anxiety disorder developed?

6. What ethical issues arise in allowing clients' self-determination in terms of avoiding stimuli that arouses anxiety in them versus helping them face triggers, if a person experiences extreme distress and emotional pain when encountering triggers for anxiety?

SUCCEED WITH

Visit **MySocialWorkLab** for more licensing-exam test questions, and to access case studies, videos, and much more.

12

Eating Disorders

Competencies Applied with Practice Behaviors — in this Chapter				
■ Professional Identity	■ Ethical Practice	☒ Critical Thinking	■ Diversity in Practice	■ Human Rights & Justice
☒ Research-Based Practice	■ Human Behavior	☒ Policy Practice	☒ Practice Contexts	■ Engage, Assess, Intervene, Evaluate

Nikki, an 18-year-old Caucasian female, came to the university counseling center at the behest of her dormitory floor's residential adviser, who was concerned about Nikki's weight loss. Nikki admitted that she was "not happy" about coming to the center, but she liked the residential adviser and didn't want to "alienate" her. When she came to her initial session, Nikki appeared visibly emaciated and was wearing a long, oversized sweater and baggy sweatpants. At the beginning of the interview, she was guarded and answered questions with only a few words. But when she realized that the social worker "was not going to tell me I needed to gain weight like everyone else," she began to open up, although she spoke in a flat, matter-of-fact tone, even about painful subjects.

Nikki said she had begun to lose weight the summer of her senior year of high school, though her concerns about her weight had begun at age 13. Before that time she had been a "skinny kid," and that's how she wanted to stay. She admitted that she didn't want to grow up and thought that staying thin was a way to achieve this. She said she admired little girls' bodies (even girls as young as three and four), and thought they looked great.

During that summer, Nikki said that she was bored because there were no jobs for high school students in the midsized city where she lived. Losing weight gave her "something to do." Every day, she ate only two meals and jumped rope for 30 minutes. If she didn't exercise daily, she felt "fat" and "disgusted" with herself. Nikki said that before the summer, she didn't have the discipline to cut back on her food intake. At the same time, she said she had exercised and weighed herself almost every day since she was 14 years old. At 5 feet, four inches, she has never weighed more than 105 pounds.

Nikki admitted with embarrassment that she did lose control of her eating on occasion, usually with sweet food (ice cream, brownies, cake) but more recently peanut butter; she could eat an entire jar at one sitting. She said that this happened "maybe once a month" and that she would atone for it by eating even less afterward. She denied using any methods of purging.

When asked how she was feeling during the summer after she finished high school, other than "bored" at the prospect of leaving for college, she seemed surprised by the question and answered, "How did I feel? I didn't feel anything."

Since entering college three and a half months ago Nikki has eaten only two meals a day, subsisting on salad, yogurt, popcorn, and Diet Coke, and has lost an additional 10 pounds (she now weighs 85 pounds). She said that she doesn't feel hungry and that the weight loss has been easy. She has also stopped exercising.

Nikki admitted she hadn't menstruated in seven months and was losing her hair. She didn't mind the lack of menstruation because she had always hated her period, a clear marker that she was a woman. Her hair loss bothered her, however, and she showered only every other day because too much hair fell out when she washed it. She said that occasionally she felt her heart rate "slow down and then speed up." On the one hand, this scared her; on the other hand, she would sometimes think, "Maybe I'll just die of a heart attack, and all this will be over." Despite these physical concerns, she had not been to a doctor.

Nikki said that in one sense she knew she was too thin and wore baggy clothes to disguise the fact, but she still felt "fat inside," recognizing that no amount of weight loss would help her feel different. Yet she didn't know anymore what normal eating was and became panicky when people pressured her about gaining weight. She denied having anorexia to anyone who pushed her about it, saying that she had read the criteria and she hadn't lost 15% of her body weight; therefore, she couldn't have it. If she ever got fat, she said, she would be totally worthless.

Eating disorders are characterized by disturbances in a person's eating behaviors and perceptions of body weight and shape (American Psychiatric Association, 2000). Pathological fears of becoming overweight lead those with eating disorders to enact extreme, potentially damaging behaviors to lose weight and keep it off. *Anorexia nervosa* (AN) and *bulimia nervosa*, the two primary eating disorders, are the focus of this chapter. A third diagnostic category, *eating disorder not otherwise specified*, is a residual category at present. It is often used to diagnose persons who engage in chronic overeating and seek help for that problem.

PREVALENCE AND COMORBIDITY

In the National Comorbidity Survey Replication, bulimia nervosa was found among 1.5% of the U.S. female population and 0.5% of the male population (Hudson, Hiripi, Pope, & Kessler, 2006). The lifetime prevalence of bulimia nervosa is 1% of the population. The prevalence of anorexia is 0.9% of females and 0.3% of men. The lifetime prevalence is 0.6% of the U.S. population. Bulimia nervosa, in particular, has increased during the second half of the 20th century (Hudson et al., 2006). Despite the two discrete eating disorders, it must be noted that the majority of treatment-seeking adolescent and adult cases qualify for Eating Disorder Not Otherwise Specified (Eddy, Doyle, Hoste, Herzog, & Le Grange, 2008).

Most people with eating disorders, especially those with bulimia nervosa, have another psychiatric disorder. Indeed, three or more diagnoses are the most common comorbidity pattern among both anorexic (33.8%) and bulimic (64.4%) clients (Hudson et al., 2006). The most common comorbid diagnoses are (in order of occurrence) anxiety disorders, impulse control disorders (oppositional defiant disorder, conduct disorder, attention-deficit hyperactivity disorder, intermittent explosive disorder), and substance use disorders (Franko et al., 2005; Hudson et al., 2006). Depression is also common, but may be a consequence of malnutrition among those with anorexia (Godart et al., 2007).

Personality disorders are often present with eating disorders, with perhaps as many as 58% of eating disorder cases (Cassin & von Ranson, 2005). People with bulimia typically suffer from cluster B (borderline) and C personality disorders (avoidant), whereas cluster C (avoidant and obsessive-compulsive) personality disorders are associated with anorexia.

General health complications, as well as mental health problems, also occur among those with eating disorders (Rome & Ammerman, 2003). Specific to bulimia are enlarged salivary glands, the erosion of dental enamel, and electrolyte imbalances, which in turn increase the likelihood of cardiac arrhythmia and renal failure. Anorexia is associated with starvation and malnutrition, amenorrhea, metabolic abnormalities, electrolyte imbalances, irregular heart rate, low body temperature, low blood pressure, heart failure, anemia, and the growth of hair over the body.

Policy Practice

Practice Behavior Example: Analyze, formulate, and advocate for policies that advance social well-being.

Critical Thinking Question: Given the fact that many people with eating disorders are involved with the health system and general practitioners are typically unable to correctly identify eating disorders, much less provide appropriate treatment or referral, how can social workers intervene—and at what levels—in order to ensure that people receive appropriate care?

ASSESSMENT

People with eating disorders tend to be underdiagnosed and undertreated. This is especially true for minority (Mexican American and African American) women (Cachelin & Striegel-Moore, 2006; Fairburn, Agras, Walsh, Wilson, & Stice, 2004; Goeree, Ham, & Iorio, 2011). Screening for the possibility of an eating disorder should routinely be done during the medical assessment of teenage girls and in situations where individuals, particularly adolescent females, have already been diagnosed with another disorder (Lewinsohn, Striegel-Moore, & Seeley, 2000), as both health (Johnston, Fornae, Cabrini, & Kendrick, 2007) and mental health professionals (Hudson et al., 2006) often overlook eating disorders. Assessment guidelines are delineated in Box 12.1.

Box 12.1 • Assessment of Eating Disorders

The assessment of a suspected eating disorder optimally involves the following components (Mizes & Palermo, 1997):

1. Clinical interview.
2. Medical evaluation that, in addition to a routine checkup, assesses for problems due to weight loss and amenorrhea, tests for electrolyte imbalance, and refers individuals with bulimia to a dentist for the examination of problems due to enamel erosion.
3. Questionnaire measures of eating disorders, body image, and related problems (see Corcoran & Walsh, 2006).
4. Assessment of concurrent psychiatric disorders.
5. Risk and resilience assessment.
6. Emphasis on times when an individual feels better about herself/her body, and times when eating disorder symptoms have not been present or are lessened.
7. Motivation to overcome the disorder.

Goals (Yager et al., 2002):

1. Restore healthy weight.
2. Reduce or eliminate binge-eating and purging behaviors.
3. Provide education on nutrition and healthy eating and exercise patterns.
4. Treat physical complications.
5. Correct core maladaptive thoughts, attitudes, and feelings related to the eating disorder.
6. Treat comorbid disorders.
7. Build coping skills and problem-solving abilities.
8. Address themes that may underlie eating disorder behaviors (developmental conflicts, identity formation, body-image concerns, self-esteem, sexual and aggressive difficulties, mood regulation, gender role expectations, and family dysfunction).
9. Enlist family support and provide family therapy where appropriate.
10. Improve interpersonal and social functioning.
11. Prevent relapse.

Nikki readily admitted to "feeling depressed" since she started high school. She said she sometimes wished she wasn't alive but wouldn't kill herself because of what it would do to her mother. She said she still felt depressed most days and that everything tended to look dark, "like the color is sucked out of everything. The dorm, all the old buildings around campus, everything looks dreary and grey."

She studied constantly, even though she found it sheer drudgery, because she wanted to get all As and felt guilty when she didn't study. If she didn't get all As, then she would be worthless. Despite all her studying, Nikki had no career plans and was undecided about a major. Therefore, all this studying "lacked meaning." She said she couldn't see a future for herself and didn't want to be married or have children.

Nikki also didn't have any other activities that she enjoyed, except for meeting boys. She was surprised that boys seemed attracted to her because she didn't think she looked sexually appealing at her current weight. She was asked out on a lot of dates and accepted these invitations, but didn't feel serious about anyone.

Nikki said her concentration was good, although she incessantly thought about food and not eating. She never went to sleep before 2:00 A.M., because that was when her dorm hall finally quieted down. She would wake up naturally at 7:00 A.M. She denied feeling tired, although she slept only five hours a night.

When asked about other symptoms of depression before the present time, Nikki said she had had chronic insomnia since becoming a teenager. She had difficulty falling asleep some nights and often woke up at 5:00 A.M. She said that beginning in her teenage years her appetite increased, and one of her few pleasures was food and eating. That was why she had become concerned about her weight; she wanted to eat so much because it made her feel better. Another thing that had made her feel better about herself in high school was male attention. When a boy she liked didn't return the feeling or something went wrong in a relationship, she felt suicidal, although she never acted on those feelings. Nikki couldn't remember a time since she was 14 when these symptoms had lifted for more than a few days at a time. She said she had never been referred for treatment, and because she followed the rules and got good grades, no one really noticed anything unusual about her.

One of Nikki's roommates in the dorm was a friend, Alice, whom she had known in high school. Her other roommate, Megan, was a "total partier," who drank a 12-pack when she went out drinking and hung around a coke dealer, "so that must mean she's doing coke, right?" According to Nikki, Megan had some kind of eating disorder. She was thin and would eat only salad and drink alcohol. Nikki said it was hard having Megan as a roommate because she stayed up all night and would come in and out of the room at all hours, disrupting Nikki's sleep. She didn't clean up after herself and constantly left the door unlocked, even though both Nikki and Alice had talked to her numerous times about this.

Nikki said that her parents didn't seem to love or even like each other, and that her mother was always afraid of her father leaving and not providing for them. He would retreat into distant silence if she challenged him, sometimes for days, until she begged forgiveness. When he was mad at her mother, he would take his anger out on the whole family and speak to no one. He typically worked 12-hour days and also went to work on Saturdays.

Nikki's mother, who was slightly overweight and was always talking about how fat and ugly she was, didn't work outside the home. Nikki said she thought her mother was depressed, although her mother never said so. Nikki said, "I could just feel it in the atmosphere" at home. Nikki said she knew her mother loved her, but she was "insane" and "paranoid." When asked what this meant, she said her mother thought people, such as their neighbors, were "out to get her" and wouldn't answer the phone or the door. She also "would get lost in her own world, and even if we jumped up and down and shouted her name, we couldn't get her attention."

Ever since Nikki was a child, her mother would sometimes tell Nikki she was the "best girl in the world," but at other times she would say that Nikki was "bad," "cold-blooded," "a user of people," and "selfish," and was critical of Nikki's schoolwork, even though Nikki received all As. Nikki feared that her mother was right about her. When asked, Nikki said her mother displayed this pattern toward other people as well. She would "feel deeply about other people's pain," but if they did something wrong in her mother's eyes, she would "write them off completely." She had cut herself off from her own family of origin as a young adult and had not had contact with them for 20 years.

Nikki had two sisters, both still in high school. The older one was a junior, and she and Nikki were close, but her other sister, a sophomore, was "spoiled" and "impossible for anyone to get along with." Nikki said that due to her father's corporate job, the family had moved around a lot so that he could "move up the ladder." The last move was in the middle of her junior year of high school.

Nikki said she had been brought up going to (Episcopalian) church every Sunday and still went to church by herself now that she was in college. She didn't get much out of going to services but did so because she was "supposed to." She reported that her parents had never considered that she go to counseling because "they didn't believe in it and thought that people should solve their own problems." She said her mother would also say that "only your family can help, not anyone on the outside."

Nikki said she hadn't made any new friends since starting college. She had moved around so much that she didn't feel like making the effort, and no one interested her. Despite this attitude, she went to all the dorm parties on the weekends because "it was something to do." She sometimes drank and felt the effects easily because of her low weight. She said she had started drinking during her junior year in high school, at times to the point of blacking out. She denied any drug use. Several of her paternal relatives (an uncle and a great-uncle) were known to the family as alcoholics.

Directions Part I, Multiaxial Diagnosis Given the case information and your responses to the following questions, prepare the following: a multiaxial diagnosis and a rationale, as well as additional information you would have wanted to know in order to make a more accurate diagnosis.

BIOPSYCHOSOCIAL RISK AND RESILIENCE INFLUENCES

Onset

For the purposes of examining the risk and protective mechanisms for the onset of eating disorders, anorexia and bulimia will be considered together, as they share overlapping risk factors, symptoms, and causes (White, 2000). However, influences on each disorder's course will be explored separately, as sufficient evidence has been gathered on each one. Box 12.2 further describes the eating disorders in various socially diverse populations.

Biology

Biological influences on eating disorders include heritability, obstetrical complications, early puberty, early eating patterns, obesity, and dieting. Anorexia is moderately heritable (Bulik, Sullivan, Tozzi, et al., 2006), and more so than bulimia (Fonagy, Target, Cottrell, Phillips, & Kurtz, 2002), although family members of individuals with eating disorders have an increased vulnerability for both disorders (Bulik et al., 2006).

Preterm birth and pregnancy complications are associated with eating disorders. A study conducted in Italy found that certain obstetrical complications, such as maternal anemia, diabetes, and preeclampsia (a hypertensive disorder), were associated

Box 12.2 • Eating Disorders and Social Diversity

Females

- Although eating disorders are more prevalent in females, about 25% of cases are represented by males.[1]

Gay and Lesbian

- Homosexual males may be at risk for eating disorders.[2]

Ethnic Minorities

- In Western countries, Asians have a similar risk to Caucasians, if not higher.[3]

- Although Caucasian women in Western countries do not have higher rates of diagnosable eating disorders than do non-Caucasian women, they do have higher rates of body dissatisfaction and eating disturbance.[4]

- Lack of existing research on eating disorders as they pertain to Hispanic, Native American, East Indian, and eastern European women.[5]

- Mexican American and African American women are underdiagnosed and undertreated.[6]

[1]Hudson et al., 2006.
[2]Muise, Stein, & Arbess, 2003.
[3]Wildes & Emery, 2001.
[4]Wildes & Emery, 2001.
[5]O'Neill, 2003.
[6]Cachelin & Striegel-Moore, 2006; Fairburn et al., 2004; Goeree, Ham, & Iorio, 2011; Keel & Brown, 2010.

with the development of anorexia, whereas others, such as placental infarction, early eating difficulties, and low birth weight for gestational age, were associated with bulimia (Favaro, Tenconi, & Santonastaso, 2006). The total number of obstetrical complications was predictive of the development of anorexia. The authors concluded that neurodevelopmental impairments could be associated with the etiology of eating disorders.

Adolescence is clearly a developmental stage that makes females vulnerable to eating disorders. The mean age of onset is 18.9 years for AN and 19.7 for bulimia nervosa (Hudson et al., 2006). Anorexia tends to have an earlier age of onset than bulimia (Lewinsohn et al., 2000). The tension between the cultural ideal of female beauty and the physical reality of the female body after puberty is magnified by female gender role expectations. That is, female identity is defined in relational terms, and beauty is a core aspect of female identity (Striegel-Moore, 1993).

Early onset of puberty (prior to age 11) confers particular risk for the development of eating disorders; conversely, later-onset menarche (age 14 and over) is protective. Interestingly, one review indicated that earlier maturation is related to increased life stress in childhood (DeRose, Wright, & Brooks-Gunn, 2006), although the mechanisms by which this happens are not well understood. Early-maturing females tend to be shorter and heavier; therefore, their body type strays further from the current body ideal (Mizes & Palmero, 1997; Striegel-Moore, 1993). In fact, a lean body build presents protection from eating disorders because this body type matches the contemporary standard. People often tease early-maturing girls for their development; they may also be exposed to experiences for which they are not psychologically prepared, such as dating and sexual pressure.

Certain food patterns, some with early onset, present risks for eating disorders. For instance, picky eating in childhood is a risk influence for thin body preoccupation and possibly anorexia (Agras, Bryson, Lawrence, Hammer, & Kraemer, 2007). Childhood obesity poses a risk for bulimia (Stice, 2002), perhaps because of its damaging effect on body image (Striegel-Moore & Cachelin, 1999). Dieting is also a risk (Lowe & Timko, 2004). "Unrealistically rigid standards of dietary restraint coupled with a sense of deprivation may leave dieters vulnerable to loss of control after perceived or actual transgression of their diet. A lapse leads to an 'all-or-nothing' cognitive reaction. . . . Dieting can also be associated with different conditioning processes that may predispose a person to binge eating. For example, it may increase the appeal of 'forbidden' or 'binge' foods (typically those high in fat and sugar). . ." (Lowe, 2002, pp. 96–97). At the same time, dieting alone will not cause an eating disorder, as dieting is fairly normative among adolescent and adult women. Among dieters, more disturbed eating habits and attitudes are associated with the development of eating disorders (Fairburn, Cooper, Doll, & Davies, 2005).

Psychology

Body dissatisfaction and distortion, negative affect, perfectionism, impulsivity, and substance use are risk factors for eating disorders (Stice, 2002). As discussed in the section Prevalence and Comorbidity, having a mental disorder puts one at risk for the development of an eating disorder. Protective factors in the psychological domain include high self-esteem, a strong sense of identity, well-developed social and coping skills, and a positive temperament (Striegel-Moore & Cachelin, 1999).

Social Influences

Family influences on eating disorders have been noted, but whether the link is due to genetic mechanisms, childhood experiences, family concerns about weight, family psychopathology, or transaction patterns is unknown (Cooper, 1995; Wilson, Heffernan, & Black, 1996). In addition, specific patterns have not been delineated, but families in which eating disorders develop tend to be dysfunctional in various ways (Mizes & Palermo, 1997). A small significant relationship exists between sexual abuse, which often occurs within the context of the family, and eating disorders (Smolak & Murnen, 2002). On the protective side, families that foster parent-child attachment and have effective discipline skills, healthy cohesion, and positive communication help buffer their children against eating disorders (Striegel-Moore & Cachelin, 1999).

Another family process involves the extent to which parents transmit societal values having to do with weight and appearance (Striegel-Moore & Cachelin, 1999). When parents focus excessively on their own or their children's shape and size, children may feel pressure to lose weight (Kotler, Cohen, Davies, Pine, & Walsh, 2001; Mizes & Palermo, 1997). Teasing by family members about a child's weight is particularly detrimental.

Of note, families tend to experience a high level of burden in terms of feeling depressed and anxious when a child in the family has an eating disorder (Zabala, Macdonald, & Treasure, 2009). Parents also experienced a high degree of expressed emotion, especially when their daughters had been ill for a long time. The Academy for Eating Disorders has recently issued a position paper on families (Le Grange, Lock, Loeb, & Nicholls, 2010). The Academy's stance is that families should not receive blame for their children's eating disorders. The rationale stems from the difficulty of specifying family mechanisms through which eating disorders develop. This rationale also avoids alienating families from treatment and invites their collaboration and compliance.

Aside from family influences, other social mechanisms include social support, extracurricular activities, societal values, and socioeconomic status (Striegel-Moore & Cachelin, 1999). A poor social support system may evolve from social isolation, social anxiety, and public self-consciousness and increased risk of eating disorders. Conversely, protective mechanisms include social skills, social connections, and social support (Stice, 2002). A recent five-year longitudinal study showed that teens are influenced by their friends' extreme weight control behaviors (Eisenberg & Nuemark-Sztainer, 2010). Adolescents (both male and female) showed more extreme control behaviors themselves at five-year follow-up if their friends performed such behaviors in adolescence.

Involvement in certain extracurricular activities that emphasize very low body fat, such as certain sports and dance, places an individual at risk for eating disorders (Striegel-Moore & Cachelin, 1999). Activities that emphasize health and fitness protect against the development of eating disorders, as well as activities that presumably involve other aspects of the individual aside from appearance and weight.

Societal overemphasis on thinness for females has resulted in widespread dissatisfaction among females concerning their body image (Mizes & Palmero, 1997). Exposure to images in the media of extremely thin women is associated with dissatisfaction concerning body image (Groesz, Levine, & Murnen, 2002). Finally, products involving weight and appearance targeted at females are big business, creating strong incentives for corporations to boost markets for products that address females' supposed flaws.

Unlike many other mental disorders, high socioeconomic status (SES) does not confer protection against the development of eating disorders (Striegel-Moore & Cachelin, 1999). Females of middle and upper SES may indeed be more vulnerable due to increased demands in terms of social compliance and perfectionism. However, Goeree et al. (2009) recently examined data from the National Heart Lung Blood Institute Growth and Health survey and found that, contrary to expectations, African Americans and girls from low-income homes had higher rates of bulimic behavior than did Caucasians and mid- to upper-income girls. The authors' contention is that the widespread belief that mid- to upper-income Caucasian girls suffer from higher rates of eating disorders is because they are more likely to come to the attention of treatment providers. In contrast, low-income girls have not been identified and treated.

Course and Recovery

Studies that follow clients over time reveal wide variations in the course of eating disorders. Less positive outcomes typically pertain to AN compared to bulimia nervosa (Keel & Brown, 2010). Eating disorder symptoms, whether low level (fasting, dieting, using weight loss drink or powder, skipping meals, smoking more cigarettes) or high level (diet pill usage, vomiting, laxative use), are associated with suicidal behavior in adolescents (Crow, Eisenberg, Story, & Neumark-Sztainer, 2008) and physical and mental health problems in adulthood (see Wilson, Grilo, & Vitousek, 2007, for a review). A U.K. study of almost 2,000 people who had been admitted to an eating disorder treatment facility found that those with anorexia had a 10-fold increased risk of early death. Very low body mass index and alcohol misuse emerged as predictors of mortality (Button, Chadala-vada, & Palmer, 2010). Suicide is the major cause of death for people with AN (Berkman, Lohr, & Bulik, 2007), and suicide rates for those with anorexia are greater than in the normal population (Pompili, Mancinelli, Girardi, Ruberto, & Tatarelli, 2004). Suicide attempts are also common among those with bulimia nervosa (25 to 35%) (Franko & Keel, 2006).

Another finding is that the "crossover" rate between anorexia and bulimia is high. Among persons with an initial diagnosis of restricting-type anorexia, 36% developed bulimia, whereas 27% of those with an initial diagnosis of bulimia developed anorexia (Tozzi et al., 2005). A typical such pattern for AN is for people to start out with the restricting type (Peat, Mitchell, Hoek, & Wonderlich, 2009). Because a high level of restriction from food is difficult to maintain, they may then experience a loss of control and binge and thus present as having the binge-purge subtype. From there, many people go on to gain weight and meet diagnostic criteria for bulimia nervosa.

Following the onset of an eating disorder, a similar combination of risk and protective mechanisms is thought to maintain the condition, determine whether a person recovers, or predict responses to particular interventions (Gowers & Bryant-Waugh, 2004). Tables 12.1 and 12.2 provide the risk and resilience factors influencing the course of AN and bulimia nervosa, respectively.

> **Directions Part II, Biopsychosocial Risk and Protective Factors Assessment**
> Formulate a risk and protective factors assessment, both for the onset of the disorder and the course of the disorder, including the strengths that you see for this individual.

Table 12.1   Risk and Resilience Factors Influencing the Course of AN

Risk	Protective
Features of the disorder	
initially lower minimum weight	shorter duration of illness before treatment
eating disorder severity	
long duration of eating disorder	
Developmental stage	
adults	adolescent (with younger adolescents having better outcome than older adolescents)
Psychological	
greater body-image disturbance	
comorbid psychological disorders, such as anxiety disorders (especially obsessive-compulsive disorder [OCD]), depression, and substance abuse	
resistance and denial	
sexual problems	
impulsivity	
Social	
disturbed family relationships before onset of the disorder	support and empathic relationships, whether professional or nonprofessional
impaired social functioning	
Treatment factors	
failure to respond to previous treatment	

Sources: Bell, 2003; Berkman et al., 2007; Gowers & Bryant-Waugh, 2004; Keel, Dorer, Franko, Jackson, & Herzog, 2005; Yager et al., 2002.

Table 12.2	**Risk and Resilience Factors Influencing the Course of Bulimia Nervosa**
Risk	**Protective**
Features of the disorder	
high baseline frequencies of bingeing and vomiting	milder symptoms
preoccupation and ritualization of eating	shorter duration of illness
long duration of symptoms	
Psychological	
substance use disorder	
depression	
personality disorder	
impulsivity	
greater body-image disturbance	
lower motivation for change	
high initial perfectionism	
Social	
interpersonal problems	support and empathic relationships, whether professional or nonprofessional
Treatment factors	
short abstinence period	early change in purging frequency
only reduction in bulimic behaviors at end of treatment	complete abstinence at end of treatment

Sources: Bell, 2003; Berkman et al., 2007; Fonagy et al., 2002; Gowers & Bryant-Waugh, 2004; Hartmann, Zeeck, & Barrett, 2009; Keel et al., 2005; Keel & Mitchell, 1997; Wilson et al., 1999; Yager et al., 2002.

INTERVENTION

The intervention research for eating disorders has suffered from certain limitations. Evidence for how to treat AN, in particular, has not been strong. Further, studies usually do not focus on adolescents, which is unfortunate for a condition that commonly arises in adolescence (Gowers & Bryan-Waugh, 2004).

The goals of intervention with clients who have eating disorders should focus, of course, on aspects of their weight and eating behaviors. However, interventions that attend to weight alone are associated with client dissatisfaction (Bell, 2003), and dietary advice as the only intervention seems particularly onerous to women (Hay, Bacaltchuk, Claudino, Ben-Tovim, & Yong, 2003).

Treatment Settings

Although outcome studies of inpatient treatment of bulimia are lacking, in the vast majority of cases (95%) outpatient treatment is sufficient (Fonagy et al., 2002). Inpatient treatment usually involves multidisciplinary services comprising psychiatry, psychology, nursing, dietetics, occupational therapy, physical therapy, social services, and general medical services (Foreyt, Poston, Winebarger, & McGavin, 1998). Inpatient treatment for anorexia is indicated with the following risk factors (Foreyt et al., 1998; Golden et al., 2003): (1) serious physical complications (malnutrition, dehydration, electrolyte disturbances, cardiac dysrhythmia, arrested growth); (2) extremely low body weight; (3) suicide risk; (4) lack of response to outpatient treatment; (5) lack of available outpatient treatment; (6) comorbid disorders that interfere with outpatient treatment (i.e., severe depression, OCD); and (7) a need to be separated from the current living situation.

Hospital stays have shortened in recent years due to changes imposed by managed care. Shorter stays make it harder for the client to achieve optimal weight, as weight should be restored at a rate of only one to three pounds per week. If the client is released before reaching optimal weight,[1] he or she may be unable to maintain the weight, which might necessitate rehospitalization (Mizes & Palmero, 1997). In addition, individuals benefit from having some control over the process and pace of intervention (Bell, 2003). Those who are resistant to weight gain may need to gain weight more slowly and have a period of weight maintenance, thus requiring a longer hospital stay (Willer, Thuras, & Crow, 2005). Still, due to patterns of insurance reimbursement, the outpatient care of anorexia will increasingly be the norm.

Psychosocial Interventions

For bulimia, two major psychosocial interventions, both delivered in a brief format (e.g., 16 sessions) have received empirical validation: cognitive-behavioral therapy (CBT) and interpersonal therapy (IPT). A review of psychotherapy studies showed that about 40% of those who complete treatment recover (this percentage is reduced to 32.6 when including dropouts from treatment) (Thompson-Brenner, Glass, & Westen, 2003).

CBT includes a "package" of strategies, among them self-monitoring, social skills training, assertiveness training, problem solving, and cognitive restructuring. A review of studies found that about one half of women with bulimia recover with a course of CBT (Hay & Bacaltchuk, 2003), which generally achieves a superior effect to medication (Whittal, Agras, & Gould, 1999).

Individual therapy seems more effective than group modalities (Thompson-Brenner et al., 2003). In addition, a self-help format is a promising approach (Hay & Bacaltchuk, 2003). These intervention procedures have been clearly outlined in treatment manuals (Fonagy et al., 2002). (See Fairburn, Marcus, & Wilson, 1993, for an example of a treatment manual.) Despite these advantages, many experienced clinicians do not find CBT as useful as described by researchers (Yager et al., 2002). This disparity may be due to lack of training, discomfort with the methods, or differences between clients seen in the community and those who participate as research subjects. In randomized controlled trials (the gold standard of intervention research), individuals with substance use disorders, bipolar disorder, or suicidality are screened out from research (Thompson-Brenner et al., 2003). Therefore, the results of such trials may not generalize to clients who are seen in clinical settings for bulimia.

---

[1]Ninety percent of normal weight, so that menstruation can resume.

Individual IPT is another empirically validated approach for bulimia (e.g., Fairburn et al., 1991; Fairburn et al., 1995), which has been adapted from the treatment of depression. (See chapter 9.) CBT and IPT compare favorably with each other, although IPT may take longer to achieve its desired outcomes.

Unfortunately, these empirically validated interventions have not typically been tested with adolescents. It seems that developmentally appropriate modifications, including a degree of parental involvement and addressing age-related motivational issues, would be necessary (Gowers & Bryant-Waugh, 2004).

A great deal of ambivalence about staying thin and getting better is typically present with eating disorders, and motivational interviewing may be necessary to engage people in treatment and to restore healthy eating patterns. Motivational interviewing, which originated in response to substance use disorders (see chapter 7), has been adapted for eating disorders (Killick & Allen, 1997; Tantillo, Bitter, & Adams, 2001; Treasure & Ward, 1997). Preliminary evidence suggests that motivational interviewing compares favorably with CBT for reducing bulimic symptoms (Treasure et al., 1999).

Empirical support for psychosocial treatment of AN is lacking. Long-term psychodynamic therapy is most often used for the outpatient treatment of anorexia, although results have not typically been examined empirically (Mizes & Palermo, 1997). A Cochrane Collaboration systematic review of outpatient psychotherapies for AN found only seven studies, with little evidence to support any particular intervention (Hay, Bacaltchuk, & Stefano, 2004).

As discussed, certain risk influences involve the family. Although there is consensus among practitioners that family involvement should be part of the treatment plan, at least for younger adolescents with anorexia (Crisp et al., 1991; Robin, Siegel, & Moye, 1995; Robin et al., 1999), methodologically strong studies have been few. More recently, a systematic review of randomized, controlled trials of family therapy for AN was conducted (Fisher, Hetrick, & Rushford, 2010). Based on 13 studies, there was some evidence that family therapy may be more effective than treatment as usual but not other psychotherapies for remission from AN, where there were no differences found in relapse rates, symptom scores, weight measures, or the number of dropouts (Fisher et al., 2010).

Despite these findings, much attention in the literature has centered on the Maudsley model, a family intervention that has been used with mainly adolescents. Influenced by Minuchin's family systems therapy (Minuchin, Rosman, & Baker, 1978), the Maudsley model was developed by Dare and Eisler at London's Maudsley Hospital in the 1980s with the main aim of getting the parents to unite to stand up to an externalized illness and re-feed their adolescent until a healthy weight is resumed (Lock, Le Grange, Agras, & Dare, 2001). Family treatment may include therapeutic techniques from traditional family therapy or other schools of psychotherapy and in this way depart from family systems therapy.

Medication

Although psychotropic medications should not stand as the primary treatment of eating disorders (Bacaltchuk, Hay, & Trefiglio, 2001; Gowers & Bryant-Waugh, 2004; Nakash-Eisikovitz, Dierberger, & Westen, 2002), selective serotonin reuptake inhibitors (SSRIs), particularly fluoxetine (Prozac), have been used to treat bulimia. Bacaltchuk and Hay (2003) examined antidepressants compared to placebo in 19 trials and found that the likelihood of short-term remission from binge episodes was increased with the use of antidepressants (70% reduction of binges) compared to placebo (50% reduction).

Critical Thinking

Practice Behavior Example: *Distinguish, appraise, and integrate multiple sources of knowledge, including research-based knowledge, and practice wisdom.*

Critical Thinking Question: Given that most of the research has centered on adult women with eating disorders rather than on adolescents, how would you decide how to adapt what you have learned to the application of adolescents with eating disorders?

Bacaltchuk et al. (2001) focused on medication compared to psychotherapy and medication in combination with psychotherapy. When medication was compared to psychotherapy, remission rates from eating disorder symptoms were higher for psychotherapy, and dropout rates were much higher for medication. However, there were no statistically significant differences between mean binge frequency and depression between people taking antidepressants and attending psychotherapy. Results of their studies lead the authors to conclude that combining medication and psychotherapy produces few consistent gains over psychotherapy alone when considering other outcomes, including depression and binge frequency.

Of note is that medication does not seem to have much impact on anorexia (Claudino et al., 2006; Gowers & Bryant-Waugh, 2004). When medications are used, it is usually because of comorbid depression or anxiety. People being treated for eating disorders, especially those with anorexia, report psychological interventions as being more helpful than medication (Bell, 2003).

Research-Based Practice

Practice Behavior Example: *Use research evidence to inform practice.*

Critical Thinking Question: How will you ensure that you apply intervention research knowledge with ethnic minority clients diagnosed with eating disorders in a culturally competent way?

> **Directions Part III, Goal Setting and Treatment Planning**   Given your risk and protective factors assessments of the individual, your knowledge of the disorder, and evidence-based practice guidelines, formulate goals and a possible treatment plan for this individual.

CRITICAL PERSPECTIVE

A major critique of the diagnosis of eating disorders that is central to the social work perspective is that it focuses on the internal deficits of those with eating disorders, rather than emphasizing social and cultural attitudes (Pratt & Woolfenden, 2003). Both anorexia and bulimia have increased throughout recent decades due to cultural standards of thinness (Keel & Klump, 2003). One of the challenges faced by those involved in prevention efforts is the difficulty of changing the dieting and weight preoccupations that are so culturally pervasive (Mizes & Palmero, 1997).

Another class of critiques has to do with the narrowness of the diagnostic criteria for anorexia and bulimia. As a result, most individuals with serious eating-related problems are diagnosed with "eating disorder not otherwise specified." This is a heterogenous group of problems for which effective treatment is needed. In *Diagnostic and Statistical Manual of Mental Disorders* (DSM-V), binge eating disorder (currently categorized in DSM-IV as an "eating disorder not otherwise specified") will likely stand alone (Wonderlich, Gordon, Mitchell, Crosby, & Engel, 2009). Binge eating disorder has similar criteria to bulimia nervosa but without the purging element.

Other suggestions include relaxing criteria for the other eating disorders; if some of these criteria were modified, a significant number of cases from the "eating disorder not otherwise specified" category would be absorbed. For AN, consideration has been made to dropping "amenorrhea" as a criterion (Attia & Roberto, 2009). Some women who are seriously underweight continue to menstruate (Striegel-Moore et al., 2005). Also, the criterion lacks relevance for prepubescent girls and for males (Franko, Wonderlich, Little, & Herzog, 2004).

For bulimia nervosa, one problem with the criteria is the term *excessive exercise* for inappropriate compensating behavior. *Excessive* implies a large amount of time dedicated to exercise, yet it is not the quantity of physical activity that is salient, but its compulsive quality (Adkins & Keel, 2005). It has been suggested that the word *compulsive* be substituted for *excessive*. Another way to define the criterion as excessive is to ask the client if the postponement of exercise results in intense guilt or if it is undertaken solely to influence weight or shape (Mond, Hay, Rodgers, & Owen, 2006).

Other critiques concerning the diagnosis for bulimia involve the duration of binges, the amount of food consumed during binges, and the frequency criterion for bulimia. Although the criterion requires that the binge eating happen "in a discrete period of time," no evidence indicates that discrete binges offer any more clinical utility than episodes that occur over an extended period of time (Franko et al., 2004). The binge is required to be "an amount that is definitely larger than what most people would eat." However, many women report subjective binge episodes and then feel compelled to purge but perhaps would not meet the criterion because their binges are not sufficiently large (Franko et al., 2004). Better indicators of a binge episode might be the level of mood disturbance involved or the sense of loss of control (Herzog & Delinsky, 2001, as cited in Franko et al., 2004). Finally, the DSM requires that the bingeing and purging episodes occur at least twice a week for a three-month period. However, the decision for this minimum frequency was not based on empirical evidence, and bulimic behaviors less frequent than this may still involve a clinically significant problem (Franko et al., 2004; Wilson & Sysko, 2009).

A final critique involves the subtyping of anorexia (whether binge eating and purging or restricting) and bulimia (purging or nonpurging). Questions have been generated as to the utility and validity of these subtypes (Franko et al., 2004; Peat et al., 2009; van Hoeken, Veling, Sinke, Mitchell, & Hoek, 2009). For example, anorexia binge eating-purging type may be more like bulimia than restricting anorexia, which may represent a discrete type of eating disorder. Additionally, the bulimia subtypes may not involve a true distinction.

A final critique has been presented by Goeree et al. (2009), economists who performed mathematical models of bulimic behaviors from a national survey. They determined that bulimic behavior could be conceptualized as an addiction because the best predictor of a continued eating disorder was current status with an eating disorder. Although eating disorder researchers have discounted an addiction hypothesis (Wilson, 1999), Goeree and colleagues argue that an addiction model would help increase insurance coverage for the treatment of eating disorders, which are not as frequently or as generously covered as the substance use disorders.

Practice Contexts

Practice Behavior Example: *Continuously discover, appraise, and attend to changing locales, populations, scientific and technological developments, and emerging societal trends to provide relevant services.*

Critical Thinking Question: Given the variety of evidence-based treatments available, how would you go about influencing the system of a facility of which you were an employer if it used only an addictions (Overeaters Anonymous) approach?

Directions Part IV, Critical Perspective   Formulate a critique of the diagnosis as it relates to this case example. Questions to consider include the following: Does this diagnosis represent a valid mental disorder from the social work perspective? Is this diagnosis significantly different from other possible diagnoses? Your critique should be based on the values of the social work profession (which are incongruent in some ways with the medical model) and the validity of the specific diagnostic criteria applied to this case.

Case 2   Off to the Races

Kelly is a 28-year-old married white female whose chief complaint is, "I can't stop eating." She loves foods rich in carbohydrates, such as sugar and flour, and claims that once she starts eating refined foods, she cannot stop (i.e., she loses the ability to control the size of her food portions). Her belief is that once she takes a bite of something that is sugary, "the bite takes me and I'm off to the races." She admits to eating when she is not hungry and reports that she eats quickly, "stuffing it into my face."

Kelly has struggled with food since she was nine years old. Kelly was always "over-weight as a child"; she is presently 5 feet 6 inches tall and weighs 200 pounds. She constantly obsesses about food, planning each day what she will eat and where she will obtain food. Often (at least four days a week) she will buy large quantities of ice cream and cake from the store, binge, and then sleep. When she wakes up, she feels depressed, guilty, and full of self-loathing. She often has crying jags because she feels so bad. When questioned, she denied any regular purging, but said that she resorted to laxatives "about once every two weeks."

In the past Kelly has attempted to lose weight. For example, when she was 10 years old she joined a recreational track team and was moderately successful in losing weight. However, although her weight began to normalize according to body mass index figures, Kelly would still binge on certain foods, such as pizza, pasta, and desserts. This pattern of behavior continued later during cross-country and cheerleading seasons. She recalls that despite the binge episodes, she would maintain a normal weight and sometimes would even weigh less than what was considered healthy for her height and frame, although she never met the criteria for anorexia. During off-seasons, when she was not participating in sports activities, however, her binge eating would result in significant weight gains.

Since her teenage years, Kelly has made multiple attempts to deal with her eating disorder. These include a "healthy" diet devised by a nutritionist; behavioral modifica-tions designed to moderate and control her intake of carbohydrate-rich foods; psycho-dynamically oriented psychotherapy to explore the causes that led to her binge eating; and CBT to examine her faulty thinking concerning food, body shape, and size. In her mid-20s she also admitted herself to a residential program that specialized in women and empowerment, and attended Overeaters Anonymous (OA), a 12-step support group for compulsive eaters.

There is a strong history of addiction-related disorders in Kelly's family, including alcoholism on the paternal side, and eating disorders, primarily binge eating, on the maternal side. Kelly's mother is a first-generation Italian immigrant who believes that food can be an "emotional comfort." Further, Kelly's mother suffered from bulimia herself; she exercised for weight compensation, even running marathons. Kelly's mother was also sexually abused by an uncle when she was a child.

Kelly has two sisters and three brothers, all of whom are obese. She is close to her sisters and less close to her brothers. All of the brothers exhibit alcoholism to varying degrees, as does her father. Additionally, some of the males in the extended paternal side of the family are described as "gutter" alcoholics.

Kelly's parents had an antagonistic relationship with each other during Kelly's forma-tive years, in which Kelly's father physically and sexually abused Kelly's mother; Kelly wit-nessed this abuse. Kelly's father works for the post office, while Kelly's mother is a school bus driver, placing the family as lower middle class. They are Catholic and attend mass regularly.

Upon graduating from high school, Kelly attended college, but after the first year, she switched to a community college in order to live at home. She told her family about her eating disorder and was able to derive some emotional support from her sisters and mother. She also attended OA meetings with her mother. Because she had to move to an-other state to attend graduate school, Kelly was lonely and would use both food and men to fill her emotional void. She also stopped going to OA.

As a result of meeting a man through a personal ad, she married within the year. She admitted that she didn't know him well because they had lived in different areas and had not spent much time together. After the wedding, Kelly discovered that her husband was controlling and verbally abusive. He ordered her around, wanted her to cater to his needs, and called her "fat" and "lazy with no willpower." Although Kelly admits that her husband "pushed and shoved her around" physically, when asked about physical abuse, Kelly became silent and repeatedly avoided talking about the subject.

Kelly recently learned that she was six weeks pregnant. In an attempt to abort the baby in utero, she repeatedly punched herself in the stomach (this was not successful) and used ipecac (an over-the-counter emetic often used by bulimic individuals) to purge after binge eating. She also felt suicidal. One day, she wrote a suicide note; placed the note beside her on the car seat in the garage, which was closed; and started the engine in an attempt to commit suicide through carbon monoxide poisoning. However, she then called one of her sisters, who was able to talk her out of the attempt.

Kelly is adamant about wanting a divorce but is concerned about her financial status. Although she has successfully completed graduate school, she has been unable to find a job. She admits that she feels too disgusted with herself even to try. "Who's going to want me when I look like this?" She feels incredibly ashamed of her appearance and her unsuccessful marriage.

Kelly made no friends at graduate school, and the phone contact she maintains with her family members is inadequate to meet her needs for social and emotional support. Kelly presents as a tearful, poorly groomed individual (her hair is not brushed, and she attended initial therapy sessions in baggy pants and an inside-out sweatshirt), with suicidal ideation because of her binge eating and deteriorating marital situation.

Please go to the Appendix for directions to this case.

Case 3 The Perfectionist

Tina, a 14-year-old biracial Asian American girl, was brought to outpatient therapy after her discharge from a two-week stay in an inpatient eating disorders unit. Six months previously, she had begun to restrict sweets and fats and drastically increased her exercise regimen (running an hour a day on average). In total, Tina lost 15 pounds from her unusually small 4-feet, 11-inch frame, bringing her weight down to 82 pounds. She had stopped menstruating for three months and had a low heart rate before her hospitalization, during which she was placed on a feeding tube and treated with an SSRI. During her hospital stay she gained 10 pounds.

Other symptoms that had developed prior to and after her hospitalization were a preoccupation with her hygiene and morning routine; she took an average of 90 minutes each morning to get ready, constantly redoing her hair and makeup. She denied that this preoccupation was due to a defect in her appearance; she just wanted to look "perfect." She didn't view these behaviors as excessive and said that all the girls at school spent a lot of time getting ready if they wanted to look good.

Additionally, if she didn't get straight As, she felt like a failure, became angry with herself, and withdrew into her room. She regularly stayed up until 2:00 A.M. doing her schoolwork until it was "perfect" or memorizing for exams until she could recite the material back word for word. She admitted that she told no one at school how much time she spent studying (six to seven hours a night) and acknowledged that by anyone's standards but her own and her father's, it was excessive.

Tina was still extremely preoccupied with her weight and shape after her hospitalization, as evidenced by her continuing restricted eating, exercising, and constant self-criticism. She often said to her mother, "I hate how I look. Do I look fat to you? Would you tell me if I did?" Her mother did not know how to respond to this "barrage of questions," and Tina remained unconvinced by her attempts at reassurance. Tina denied bingeing or purging, and her mother confirmed this report.

The above behaviors and ideas were not bothersome to Tina; in fact she didn't understand why her parents and psychiatrist were making such a fuss over them, as she had always been this way. "My father is a perfectionist, too," she said. Her parents were stymied by her behaviors and especially angered by her monopolization of the bathroom in the morning. Yelling at her, punishing her, reprimanding her—all came to naught. Tina was "stuck" in her behaviors despite her stated desire to change them. She worried constantly that she was fat and had a great deal of difficulty accepting the recommendation of continued weight gain.

Tina is the younger of two children and reports being close to her brother, three years her senior. Her parents are of mixed ethnicity; her father is a second-generation Korean and her mother is American. Both parents are intelligent and accomplished; her father is an academic scientist and her mother a pianist who limits herself to teaching students privately, having given up her career when the children were born. Tina's relatives lived across the United States, and she typically saw them only once a year. She said she doesn't feel particularly close to anyone in her extended family. Tina has never drunk alcohol or used drugs, and her parents report being social drinkers, which they define as an occasional glass of wine.

Tina's father is obsessed with being thin and in shape and gives her mixed messages about food. He wants her to eat, but is not unhappy that she eliminated "fatty, junk food" and is critical of "the American diet." His wife is of healthy weight, although she gained weight after having children. The household environment is conflicted, angry, and tense due to their marital problems, mostly about parenting differences. Tina's father is often critical of her mother for being too "permissive" with the children and for letting herself go. He feels that children are raised too loosely in the United States, whereas Tina's mother feels that he is too hard on them, often putting them down and calling them "lazy failures," among other pejorative terms. She also reported feeling very controlled by her husband's criticisms and demands. "Nothing I do is right." She reported having thoughts about leaving him many times, and he, too, often feels hopeless and resigned to a disappointing marriage. Tina's mother has a history of depression, which has been treated with medication in the past; her father has refused to consider the possibility of any emotional difficulties in himself.

In the initial session Tina spoke flatly, showing little expression and eye contact as she talked about what she had been through for the last six months. She gave minimal answers to questions and displayed little response to empathic statements made by the therapist. She said that art was an outlet for her and showed some energy when the therapist suggested she draw a picture in the session to indicate how she felt. When she talked about her drawing, she described feeling "trapped" and "frightened." When questioned further about these feelings, she said that she hated her family and felt no future for herself. Despite this statement, she said she had never felt suicidal or depressed. She also denied having been sexually abused.

Tina described having only one friend, a second-generation Korean girl her age, and said she wasn't interested in having a boyfriend. She said, "What's the point of a relationship? Look at my parents and how their marriage turned out." Tina liked participating in track and cross-country at school for the exercise it provided; she said that she liked long-distance running, although she never placed in races. She admitted that this made her feel like a "failure."

Please go to the Appendix for directions to this case.

PRACTICE TEST The following questions will test your knowledge of the content found within this chapter. For additional assessment, including licensing-exam type questions on applying chapter content to practice behaviors, visit **MySocialWorkLab.com**

1. Most people who present to treatment for eating disorders have what diagnosis?

   a. Anorexia

   b. Eating Disorder NOS

   c. Bulimia

   d. Binge Eating Disorder

2. What is true of the diagnosis of anorexia nervosa?

   a. Females can experience normal menstrual cycles

   b. The person continues to lose weight until becoming satisfied with his or her appearance

   c. The person cannot engage in purging behavior on a regular basis

   d. The person is significantly underweight according to health standards

3. Mayumi was a high school senior who sought help to get control of her purging behaviors. Two years ago she became obsessed with her weight, believing she needed to lose "about ten pounds." She watched her diet carefully and exercised daily, but she began eating cookies and cakes as well. Mayumi became concerned that this eating of sweets was getting out of her control, so she began purging through self-induced vomiting. In addition to the vomiting, Mayumi might also purge by which of the following means?

   a. Laxatives

   b. Exercise

   c. Cooking only low-calorie meals

   d. Avoiding sweets

4. Mayumi did lose weight but it never fell below the normal range for her height and build. She finally confided to several close friends that she was engaging in purging behavior about three times per week and needed help. An appropriate evidence-based intervention for Mayumi would be:

   a. A brief inpatient stay to get her weight fluctuations under control

   b. Individual psychodynamic therapy

   c. IPT

   d. Nutritional education

5. In the cases presented in this chapter, what role do you believe the comorbid mental health disorders played in the development of the eating disorders? Do you see any opportunities in these cases for intervention before the eating disorders developed?

6. Given that there are few empirically validated treatments found yet for AN, what factors will determine your decision making for appropriate treatment for a young adult woman who first presents with anorexia?

SUCCEED WITH

Visit **MySocialWorkLab** for more licensing-exam test questions, and to access case studies, videos, and much more.

13

Borderline Personality Disorders

Competencies Applied with Practice Behaviors — in this Chapter				
■ Professional Identity	■ Ethical Practice	■ Critical Thinking	■ Diversity in Practice	■ Human Rights & Justice
■ Research-Based Practice	✖ Human Behavior	■ Policy Practice	■ Practice Contexts	✖ Engage, Assess, Intervene, Evaluate

Kenda Starnes is a 19-year-old single Caucasian female referred to the mental health center by a housemate, a 42-year-old man named John. When John called the agency, he was told that he could not make an appointment on behalf of a nonrelative. "But she's threatening to kill herself," he pleaded. He added that Kenda had recently spent one week in a psychiatric hospital and was refusing to take the antidepressant medications the doctor had prescribed. "She won't listen to the doctor. She won't listen to me. She jerks everyone around, trying to get her way." John was about to arrange to have the discharge summary sent to this agency, but he apparently persuaded Kenda to call on her own behalf, because she contacted the social worker the next day.

Kenda came to her first appointment dressed casually and appeared her stated age. During the meeting she seemed uncomfortable and suspicious. Her affect was grim, and she rarely made eye contact. Kenda admitted to the social worker that she was in a lot of emotional pain. "I feel so lonely sometimes. I don't know if it will ever go away. I used to wish someone would rescue me, but really I don't think anyone understands me." Kenda added that she tried to stay active, to "keep my mind off myself," spending most of her time with John, his six-year-old daughter, and the two other young adult women who lived at the house. "All of us work as volunteer emergency medical technicians (EMTs) for the Fire Department. That's where we met. John had just gotten divorced and was looking for housemates."

Asked about her current relationships, Kenda said that she liked the other women in the house "OK" but didn't feel that she knew them very well. She was quick to say, "They're not trustworthy." She added, "John is divorced. He's just a friend to all of us." About that relationship, she said, "I don't know what he wants from me, but it's a place to stay.

Actually, I think he wants sex from me, but I don't like him that way. He's kind of creepy. But it's nice to have people around, even though they don't care much about me. In fact, it's terrible when I'm by myself." When asked to elaborate on that point, Kenda said, "I feel lonely all the time. I need people to be with me. Sometimes I feel I'm disintegrating when I'm alone, as though I'm just fading into nothingness. It's scary. It's why I hate to go to bed at night. I have to lie there alone in the dark and think. I get more and more afraid, because I'm so empty." Kenda admitted that she feels tired almost all the time, partly because of poor sleep but also because of "feeling frustrated so often."

When asked about other friends, Kenda said, "People don't like me. You can't trust them anyway. In fact, people are always letting me down. I don't do anything to hurt them, but they're always abandoning me when I need them the most. I call them and they can't talk, or I stop by their apartments and they're not home, even when they've said they would be. I don't know why people don't treat me better. I'm a good person."

Alarmingly, the hospital records, which arrived after the first visit, indicated that Kenda had been hospitalized 10 times in the year since her high school graduation. These inpatient stays were all precipitated by the onset of depression, fears of losing self-control, and the alarming anxiety she experienced when alone. The episodes often occurred during her chronically sleepless nights. The hospital report also indicated that Kenda was prone when upset to strike her fist into concrete walls. She had broken bones in her hand on at least five occasions by doing this. When the social worker asked about this, Kenda responded, "When I get upset, I have to do something. I'm afraid I'll lose control or fall apart. Sometimes when I hit the wall it brings me back down to earth." There was no history of any mental health intervention prior to her leaving her family's home.

Personality is a difficult concept to define. One noted theorist defined it as a stable set of tendencies and characteristics or thoughts, beliefs, and actions that have continuity over time (Maddi, 2007). The *Diagnostic and Statistical Manual of Mental Disorders* (DSM-IV) category of personality disorders represents an attempt to identify persons whose chronic problems in social functioning are related to ingrained patterns of thinking, behaving, and feeling. The idea of a personality as *disordered* is controversial, however (Millon & Grossman, 2006). Social workers should be concerned about using these diagnoses because they appear to describe the *total person*, rather than a particular aspect of the person or the result of person-in-environment processes. In this chapter we consider the concept of personality disorder and, more specifically, one personality disorder that is often encountered by clinical practitioners: the borderline type.

CHARACTERISTICS OF PERSONALITY DISORDERS

According to the American Psychiatric Association [APA] (2000), all of the personality disorders are characterized by enduring cognitions and behaviors that deviate from cultural standards, are pervasive and rigid, are stable over time, have an onset in adolescence or early adulthood, and lead to unhappiness and impairment. They must include maladaptive behavior in at least two of the following areas: *affect* (range and intensity of emotions), *cognition* (how the self and others are perceived), *impulse control*, and *interpersonal functioning*. The DSM-V Personality Disorders Work Group, however, is considering a revised focus on the "disturbance of self" and "interpersonal" domains (American Psychiatric Association [APA], 2010). The DSM classifies the personality disorders into three *clusters*, based on shared core characteristics. Cluster A includes the paranoid, schizoid, and schizotypal disorders. These disorders are believed to have a genetic base and are more common in the biological relatives of people with schizophrenia. People with these disorders are considered by others to be odd and eccentric. The cluster B disorders (anti-social, borderline, histrionic, and narcissistic) are characterized by dramatic, emotional, and erratic presentations. These disorders may have a partial genetic base, in that they have associations with other DSM Axis I disorders (such as substance abuse, mood, and somatic disorders). The cluster C disorders (avoidant, dependent, and obsessive-compulsive) feature anxious or fearful presentations and are associated with the anxiety disorders. It is estimated that about 9.1% of the adult U.S. population has a personality disorder (Lenzenweger, Lane, Loranger, & Kessler, 2007).

All personality disorder diagnoses are recorded on Axis II. The practitioner must be cautious about diagnosing a specific personality disorder, because there is much overlap among the symptoms of the different personality disorders (Skodol, 2005). If the social worker plans to focus intervention on the personality disorder, the term *principal diagnosis* should be included. The cluster A disorders may be specified as *premorbid* if they were present before the symptoms of the Axis I diagnosis (if the latter will be the primary focus of intervention).

The diagnosing clinician must make judgments about personality functioning in the context of the client's ethnic, cultural, and social background. Some cultures, for example, value interpersonal dependency more than others do. Disproportionately high rates of personality disorders are diagnosed in African American populations, but no such differences are evident among the Caucasian, Asian, and Hispanic populations (McGilloway, Hall, Lee, & Bhui, 2010). Hispanic clients have more symptoms reflecting anger, affective instability, and unstable relationships than Caucasians do. African Americans are more likely than Caucasians or Hispanics to be diagnosed with the paranoid and schizotypal personality disorders (Whaley, 2001).

Personality disorder diagnoses should rarely be applied to children and adolescents. Personality patterns are not considered to reach a state of constancy until late adolescence or young adulthood. Further, the diagnosis lacks validity in young people because many symptoms occur in the course of normal adolescence (Chabrol et al., 2004). To diagnose a personality disorder in a client under age 18, the symptoms must have been present for a full year.

Human Behavior

Practice Behavior Example: *Critique and apply knowledge to understand person and environment.*

Critical Thinking Question: What is your perspective on the issue of a personality being disordered? To what extent are one's personality characteristics related to their environments? To what extent is a personality fluid rather than rigid?

BORDERLINE PERSONALITY DISORDER

With this introduction we now move into a discussion of borderline personality disorder (BPD). Persons with this disorder are frequently encountered in clinical settings and are often difficult to engage in an intervention process. Many of the principles of assessment and intervention described here are also relevant to clients with other personality disorders, however.

BPD is characterized by a pattern of instability in interpersonal relationships and self-image and a capacity for frequent and intense negative emotions. Although there is disagreement about the core features of the disorder, most observers agree on the characteristics of *highly variable mood* and *impulsive behavior* (Hopwood & Zanarini, 2010).

PREVALENCE AND COMORBIDITY

BPD is a significant mental health problem present in many cultures around the world (Freeman, Stone, & Martin, 2005). A recent national study found that it can be diagnosed in 5.9% of adults, and it is the most common personality disorder found in clinical settings (Grant et al., 2008). BPD is diagnosed predominantly in women; the estimated gender ratio is 3:1 (Freeman et al., 2005). Actual population rates are comparable in women and men (Lenzenweger et al., 2007), but clinical samples include more women.

Many disorders are often comorbid with BPD. A majority (84.5%) of cases meet criteria for at least one Axis I disorder in the past year, and the mean number is 3.2 (Lenzenweger et al., 2007). The most commonly seen Axis I disorders include the mood, anxiety, and substance use disorders, with 29.4, 21.5, and 14.1% one-year comorbidity rates, respectively (Grant et al., 2008). There is overlap among the symptoms of the personality disorders as well, and BPD most often co-occurs with the antisocial and avoidant types (Grilo, Sanislow, & McGlashan, 2002).

Up to 55% of inpatients with BPD have a history of suicide attempts, and the actual suicide rate is between 5 and 10% (APA, 2000). Up to 80% have committed acts of self-mutilation (such as cutting the forearms or face). Studies have shown that nonsuicidal acts of self-mutilation are intended to express anger, punish oneself, generate normal feelings when experiencing depersonalization, or distract oneself from painful feelings (Brown, Comtois, & Linehan, 2002). The risk of suicide appears to be highest when clients are in their 20s. The presence of substance use has major implications for treatment, because clients with BPD who abuse substances generally have a poor outcome and are at higher risk for suicide and death or injury from accidents (Kolla, Eisenberg, & Links, 2008).

ASSESSMENT

Although general assessment guidelines for BPD are offered in Box 13.1, a particular challenge for assessment is to determine whether Axis I symptoms are circumscribed enough to justify a diagnosis of the disorder. When the practitioner combines an Axis I disorder with BPD, intervention should focus on both disorders, because the presence of BPD is a risk influence for recovery from an Axis I disorder (Livesley, 2004).

Depressive disorders are strongly associated with BPD. Features of depression that are particularly characteristic of BPD are emptiness, self-condemnation, abandonment fears, hopelessness, self-destructiveness, and repeated suicidal gestures (Berrocal, Moreno, Rando, Benvenuti, & Cassano, 2008). In this type of presentation, one would diagnose only BPD and not a separate major depressive disorder.

Box 13.1 • Assessment of BPD

- Do the client's presenting problems result from patterns of interaction with others?

- Are there recent stressors that may account for the client's symptom presentation? If so, is this an isolated situation or part of a general pattern?

- Is the client under the influence of any substances (alcohol, drugs, or medicine) that may account for the symptoms of anxiety and depression?

- Has the client's personality changed as a result of the presence of a medical condition (in which case the appropriate diagnosis would be a personality change due to a general medical condition)?

- Is there evidence of a history of hypomanic or manic episodes (which may suggest a diagnosis of bipolar disorder)?

- Is the client experiencing a major depressive episode? (Note that features of depression particularly characteristic of BPD are emptiness, self-condemnation, fears of abandonment, sense of hopelessness, self-destructiveness, and repeated suicidal gestures; these would not be diagnosed as a separate major depressive disorder but as indicative of BPD.)

- If the client is an older adolescent/young adult, are the identity concerns related to a developmental phase?

- If there are manipulative behaviors displayed by the client, are they related to a desire for nurturance or to a desire for power, profit, or personal gain?

Sources: Yen et al., 2004.

Kenda volunteered that she was the fourth of eight children (five girls and three boys) born to a Catholic couple, and the fourth girl. The family was lower middle class. Her father is a struggling furniture salesman. Her parents had a rural background and moved to their present suburban area when Kenda was a few years old. "My dad never felt accepted in the city, because we were country people. He seemed to take his frustrations out on me." Kenda added, "I was always the black sheep. I didn't do anything bad, but that's what my folks always told me. I was always getting yelled at for no reason. They used to get mad, saying I was a dangerous driver. I liked to drive my car fast, but I only did that late at night, and I never had a serious accident. It was fun, and I knew what I was doing. But no one in my family would ride with me. I used to like when people rode with me, because I liked to scare them." Kenda added that she was at best cordial with her family and had little contact with her parents and siblings. She described her parents as "mean." When pressed about this, Kenda shared that "My parents were together all the time and didn't pay much attention to us. We all had to raise ourselves." Kenda said that she moved out of the house the day after her high school graduation. "I stayed away from home as much as I could all through high school, and I couldn't wait to get away." Kenda stated again that she was frequently singled out as the family scapegoat. Her father in particular always criticized her and told the others that she was worthless. "He's like a lot of people, who don't want to give credit to me when it's due."

During the second interview Kenda was more verbal and the social worker learned more about her background. In high school Kenda showed remarkable athletic ability, starring on her high school's state championship softball team two years in a row. Another impressive accomplishment was her work on the town's volunteer rescue squad. Kenda developed an early interest in nursing and intentionally sought out the EMT position. She hoped to become a registered nurse one day. She admitted to being a bit of a daredevil as well, jumping off high cliffs into reservoirs and sometimes starting fights with other young women she didn't know "just for the excitement of seeing what happens."

Kenda smiled when she talked about her fights but downplayed her accomplishments, saying that "I'm not really good at anything. I don't have any skills. I'm kind of a nobody." Yet, beginning at the age of 18, Kenda had been making emergency squad runs, going to the sites of heart attacks and car accidents and participating in dramatic rescues. Further, she seemed to be very effective in that capacity. "I like to keep busy," she said. "I don't feel so good when I just sit around." Indeed, Kenda and her housemates worked long hours at the Fire Department, attended parties, played sports, and took weekend trips together. When asked if she took pride or pleasure in these activities, she replied, "No. I'm just filling time. If I stop doing things I feel so empty." Kenda did say that she missed a lot of work due to her inability to concentrate on external events and function interpersonally when she felt sad, frightened, or irritable. She usually missed several days of work each week and thus had an unsteady income, which was a concern to her.

Kenda suggested that her parents could provide the social worker with more accurate background information and invited the social worker to meet with them, as long as she didn't have to be present. The social worker had one meeting with her parents and was struck by their defensiveness. Her father said, "Whatever Kenda tells you, don't believe it. I always provided very well for her. We always had food on the table and clothes in the closet. I never cared that Kenda never appreciated anything, She was an ungrateful girl." Kenda's mother agreed that she was not one to nurture or be soft with her kids. She said, "Children cannot learn too early to stand on their own two feet, and I ran my household accordingly. They had to learn early to take care of themselves." The social worker gained the impression that Kenda's description of an emotionally cold household was accurate.

During the third assessment meeting, Kenda said again that she sometimes felt she deserved to be lonely, because "I'm a bad person," even though she was not able to elaborate on this point. At other times, however, she felt she was "an OK person." Kenda talked about a series of short-term relationships with boys during her last two years of high school, but she insisted that they were superficial. She never let her boyfriends get to know her well and was never physically intimate with them. She said, "They were always smothering me, wanting to be with me all the time, but who wants that? They all seemed nice at first, but then I realized I couldn't count on them for anything, and they eventually wanted sex. That's probably all they ever wanted. So we wound up having lots of arguments and I had to push them away." Still, Kenda said that she always had a new boyfriend within a few weeks of a breakup. She said, somewhat sarcastically, "It was a way for me to pass the time."

After this third visit, the social worker received a letter from Kenda detailing her history of sexual abuse by her father that spanned the ages of 5 through 17. She had never discussed these incidents with anyone. Kenda added that the incest was her own fault, proof that she was a bad person. The social worker asked Kenda why she had finally decided to tell her about the incest. Kenda said she had never trusted anyone and assumed that anyone who knew her secret would reject her. She perceived that the social worker was genuinely interested in her, although she admitted to feeling confused by the social worker's concern. "You're the best therapist I've ever known, and I'm really trusting you with something here. You'd better not let me down."

During the fourth meeting Kenda was again experiencing thoughts of death and fears of losing control. They began the process of writing up a treatment contract and plan, and the social worker arranged for Kenda to be seen by the agency physician for a medication evaluation. "I'll see him," Kenda said, but I've taken meds before and they never do anything for me."

Engage, Assess, Intervene, Evaluate

Practice Behavior Example: *Use empathy and other interpersonal skills.*

Critical Thinking Question: Clients with BPD are said to trigger some negative reactions in their social workers (anger, frustration, anxiety). What could you do to insure that such unavoidable feelings do not negatively affect your ability to empathize with, and feel positively toward, your clients? Would it be productive to share your reactions with the client?

Directions Part I, Multiaxial Diagnosis   Given the case information, prepare the following: a multiaxial diagnosis, the rationale for the diagnosis and global assessment of functioning score, and additional information you would have wanted to know in order to make a more accurate diagnosis.

Multiaxial Diagnosis

Axis I:
Axis II:
Axis III:
Axis IV:
Axis V:

Rationale and Differential Diagnosis

Additional Information Needed

BIOPSYCHOSOCIAL RISK AND RESILIENCE INFLUENCES

Onset

BPD most likely results from a combination of biological and environmental processes. It is approximately five times more common among first-degree biological relatives of those with the disorder than in the general population (APA, 2000). BPD also increases familial risk for substance abuse, antisocial personality, and mood disorders. Still, these risks may be related to environmental conditions as well as personal constitution. A recent large-scale study of the genetic and environmental risk influences among twins found that BPD appears to be approximately 38% genetic and 63% environmental (Kendler et al., 2008). Additional risks for people from oppressed and vulnerable populations are listed in Box 13.2.

Biological influences

The biological causes of BPD are speculative. Some of its symptoms (impulsivity, irritability, hypersensitivity, emotional lability, and intensity) are associated with a biological foundation. Researchers have studied the link between BPD and two neurotransmitters: serotonin (which is diminished) and norepinephrine (which is overactive) (Goodman, Triebwasser, & New, 2008). Serotonin has been linked to both external and self-directed aggression. As noted earlier, a relationship between the personality and affective disorders has long been argued (Mackinnon & Pies, 2006). Persons with BPD are said to have mood swings that resemble bipolar disorder (the interpersonal conflicts are a differentiating factor). Biological contributors to this process may include elevations of the person's catecholamines (neurotransmitters that mediate mood states and aggression) and dysfunctions in the locus coeruleus (used for information processing and memory), the amygdala in the limbic system (that manages fear and anxiety), and the hippocampus (a center of emotional experience) (Skodol et al., 2002).

Psychological influences

Although there is limited evidence to support their validity, psychodynamic theorists have produced a rich literature on persons with BPD (e.g., Clarkin, Yeomans, & Kernberg, 2006; Gabbard & Horowitz, 2009). These clients are said to have failed to negotiate successfully the delicate task of separating from primary caregivers while maintaining an internalized sense of being cared for. During infancy they either were or felt themselves to be

---

Box 13.2 • BPD in Vulnerable and Oppressed Populations

Youths

- Childhood history of neglect, abuse, loss, or lack of validation places youths at risk for development of BPD.[1]
- Ongoing sexual abuse in childhood is a major predictor of the severity of borderline syndromes.[2]

Females

- BPD is diagnosed more often in women,[3] although in a national study, rates were comparable for men and women living in the community.[4]
- Men with BPD are more likely to present with comorbid substance abuse disorders, whereas women are more likely to present with PTSD and eating disorders.[5]

Racial Minorities

- Hispanic persons have a disproportionately higher rate of BPD when compared with Caucasian and African American groups.[6]

Low Socioeconomic Status (SES)

- A background of poverty places a person with BPD at risk of lower success rates in the realms of intimacy and work because of additional stresses associated with low SES.[7]
- Out of all the personality disorders, BPD puts people at greatest risk for unemployment, which is associated with low SES.[8]

---

[1]Yen et al., 2004.
[2]Zanarini, Frankenburg, Reich, & Fitzmaurice, 2010.
[3]APA, 2000.
[4]Lenzenweger et al., 2007.
[5]Skodol et al., 2005.
[6]Skodol et al., 2005.
[7]Skodol et al., 2005.
[8]Lenzenweger et al., 2007.

abandoned. They feel that when a parent or other close attachment figure is not physically present or immediately available, he or she may be gone forever. The person often experiences intense separation anxiety as a result. For these reasons, the person carries into new relationships the sense that abandonment by significant others is always a real threat.

Social influences

Most empirical research shows a positive relationship between childhood trauma and borderline symptoms (Holm & Severinsson, 2008). Such trauma includes loss, sexual and physical violence, neglect, abuse, firsthand observation of domestic violence, and parental substance abuse or criminality. In general, clients with BPD report significantly more negative life events than do persons with other personality disorders or depression (Skodol et al., 2005). Ongoing sexual abuse in childhood is a major predictor of the severity of borderline syndromes (Schulte-Herbrüggen et al., 2009). Dissociative symptoms are positively associated with inconsistent treatment by a caregiver, sexual abuse by a caregiver, firsthand observation of sexual violence as a child, and an adult rape history (Zanarini & Jager-Hyman, 2009).

The role of childhood trauma as a risk mechanism also appears to be related to the person's biological sensitivity to environmental stimuli. This mechanism is thought to act through the neurotransmitters described earlier during the person's physical development. In studies of predictor variables for the BPD diagnosis, *interpersonal sensitivity* emerged as most significant (Gratz, Tull, & Gunderson, 2008). Sensitivity to intense experiences of negative emotions may be a stronger predictor of the disorder than childhood sexual abuse. When experiencing intense emotions, persons with this disorder tend to lose their sensitivity to the feelings of others (Bland, Williams, Scharer, & Manning, 2004). This may produce a situation in which the person uses impulsive and self-destructive behavior to manage the stress related to his or her hypersensitive reactions to negative stimuli.

Another risk influence for BPD is the familial structure of Western society, in which the upbringing of most children is limited to one or two primary caregivers, without other consistent parent figures to assist when these caregivers prove to be inadequate (Millon, 2010). This is in contrast to some cultural groups where extended family routinely provide major parenting roles.

Course and Recovery

Long-term studies of clients with BPD indicate that its course is variable (Zanarini et al., 2010) (See Table 13.1). The person's early adulthood is often characterized by instability, episodes of affective and impulse control problems, and high usage of general health and mental health resources. One study of young adults found that BPD predicted negative outcomes in the areas of academic achievement and social maladjustment over the subsequent two years, regardless of the presence of any other diagnoses (Bagge et al., 2004).

There is some evidence, however, that the course of BPD is more benign than formerly believed, in part because of the availability of effective interventions (Fonagy & Bateman, 2006). Later in life, a majority of individuals with the disorder attain greater stability in social and occupational functioning, even in the absence of intervention, in part because their acting-out symptoms tend to decrease (Himelick & Walsh, 2002). It has also been found that the symptoms of this disorder may wax and wane throughout its course. In a longitudinal study of clients with a variety of personality disorders, affective instability and inappropriate anger were the most stable characteristics over a two-year span for persons with BPD, whereas self-injury and efforts to avoid abandonment were the least stable (Skodol et al., 2005).

Longitudinal studies also indicate that about one third of clients with BPD appear to recover from the disorder within 10 years after initial diagnosis, solidifying their identities and replacing self-damaging acts with modulated behavior patterns (Zanarini et al., 2010). After 10 years of intervention, 50% of clients no longer meet the full criteria for the disorder. Studies of hospitalized clients with BPD indicate that even though they may gradually

Table 13.1   Risk and Resilience Influences for Course of the Disorder

Risk influences	Resilience influences
Biological	
Estimated 37% genetic heritability	Healthy prenatal environment
Sensitive temperament	
Elevated risk of mood disorders among first-degree relatives	
Psychological	
Attachment deficits	Resolution of attachment issues, childhood trauma, and neglect
Abuse, neglect	
Chaotic family environment	Absence of substance use
Presence of a comorbid disorder	Major symptoms: self-injury, efforts to avoid abandonment
Substance use	
Major symptoms: higher levels of affective instability, identity disturbance, and impulsivity	Stable family environment
Social	
Invalidating early environment	Structured lifestyle
Lack of structure in daily life	Some stable relationships
Failure to establish relationships with others	High academic achievement
Absence of enduring relationships	Stable occupational functioning
Poor academic achievement	Absence of poverty conditions
Poor occupational functioning	
Living in poverty	

Sources: Bagge et al., 2004; Fonagy & Bateman, 2006; Livesley, 2004; Paris, 2003; Skodol et al., 2005; Zanarini et al., 2010.

attain functional roles 10 to 15 years after admission to psychiatric facilities, only about 50% of the women and 25% of the men will have attained enduring success in intimacy (as indicated by marriage or long-term partnership) (Paris, 2003). From 50 to 75% of clients will have achieved stable, full-time employment by that time. Clients with the disorder from backgrounds of poverty may have substantially lower success rates in the spheres of intimacy and work because of the additional stresses associated with that condition. Clients with comorbid drug use disorders have a higher risk of suicide attempts, as do those with affective instability, identity disturbance, and impulsivity (Skodol et al., 2005).

Human Behavior

Practice Behavior Example: *Utilize conceptual frameworks to guide the processes of assessment, intervention, and evaluation.*

Critical Thinking Question: What changes in Kenda's social environment might facilitate recovery from her major symptoms? Would any changes in her major symptoms likely be lasting?

Directions Part II, Biopsychosocial Risk and Resilience Assessment   Using Table 13.1 formulate a risk and resilience assessment, both for the onset of the disorder and the course of the disorder, including the strengths that you see for this individual. What techniques could you use to elicit additional strengths in this client?

INTERVENTION

Clients with BPD show a greater lifetime use of most categories of medication, and most types of psychotherapy, than clients with other personality disorders or major depressive disorder (Zanarini, Frankenburg, Hennen, Reich, & Silk, 2004). According to the National Comorbidity Replication Survey, 42.4% of those with BPD were in treatment during the past year (Lenzenweger et al., 2007). Still, it is challenging for practitioners to engage them in a sustained process of intervention. It is estimated that 40 to 60% of these clients drop out of intervention prematurely (Marziali, 2002). Further, there is a dearth of empirically validated methods of intervention, although psychodynamic writers have theorized extensively about clinical intervention (Levy & Ablon, 2009). Much of this literature is case studies and small samples.

Between 1974 and 1998, 15 clinical studies that included pre- and posttreatment effects were conducted (Perry, Banon, & Ianni, 1999). All of the studies were based on psychodynamic, interpersonal, cognitive-behavioral, and supportive therapies and reported positive outcomes. Four studies focused specifically on BPD, and although all of these had limitations, their pooled results indicate a 25% recovery rate per year for clients receiving intervention. This finding about the utility of a variety of interventions for persons with BPD has been supported more recently for cognitive therapy (Wenzel, Chapman, Newman, Back, & Brown, 2006) and interpersonal therapy (Markowitz, Bleiberg, Pessin, & Skodol, 2007). Psychodynamic approaches will be discussed later.

In standard interventions the practitioner establishes and maintains a therapeutic alliance, responds to crises, monitors the client's safety, provides education about the disorder, offers consistent supportive or insight-oriented therapy, and coordinates interventions by other providers (Livesley, 2004). In one research study, clients and practitioners alike emphasized the theme of trust as crucial for the establishment and maintenance of a therapeutic relationship (Langley & Klopper, 2005). In his review of outcome studies, Livesley (2004) concluded that comprehensive intervention in BPD requires an array of interventions from different therapeutic models, delivered in a coordinated way. The practitioner must be able to build an effective alliance with the client and then treat both the core interpersonal pathology and the various behavioral manifestations of the disorder. Group interventions are often productive for persons with BPD (Marziali, 2002). They can provide opportunities for identification with other members, more opportunities for learning and experimenting with new patterns of behaviors, and opportunities to provide and receive empathic feedback in a supportive environment.

Because of clients' labile moods, changing motivation, and self-harm tendencies, many practitioners establish an explicit "contract" agreement with the client about how the relationship will proceed (Levy, Hay, & Bennett, 2006). The contract should address the timing and frequency of sessions; plans for crisis management; the practitioner's after-hours availability (if any); and expectations about scheduling, attendance, and payment. Because of the client's potential for impulsive behavior, practitioners must be comfortable with setting limits on self-destructive behaviors.

Psychosocial Interventions

While validating clients' suffering, practitioners must also help them take appropriate responsibility for their actions. Effective intervention helps clients realize that although they are not responsible for their past traumas, they are responsible for controlling self-destructive patterns in the present and future (Ryle, 2004). Interpretations of here and now behavior as it links to events in the past are useful for helping clients learn about their repetitive and maladaptive behavior patterns. As previously noted, splitting is a major defense mechanism of clients with BPD. Intervention must be geared toward helping the client begin to experience the shades of gray between these extremes and integrate the positive and negative aspects of the self and others.

Some clients with BPD may need to be seen in protective environments, usually for short periods of time until their mood symptoms stabilize. Indications for partial or brief hospitalization include dangerous, impulsive behavior that cannot be managed in an out-patient setting; nonadherence to outpatient intervention and a deteriorating clinical pic-ture; complex comorbidity that requires intensive assessment of response to intervention; symptoms that significantly interfere with functioning and are unresponsive to outpatient intervention; and transient psychotic episodes associated with a loss of impulse control or impaired judgment (Friedman, 2008).

Psychodynamic intervention

Psychodynamic interventions involve careful attention to the therapist–client relationship with thoughtfully timed interpretations of the client's transference. They draw from the theoretical perspectives of ego psychology, object relations, and self-psychology. Psycho-dynamic intervention is usually conceptualized as operating on an exploratory-supportive continuum of interventions (Berzoff, 2007). On the supportive end of the continuum, goals involve the strengthening of defenses and self-esteem, validation of feelings, internalization of the therapeutic relationship, and development of a greater capacity to cope with disturb-ing feelings. At the exploratory end of the continuum the goals are to make unconscious patterns more consciously available, increase affect tolerance, build a capacity to delay im-pulsive action, provide insight into relationship problems, and develop reflective functioning toward a greater appreciation of internal motivation in the self and others. A meta-analysis of psychological therapies for BPD showed that psychodynamic interventions lower levels of anxiety and depression and reduce use of medications (Binks et al., 2006b).

A form of psychodynamic intervention known as mentalization-based treatment (MBT) consists of 18 months of individual and group therapy provided by a supervised team of professionals (Bateman & Fonagy, 2008). A primary theme of the program is that client behavior must be understood in terms of underlying mental states, and the focus of therapy is the client's moment-to-moment state of mind. The client and practitioner col-laboratively generate alternate perspectives on the client's experience of himself or herself and others by moving from validating and supportive interventions to exploring the prac-tice relationship itself. MBT was found superior to "treatment as usual" in an eight-year, randomized controlled study involving 41 clients. Participants were assessed at three times following the completion of treatment on measures of suicidality, symptoms scales, BPD rating scales, and global assessment of functioning, and significant differences were found between the groups.

Dialectical behavior therapy

This intervention approach assumes that the client's core difficulty is one of affective in-stability (Linehan, 1993; Robins & Chatman, 2002). Dialectical behavior therapy (DBT) is based on cognitive-behavioral and learning theories and is an intensive, one-year outpatient intervention that combines weekly individual sessions with skills-training groups. The purposes of the groups are to teach adaptive coping skills in the areas of emotional regulation, distress tolerance, interpersonal effectiveness, and identity con-fusion, and to correct maladaptive cognitions. The individual interventions, provided by the same practitioner, address maladaptive behaviors while strengthening and gen-eralizing coping skills. Some client–practitioner phone contact is permitted between sessions for support and crisis intervention. An important component of DBT is the consultation team, which can help the practitioner maintain objectivity during the often intensive intervention process.

DBT can be considered a well-established intervention for a client with BPD as evidenced by seven randomized clinical trials across four different research teams (Lynch, Chapman, & Rosenthal, 2006). Another summary of studies that compared DBT with other treatments indicated that DBT is more effective than less structured interventions in reducing client suicidality, although overall outcome differences were modest (Binks et al., 2006a). A more recent meta-analysis of 16 randomized studies concluded as well that DBT had a moderate effect on reducing participants' self-injurious and suicidal behaviors (Kliem, Kröger, & Kosfelder, 2010). The same study found a 27% dropout rate, however, across studies. Finally, a 12-week psychoeducational family intervention program based on the DBT model has been developed for parents and spouses, family member burden and grief, as well as increased coping skills for family members (Fruzzetti & Boulanger, 2005).

Engage, Assess, Intervene, Evaluate

Practice Behavior Example: Use empathy and other interpersonal skills.

Critical Thinking Question: Clients with BPD frequently drop out of treatment due to their changing moods and motivations. What preventive strategies might the social worker offer? To what extent should the social worker provide outreach to those clients who repeatedly engage in that behavior?

Medications

Many clients with BPD receive medications to help manage their symptoms of depression, suicidal ideation, anger, and impulsive behavior. In fact, because of their problematic behaviors and frequency of comorbid symptoms, clients with BPD are prescribed more psychotropic medications than are other psychiatric outpatients (Sansone, Rytwinski, & Gaither, 2003). Medications generally target cognitive symptoms, mood lability, and impulsivity. Prescribing effective medications is difficult, however, because of the disorder's symptom heterogeneity, diagnostic unreliability, presence of comorbid disorders, and potential for self-destructiveness.

Only 40 to 50 studies have been done on the drug treatment of BPD, and drug effects are modest (Soloff, 2005). In a recent meta-analysis of the effects of various medications on the symptoms of anger and depression, however, it was found that the class of mood stabilizers had a significant positive effect on both symptoms (Mercer, Douglass, & Links, 2009). Antidepressant and antipsychotic (especially aripiprazole) medications had positive effects on anger, but not depression.

Several other meta-analyses of comparison group studies support the above points. One such study found that selective serotonin reuptake inhibitors (SSRIs) (particularly fluoxetine) appear to be helpful in reducing anger and hostility, but that haloperidol may be a better choice for controlling hostility and psychotic symptoms (Binks et al., 2006b). Another meta-analysis of 22 randomized, placebo-controlled clinical trials concluded that antidepressant and mood-stabilizing drugs were mildly effective against affective instability and anger but did not produce significant benefits in relation to impulsivity, aggression, unstable relationships, suicidal ideation, and global functioning (Nose, Cipriani, Biancosino, Grassi, & Barbui, 2006). Antipsychotic drugs as a class had a positive effect in terms of impulsivity, aggression, interpersonal relationships, and global functioning.

Directions Part III, Goal Setting and Treatment Planning   Given your risk and resilience assessment of the individual, your knowledge of the disorder, and evidence-based practice guidelines, formulate goals and a possible treatment plan for this individual.

CRITICAL PERSPECTIVE

BPD, like all of the personality disorders, is a highly problematic diagnostic category. First, it is based on a concept (personality) that is itself difficult to capture. Second, a personality disorder is supposed to represent an enduring pattern of experience and behavior. However, the DSM does not specify how long the pattern needs to persist. Without stating a time frame, clinicians may make a diagnosis without a history of interactions with the client. Specifically, the BPD diagnosis lacks strong validity and reliability in research studies (Skodol et al., 2005). Different clients with this diagnosis may have quite different symptom clusters and as a result present very differently to practitioners. Indeed, considering the different symptoms, people can meet the criteria in 126 different ways (Asnaani, Chelminski, Young, & Zimmerman, 2007). Further, because one's *personality* is synonymous with the *person*, the diagnosis seems to present practitioners with an ethical dilemma in reinforcing a deficits perspective on human functioning.

Third, some researchers and theorists believe that personality disorders would be more legitimately conceptualized as *dimensional* rather than categorical (Skodol et al., 2005). That is, clients should be assessed with regard to the functionality of each one of a stable set of common personality traits, rather than as having a disorder relating to all of them. In other words, personality disorders could be redefined as sets of generally stable personality traits with intermittent symptomatic behaviors tied to some of these traits. Such a conceptual shift would also create a diagnostic practice that was less stigmatizing to clients.

Finally, and related to the previous criticism, the division in the DSM between Axis I disorders and Axis II personality disorders seems somewhat arbitrary. Originally, this division was based on psychodynamic notions, although now the DSM promotes itself as an atheoretical manual. More recently, the National Comorbidity Replication Survey results showed that impairment displayed by people with personality disorders was due largely to a high number of Axis I disorders in such persons rather than the effect of the personality disorder itself (Lenzenweger et al., 2007). This evidence of frequent Axis I comorbidity further raises questions about the separation of personality disorders from Axis I disorders in the DSM nomenclature.

In spite of these concerns, clients with symptoms of BPD have very real, ongoing problems, and practitioners should remain committed to working with them so that they can achieve their goals of improved relationships and social integration.

> **Directions Part IV, Critical Perspective**   Formulate a critique of the diagnosis as it relates to this case example. Questions to consider include the following: Does this diagnosis represent a valid mental disorder from the social work perspective? Is this diagnosis significantly different from other possible diagnoses? your critique should be based on the values of the social work profession (which are incongruent in some ways with the medical model) and the validity of the specific diagnostic criteria applied to this case.

Case 2   The Only Child

Marcy is a 36-year-old Caucasian woman who came to the women's counseling center several weeks ago reporting feelings of anger and "wanting an outlet to vent" about several of her relationships. She has never seen a psychiatrist or counselor before coming to the counseling center.

Marcy's childhood years were riddled with stresses. Her mother, Gloria, was "beauti-ful," "high-spirited," "highly dramatic," and an alcoholic. Her father, Michael, was (and remains, accordingly to Marcy) emotionally immature and ineffectual in his career, parent-ing, and many of his relationships. He was emotionally bereft over the marriage's dissolu-tion, which came about because of Gloria's drinking. The couple divorced when Marcy was two years old.

Marcy was an only child, and when her parents divorced she remained in her mother's custody. Gloria's addiction caused a rapid deterioration in her physical and emotional state, to the extent that when Michael's mother (Marcy's paternal grand-mother) came to visit several years later, after not having seen her granddaughter in several months, she found Marcy emaciated with sores over much of her body. Marcy's paternal grandparents took temporary custody of her but made it clear to Gloria that they wanted her "to get herself together" so that Marcy could eventually return to her mother. Her grandparents described Marcy as a "difficult child," in that she cried easily and was hard to soothe. Gloria's former in-laws ended up paying for two lengthy stays in a drug and alcohol rehabilitation center for Gloria; however, she was unable to stop drinking.

Within several years of Marcy's arrival in their lives, her grandparents sought perma-nent legal custody through the judicial system to facilitate certain decisions for Marcy, such as schooling and medical care. But they still hoped Gloria would "dry out" and "get herself together" so that she and Marcy could be together again. These hopes were dashed when Gloria died in a Las Vegas hotel room, "unintentionally drinking herself to death," when Marcy was ten.

It is clear that from the time Marcy's grandparents took custody of her, they were her primary caregivers. She refers to them as Mom and Dad and refers to her biological father (Michael) as "the big kid." Michael, who also lived with his parents through much of the rest of Marcy's childhood, was always in the background of her life. He took no visible parenting role, for which Marcy continues to hold him in contempt.

Three years ago Marcy married a man named Zach, six years her junior. Marcy has no female friends and professes to dislike most women strongly. She rarely drinks alcohol and no longer uses illicit substances, as she fears she may have inherited a propensity toward addiction from her mother. She admitted to drinking "a great deal," and doing her "fair share of drugs" in college, but she now avoids drugs and (mostly) alcohol. She admits to impulsivity in "binge shopping," but the behavior does not appear to cause marital strife, presumably because her grandmother continues to allow Marcy to use her credit cards at several fine department stores.

Marcy admits to a lengthy history of instability in her interpersonal relationships, dating back to when she was in high school, until she married. Whenever she became convinced that a boyfriend was going to leave her, she would "beg and humiliate her-self." If that didn't work, she said, she would "dump him before he could do it to me." Her romantic relationships prior to her marriage lasted for six months at the most.

At some point in college, she reported "getting really skinny. It was great! I would run a few miles a day, eat next to nothing, and drink my dinner at bars every night." She was not diagnosed or treated for an eating disorder, and the behavior seemed to resolve itself after graduation.

Marcy acknowledges that she goes through periods of feeling profoundly depressed, empty, and abandoned, no matter how her husband Zach tries to console her. She fears that "something," by which she means death, will "happen to my husband." In the ses-sion she emphasized loudly, "I would kill myself if anything happened to my Zach. He's my world. He fills me up. Every day, I live for the moment he gets home from work. I get so lonely and depressed whenever I am apart from him." She then quickly asserted, "He knows better than to have an affair. I would throw him out, scratch his eyes out, and liter-ally cut the crotches of every pair of pants he owns. He knows better than to fuck with me. I'd make him wish he'd never been born!"

Marcy claims she and her husband are very happy and do everything together. They have no outside friends but feel that their family (of two dogs and a cat) is their world. When Marcy mentioned that she had thrown a party for her husband recently on his birthday, the social worker asked who was invited. Marcy retorted that it was only she and Zach and their animals. "Why the hell would I want to invite anyone else? Zach is my world."

Early in Marcy's counseling, she confided that until very recently, she was quite close to her husband's sister, Jessica, but that she had flown into a rage when Jessica apparently set personal boundaries related to Marcy's unsolicited and disparaging advice about Jessica's new boyfriend, whom Marcy had never met. Marcy felt disrespected, that Jessica was "treating me like a neighbor, not like a sister. I hate her. I hate all of my husband's family. Zach and I decided it's just us against the world, and I am fine with that. We don't need anyone else." Since then the two women have "made up," and Marcy has changed her perception of Jessica to one of adoration and admiration. "I can't live without my sister." She also has fluctuated between adoration and devaluation of her mother-in-law during her short tenure at the counseling center.

Marcy says that she made clear to her husband's family when she and Zach became engaged that once her grandparents were gone, she was completely alone and she expected them to be her family. She forbade them to refer to her as an "in-law," stated that she was their daughter or sister, and declared that she wanted a family with whom she could be "naked and vulnerable."

Marcy readily acknowledges that her feelings about people are very "all or nothing," that she "is pretty honest," that she "either loves you or hates you," a quality she highly values in herself.

Marcy has been fired from two jobs in the past two years. Marcy's version of events is, "They're all a bunch of assholes anyway, who set me up to fail from the beginning." She is not receptive to seeing any other possible interpretation and denies the possibility that she may have had any culpability in the outcomes.

Three months ago Marcy secured a software training position that allows her to work from home, which minimizes her interpersonal actions with supervisors and coworkers. This arrangement has apparently worked out quite well for her. Some strife and friction occurred recently, however, in her relationships with her employers and coworkers, with whom she deals primarily via e-mail, telephone, and biweekly meetings. Concurrently, Marcy was under significantly increased stress with a heavy travel and training schedule.

Marcy exhibits remarkably little insight into her behavior, and her husband appears to align with Marcy's interpretations in all instances, whether regarding her troubled career path or her relationships with coworkers, former friends, or even his sister. Marcy acknowledges that early in their relationship, she demanded that of him (as she did of her grandmother): "You are either with me or you are against me. I mean, if I can't count on him to side with me no matter what, who can I count on?"

Please go to the Appendix for directions to this case.

Case 3   The "Passive" Waitress

Erica is a 23-year-old single Jewish Caucasian woman who says she's "devastated" over her recent breakup with her boyfriend and her sudden relocation to Virginia from Florida two months ago. She is currently staying with her sister and her sister's fiancé in a suburb of Washington, D.C., while she assesses her future. Their relationship is contentious; Erica feels "controlled by her sister," who she says "nags" her to "clean" around the house and "judges" her when she spends money going clubbing with her new friends instead of on groceries for the household. Erica admits that her sister feels she abuses her hospitality.

Erica graduated from college a year ago with a degree in criminal justice, which is a field she claims to feel "passionate" about. After graduation, Erica spent June in Europe with her father. Upon returning to the United States she began an intimate relationship with a man who had recently been released from prison and needed a place to stay. She allowed him to move into her apartment and paid for his room and board over the summer, using her father's credit card to pay for their expenses. In early September, upon realizing that the man was cheating on her, she abruptly moved out and came to Virginia because she wanted "to show him that I didn't care" and because "I wanted to escape." At the same time, her father cut off her access to his credit card. Currently, her mother is helping her with basic expenses but is threatening to stop supporting her as well. Her sister has given her a deadline of two months to move out on her own.

Erica details a history of unstable relationships and making "unhealthy" choices in her relationships, with men in particular. She had a boyfriend throughout high school, by whom she became pregnant twice (she aborted in each case) and comments that he was similar in character to her most recent boyfriend. She remained emotionally involved in that relationship throughout college. She is puzzled by the men she dates, stating, "I don't know why I always like the guys that I know my father won't approve of." Erica remained sexually active in college, "You know, getting drunk and sleeping with guys I didn't even know," but did not have a monogamous relationship with anyone. She has been in "almost daily" phone contact with a young African American man who lives in New Jersey whom she met two years ago over spring break. Despite admitting that this man "has some problems"—he still lives at home, is in debt, is a heavy drinker, dropped out of college, and never comes to see her (she always drives to see him)—she has strong feelings for him and is considering moving to New Jersey to be near him.

She now holds a part-time job waiting tables at an area bar, for which she receives no health insurance. After one week at her new job, she began dating one of the waiters, a 27-year-old African American male who has a four-year-old daughter. Erica states that she wants to "take it slow," yet she is already intensely emotional about the course of the relationship and had sex with him within their first week of dating. She says "she just knows" they are supposed to be together. She worries about what her family will think of these relationships, because they want her to marry a white Jewish man.

Erica grew up in Miami, Florida, the younger of two sisters. Her parents divorced when she was six years old and shared custody of her. She denies any history of sexual or physical abuse. Her father fought her mother over child support for many years, and money is a controlling force in Erica's relationship with her father. Erica has "many issues" with her father, and her feelings about him tend to shift. When he is financing her lifestyle, he is a "good guy." When she does something he does not approve of, he cuts off contact with her and she views him as "Castro." She repeatedly asked the social worker if her father is to blame for her problems.

Erica chose to live with her father and his new wife and stepchildren through most of her high school years, because his rules and supervision were much more lax than those of her mother. She used marijuana heavily throughout high school and began using other drugs (alcohol, Ecstasy, cocaine, acid) extensively in college. In her junior year in college Erica started experiencing panic attacks and was unable to attend classes. She was given paroxetine, which she took for six months, and her symptoms alleviated. She said her doctor told her the panic attacks could have been caused by her recreational drug use. She denies current drug use at this time and continues to drink socially. She is no longer taking any psychoactive medications and stated a strong aversion to taking any at this time. She declined to see the staff psychiatrist for a consultation.

Erica describes a close and supportive relationship with her mother. She says she has a similar personality to her mother and that they are both "passive," although she wasn't able to provide any details about what this meant. She believes her father resents her because she is so much like her mother. Erica reports that her mother suffered from major depression for over two years after breaking up with a long-term boyfriend and was finally helped through therapy. Her mother is currently remarried and has stepchildren much younger than Erica.

Erica's mother sent her to therapy numerous times when she was growing up, blaming Erica's problems on the divorce. Erica has little recollection of the therapy and usually stopped attending after only a few visits. She reports several traumatic events in her life thus far: having a driver on her street pull out a gun at her and her mother while at a stop sign when she was in the fifth grade; allowing gang members to come to a party held at her mother's house (while her mother was away), which resulted in the house being robbed; and undergoing two abortions while in high school.

Erica says she doesn't think about these past events in more than fleeting ways, and she doesn't have bad dreams about them. She recounted the events in detail and did not, in session, seem to be avoiding memories of them. Erica states that while she has thought about "what it would be like if I was no longer here," she has never had suicidal ideation with a plan or intent to carry it out.

Erica is an intelligent young woman with an engaging and outgoing personality and a good sense of humor. When asked how these traits were "passive," as she had described herself earlier, Erica wasn't able to reconcile these aspects of herself. Erica admits to having very low self-esteem and no sense of "who I am" beyond what others identify for her. Her values and goals change from day to day depending on whom she is talking to. She describes herself as "too generous and kind," but has strong expectations about what she must get in return for her nurturance of others.

Erica states that she has a group of close friends in Florida with whom she maintains contact, but she is reluctant to move back to Florida because of their negative influence on her life (excessive partying). Still, she is bored in Virginia and "just wants to go out and have some fun." She says she goes clubbing with her coworkers most nights after work and likes the restaurant trade for that reason; there is typically an instant social life attached to it. She says she feels bored and empty when she stays home at night and then usually spends her time talking on the phone to the young man in New Jersey or her friends in Florida. She says she feels restless, tense, and "empty" when there is no one in the house and she is alone. Because she doesn't like feeling this way, she says that she avoids the feelings by being with other people as much as possible and talks on the phone almost constantly when she is by herself. She states that one of the reasons she moved to Virginia is that she didn't want to live by herself in the apartment after she broke up with her boyfriend.

Erica believes that money would answer all of her problems and yearns for life in college when she could do whatever she wanted and her father paid her expenses. She has little insight into her pattern of behaviors in relationships and seeks therapy hoping that the social worker can advise her "what to do." Erica identifies "figuring out what I want to do with my life" as her major goal and is also interested in having a "healthy relationship." Erica has committed to only eight therapy sessions because of her financial situation, and since beginning therapy two months ago she has either missed or rescheduled half her appointments, allegedly due to work conflicts.

Erica completed a Beck's Assessment for depression and scored a 19 out of 60, putting her in the low-depression range. She denied insomnia, decreased or increased appetite, lack of energy, an inability to concentrate, or recurrent thoughts of death. When asked about episodes of major depression in the past, she said she has sometimes "felt depressed" but can "snap out of it" if she talks to a boyfriend or meets someone new.

Please go to the Appendix for directions to this case.

PRACTICE TEST

The following questions will test your knowledge of the content found within this chapter. For additional assessment, including licensing-exam type questions on applying chapter content to practice behaviors, visit **MySocialWorkLab.com**

1. Which of the following is NOT true about BPD?

   a. Women receive treatment more than men do

   b. Rates of BPD are comparable between men and women in the community

   c. If criteria for BPD is met, it is usually the only diagnosis a client will receive

   d. The course of BPD may be more benign than has been generally believed

2. Critiques of personality disorders include the following EXCEPT:

   a. Social workers don't believe in personality disorders

   b. Personality disorders originally were developed from psychodynamic theory and so may have limited usefulness in a manual that is now atheoretical

   c. The distinction between Axis I and Axis II disorders is not clear

   d. People may recover from personality disorders

3. Anna was a 46-year-old woman with medical diagnoses of hypertension and arthritis who was admitted to a center for rehabilitative services. A pattern emerged that whenever Anna made gains, she sabotaged her progress by

   complaining of anxiety, stress, depression, and a lack of support from staff and residents. She had a poor tolerance of being alone, a pervasive sense of emptiness, and fears of abandonment. Her fears of progressing in the facility were indicators of her need to remain involved with an attentive staff. Anna's moods were prone to change abruptly, as were her attitudes toward other persons. Which of the following is a symptom of Anna's personality disorder?

   a. Severe interpersonal disturbances

   b. Medical problems

   c. Poor occupational functioning

   d. Cognitive distortions

4. Anna agreed to accept psychological counseling services while in the facility, but she disapproved of five separate counselors who arranged to meet with her. The social worker was reluctant to refer to a DBT program, due to his concerns about:

   a. Her problems with emotional regulation

   b. Her motivation to persist in treatment

   c. Her ability to communicate verbally

   d. Her absence of personal strengths

5. Consider the three clients described in this chapter. What symptoms of BPD are common to all of them? In what ways are they distinct from each other? Which of the symptoms appear to cause their most serious problems in everyday life?

6. The symptoms of personality disorders are spread out among many other Axis I diagnostic categories. Do you think this diagnosis is valid, or can the symptoms be "captured" just as well by existing diagnostic categories?

SUCCEED WITH

Visit **MySocialWorkLab** for more licensing-exam test questions, and to access case studies, videos, and much more.

Appendix

CASE WORKBOOK

Please copy and use these workbook pages for the second and third cases in each chapter.

Directions Part I, Multiaxial Diagnosis   Given the case information, prepare the following: a multiaxial diagnosis, the rationale for the diagnosis, global assessment of functioning score, and additional information you would have wanted to know in order to make a more accurate diagnosis.

Multiaxial Diagnosis

Axis I:

Axis II:

Axis III:

Axis IV:

Axis V:

Rationale

Additional Information Needed

Directions Part II, Strengths-Based Assessment   Using Tables 1 & 2, formulate a risk and resilience assessment, both for the onset of the disorder and for the course of the disorder. What additional techniques could you use to elicit strengths in this client and how would you use them?

Table 1   Biopsychosocial Risk and Resilience Assessment for the Onset of the Disorder

Risk influences	Protective influences
Biological	
Psychological	
Social	

Table 2   Biopsychosocial Risk and Resilience Assessment for the Course of the Disorder

Risk influences	Protective influences
Biological	
Psychological	
Social	

Additional Strengths-Based Assessment Techniques

Directions Part III, Goal Setting and Treatment Planning   Given your risk and resilience assessments of the individual, your knowledge of the disorder, and evidence-based practice guidelines, formulate goals and a possible treatment plan for this individual.

Directions Part IV, Critical Perspective   Formulate a critique of the diagnosis as it relates to this case example. Questions to consider include the following: Does this diagnosis represent a valid mental disorder from the social work perspective? Is this diagnosis significantly different from other possible diagnoses? Your critique should be based on the values of the social work profession (which are incongruent in some way with the medical model) and the validity of the specific diagnostic criteria applied to this case.

References

Abela, J. R. Z., Brozina, K., & Haigh, E. P. (2002). An examination of the response styles theory of depression in third- and seventh-grade children: A short-term longitudinal study. *Journal of Abnormal Child Psychology, 30(5)*, 515–527.

Abraham, R. (2005). *When words have lost their meaning: Alzheimer's patients communicate through art.* Westport, CT: Prager Publishers.

Adkins, E. C., & Keel, P. K. (2005). Does "excessive" or "compulsive" best describe exercise as a symptom of bulimia nervosa? *International Journal of Eating Disorders, 38*, 24–29.

Agency for Health Care Policy and Research. (1993). Depression in primary care. Volume 1. Detection and Diagnosis Clinical Practice Guideline. Retrieved April 9, 2004, from http://www.mentalhealth.com/bookah/p44-d1.html.

Agras, W. S., Bryson, S., Lawrence, D., Hammer, L. D., & Kraemer, H. C. (2007). Childhood risk factors for thin body preoccupation and social pressure to be thin. *Journal of American Academy of Child and Adolescent Psychiatry, 46*, 171–178.

Akshoomoff, N. (2006). Autism spectrum disorders: Introduction. *Child Neuropsychology, 12*, 245–246.

Alarcon, R. (2005). Cross-cultural issues. In J. M. Oldham, A. E. Skodol, & D. S. Bender (Eds.), *The American Psychiatric Publishing textbook of personality disorders* (pp. 561–578). Washington, DC: American Psychiatric Publishing.

Alexander, J., & Parsons, B. V. (1982). *Functional family therapy.* Monterey, CA: Brooks/Cole.

Alexandre, P. K., Martins, S. S., & Richard, P. (2009). Disparities in adequate mental health care for past-year major depressive episodes among Caucasian and Hispanic youths [Abstract]. *Psychiatric Services, 60(10)*, 1365–1371.

Alexopoulos, G. S., Katz, I. R., Reynolds, C. F., Carpenter, D., Docherty, J. P., & Ross, R. W. (2001). Pharmacotherapy of depression in older patients: A summary of the expert consensus guidelines. *Journal of Psychiatric Practice, 7(6)*, 361–376.

Allegri, R. F., Sarasola, D., Serrano, C. M., Taragano, F. E., Arizana, R. L., Butman, J., et al. (2006). Neuropsychiatric symptoms as a predictor of caregiver burden in Alzheimer's disease. *Neuropsychiatric Disease and Treatment, 2(1)*, 105–110.

Altman, S., Haeri, S., & Cohen, L. J. (2006). Predictors of relapse in bipolar disorder: A review. *Journal of Psychiatric Practice, 12(5)*, 269–282.

Alvarez, H., & Ollendick, T. (2003). Individual and psychosocial risk factors. In C. A. Essau (Ed.), *Conduct and oppositional defiant disorders: Epidemiology, risk factors, and treatment* (pp. 61–98). Mahwah, NJ: Lawrence Erlbaum.

Amato, L., Minozzi, S., Davoli, M., Vecchi, S., Ferri, M., & Mayet, S. (2009). Psychosocial and pharmacological treatments versus pharmacological treatments for opioid detoxification: A review. *The Cochrane Library 2009, 3*, 1–36.

American Academy of Pediatrics. (2000). Clinical practice guideline: Diagnosis and evaluation of the child with attention-deficit/hyperactivity disorder committee on quality improvement, subcommittee on attention-deficit/hyperactivity disorder. *Pediatrics, 105*, 1158–1170.

American Psychiatric Association. (2000). *Diagnostic and statistical manual of mental disorders* (4th ed., text revision). Washington, DC: Author.

American Psychiatric Association. (2010). *DSM-5 development.* http://www.dsm5.org/Pages/Default.aspx.

Andersen, A. E., Bowers, W. A., & Watson, T. (2001). A slimming program for eating disorders not otherwise specified: Reconceptualizing a confusing, residual diagnostic category. *Psychiatric Clinics of North America, 24(2)*, 271–280.

Anderson, I. (2000). Selective serotonin reuptake inhibitors versus tricyclic antidepressants: A meta-analysis of efficacy and tolerability. *Journal of Affective Disorders, 58*, 19–36.

Andreasen, N. C. (2001). *Brave new brain: Conquering mental illness in the era of the genome.* New York: Oxford University Press.

Andreasen, N. C., Carpenter, W. T., Kane, J. N., Lasser, R. A., Marder, S. R., & Weinberger, D. R. (2005). Remission in schizophrenia: Proposed criteria and rationale for consensus. *American Journal of Psychiatry, 162,* 441–449.

Angell, M. (2004). *The truth about drug companies: How they deceive us and what to do about it.* New York, NY: Crown Publishing Group/Random House.

Anton, R. F., O'Malley, S. S., Ciraulo, D. A., Cisler, R. A., Couper, D., Donovan, D. M., et al. (2006). Combined pharmacotherapies and behavioral interventions for alcohol dependence. *Journal of American Medical Association, 295(17),* 2003–2017.

Antonuccio, D., Thomas, M., & Danton, W. (1997). A cost-effectiveness analysis of cognitive behavior therapy and fluoxetine (Prozac) in the treatment of depression. *Behavior Therapy, 28,* 187–210.

Appleyard, K., Egeland, B., Van Dulmen, M. H., & Sroufe, L. A. (2005). When more is not better: The role of cumulative risk in child behavior outcomes. *Journal of Child Psychology and Psychiatry, 46(3),* 235–245.

Arc. (2007). Causes and prevention. Retrieved 2007, from http://www.thearc.org/NetCommunity/Page.aspx?&pid=1433&srcid=1386.

Armstrong, T., & Costello, J. (2002). Community studies on adolescent substance use, abuse, or dependence and psychiatric comorbidity. *Journal of Consulting and Clinical Psychology, 70,* 1224–1239.

Arnett, P. A., & Randolph, J. J. (2006). Longitudinal course of depression symptoms in multiple sclerosis. *Journal of Neurology, Neurosurgery, and Psychiatry, 77,* 606–610.

Arnold, L. (1996). Sex differences in ADHD. *Journal of Abnormal Child Psychology, 24,* 555–569.

Ascher-Svanum, H., Faries, D., Zhu, B., Ernst, F., Swartz, M., & Swanson, J. (2006). Medication adherence and long-term functional outcomes in the treatment of schizophrenia in usual care. *Journal of Clinical Psychiatry, 67(3),* 453–460.

Ashley, O., Marsden, M. E., & Brady, T. (2003). Effectiveness of substance abuse treatment programming for women: A review. *American Journal of Drug and Alcohol Abuse, 29,* 19–54.

Asnaani, A., Chelminski, I., Young, D., & Zimmerman, M. (2007). Heterogeneity of borderline personality disorder: Do the number of criteria met make a difference? *Journal of Personality Disorders, 21(6),* 615–625.

Attia, E., & Roberto, C. A. (2009). Should amenorrhea be a diagnostic criterion for anorexia nervosa? *International Journal of Eating Disorders, 42,* 581–589.

Bacaltchuk, J., & Hay, P. (2003). Antidepressants versus placebo for people with bulimia nervosa (Cochrane Review). *The Cochrane Library,* Issue 4. Chichester, UK: Wiley.

Bacaltchuk, J., Hay, P., & Trefiglio, R. (2001). Antidepressants versus psychological treatments and their combination for bulimia nervosa (Cochrane Review). *The Cochrane Library,* Issue 4. Chichester, UK: Wiley.

Bachman, D. L., Green, R. C., Benke, K. S., Cupples, L. A., & Farrer, L. A. (2003). Comparison of Alzheimer's disease risk factors in White and African American families. *Neurology, 60(8),* 1372–1374.

Bagge, C., Nickell, A., Stepp, S., Durrett, C., Jackson, K., & Trull, T. J. (2004). Borderline personality disorder features predict negative outcomes 2 years later. *Journal of Abnormal Psychology, 113(2),* 279–288.

Bahr, S. J., & Hoffmann, J. P. (2010). Parenting style, religiosity, peers, and adolescent heavy drinking. *Journal of Studies on Alcohol and Drugs, 1(4),* 539–543.

Bains, J., Birks, J. S., & Dening, T. T. (2005). Antidepressants for treating depression in dementia (Review). *Cochrane Database of Systematic Reviews, 2002, 4.* Art. No. CD003944.

Baker, L. L., & Scarth, K. D. (2002). *Cognitive behavioural approaches to treating children and adolescents with conduct disorder.* Toronto: Children's Mental Health Ontario.

Baker-Ericzén, M. J., Stahmer, A. C., & Burns, A. (2007). Child demographics associated with outcomes in a community-based pivotal response training program. *Journal of Positive Behavior Interventions, 9(1),* 52–60.

Bakker, A., van Balkom, A., & Spinhoven, P. (2002). SSRIs vs. TCAs in the treatment of panic disorder: A meta-analysis. *Acta Psychiatrica Scandinavica, 106(3),* 163–167.

Baldessarini, R. J., Tondo, L., Davis, P., Pompili, M., Goodwin, F. K., & Henne, J. (2006). Decreased risk of suicides and attempts during long-term lithium treatment: A meta-analytic review. *Bipolar Disorders, 2006, 8*[5, Pt. 2], 625–639.

Ballard, C., & Howard, R. (2006). Neuroleptic drugs in dementia: Benefits and harm. *Nature Reviews Neuroscience, 7(6),* 492–500.

Ballard, C., & Waite, J. (2006). The effectiveness of atypical antipsychotics for the treatment of aggression and psychosis in Alzheimer's disease. *Cochrane Database of Systematic Reviews, 1.* Art. No. CD003476.

Bandelow, B., Spath, C., Tichauer, A., Broocks, A., Hajak, G., & Ruther, E. (2002). Early traumatic life events, parental attitudes, family history, and birth risk factors in patients with panic disorder. *Comprehensive Psychiatry, 43,* 269–278.

Barkley, R. A. (2000). *Taking charge of ADHD* (Rev. ed.). New York: Guilford Press.

Barkley, R. A. (2004). Adolescents with attention-deficit/hyperactivity disorder: An overview of empirically based treatments. *Journal of Psychiatric Practice, 10,* 39–56.

Barkley, R. A. (2006). Attention-deficit/hyperactivity disorder. In D. A. Wolfe & E. J. Mash (Eds.), *Behavioral and emotional disorders in adolescents: Nature, assessment, and treatment* (pp. 91–152). New York: Guilford Press.

Barkley, R. A., Fischer, M., & Smallish, L. (2006). Young adult outcome of hyperactive children: Adaptive functioning in major life activities. *Journal of the American Academy of Child and Adolescent Psychiatry, 45(2),* 192–202.

Barkley, R. A., & Murphy, K. R. (2006). *Attention-deficit hyperactivity disorder: A clinical workbook* (3rd ed.). New York: Guilford Press.

Barnes, C., & Mitchell, P. (2005). Considerations in the management of bipolar disorder in women. *Australian and New Zealand Journal of Psychiatry, 39(8),* 662–673.

Barnett, S. M., Sirey, J. A., Bruce, M., Hamilton, M., Raue, P., Friedman, S. J., et al. (2002). Predictors of early recovery from major depression among persons admitted to community-based clinics. *Archives of General Psychiatry, 59,* 729–735.

Barnhill, G. (2007). Outcomes in adults with Asperger syndrome. *Focus on Autism and Other Developmental Disabilities, 22(2),* 116–126.

Baron-Cohen, S., Ring, H. A., & Bullmore, E. T. (2000). The amygdala theory of autism. *Neuroscience & Biobehavioral Reviews, 24(3),* 355–364.

Basco, M. R., & Rush, A. J. (2005). *Cognitive-behavioural therapy for bipolar disorder* (2nd ed.). New York: Guilford Press.

Bateman, A., & Fonagy, P. (2008). 8-year follow-up of patients treated for borderline personality disorder: Mentalization-based treatment versus treatment as usual. *American Journal of Psychiatry, 165,* 631–638.

Beattie, E. R. A., Algase, D. L., & Song, J. (2004). Keeping wandering nursing home residents at the table: Improving food intake using a behavioral communication intervention. *Aging and Mental Health, 8(2),* 109–116.

Beatty, R., Geckle, M., Huggins, J., Kapner, C., Lewis, K., & Sandstrom, D. (1999). Gay men, lesbians, and bisexuals. In B. McCrady & E. Epstein (Eds.), *Addictions: A comprehensive guidebook* (pp. 542–551). New York: Oxford University Press.

Beck, A., Rush, A., Shaw, B., & Emery, G. (1979). *Cognitive therapy of depression.* New York: Guilford Press.

Bell, L. (2003). What can we learn from consumer studies and qualitative research in the treatment of eating disorders? *Eating and Weight Disorders, 8,* 181–187.

Benjet, C., Thompson, R. J., & Gotib, I. H. (2010). 5-HTTLPR moderates the effects of relational peer victimization of the depressive symptoms in adolescent girls. *Journal of Child Psychology and Psychiatry, 51(2),* 173–179. DOI: 10.1111/j.1469-7610.2009.02149.x.

Bentley, K., & Walsh, J. (2006). *The social worker and psychotropic medication* (3rd ed.). Pacific Grove, CA: Brooks/Cole.

Berk, M., Conus, P., Lucas, N., Hallam, K., Malhi, G. S., Dodd, S., et al. (2007). Setting the stage: From prodrome to treatment resistance in bipolar disorder. *Bipolar Disorders, 9,* 671–678.

Berkman, N. D., Lohr, K. N., & Bulik, C. M. (2007). Outcomes of eating disorders: A systematic review of the literature. *International Journal of Eating Disorders, 40(4),* 293–309.

Bernard, L., Young, A. H., Pearson, J., Geddes, J., & O'Brien, G. (2002). Systematic review of the use of atypical antipsychotics in autism. *Journal of Psychopharmacology, 16(1),* 93–101.

Bernstein, G., & Shaw, K. (1997). Practice parameters for the assessment and treatment of children and adolescents with anxiety disorders. *Journal of the American Academy of Child and Adolescent Psychiatry, 36* (10 Suppl), 69S–84S.

Berrocal, C., Moreno, M. A. R., Rando, M. A., Benvenuti, A., & Cassano, G. B. (2008). Borderline personality disorder and mood spectrum. *Psychiatry Research, 159(3),* 300–307.

Bertolino, B., & O'Hanlon, B. (2002). *Collaborative, competency-based counseling and therapy.* Boston: Allyn & Bacon.

Berument, S., Rutter, M., Lord, C., Pickles, A., & Bailey, A. (1999). Autism Screening Questionnaire: Diagnostic validity. *British Journal of Psychiatry, 175,* 444–451.

Berzoff, J. (Ed.). (2007). *Inside out and outside in: Psychodynamic clinical theory and practice in contemporary multicultural contexts* (2nd ed.). Northvale, NJ: Jason Aronson.

Bhutta, A., Cleves, M., Casey, P., Cradock, M., & Anand, K. (2002). Cognitive and behavioral outcomes of school-aged children who were born preterm: A meta-analysis. *Journal of the American Medical Association, 288,* 728–737.

Biederman, J., Petter, C. R., Monuteaux, M. C., Fried, R., Byrne, D., Mirto, T., et al. (2010). Adult psychiatric outcomes of girls with attention deficit hyperactivity disorder: 11-year follow-up in a longitudinal case-control study. *American Journal of Psychiatry, 167(4),* 409–417. Retrieved from http://ajp.psychiatryonline.org.

Biederman, J., Petty, C. R., Dolan, C., Hughes, S., Mick, M., Monuteaux, M. C., et al. (2008). The long-term longitudinal course of oppositional defiant disorder and conduct disorder in ADHD boys: Findings from a controlled 10-year prospective longitudinal follow-up study. *Psychological Medicine, 38,* 1027–1036. DOI: 10.1017/S0033291707002668.

Billstedt, E., Gillberg, C., & Gillberg, C. (2005). Autism after adolescence: Population-based 13- to 22-year follow-up study of 120 individuals with autism diagnosed in childhood. *Journal of Autism and Developmental Disorders, 35(3),* 351–360.

Binks, C., Fenton, M., McCarthy, L., Lee, T., Adams, C., & Duggan, C. (2006a). Psychological therapies for people with borderline personality disorder. *The Cochrane Database System Review, 1.* Art. No. CD005652.

Binks, C., Fenton, M., McCarthy, L., Lee, T., Adams, C., & Duggan, C. (2006b). Pharmacological interventions for people with borderline personality disorder. *Cochrane Database of Systematic Reviews.* Art. No. CD005653.

Bird, M., & Parslow, R. (2002). Potential for community programs to prevent depression in older people. *The Medical Journal of Australia, 7,* 107–110.

Birks, J., Grimley-Evans, J., Iakovidou, V., & Tsolaki, M. (2007). Rivastigmine for Alzheimer's disease. *The Cochrane Database of Systematic Reviews,* Issue 1. DOI: 10.1002/14651858. CD001191.

Birmaher, B., Axelson, D., Monk, K., Kalas, C., Goldstein, B., Hickey, M. B., et al. (2009). Lifete psychiatric disorders in school-age offspring of parents with bipolar disorder. *Archives of Genera Psychiatry, 66(3),* 287–296.

Birmaher, B., Axelson, D., Strober, M., Gill, M. K., Valeri, S., Chiapetta, L., et al. (2006). Clinical course of children and adolescents with bipolar spectrum disorders. *Archives of General Psychiatry, 63(2),* 175–183.

Bishop, A. J., Martin, P., MacDonald, M., & Poon, L. (2010). Predicting happiness among centenarians. *Gerontology, 56,* 88–92. DOI: 10.1159/000272017.

Bishop, D. V. M. (1998). Development of the Children's Communication Checklist (CCC): A method for assessing qualitative aspects of communicative impairment in children. *Journal of Child Psychology and Psychiatry, 39,* 879–891.

Bishop, S. L., Luyster, R., Richler, J., & Lord, C. (2008). Diagnostic assessment. In K. Chawarsks, A. Klin, & F.

R. Volkmar (Eds.), *Autism spectrum disorders in infants and toddlers: Diagnosis, assessment, and treatment* (pp. 23–49). New York: Guilford Press.

Bisson, J., & Andrew, M. (2005). Psychological treatment of post-traumatic stress disorder (PTSD). *Cochrane Database of Systematic Reviews, 3,* 1–2.

Bisson, J., & Andrew, M. (2007). Psychological treatment of post-traumatic stress disorder (PTSD). *Cochrane Database of Systematic Reviews, 2007, 3.*

Bland, A. R., Williams, C. A., Scharer, K., & Manning, S. (2004). Emotion processing in borderline personality disorder. *Issues in Mental Health Nursing, 25,* 655–672.

Blazer, D. G., & Wu, L. T. (2009). The epidemiology of substance use and disorders among middle aged and elderly community adults: National survey on drug use and health. *American Journal of Geriatric Psychiatry, 17,* 237–245.

Blehar, M. C. (2006). Women's mental health research: The emergence of a biomedical field. *Annual Review of Clinical Psychology, 2,* 135–160.

Boden, J. M., Fergusson, D. M., & Horwood, L. J. (2007). Anxiety disorders and suicidal behaviours in adolescence and young adulthood: Findings from a longitudinal study. *Psychological Medicine, 37,* 431–440.

Bogenschneider, K. (1996). An ecological risk/protective theory for building prevention programs, policies, and community capacity to support youth. *Family Relations: Journal of Applied Family & Child Studies, 45,* 127–138.

Bohlmeijer, E., Smit, F., & Cuijpers, P. (2003). Effects of reminiscence and life review on late-life depression: A meta-analysis. *International Journal of Geriatric Psychiatry, 18,* 1088–1094.

Boise, L., Neal, M. B., & Kaye, J. (2004). Dementia assessment in primary care: Results from a study in three managed care systems. *The Journals of Gerontology Series A: Biological Sciences and Medical Sciences, 59,* M621.

Bolen, R., & Scannapieco, M. (1999). Prevalence of child sexual abuse: A corrective meta-analysis. *Social Service Review, 73,* 281–301.

Bond, G. R. (2004). Supported employment: Evidence for and against evidence-based practice. *Psychiatric Rehabilitation Journal, 27(4),* 345–359.

Bond, J., Kaskutas, L., & Weisner, C. (2003). The persistent influence of social networks and Alcoholics Anonymous on abstinence. *Quarterly Journal of Studies on Alcohol, 64,* 579–588.

Boomsma, D., van Beijsterveldt, C., & Hudziak, J. (2005). Genetic and environmental influences on anxious/depression during childhood: A study from the

Netherlands twin register. *Genes, Brain, & Behavior, 4*, 466–481.

Borges, G., Angst, J., Nock, M., Ruscio, A. M., Walters, E., & Kessler, R. (2006). A risk index for 12-month suicide attempts in the National Comorbidity Survey Replication (NCR-S). *Psychological Medicine, 36(12),* 1747–1757.

Bosquet, M., & Egeland, B. (2006). The development and maintenance of anxiety symptoms from infancy through adolescence in a longitudinal sample. *Development and Psychopathology, 18,* 517–550.

Bouchard, M. F., Bellinger, D. C., Wright, R. O., & Weisskopf, M. G. (2010). Attention-deficit/hyperactivity disorder and urinary metabolites of organophosphate pesticides. *Pediatrics, 125(6),* 1270–1277. DOI: 10.1542/peds.2009-3058.

Bourgeois, M. S., Dijkstra, K., & Hickey, E. M. (2005). Impact of communication interaction on measuring self- and proxy-related depression in dementia (electronic version). *Journal of Medical Speech-Language Pathology, 13,* 37–51.

Bowden, C. L. (2000). Efficacy of lithium in mania and maintenance therapy of bipolar disorder. *Journal of Clinical Psychiatry, 61*(Suppl. 9), 35–40.

Bowden, C. L. (2005). Treatment options for bipolar depression. *Journal of Clinical Psychiatry, 66* (Suppl. 1), 3–6.

Bowlby, J. (1969). *Attachment and loss: Vol. 1. Attachment.* New York: Basic Books.

Bowlby, J. (1973). *Attachment and loss: Vol. 2. Separation: Anxiety and anger.* New York: Basic Books.

Bowlby, J. (1980). *Attachment and loss: Vol. 3. Loss.* New York: Basic Books.

Bradizza, C. M., Stasiewicz, P. R., & Paas, N. D. (2006). Relapse to alcohol and drug use among individuals diagnosed with co-occurring mental health and substance use disorder: A review. *Clinical Psychology Review, 26(2),* 162–178.

Bradley, R., Greene, J., Russ., E., Dutra, L., & Westen, D. (2005). *American Journal of Psychiatry, 162(2),* 214–227.

Bradshaw, C., & Thomlison, B. (1996). Posttraumatic stress disorder conceptualized as a problem in the person-environment system. In F. Turner (Ed.), *Adult psychopathology: A social work perspective* (pp. 638–660). New York: Free Press.

Brady, K. T., & Back, S. E. (2008). Women and addiction. In H. D. Kleber & M. Galanter (Eds.), *The American Psychiatric Publishing textbook of substance abuse treatment* (4th ed.) (pp. 555–564). Arlington, VA: American Psychiatric Publishing.

Breslau, J., Kendler, K. S., & Su, M. (2005). Lifetime risk and persistence of psychiatric disorders across ethnic groups in the United States. *Psychological Medicine, 35(3),* 317–327.

Breslau, J., Kendler, K. S., Su, M., Gaxiola-Aguilar, S., & Kessler, R. C. (2005). Lifetime risk and persistence of psychiatric disorders across ethnic groups in the United States. *Psychological Medicine, 35,* 317–327.

Breslau, J., Miller, E., Chung, W., & Schweitzer, J. B. (2011). Childhood and adolescent onset psychiatric disorders, substance use, and failure to graduate high school on time. *Journal of Psychiatric Research, 45(3),* 295–301.

Brestan, E., & Eyberg, S. (1998). Effective psychological treatments of conduct-disordered children and adolescents: 29 years, 82 studies, and 5,272 kids. *Journal of Clinical Child Psychology, 27,* 180–189.

Brewin, C., Andrews, B., & Valentine, J. (2000). Meta-analysis of risk factors for posttraumatic stress disorder in trauma-exposed adults. *Journal of Consulting and Clinical Psychology, 68,* 748–766.

Bridge, J. A., Iyengar, S., Salary, C. B., Barbe, R. P., Birmaher, B., Pincus, H. A., et al. (2007). Clinical response and risk for reported suicidal ideation and suicide attempts in pediatric antidepressant treatment. *Journal of American Medical Association, 297(15),* 1683–1700.

Briggs-Gowan, M. J., Carter, A. S., Clark, R., Augustyn, M., McCarthy, K., & Ford, J. D. (2010). Exposure to potentially traumatic events in early childhood: Differential links to emergent psychopathology. *Journal of Child Psychology and Psychiatry, 51(10),* 1132–1140. DOI: 10.1111/j.1469-7610.2010.02256.x.

Brodaty, H., Luscombe, G., Peisah, C., Anstey, K., & Andrews, G. (2001). A 25-year longitudinal, comparison study of the outcome of depression. *Psychological Medicine, 31(8),* 1347–1359.

Brookmeyer, R., Evans, D. A., Hebert, L., Langa, K. M., Heeringa, S. G., Plassman, B. L., et al. (2011). National estimates of the prevalence of Alzheimer's disease in the United States. *Alzheimer's & Dementia, 7(1),* 61–73.

Brown, M. Z., Comtois, K. A., & Linehan, M. M. (2002). Reasons for suicide attempts and nonsuicidal self-injury in women with borderline personality disorder. *Journal of Abnormal Psychology, 111(1),* 198–202.

Brown, R. T., Amler, R. W., Freeman, W. S., Perrin, J., Stein, M., Feldman, H., et al. (2005). Treatment of attention-deficit/hyperactivity disorder: Overview of the evidence. *Pediatrics, 115,* 749–775.

Bruce, S. E., Yonkers, K. A., Otto, M. W., Eisen, J. L., Weisberg, R. B., Pagano, M., et al. (2005). Influence of psychiatric comorbidity on recovery and recurrence in generalized anxiety disorder, social phobia, and panic disorder: A 12-year prospective study. *American Journal of Psychiatry, 162,* 1179–1187.

Bryant, R. A., Felmingham, K. L., Falconer, E. M., Benito, L. P., Dobson-Stone, C., Pierce, K. D., et al. (2010). Preliminary evidence of the short allele of the serotonin transporter gene predicting poor response to cognitive behavior therapy in posttraumatic stress disorder. *Biological Psychiatry, 67(12),* 1217–1219.

Buckley, P. (2006). Prevalence and consequences of the dual diagnosis of substance abuse and severe mental illness. *Journal of Clinical Psychiatry, 67,* 5–9.

Bukstein, O., Dunne, J., Ayres, W., Arnold, V., Benedek, E., Bensenn, R., et al. (1997). Practice parameters for the assessment and treatment of children and adolescents with substance use disorders. *Journal of the American Academy of Child and Adolescent Psychiatry, 36,* 140–157.

Bukstein, O. G., & Cornelius, J. (2006). Psychopharmacology of adolescents with substance use disorders: Using diagnostic-specific treatments. In Howard A. Liddle & Cynthia L. Rowe (Eds.), *Adolescent substance abuse: Research and clinical advances* (pp. 241–263). New York: Cambridge University Press.

Bukstein, O. G., Cornelius, J., Trunzo, A. C., Kelly, T. M., & Wood, D. S. (2005). Clinical predictors of treatment in a population of adolescents with alcohol use disorders. *Addictive Behaviors, 30,* 1663–1673.

Bulik, C. (2004). Genetic and biological risk factors. In J. K. Thompson (Ed.), *Handbook of eating disorders and obesity* (pp. 3–16). Hoboken, NJ: Wiley.

Bulik, C. M., Sullivan, P. F., Tozzi, F., Furberg, H., Lichtenstein, P., & Pedersen, N. L. (2006). Prevalence, heritability, and prospective risk factors for anorexia nervosa. *Archives of General Psychiatry, 63,* 305–312.

Burdick, K. E., Braga, R. J., Goldberg, J. F., & Malhotra, A. K. (2007). Cognitive dysfunction in bipolar disorder: Future place of pharmacotherapy. *CNS Drugs, 21(12),* 971–981.

Burke, J., Loeber, R., & Birmaher, B. (2002). Oppositional defiant disorder and conduct disorder: A review of the past 10 years, part II. *Journal of the American Academy of Child and Adolescent Psychiatry, 41,* 1275–1294.

Burns, A., Guthrie, E., Marino-Francis, F., Susby, C., Morris, J., Russell, E., et al. (2005). Brief psychotherapy in Alzheimer's disease: Randomized controlled trial. *British Journal of Psychiatry, 187(2),* 143–147.

Button, E. J., Chadalavada, B., & Palmer, R. L. (2010). Mortality and predictors of death in a cohort of patients presenting to an eating disorders service. *International Journal of Eating Disorders, 43(5),* 387–392. DOI: 10.1002/eat.20715.

Butzlaff, R. L., & Hooley, J. M. (1998). Expressed emotion and psychiatric relapse. *Archives of General Psychiatry, 55,* 547–552.

Byrne, M., Agerbo, E., & Mortensen, P. B. (2002). Family history of psychiatric disorders and age at first contact in schizophrenia: An epidemiological study. *British Journal of Psychiatry, 181(43),* 19–25.

Cachelin, F. M., & Striegel-Moore, R. H. (2006). Help seeking and barriers to treatment in a community sample of Mexican American and European American women with eating disorders. *International Journal of Eating Disorders, 39,* 154–161.

Cardno, A., & Murray, R. M. (2003). The "classic" genetic epidemiology of schizophrenia. In R. M. Murray & P. B. Jones (Eds.),*The epidemiology of schizophrenia* (pp. 195–219). New York: Cambridge University Press.

Carlson, C. L., Tamm, L., & Gaub, M. (1997). Gender differences in children with ADHD, ODD, co-occurring ADHD/ODD identified in a school population. *Journal of the American Academy of Child and Adolescent Psychiatry, 36(12),* 1706–1714.

Carlson, G. A. (2002). Bipolar disorder in children and adolescents: A critical review. In D. Shaffer & B. D. Waslick (Eds.), *The many faces of depression in children and adolescents* (pp. 105–123). Washington, DC: American Psychiatric Publishing.

Carpenter, L. L., Gawuga, C. E., Tyrka, A. R., Lee, J. K., Anderson, G. M., & Price, L. H. (2010). Association between plasma IL-6 response to acute stress and early-life adversity in healthy adults. *Neuropsychopharmacology, 35,* 2617–2623. DOI: 10.1038/npp.2010.159.

Carter, B., & McGoldrick, M. (2005). *The expanded family life cycle: Individual, family, and social perspectives* (3rd ed.). Boston: Allyn & Bacon.

Cartwright-Hatton, S., McNicol, K., & Doubleday, E. (2006). Anxiety in a neglected population: Prevalence of anxiety disorder in pre-adolescent children. *Clinical Psychology Review, 26(7),* 817–833.

Caspi, A., Sugden, K., Moffit, T. E., Taylor, A., Craig, I. W., Harrington, H., et al. (2003). Influence of life stress on depression: Moderation by a polymorphism in the 5-TT gene. *Science, 301(5631),* July 18, 386–389.

Cassin, S. E., & von Ranson, K. M. (2005). Personality and eating disorders: A decade in review. *Clinical Psychology Review, 25(7),* 895–916.

Castro, F., Proescholdbell, R. J., Abeita, L., & Rodriquez, D. (1999). Ethnic and cultural minority groups. In B. McCrady & E. Epstein (Eds.), *Addictions: A comprehensive guidebook* (pp. 499–526). New York: Oxford University Press.

Cataldo, J. K., Prochaska, J. J., & Glantz, S. A. (2010). Cigarette smoking is a risk factor for Alzheimer's disease: An analysis controlling for tobacco industry affiliation. *Journal of Alzheimer's Disease, 19(2),* 465–480.

Cederlund, M., Hagberg, B., Billstedt, E., Gillberg, I. C., & Gillberg, C. (2008). Asperger syndrome and autism: A comparative longitudinal follow-up study more than 5 years after original diagnosis. *Journal of Autism and Developmental Disorders, 38(1),* 72–85.

Centers for Disease Control and Prevention. (2004). *Youth risk behavior surveillance. Surveillance summaries,* May 21. MMWR 2004: 53(No. SS-2).

Centers for Disease Control and Prevention. (2005). Mental health in the United States. Prevalence of diagnosis and medication treatment for attention-deficit/hyperactivity disorder. United States, 2003. *Morbidity and Mortality Weekly Report, 54,* 842–847.

Chabrol, H., Montovany, A., Duconge, E., Kallmeyer, A., Mullet, E., & Leichsenring, M. (2004). Factor structure of the borderline personality inventory in adolescents. *European Journal of Psychological Assessment, 20(1),* 9–65.

Chue, P. (2006). The relationship between patient satisfaction and treatment outcomes in schizophrenia. *Journal of Psychopharmacology, 20(6),* 38–56.

Chung, T., & Maisto, S. A. (2006). Relapse to alcohol and other use in treated adolescents: Review and reconsideration of relapse as a change point in clinical course. *Clinical Psychology Review, 26,* 149–161.

Ciesla, J. A., & Roberts, J. E. (2001). Meta-analysis of the relationship between HIV infection and risk for depressive disorders. *American Journal of Psychiatry, 158(5),* 725–730.

Cipriani, A., Pretty, H., Hawton, K., & Geddes, J. R. (2005). Lithium in the prevention of suicidal behavior and all-cause mortality in patients with mood disorders: A systematic review of randomized trials. *American Journal of Psychiatry, 162(10),* 1805–1819.

Cipriani, A., Smith, K., Burgess, S., Carney, S., Goodwin, G., & Geddes, J. (2006). Lithium versus antidepressants in the long-term treatment of unipolar affective disorder. *Cochrane Database of Systematic Reviews,* Issue 4. Art. No. CD003492. DOI: 10.1002/14651858.CD003492. pub2.

Claire, L., Wilson, B. A., Carter, G., Roth, I., & Hodges, J. R. (2004). Awareness in early-stage Alzheimer's disease: Relationship to outcome of cognitive rehabilitation. *Journal of Clinical and Experimental Neuropsychology, 26(2),* 215–226.

Clare, L., Woods, R. T., Moniz-Cook, E. D., Orrell, M., & Spector, A. (2007). Cognitive rehabilitation and cognitive training for early-stage Alzheimer's disease and vascular dementia. *The Cochrane Database of Systematic Reviews,* Issue 1. DOI: 10.1002/14651858.

Clarkin, J. F., Yeomans, F. E., & Kernberg, O. F. (Eds.). (2006). *Psychotherapy for borderline personality: Focusing on object relations.* Arlington, VA: American Psychiatric Publishing.

Claudino, A. M., Hay, P., Lima, M. S., Bacaltchuk, J., Schmidt, U., & Treasure, J. (2006). Antidepressants for anorexia nervosa. *Cochrane Database of Systematic Reviews, 25,* 1–2.

Clavarino, A. M., Mamun, A. A., O'Callaghan, M., Aird, R., Bor, W. l., O'Callaghan, F., et al. (2010). Maternal anxiety and attention problems in children at 5 and 14 years. *Journal of Attention Disorders, 13(6),* 658–667. DOI: 10.1177/1087054709347203.

Cleveland, H. H., & Harris, K. S. (2010). The role of coping in moderating within-day associations between negative triggers and substance use cravings: A daily diary investigation. *Addictive Behaviors, 35(1),* 60–63.

Cohen, A., Houck, P. R., Szanto, K., Dew, M. A., Gilman, S. E., & Reynolds, C. F. (2006). Social inequalities in response to antidepressant treatment in older adults. *Archives of General Psychiatry, 63(1),* 50–56.

Cohen, D. (2002). Research on the drug treatment of schizophrenia: A critical reappraisal and implications for social work education. *Journal of Social Work Education, 38(2),* 217–239.

Cohen, J. A. (1998). Summary of the practice parameters for the assessment and treatment of children and adolescents with posttraumatic stress disorder. *Journal of the American Academy of Child and Adolescent Psychiatry, 37(9),* 997–1001.

Cohen, J. A. (2005). Treating traumatized children: Current status and future directions. *Journal of Trauma and Dissociation, 6(2),* 109–121.

Cohen, J. A., & Mannarino, A. P. (1996). A treatment outcome study for sexually abused preschool children: Initial findings. *Journal of the American Academy of Child and Adolescent Psychiatry, 35,* 42–50.

Cohen, J., Mannarino, A., & Rogal, S. (2001). Treatment practices for childhood posttraumatic stress disorder. *Child Abuse and Neglect, 25,* 123–135.

Cole, M. G. (2005). Evidence-based review of risk factors for geriatric depression and brief preventive interventions. *Psychiatric Clinics of North America, 28*, 785–803.

Compton, W. M., Thomas, Y. F., Stinson, F. S., & Grant, B. F. (2007). Prevalence, correlates, disability, and comorbidity of DSM-IV drug abuse and dependence in the United States: Results from the national epidemiologic survey on alcohol and related conditions. *Archives of General Psychiatry, 64*, 566–576.

Conklin, H. M., & Iacono, W. G. (2003). At issue: Assessment of schizophrenia: Getting closer to the cause. *Schizophrenia Bulletin, 29(3)*, 409–412.

Conn, D. K., & Seitz, D. P. (2010) Advances in the treatment of psychiatric disorders in long-term care homes. *Current Opinion in Psychiatry, 23(6)*, 516–521.

Conner, K. R., Sorensen, S., & Leonard, K. E. (2005). Initial depression and subsequent drinking during alcoholism treatment. *Journal of Studies on Alcohol*, 401–406.

Connolly, S. A., & Bernstein, G. A. (2007). Practice parameters for the assessment and treatment of children and adolescents with anxiety disorders. *Journal of the American Academy of Child and Adolescent Psychiatry, 46*, 267–283.

Connor, D., Steeber, J., and McBurnett, K. (2010). A review of attention-deficit/hyperactivity disorder complicated by symptoms of oppositional defiant disorder or conduct disorder. *Journal of Developmental and Behavioral Pediatric, 31*, 427–440.

Constantino, J. N., & Todd, R. D. (2003). Autistic traits in the general population: A twin study. *Archives of General Psychiatry, 60(5)*, 524–530.

Cook, J. A., Mock, L. O., Jonikas, J. A., Burke-Miller, J. K., Carter, T. M., Taylor, A., et al. (2009). Prevalence of psychiatric and substance use disorders among single mothers nearing lifetime welfare eligibility limits. *Archives of General Psychiatry, 66(3)*, 249–258.

Cooper, C., Katone, C., Orrell, M., & Livingston, G. (2004). Coping strategies and anxiety in caregivers of people with Alzheimer's disease: The LASER-AD study. *Journal of Affective Disorders, 90(1)*, 15–20.

Cooper, R. (2004). What is wrong with the DSM? *History of Psychiatry, 15(57, Pt. 1)*, 5–25.

Cooper, Z. (1995). The development and maintenance of eating disorders. In K. D. Brownell & C. G. Fairburn (Eds.), *Eating disorders and obesity: A comprehensive handbook* (pp. 199–206). New York: Guilford Press.

Copeland, W. E., Miller-Johnson, S., Keeler, G., & Angold, A. (2007). Childhood psychiatric disorders and young adult crime: A prospective, population-based study. *American Journal of Psychiatry, 164*, 1668–1675.

Copeland, W. E., Shanahan, L., Costello, E. J., and Angold, A. (2009).Childhood and adolescent psychiatric disorders as predictors of young adult disorders. *Archives of General Psychiatry, 66(7)*, 764–772. Retrieved from http://www.archgenpsychiatry.com.

Corcoran, J. (2011). *Mental health treatment for children and adolescents.* New York: Oxford University Press.

Corcoran, J., & Dattalo, P. (2006). Parent involvement in treatment for ADHD: A meta-analysis of the published studies. *Research in Social Work Practice, 16(6)*, 561–570.

Corcoran, J., & Walsh, J. (2006). *Clinical assessment and diagnosis in social work practice.* New York: Oxford University Press.

Corrao, G., Bagnardi, V., Zambon, A., & Arico, S. (1999). Exploring the dose–response relationship between alcohol consumption and the risk of several alcohol-related conditions: A meta-analysis. *Addiction, 94*, 1551–1573.

Costello, E. J., Erkanli, A., & Angold, A. (2006). Is there an epidemic of child or adolescent depression? *Journal of Child Psychology and Psychiatry and Allied Disciplines, 47*, 1263–1271.

Counts, C. A., Nigg, J. T., Stawicki, J. A., Rappley, M., & Eye, A. V. (2005). Family adversity in DSM-IV ADHD combined and inattentive subtypes and associated disruptive behavior problems. *Journal of the American Academy of Child and Adolescent Psychiatry, 44(7)*, 690–698.

Cozolino, L. (2002). The neuroscience of psychotherapy: *Building and rebuilding the human brain.* New York: W. W. Norton.

Creamer, M., McFarlane, A. C., & Burgess, P. (2005). Psychopathology following trauma: The role of subjective experience. *Journal of Affective Disorders, 86(2–3)*, 175–182.

Crisp, A. H., Norton, K., Gowers, S., Halek, C., Bowyer, C., Yeldham, D., et al. (1991). A controlled study of the effect of therapies aimed at adolescent and family psychopathology in anorexia nervosa. *British Journal of Psychiatry, 159*, 325–333.

Cronk, N., Slutske, W., Madden, P., Bucholz, K., & Heath, A. (2004). Risk for separation anxiety disorder among girls: Paternal absence, socioeconomic disadvantage, and genetic vulnerability. *Journal of Abnormal Psychology, 113*, 237–247.

Crow, S., Eisenberg, M. E., Story, M., & Neumark-Sztainer, D. (2008). Suicidal behavior in adolescents: Relationship to weight status, weight control behaviors, and body dissatisfaction. *International Journal of Eating Disorders, 41(1)*, 82–87.

Crow, T. J., Honea, R., Passingham, D., & Mackay, C. E. (2005). Regional deficits in brain volume in schizophrenia: A meta-analysis of voxel-based morphometry studies. *American Journal of Psychiatry, 162,* 2233–2245.

Crum, R. M., Green, K. M., Storr, C. L., Chan, Y. F., Ialongo, N., Stuart, E. A., et al. (2008). Depressed mood in childhood and subsequent alcohol use through adolescence and young adulthood. *Archives of General Psychiatry, 65(6),* 702–712.

Crumlish, N., & O'Rourke, K. (2010). A systematic review of treatments for post-traumatic stress disorder among refugees and asylum-seekers. *The Journal of Nervous and Mental Disease, 198(4),* 237–251. DOI: 10.1097/NMD.0b013e3181d61258.

Cuffe, S. P., McKeown, R. E., Jackson, K. L., Addy, C. L., Abramson, R., & Garrison, C. Z. (2001). Prevalence of attention-deficit/hyperactivity disorder in a community sample of older adolescents. *Journal of the American Academy of Child and Adolescent Psychiatry, 40(9),* 1037–1044.

Cuijpers, P., van Straten, A., Andersson, G., & van Oppen, P. (2008b). Psychotherapy for depression in adults: A meta-analysis of comparative outcome studies. *Journal of Consulting and Clinical Psychology, 76,* 909–922.

Currie, J., & Thomas, D. (1995). Does Head Start make a difference? *American Economic Review, 85(3),* 341–365.

Davidson, P., & Parker, K. (2001). Eye movement desensitization and reprocessing (EMDR): A meta-analysis. *Journal of Consulting and Clinical Psychology, 69,* 305–316.

Davila, J., Ramsay, M., Stroud, C. B., & Steinberg, S. J. (2005). Attachment as vulnerability to the development of psychopathology. In B. L. Hankin & J. R. Z. Abela (Eds.), *Development of psychopathology: A vulnerability-stress perspective* (pp. 215–242). Thousand Oaks, CA: Sage Publications.

De Beurs, E., Beekman, A., Geerlings, S., Deeg, D., Van Dyck, R., & Van Tilburg, W. (2001). On becoming depressed or anxious in late life: Similar vulnerability factors but different effects of stressful life events. *British Journal of Psychiatry, 179(5),* 426–431.

Deater-Deckard, K., Dodge, K. A., & Sorbring, E. (2005). Cultural differences in the effects of physical punishment. In M. Rutter & M. Tienda (Eds.), *Ethnicity and causal mechanisms* (pp. 204–226). New York: Cambridge University Press.

Deater-Deckard, K., Ivy, L., & Smith, J. (2005). Resilience in gene–environment transactions. In S. Goldstein & R. B. Brooks (Eds.), *Handbook of resilience in children* (pp. 49–63). New York: Kluwer Academic/Plenum Publishers.

DeGrandpre, R. (1999). *Ritalin nation: Rapid fire culture and the transformation of human consciousness.* New York: W. W. Norton.

deJong, P., & Berg, I. K. (2008). *Interviewing for solutions* (3rd ed.). Pacific Grove, CA: Brooks/Cole.

Dekovic, M. (1999). Risk and protective factors in the development of problem behavior during adolescence. *Journal of Youth and Adolescence, 28(6),* 667–685.

DeRose, L., Wright, A., & Brooks-Gunn, J. (2006). Does puberty account for the gender differential in depression? In C. L. M. Keyes & S. H. Goodman (Eds.), *Women and depression: Handbook for the social, behavioral, and biomedical sciences* (pp. 89–128). New York: Cambridge University Press.

Desai, H., & Jann, M. (2000). Major depression in women: A review of the literature. *Journal of the American Pharmaceutical Association, 40,* 525–537.

Detera-Wadleigh, S. D., & McMahon, F. J. (2006). G72/G30 in schizophrenia and bipolar disorder: Review and meta-analysis. *Biological Psychiatry, 60(2),* 106–114.

DeVane, C. L., Chiao, E., Franklin, M., & Kru, E. J. (2005). Anxiety disorders in the 21st century: Status, challenges, opportunities, and comorbidity with depression. *American Journal of Managed Care,* 344–353.

Dieterich, M., Irving, C. B., Park, B., & Marshall, M. (2010). Intensive case management for severe mental illness. *Cochrane Database of Systematic Reviews,* Issue 10. Art. No. CD007906.

Dodge, K. (2003). Do social information-processing patterns mediate aggressive behavior? In B. Lahey, T. E. Moffitt, & A. Caspi (Eds.), *Causes of conduct disorder and juvenile delinquency* (pp. 254–276). New York: Guilford Press.

Donovan, C., & Spence, S. (2000). Prevention of childhood anxiety disorders. *Clinical Psychology Review, 20,* 509–531.

Dosreis, S., Weiner, C. L., Johnson, L., & Newschaffer, C. J. (2006). Autism spectrum disorder screening and management practices among general pediatric providers. *Journal of Developmental and Behavioral Pediatrics, 27*(Suppl. 2), S88–S94.

Dretzke, J., Davenport, C., Frew, E., Barlow, J., Stewart-Brown, S., Bayliss, S., et al. (2009). The clinical effectiveness of different parenting programmes for children with conduct problems: A systematic review of randomised controlled trials. *Child and Adolescent Psychiatry and Mental Health, 3,* 7.

Duffy, M., Gillig, S. E., & Tureen, R. M. (2002). A critical look at the DSM-IV. *Journal of Individual Psychology, 58(4),* 363–373.

DuPaul, G. J., & Power, T. J. (2000). Educational interventions for students with attention-deficit disorders. In T. Brown (Ed.), *Attention-deficit disorders and comorbidities in children, adolescents, and adults* (pp. 607–634). Washington, DC: American Psychiatric Publishing.

Ebmeier, K. P., Donaghey, C., & Steele, J. D. (2006). Recent developments and current controversies in depression. *Lancet, 367,* 153–167.

Eddy, K., Celio Doyle, A., Hoste, A., Herzog, D., & Le Grange, D. (2008). Eating disorder not otherwise specified (EDNOS): An examination of EDNOS presentations in adolescents. *Journal of the American Academy of Child and Adolescent Psychiatry, 47(2),* 156–164.

Egger, H., & Angold, A. (2006). Common emotional and behavioral disorders in preschool children: Presentation, nosology, and epidemiology. *Journal of Child Psychology and Psychiatry, 47(3–4),* 313–337.

Ehrensaft, M. K. (2005). Interpersonal relationships and sex differences in the development of conduct problems. *Clinical Child and Family Psychology Review, 8(1),* 39–63.

Eisenberg, M. E., & Nuemark-Sztainer, D. (2010). Friends' dieting and disordered eating behaviors among adolescents five years later: Findings from Project EAT. *Journal of Adolescent Health, 47,* 67–73.

Ekblad, M., Gissler, M., Lehtonen, L., & Korkeila, J. (2010). The effect of prenatal smoking exposure on adolescents' use of psychiatric drugs. *Pediatric Academic Societies Abstracts,* 4401.56. Abstract retrieved from http://www.abstracts2view.com/pasall/view.php?nu=PAS10L1_513.

Elder, T. E. (2010). The importance of relative standards in ADHD diagnose: Evidence based on exact birth dates. *Journal of Health Economics, 29(5),* 641–656.

Ellen, I. G. (2000). *Sharing America's neighborhoods: The prospects for stable racial integration.* Cambridge, MA: Harvard University Press.

Ennett, S. T., Foshee, V. A., Bauman, K. E., Hussong, A., Cai, L., McNaughton, et al. (2008). The social ecology of adolescent alcohol misuse. *Child Development, 79(6),* 1777–1791.

Epps, S., & Jackson, B. (2000). *Empowered families, successful children.* Washington, DC: American Psychiatric Publishing.

Essex, M. J., Klein, M. H., Slattery, M. J., Goldsmith, H. H., and Kalin, N. H. (2010). Early risk factors and developmental pathways to chronic high inhibition and social anxiety disorder in adolescence. *American Journal of Psychiatry, 167(1),* 40–46. Retrieved from http://ajp.psychiatryonline.org.

Eyberg, S. M., Nelson, M. M., & Boggs, S. R. (2008). Evidenced-based psychosocial treatments for children and adolescents with disruptive behavior. *Journal of Clinical Child and Adolescent Psychology, 37,* 215–237.

Fairburn, C. G., Agras, W. S., Walsh, B. T., Wilson, G. T., & Stice, E. (2004). Prediction of outcome in bulimia nervosa by early change in treatment. *American Journal of Psychiatry, 161,* 2322–2324.

Fairburn, C. G., Cooper, Z., Doll, H. A., & Davies, B. A. (2005). Identifying dieters who will develop an eating disorder: A prospective, population-based study. *American Journal of Psychiatry, 162,* 2249–2255.

Fairburn, C. G., Jones, R., Peveler, R. C., Carr, S. J., Solomon, R. A., O'Connor, M. E., et al. (1991). Three psychological treatments for bulimia nervosa: A comparative trial. *Archives of General Psychiatry, 48(5),* 463–469.

Fairburn, C. G., Marcus, M. D., & Wilson, G. T. (1993). Cognitive-behavioral therapy for binge eating and bulimia nervosa: A comprehensive treatment manual. In C. G. Fairburn & G. T. Wilson (Eds.), *Binge eating: Nature, assessment, and treatment* (pp. 361–404). New York: Guilford Press.

Fairburn, C. G., Norman, P. L., Welch, S. L., O'Connor, M. E., Doll, H. A., & Peveler, R. C. (1995). A prospective study of outcome in bulimia nervosa and the long-term effects of three psychological treatments. *Archives of General Psychiatry, 52(4),* 304–312.

Fals-Stewart, W., Birchler, G., & Kelley, M. (2006). Learning sobriety together: A randomized clinical trial examining behavioural couples therapy with alcoholic female patients. *Journal of Consulting and Clinical Psychology, 74,* 579–591.

Faraone, S. V., Biederman, J., Spencer, T., Mick, E., Murray, K., Petty, C., et al. (2006). Diagnosing adult attention deficit hyperactivity disorder: Are late onset and subthreshold diagnoses valid? *American Journal of Psychiatry, 163(10),* 1720–1729.

Faraone, S. V., & Khan, S. A. (2006). Candidate gene studies of attention-deficit/hyperactivity disorders. *Journal of Clinical Psychiatry, 67(8),* 13–20.

Faravelli, C., Rosi, S., & Scarpato, M. A. (2006). Threshold and subthreshold bipolar disorders in the Sesto Fiorentino Study. *Journal of Affective Disorders, 94(1–3),* 111–119.

Fatjó-Vilas, M., Gourion, D., Campanera, S., Mouaffak, F., Levy-Rueff, M., Navarro, M. E., et al. (2008). New evidences of gene and environment interactions affecting prenatal neurodevelopment in schizophrenia-spectrum disorders: A family dermatoglyphic study. *Schizophrenia Research, 103(1–3),* 209–217.

Fava, G. A., Ruini, C., & Rafanelli, C. (2005). Sequential treatment of mood and anxiety disorder. *Journal of Clinical Psychiatry, 66(11),* 1392–1400.

Favaro, A., Tenconi, E., & Santonastaso, P. (2006). Prenatal factors and the risk of developing anorexia nervosa and bulimia nervosa. *Archives of General Psychiatry, 63,* 82–88.

Fawcett, J. (2006). Depressive disorders. In R. L. Simon & R. E. Hales (Eds.), *The American Psychiatric Publishing textbook of suicide assessment and management* (1st ed.) (pp. 255–275). Washington, DC: American Psychiatric Publishing.

Fazel, S., Doll, H., & Langstrom, N. (2008). Mental disorders among adolescents in juvenile detention and correctional facilities: A systematic review and metaregression analysis of 25 surveys. *Journal of the American Academy of Child and Adolescent Psychiatry, 47,* 1010–1019.

Fergusson, D., Horwood, L., & Lynskey, M. (1996). Childhood sexual abuse and psychiatric disorder in young adulthood: II. Psychiatric outcomes of childhood sexual abuse. *Journal of the American Academy of Child and Adolescent Psychiatry, 35,* 1365–1374.

Fergusson, D. M., Boden, J. M., & Horwood, L. J. (2008). Exposure to childhood sexual and physical abuse and adjustment in early adulthood. *Child Abuse and Neglect, 32,* 607–619.

Findling, R. L. (2009). Treatment of childhood-onset bipolar disorder. In C. A. Zarate & H. K. Manji (Eds.), *Bipolar depression: Molecular neurobiology, clinical diagnosis and pharmacotherapy* (pp. 241–252). Cambridge, MA: Birkhäuser.

Findling, R. L., Youngstrom, E. A., Fristad, M. A., Birmaher, B., Kowatch, R. A., Frazier, A. E., et al. (2010). Characteristics of children with elevated symptoms of mania: The Longitudinal Assessment of Manic Symptoms (LAMS) Study. *Journal of Clinical Psychiatry, 71(12),* 1664–1672.

Fink, M. (2006). ECT in therapy-resistant mania: Does it have a place? *Bipolar Disorders, 8(3),* 307–309.

Finlay, J. M. (2001). Mesoprefontal dopamine neurons and schizophrenia: Roles of developmental abnormalities. *Schizophrenia Bulletin, 27(3),* 431–442.

Finnegan, L. P., & Kandall, S. R. (2008). Perinatal substance abuse. In H. D. Kleber & M. Galanter (Eds.), *The American Psychiatric Publishing textbook of substance abuse treatment* (4th ed.). Washington, DC: American Psychiatric Publishing.

First, M. B., Frances, A., & Pincus, H. A. (2002). *DSM-IV-TR handbook of differential diagnosis.* Arlington, VA: American Psychiatric Publishing.

Fischer, J., & Corcoran, K. (2007). *Measures for clinical practice and research: A sourcebook: Volume 1 and Volume 2: Couples, families, and children* (4th ed.). New York: Oxford University Press.

Fisher, C. A., Hetrick, S. E., & Rushford, N. (2010). Family therapy for anorexia nervosa. *The Cochrane Database of Systematic Reviews, 2010, 4.*

Fitzsimmons, S., & Buettner, L. L. (2003). Therapeutic recreation intervention for need-driven dementia-compromised behaviors in community dwellers. *American Journal of Alzheimer's Disease and Other Dementias, 17(6),* 367–381.

Fletcher, K. (1996). Childhood post-traumatic stress disorder. In E. J. Mash & R. Barkley (Eds.), *Child psychopathology* (pp. 248–276). New York: Guilford Press.

Floersch, J. (2003). The subjective experience of youth psychotropic treatment. *Social Work in Mental Health, 1(4),* 51–69.

Floyd, M. (2003). Bibliotherapy as an adjunct to psychotherapy for depression in older adults. *Journal of Clinical Psychology, 59(2),* 187–195.

Foa, E. B., Keane, T. M., & Friedman, M. J. (Eds.). (2000). *Effective treatments for PTSD: Practice guidelines from the International Society for Traumatic Stress Studies.* New York: Guilford Press.

Fonagy, P., & Bateman, A. W. (2006). Progress in the treatment of borderline personality disorder. *British Journal of Psychology, 188(1),* 1–3.

Fonagy, P., & Kurtz, Z. (2002). Disturbance of conduct. In P. Fonagy, M. Target, D. Cottrell, J. Phillips, & Z. Kurtz (Eds.), *What works for whom? A critical review of treatments for children and adolescents.* New York: Guilford Press.

Fonagy, P., Target, M., Cottrell, D., Phillips, J., & Kurtz, Z. (2002). *What works for whom? A critical review of treatments for children and adolescents.* New York: Guilford Press.

Fonseca, A. C., & Perrin, S. (2001). Clinical phenomenology, classification and assessment of anxiety disorders in children and adolescents. In W. K. Silverman & P. D. A. Treffers (Eds.), *Anxiety disorders in children and adolescents: Research, assessment and intervention* (pp. 126–158). New York: Cambridge University Press.

Ford, J. D., Stockton, P., & Kaltman, S. (2006). Disorders of extreme stress (DESNOS) symptoms are associated with type and severity of interpersonal trauma exposure in a sample of healthy young women. *Journal of Interpersonal Violence, 21(11),* 1399–1416.

Ford, T., Goodman, R., & Meltzer, H. (2004). The relative importance of child, family, school and neighborhood correlates of childhood psychiatric disorder. *Social Psychiatry and Psychiatric Epidemiology, 39(6),* 487–496.

Foreyt, J., Poston, W., Winebarger, A., & McGavin, J. (1998). Anorexia nervosa and bulimia nervosa. In E. Mash & R. Barkley (Eds.), *Treatment of childhood disorders* (2nd ed.) (pp. 647–691). New York: Guilford Press.

Franco, K. N., & Messinger-Rapport, B. (2005). Pharmacological treatment of neuropsychiatric symptoms of dementia: A review of the evidence. *Journal of the American Medical Association, 293(5),* 596–608.

Frank, E. (2007). Interpersonal and social rhythm therapy: A means of improving depression and preventing relapse in bipolar disorder. *Journal of Clinical Psychology: In Session, 63(5),* 463–473.

Franko, D. L., Dorer, D. J., Keel, P. K., Jackson, S., Manzo, M. P., & Herzog, D. B. (2005). How do eating disorders and alcohol use disorder influence each other? *International Journal of Eating Disorders, 38,* 200–207.

Franko, D. L., & Keel, P. K. (2006). Suicidality in eating disorders: Occurrence, correlates, and clinical implications. *Clinical Psychology Review, 26,* 769–782.

Franko, D., Wonderlich, S., Little, D., & Herzog, D. (2004). Diagnosis and classification of eating disorders. In J. K. Thompson (Ed.), *Handbook of eating disorders and obesity* (pp. 58–80). Hoboken, NJ: Wiley.

Freeman, A., Stone, M., & Martin, D. (2005). Introduction: A review of borderline personality disorder. In A. Freeman, M. H. Stone, & D. Martin (Eds.), *Comparative treatments for borderline personality disorder* (pp. 1–20). New York: Springer.

Frick, P. J. (2006). Developmental pathways to conduct disorder. *Child and Adolescent Psychiatric Clinics of North America, 15,* 311–331.

Friedman, E. S., Wisniewski, S. R., Gilmer, W., Nierenberg, A. A., Rush, A. J., Fava, M., et al. (2009). Sociodemographic, clinical, and treatment characteristics associated with worsened depression during treatment with citalopram: Results of the NIMH STAR*D trial. *Depression and Anxiety, 26(7),* 612–621.

Friedman, F. B. (2008). Borderline personality disorder and hospitalization. *Social Work in Mental Health, 6(1–2),* 67–84.

Fruzzetti, A. E.., & Boulanger, J. L. (2005). Family involvement in treatment. In J. G. Gunderson & P. D. Hoffman (Eds.),*Understanding and treating borderline personality disorder: A guide for professionals and families* (pp. 151–164). Arlington, VA: American Psychiatric Publishing.

Fuller, R., & Hiller-Sturmhofel, S. (1999). Alocholism treatment in the United States: An overview. *Alcohol Research and Health, 23,* 69–77.

Gabbard, G. O., & Horowitz, M. J. (2009). Insight, transference interpretation, and therapeutic change in the dynamic psychotherapy of borderline personality disorder. *American Journal of Psychiatry, 66(5),* 517–521.

Gadow, K., DeVincent, C., & Schneider, J. (2008). Predictors of psychiatric symptoms in children with an autism spectrum disorder. *Journal of Autism and Developmental Disorders, 38(9),* 1710–1720.

Gangwisch, J. E., Babiss, L. A., Malaspina, D., Turner, J. B., Zammit, G. K., & Posner, K. (2010). Earlier parental set bedtimes as a protective factor against depression and suicidal ideation. *Sleep, 33(1),* 97–106. Retrieved from http://www.ncbi.nlm.nih.gov/pmc/articles/PMC2802254/.

Garfinkel, I., Heintze, T., & Huang, C. (2001). The effects of child support enforcement on women's incomes. *Poverty Research News, 5(3),* 5–7.

Garmezy, N. (1993). Children in poverty: Resilience despite risk. *Psychiatry, 56,* 127–136.

Gatz, J. L., Tyas, S. L., St. John, P., & Montgomery, P. (2005). Do depressive symptoms predict Alzheimer's disease and dementia? *Journal of Gerontology: Medical Sciences, 60A(6),* 744–747.

Gatz, M., Reynolds, C. A., Fratiglioni, L., Johansson, B., Mortimer, J. A., Berg, S., et al. (2006). Role of genetics and environments for explaining Alzheimer's disease. *Archives of General Psychiatry, 63,* 168–174.

Geanellos, R. (2005). Adversity as opportunity: Living with schizophrenia and developing a resilient self. *International Journal of Mental Health Nursing, 14(1),* 7–15.

Geddes, J. R., Burgess, S., Hawton, K., Jamison, K., & Goodwin, G. M. (2004). Long-term lithium therapy for bipolar disorder: Systematic review and meta-analysis of randomized controlled trials. *American Journal of Psychiatry, 161(2),* 217–222.

Gelhorn, H., Stallings, M., Young, S., Corley, R., Rhee, S. H., Christian, H., et al. (2006). Common and specific genetic influences on aggressive and nonaggressive conduct disorder domains. *Journal of the American Academy of Child and Adolescent Psychiatry, 45(5),* 570–577.

Geller, B., Tillman, R., Bolhofner, K., & Zimerman, B. (2008). Child bipolar I disorder: Prospective continuity with adult bipolar I disorder; characteristics of second and third episodes; predictors of 8-year outcome. *Archives of General Psychiatry, 65(10),* 1125–1133.

Ginsberg, L. D. (2006). Carbamazepine extended-release capsules: A retrospective review of its use in children and adolescents. *Annals of Clinical Psychiatry, 18*(Suppl. 1), 9–14.

Ginsburg, G. S., Kingeiy, J. N., Drake, K. L., & Grados, M. A. (2008). Predictors of treatment response in pediatric obsessive-compulsive disorder. *Journal of the American Academy of Child and Adolescent Psychiatry, 47,* 868–878.

Girgus, J. S., & Nolen-Hoeksema, S. (2006). Cognition and depression. In C. L. Keyes & S. H. Goodman (Eds.), *Women and depression: A handbook for the social, behavioral, and biomedical sciences* (pp. 147–175). New York: Cambridge University Press.

Gizer, I. R., Ficks, C., & Waldman, I. D. (2009). Candidate gene studies of ADHD: A meta-analytic review. *Human Genetics, 126,* 51–90. DOI: 10.1007/s00439-009-0694x.

Glueckauf, R. L., Stine, C., Bourgeois, M., Pomedor, A., Rom, P., Young, M. E., et al. (2005). Alzheimer's rural care healthline: Linking rural caregivers to cognitive-behavioral intervention for depression. *Rehabilitation Psychology, 50(4),* 346–354.

Godart, N. T., Perdereau, F., Rein, Z., Berthoz, S., Wallier, J., Jeammet, P. H., et al. (2007). Comorbidity studies of eating disorders and mood disorders. Critical review of the literature. *Journal of Affective Disorders, 97,* 37–49.

Goeree, M. S., Ham, J. C., & Iorio, D. (2009, November 6). Caught in the bulimic trap? On the incidence, persistence, and state dependence of bulimia among blacks and whites. Retrieved from http://www-bcf.usc.edu/~goeree/bn.pdf.

Goeree, M. S., Ham, J. C., & Iorio, D. (2011). Race, social class, and bulimia nervosa. *IZA Discussion Papers, 5823,* 1–36.

Golden, N., Katzman, D., Kreipe, R., Stevens, S., Sawyer, S., Rees, J., et al. (2003). Eating disorders in adolescents: Position paper of the Society for Adolescent Medicine. *Journal of Adolescent Health, 33,* 496–503.

Golding, J. M. (1999). Intimate partner violence as a risk factor for mental disorders: A meta-analysis. *Journal of Family Violence, 14(2),* 99–132.

Goldstein, A. P., Glick, B., & Gibb, J. C. (1998). *Aggression replacement training: A comprehensive intervention for aggressive youth.* Champaign, IL: Research Press.

Goldstrom, I. D., Campbell, J., Rogers, J. A., Lambert, D. B., Blacklow, B., Henderson, M. J., et al. (2006). National estimates for mental health mutual support groups, self-help organizations, and consumer-operated services. *Administration and Policy in Mental Health, 33,* 92–103.

Glodzick-Sobanska, L., Pirraglia, E., Brys, M., de Santi, S., Mosconi, L., Rich, K. E., et al. (2009). The effects of normal aging and ApoE genotype on the levels of CSF biomarkers for Alzheimer's disease. *Neurobiology of Aging, 30(5),* 672–681.

Gonzalez-Tejara, G., Canino, G., Ramirez, R., Chavez, L., Shrout, P., Bird, H., et al. (2005). Examining minor and major depression in adolescents. *Journal of Child Psychology and Psychiatry, 46,* 888–899.

Goodman, M., Triebwasser, J., & New, A. (2008). Biological underpinnings of borderline personality disorder. *Social Work in Mental Health, 6(1–2),* 33–47.

Goodman, S. H. (2007). Depression in mothers. In S. Nolen-Hoeksema, T. D. Cannon, & T. Widiger (Eds.), *Annual Review of Clinical Psychology, 3,* 107–135.

Gorman, J., Shear, K., Cowley, D., Cross, C. D., March, J., Roth, W., et al. (2002). Practice guidelines for the treatment of patients with panic disorder. *American Psychiatric Association practice guidelines for the treatment of psychiatric disorders. Compendium 2002* (pp. 635–696). Washington, DC: American Psychiatric Publishing.

Gould, M. S., Walsh, B. T., Munfakh, J. L., Kleinman, M., Duan, N., Olfson, M., et al. (2009). Sudden death and use of stimulant medications in youths. *American Journal of Psychiatry, 166,* 992–1001. DOI: 10.1176/appi.ajp.2009.09040472.

Gowers, S., & Bryant-Waugh, R. (2004). Management of child and adolescent eating disorders: The current evidence base and future directions. *Journal of Child Psychology and Psychiatry, 45,* 63–83.

Grant, B. F., Chou, S. P., Goldstein, R. B., Huang, B., Stinson, F. S., Saha, T. D., et al. (2008). Prevalence, correlates, and comorbidity of DSM-IV borderline personality disorder: Results from the wave 2 national epidemiologic survey on alcohol and related conditions. *Journal of Clinical Psychiatry, 69(4),* 533–545.

Grant, B. F., Hasin, D. S., Blanco, C., Stinson, F. S., Chou, S. P., Goldstein, R. B., et al. (2005). The epidemiology of social anxiety disorder in the United States: Results from the National Epidemiologic Survey on Alcohol and Related Conditions. *Journal of Clinical Psychiatry, 66,* 1351–1361.

Grant, B. F., Hasin, D. S., Stinson, F. S., Dawson, D. A. S., Chou, P. W., Ruan, J., et al. (2005). Co-occurrence of 12-month mood and anxiety disorders and personality disorders in the US: Results from the national epidemiologic survey on alcohol and related conditions. *Journal of Psychiatric Research, 39(1),* 1–9.

Grant, B. F., Stinson, F. S., Hasin, D. S., Dawson, D. A., Chou, S. P., Ruan, W. J., et al. (2005). Prevalence, correlates, and comorbidity of bipolar I disorder and axis I and II disorder: Results from the national epidemiological survey on alcohol and related conditions. *Journal of Clinical Psychiatry, 66,* 1205–1215.

Gratz, K. L., Tull, M. T., & Gunderson, J. G. (2008). Does anxiety sensitivity help us to understand borderline personality disorder? *Clinician's Research Digest, 26(11)*, 2.

Graybeal, C. (2001). Strengths-based social work assessment: Transforming the dominant paradigm. *Families in Society, 82*, 233–242.

Green, J. G., McLaughlin, K. A., Berglund, P. A., Gruber, M. J., Sampson, N. A., Zaslavsky, A. M., et al. (2010). Childhood adversities and adult psychiatric disorders in the national comorbidity survey replication I: Associations with first onset of DSMTV disorders. *Archives of General Psychiatry, 67*, 113–123.

Greene, R. R., & Livingston, N. (2002). A social construct. In R. R. Greene (Ed.), *Resiliency theory: An integrated framework for practice, research, and policy.* Washington, DC: NASW Press.

Greenberg, M., Speltz, M., DeKlyen, M., & Jones, K. (2001). Correlates of clinic referral for early conduct problems: Variable-
and person-oriented approaches. *Development and Psychopathology, 13*, 255–276.

Griffiths, C. A. (2006). The theories, mechanisms, benefits, and practical delivery of psychosocial educational interventions for people with mental health disorders. *International Journal of Psychosocial Rehabilitation, 11(1)*, 21–28.

Grilo, C. M., Sanislow, C. A., & McGlashan, T. H. (2002). Co-occurrence of DSM-IV personality disorders with borderline personality disorder. *Journal of Nervous and Mental Disease, 190(8)*, 552–553.

Groesz, L. M., Levine, M. P., & Murnen, S. K. (2002). The effect of experimental presentation of thin media images on body satisfaction: A meta-analytic review. *International Journal of Eating Disorders, 31*, 1–16.

Guo, W., & Tsui, M. (2010). From resilience to resistance: A reconstruction of the strengths perspective in social work practice. *International Social Work, 53(2)*, 233–245.

Gurvits, I. G., Koenigsberg, H. W., & Siever, L. J. (2000). Neurotransmitter dysfunction in patients with borderline personality disorder. *Psychiatric Clinics of North America, 23(1)*, 27–40.

Gutman, L. M., & Sameroff, A. J. (2004). Continuities in depression from adolescence to young adulthood: Contrasting ecological influences. *Development and Psychopathology, 16*, 967–984.

Hagopian, L., & Ollendick, T. (1997). Anxiety disorders. In R. Ammerman & M. Hersen (Eds.), *Handbook of prevention and treatment with children and adolescents: Intervention in the real world context* (pp. 431–454). New York: Wiley.

Hammen, C., Brennan, P., & Keenan-Miller, D. (2008). Patterns of adolescent depression to age 20: The role of maternal depression and youth interpersonal dysfunction. *Journal of Abnormal Child Psychology, 36*, 1189–1198.

Hamrin, V., & Pachler, M. (2007). Pediatric bipolar disorder: Evidence-based psychopharmalogical treatments. *Journal of Child and Adolescent Psychiatric Nursing, 20(1)*, 40–58.

Hanes, R. B., Yao, X., Degani, A., Kripalani, S. Garb, A., & McDonald, H. P. (2005). Interventions to enhance medication adherence. *Cochrane Database of Systematic Reviews, 4*. Art. No. CD000011.

Hankin, B. L., & Abela, J. R. Z. (2005). Depression from childhood through adolescences and adulthood: A developmental vulnerability and stress perspective. In B. L. Hankin & J. R. Z. Abela (Eds.), *Development of psychopathology: A vulnerability-stress perspective* (pp. 245–288). Thousand Oaks, CA: Sage Publications.

Hankin, B. L., Abela, J. R. Z., Auerbach, R. P., McWhinnie, C. M., & Skitch, S. A. (2005). Development of behavioral problems over the life course: A vulnerability and stress perspective. In B. L. Hankin & J. R. Z. Abela (Eds.), *Development of psychopathology: A vulnerability-stress perspective* (pp. 385–416). Thousand Oaks, CA: Sage Publications.

Hanklin, B., Kassel, J. D., & Abela, J. R. (2005). Adult attachment dimensions and specificity of emotional distress symptoms: Prospective investigations of cognitive risk and interpersonal stress generation as mediating mechanisms. *Personality and Psychology Bulletin, 31*, 136–151.

Hanson, E., Kalish, L. A., Bunce, E., Curtis, C., McDaniel, S., Ware, J., et al. (2007). Use of complementary and alternative medicine among children diagnosed with autism spectrum disorder. *Journal of Autism and Developmental Disorders, 37(4)*, 628–636.

Happe, F., & Ronald, A. (2008). The "fractionable autism triad"s: A review of evidence from behavioural, genetic, cognitive and neural research. *Neuropsychology Review, 18(4)*, 287–304.

Harrington, J., Rosen, L., Garnecho, A., & Patrick, P. (2006). Parental perceptions and use of complementary and alternative medicine practices for children with autistic spectrum disorders in private practice. *Journal of Developmental and Behavioral Pediatrics, 27*(2 Suppl.), S156–61.

Hartmann, A., Zeeck, A., & Barrett, M. S. (2009). Interpersonal problems in eating disorders. *International Journal of Eating Disorders, 43(7)*, 619–627.

Hasin, D. S., Stinson, F. S., Ogburn, E., & Grant, B. F. (2007). Prevalence, correlates, disability, and comorbidity of DSM-IV
alcohol abuse and dependence in the United States: Results from the national epidemiologic survey on alcohol and related conditions. *Archives of General Psychiatry, 64(7),* 830–842.

Hawton, K., Sutton, L., Haw, C., Sinclair, J., & Harriss, L. (2005). Suicide and attempted suicide in bipolar disorder: A
systematic review of risk factors. *Journal of Clinical Psychiatry, 66(6),* 693–704.

Hay, P., Bacaltchuk, J., Claudino, A., Ben-Tovim, D., & Yong, P. (2003). *Individual psychotherapy in the outpatient treatment of adults with anorexia nervosa* (Cochrane Review). *The Cochrane Library,* Issue 4. Chichester, UK: Wiley.

Hay, P. J., & Bacaltchuk, J. (2003). Psychotherapy for bulimia nervosa and binging (Cochrane Review). *The Cochrane Library,* Issue 1. Oxford: Update Software.

Hay, P. J., Bacaltchuk, J., & Stefano, S. (2004). Psychotherapy for bulimia nervosa and binging. *Cochrane Database of Systematic Reviews, 2004, 3.*

Hayward, C., Wilson, K. A., Lagle, K., Killen, J. D., & Taylor, C. B. (2004). Parent-reported predictors of adolescent panic attacks. *Journal of the American Academy of Child and Adolescent Psychiatry, 43,* 613–620.

Hayward, C., Wilson, K. A., Lagle, K., Kraemer, H. C., Killen, J. D., & Taylor, C. B. (2008). The developmental psychopathology of social anxiety in adolescents. *Depression and Anxiety, 25,* 200–206. DOI: 10.1002/da.20289.

Hazan, C., Campa, M., & Gur-Yaish, N. (2006). Attachment across the lifespan. In P. Noller & J. Feeney (Eds.), *Close relationships: Functions, form and processes* (pp. 189–209). Hove, England: Psychology Press/Taylor & Francis.

Hazell, P., O'Connell, D., Heathcote, D., & Henry, D. (2003). Tricyclic drugs for depression in children and adolescents (Cochrane Review). *The Cochrane Library,* Issue 1, 2003. Oxford: Update Software.

He, G., Luo, W., Li, P., Remmers, C., Netzer, W. J., Hendrick, J., et al. (2010). Gamma-secretase activating protein is a therapeutic target for Alzheimer's disease. *Nature, 467(7311),* 95–98.

Healy, D. (2002). *The creation of psychopharmacology.* Cambridge, MA: Harvard University Press.

Helgeson, V., Reynolds, K., & Tomich, P. (2006). A meta-analytic review of benefit finding and growth. *Journal of Consulting and Clinical Psychology, Special issue: Benefit-Finding, 74,* 797–816.

Henggeler, S. W., Schoenwald, S. K., Borduin, C., Rowland, M., & Cunningham, P. B. (1998). *Multisystemic treatment of antisocial behavior in children and adolescents.* New York: Guilford Press.

Henry, J. D., Rendell, P. G., Scicluna, A., Jackson, M., & Phillips, L. H. (2009). Emotion experience, expression, and regulation in Alzheimer's disease. *Psychology and Aging, 24(1),* 252–257.

Hersen, M. (2006). *Clinician's handbook of child behavioral assessment.* San Diego, CA: Elsevier.

Herzog, D. B., & Delinsky, S. S. (2001). Classification of eating disorders. In R. Striegel-Moore & L. Smolak (Eds.), *Eating disorders: Innovative directions for research and practice* (pp. 31–50). Washington, DC: American Psychological Association.

Hettema, J. M., Neale, M. C., & Kendler, K. S. (2001). A review and meta-analysis of the genetic epidemiology of anxiety disorders. *American Journal of Psychiatry, 1574,* 1568–1578.

Heyn, P. (2003). The effect of a multisensory exercise program on engagement, behavior, and selected physiological indexes in persons with dementia. *American Journal of Alzheimer's Disease and Other Dementias, 18(4),* 247–251.

Hicks, B. M., South, S. C., DiRago, A. C., Iacono, W. G., & McGue, M. (2009). Environmental adversity and increasing genetic risk for externalizing disorders. *Archives of General Psychiatry, 66,* 640–648.

Hill, D., Rozanski, C., Carfagnini, J., &Willoughby, B. (2005). Gender identity disorders in childhood and adolescence: A
critical inquiry. *Journal of Psychology and Human Sexuality, 17(3/4),* 7–33.

Hill, J. (2002). Biological, psychological and social processes in conduct disorders. *Journal of Child Psychology and Psychiatry, 43(1),* 133–164.

Hillman, J. (2007). Grandparents of children with autism: A review with recommendations for education, practice, and policy. *Educational Gerontology, 33(6),* 513–527.

Hilty, D., Brady, K., & Hales, R. (1999). A review of bipolar disorder among adults. *Psychiatric Services, 50,* 201–213.

Himelick, A. J., & Walsh, J. (2002). Nursing home residents with borderline personality traits: Clinical social work interventions. *Journal of Gerontological Social Work, 37(1),* 49–63.

Hino, T., Takeuchi, T., & Yamanouchi, N. (2002). A 1-year follow-up study of coping in patients with panic disorder. *Comprehensive Psychiatry, 43,* 279–284.

Hinshaw, S. P., Owens, E. B., Sami, N., & Fargeon, S. (2006). Prospective follow-up of girls with attention-deficit/hyperactivity disorder into adolescence: Evidence for continuing cross-domain impairment. *Journal of Consulting and Clinical Psychology, 74(3),* 489–499.

Hirschfeld, R. M. A., Lewis, L., & Vornik, L. A. (2003). Perceptions and impact of bipolar disorder: How far have we come? Results of the National Depressive and Manic Depressive Association's 2000 survey of individuals with bipolar disorder. *Journal of Clinical Psychiatry, 64(2),* 161–174.

Hirschowitz, J., Kolevzon, A., & Garakani, A. (2010). The pharmacological treatment of bipolar disorder: The question of modern advances. *Harvard Review of Psychiatry, 18(5),* 266–278.

Hjern, A., Weitoft, G. R., & Lindblad, F. (2010). Social adversity predicts ADHD-medication in school children—A national cohort study. *Acta Paediatrica, 99(6),* 920–924. DOI: 10.1111/j.1657-2227.2009.01638.x.

Hoffman, S. G., & Smits, J. A. J. (2008). Cognitive-behavioral therapy for adult anxiety disorders: A meta-analysis of randomized placebo-controlled trials. *Journal of Clinical Psychiatry, 69,* 621–632.

Holahan, C. J., Moos, R. H., Holahan, C. K., Brennan, P. L., & Schutte, K. K. (2005). Stress generations, avoidance coping, and depressive symptoms: 10-year model. *Journal of Consulting and Clinical Psychology, 73(4),* 658–666.

Holahan, C. J., Schutte, K. K., Brennan, P. L., Holahan, C. K., Moos, B. S., & Moos, R. H. (2010). Late-life alcohol consumption and 20-year mortality. *Alcoholism: Clinical and Experimental Research, 34(11),* 1961–1971.

Holm, A. L., & Severinsson, E. (2008). The emotional pain and distress of borderline personality disorder: A review of the literature. *International Journal of Mental Health Nursing, 17(1),* 27–35.

Holter, M. (2004). Autistic spectrum disorders: Assessment and intervention. In P. Allen-Meares & M. Fraser (Eds.), *Intervention with children and adolescents: An interdisciplinary perspective* (pp. 205–228). Washington, DC: NASW Press.

Hopfer, C. J., Stallings, M. C., Hewitt, J. K., &Crowley, T. J. (2003). Family transmission of marijuana use, abuse, and dependence. *Journal of the American Academy of Child and Adolescent Psychiatry, 42,* 834–841.

Hopwood, C. J., & Zanarini, M. C. (2010). Borderline personality traits and disorder: Predictive prospective patient functioning. *Journal of Consulting and Clinical Psychology, 78(4),* 585–589.

Howlin, P. (2005). Outcomes in autism spectrum disorders. In F. R. Volkmar, R. Paul, A. Klin, & D. Cohen (Eds.), *Handbook of autism and pervasive developmental disorders Vol. 1: Diagnosis, development, neurobiology, and behavior* (3rd ed.) (pp. 201–220). Hoboken, NJ: Wiley.

Huang, B., Grant, B. F., Dawson, D. A., Frederick, F. S., Chou, S. P., Saha, T. D., et al. (2006). Race-ethnicity and the prevalence and co-occurrence of *Diagnostic and Statistical Manual of Mental Disorders,* alcohol and drug use disorders and Axis I and II disorders.

Huang, X., Lei, Z., & El-Mallach, R. S. (2007). Lithium normalizes elevated intracellular sodium. *Bipolar Disorder, 9(3),* 298–300.

Hudson, J., Hiripi, E., Pope, H., & Kessler, R. (2006). The prevalence and correlates of eating disorders in the National Comorbidity Survey Replication. *Biological Psychiatry, 61,* 348–358.

Humphreys, K., Wing, S., McCarty, D., Chappel, J., Gallant, L., Haberle, B., et al. (2004). Self-help organizations for alcohol and drug problems: Towards evidence-based practice. *Journal of Substance Abuse Treatment, 26,* 151–158.

Hutsler, J., & Zhang, H. (2010). Increased dendritic spine densities on cortical projection neurons in autism spectrum disorders. *Brain Research, 1309(14),* 83–94.

Ingram, R., & Smith, L. T. (2008). Mood disorders. In J. E. Maddux & B. A. Winstead (Eds.), *Psychopathology: Foundations for a contemporary understanding* (2nd ed.) (pp. 171–197). New York: Routledge/Taylor & Francis Group.

Ivleva, E., Thaker, G., & Tamminga, C. A. (2008). Comparing genes and phenomenology in the major psychoses: Schizophrenia and bipolar 1 disorder. *Schizophrenia Bulletin, 34(4),* 734–742.

Jackson, A., Cavanaugh, J., & Scott, J. (2003). A systematic review of manic and depressive prodromes. *Journal of Affective Disorders, 74(3),* 209–217.

Jacobvitz, D., Hazen, N., Curran, M., & Hitchens, K. (2004). Observations of early triadic family interactions: Boundary disturbances in the family predict symptoms of depression, anxiety, and attention-deficit/hyperactivity disorder in middle childhood. *Development and Psychopathology, 16,* 577–592.

Jaffee, S. R., Caspi, A., & Moffitt, T. E. (2005). Nature x nurture: Genetic vulnerabilities interact with physical maltreatment to promote conduct problems. *Development and Psychopathology, 17(1),* 67–84.

James, A., Soler, A., & Weatherall, R. (2005). Cognitive behavioural therapy for anxiety disorders in children and adolescents. *Cochrane Database of Systematic Reviews, 4*. Art. No. CD004690.

Jané-Llopis, E., & Matytsina, I. (2006). Mental health and alcohol, drugs and tobacco: A review of the comorbidity between mental disorders and the use of alcohol, tobacco and illicit drugs. *Drug and Alcohol Review, 25*, 515–536.

Jatzko, A., Rothenhofer, S., & Schmitt, A. (2006). Hippocampal volume in chronic posttraumatic stress disorder (PTSD): MRI
study using two different evaluation methods. *Journal of Affective Disorders, 94(1–3)*, 121–126.

Jedrziewski, M. K., Lee, V. M., & Trojanowski, J. Q. (2005). Lowering the risk of Alzheimer's disease: Evidence-based practices emerging from new research. *Alzheimer's and Dementia, 1(2)*, 152–160.

Jensen, P. S., Arnold, L. E., Swanson, J. M., Vitiello, B., Abikoff, H. B., Greenhill, L. L., et al. (2007). 3-Year follow-up of the NIMH MTA Study. *Journal of the American Academy of Child and Adolescent Psychiatry, 46*, 989–1002.

Jesner, O. S., Aref-Adib, M., & Coren, E. (2007). Risperidone for autism spectrum disorder. *Cochrane Database of Systematic Reviews 2007*, Issue 1. Art. No. CD005040. DOI: 10.1002/14651858.CD005040.pub2.

Jessor, R., Van Den Bos, J., Vanderryn, J., Costa, F. M., & Turbin, M. S. (1997). Protective factors in adolescent problem behavior: Moderator effects and developmental change. In G. A. Marlatt & G. R. Van Den Bos (Eds.), *Addictive behaviors: Readings on etiology, prevention, and treatment* (pp. 239–264). Washington, DC: American Psychological Association.

Jobe, T., &Harrow, M. (2005). Long-term outcome of patients with schizophrenia: A review. *Canadian Journal of Psychiatry, 50(14)*, 892–900.

Johnson, B. R., Jang, S. J., Li, S. D., & Larson, D. (2000). The "invisible institution" and black youth crime: The church as an agency of local social control. *Journal of Youth and Adolescence, 29(4)*, 479–498.

Johnson, C. P., & Myers, S. M. (2007). Identification and evaluation of children with autism spectrum disorders. Council on Children with Disabilities. *Pediatrics, 120(5)*, 1183–1215.

Johnson, D. R., & Lubin, H. (2006). The counting method: Applying the rule of parsimony to the treatment of posttraumatic stress disorder. *Traumatology, 12(1)*, 83–99.

Johnson, J. G., McGeoch, P. G., Caskey, V. P., Abhary, S. G., Sneed, J. R., & Bornstein, R. F. (2005). The developmental psycho-pathology of personality disorders. In B. L. Hankin & J. R. Z. Abela (Eds.), *Development of
psychopathology: A vulnerability-stress perspective* (pp. 417–464). Thousand Oaks, CA: Sage Publications.

Johnson, K. A., Wiersema, J. R., & Kuntsi, J. (2009). What would Karl Popper say? Are current psychological theories of ADHD
falsifiable? *Behavioral and Brain Functions, 5*, 15, 1–11.

Johnston, L. (2000). *Users and abusers of psychiatry: A critical look at psychiatric practice* (2nd ed.). Philadelphia: Routledge.

Johnston, O., Fornae, G., Cabrini, S., & Kendrick, T. (2007). Feasibility and acceptability of screening for eating disorders in primary care. *Family Practice, 24(5)*, 511–517.

Johnstone, P., & Zolese, G. (2005). Length of hospitalization for people with severe mental illness. *The Cochrane Database of Systematic Reviews, 2*. Art. No. CD000384.

Joiner, T. E., Walker, R. L., Pettit, J. W., Perez, M., & Cukrowicz, K. (2005). Evidence-based assessment of depression in adults. *Psychological Assessment, 17(3)*, 267–277.

Jones, C., Cormac, I., Silvera da Monta Neto, J. I., & Campbell, C. (2004). Cognitive behavior therapy for schizophrenia. *Cochrane Database of Systematic Reviews, 4*. Art. No. CD000524.

Jones, R. S., Chow, T. W., & Getz, M. (2005). Asian Americans and Alzheimer's disease: Assimilation, culture, and beliefs. *Journal of Aging Studies, 20(1)*, 11–25.

Jorm, A. F., & Griffiths, K. M. (2006). Population promotion of informal self-help strategies for early intervention against depression and anxiety. *Psychological Medicine, 36(1)*, 3–6.

Justo, L., Soares, B., & Calil, H. (2009). Family interventions for bipolar disorder. *Cochrane Database of Systematic Reviews*, Issue 4. Art. No.: CD005167.

Kahn, R. S., Khoury, J., Nichols, W. C., & Lanphear, B. P. (2003). Role of dopamine transporter genotype and maternal prenatal smoking in childhood hyperactive-impulsive, inattentive, and oppositional behaviors. *Journal of Pediatrics, 143(1)*, 104–110.

Kaminer, Y., & Waldron, H. B. (2006). Evidence-based cognitive-behavioral therapies for adolescent substance use disorders: Applications and challenges. In H. Liddle & C. Rowe (Eds.), *Adolescent substance abuse: Research and clinical advances* (pp. 396–420). New York: Cambridge University Press.

Kanas, N. (2005). Evidential support for the value of integrative group therapy for patients with schizophrenia. *Directions in Psychiatry, 25(3)*, 231–239.

Kaplow, J., Curran, P., & Dodge, K. (2002). Conduct problems prevention research group. Child, parent, and peer predictors of early-onset substance use: A multisite longitudinal study. *Journal of Abnormal Child Psychology, 30,* 199–216.

Karageorge, K., & Wisdom, G. (2001). *Physically and sexually abused women in substance abuse treatment: Treatment services and outcomes.* Report to the Center for Substance Abuse Treatment. Fairfax, VA: Caliber Associates.

Karasu, T. B., Gelenberg, A., Merriam, A., & Wang, P. (2002). Practice guidelines for the treatment of patients with major depressive disorder. *American Psychiatric Association practice guidelines for the treatment of psychiatric disorder: Compendium 2002* (2nd ed.) (pp. 463–545). Washington, DC: American Psychiatric Publishing.

Kasari, C., & Rotheram-Fuller, E. (2005). Current trends in psychological research on children with high-functioning autism and Asperger disorder. *Current Opinion in Psychiatry, 18(5),* 497–501.

Kazdin, A. (2001). Treatment of conduct disorders. In J. Hill & B. Maughan (Eds.), *Conduct disorders in childhood and adolescence* (pp. 408–448). New York: Cambridge University Press.

Keefe, R. S., & Fenton, W. S. (2007). How should DSM-V criteria for schizophrenia include cognitive impairment? *Schizophrenia Bulletin, 33(4),* 912–920.

Keel, P., & Mitchell, J. (1997). Outcome in bulimia nervosa. *American Journal of Psychiatry, 154,* 313–321.

Keel, P., Dorer, D., Franko, D., Jackson, S., & Herzog, D. (2005). Postremission predictors of relapse in women with eating disorders. *American Journal of Psychiatry, 162,* 2263–2268.

Keel, P. K., & Brown, T. A. (2010). Update on course and outcome in eating disorders. *International Journal of Eating Disorders, 43(3),* 195–204. DOI: 10.1002/eat.20810.

Keel, P. K., & Klump, K. L. (2003). Are eating disorders culture-bound syndromes? Implications for conceptualizing their etiology. *Psychological Bulletin, 129,* 747–769.

Keeley, M. L., Storch, E. A., Merlo, L. J., & Geffken, G. R. (2008). Clinical predictors of response to cognitive-behavioral therapy for obsessive-compulsive disorder. *Clinical Psychology Review, 28,* 118–130.

Kelly, J., Myers, M., & Brown, S. (2002). Do adolescents affiliate with 12-step groups? A multivariate process model of effects. *Journal of Studies on Alcohol, 63,* 293–305.

Kelly, J. F., Stout, R., Magill, M., Tonigan, J. S., & Pagano, M. (2010). Mechanisms of behavior change in Alcoholics Anonymous: Does AA improve alcohol outcomes by reducing depression symptoms? *Addiction, 105,* 626–636.

Kendall, P. C., Hudson, J., Gosch, E., Flannery-Schroeder, E., & Suveg, C. (2008). Child and family therapy for anxiety-disordered youth: Results of a randomized clinical trial. *Journal of Consulting and Clinical Psychology, 76,* 282–297.

Kendler, K. S., Aggen, S. H., Czajkowski, N., Raysamb, E., Tambs, K., Torgersen, S., et al. (2008). The structure of genetic and environmental risk factors for DSM-IV personality disorders. *Archives of General Psychiatry, 65(12),* 1438–1446,

Keshavan, M. S., Gilbert, A. R., & Diwadkar, V. A. (2006). Neurodevelopmental theories. In J. A. Lieberman, T. S. Stroup, & D. O. Perkins (Eds.), *The American Psychiatric publishing textbook of schizophrenia* (pp. 69–83). Arlington, VA: American Psychiatric Publishing.

Kessler, R. (2004). The epidemiology of dual diagnosis. *Biological Psychiatry, 56,* 730–737.

Kessler, R., Adler, L., Barkley, R., Biederman, J., Conners, K., Demler, O., et al. (2006). The prevalence and correlates of adult ADHD in the United States: Results from the National Comorbidity Survey Replication. *American Journal of Psychiatry, 163,* 716–723.

Kessler, R. C. (2003). Epidemiology of women and depression. *Journal of Affective Disorders, 74(1),* 5–13.

Kessler, R. C., Adler, L. A., Barkely, R., Biederman, J., Conners, C. K., Faraone, S. V., et al. (2005). Patterns and predictors of attention deficit/hyperactivity disorder persistence into adulthood: Results from National Comorbidity Survey Replication. *Biological Psychiatry, 57,* 1442–1451.

Kessler, R. C., Berglund, P., Demler, O., Jin, R., Merikangas, K. R., & Walters, E. E. (2005). Lifetime prevalence and age-of-onset distributions of DSM-IV disorders on the National Comorbidity Survey Replication. *Archives of General Psychiatry, 62(6),* 593–602.

Kessler, R. C., Chiu, W. T., Demler, O., & Walters, E. E. (2005). Prevalence, severity, and comorbidity of 12-month *DSM-IV* disorders in the National Comorbidity Survey Replication. *Archives of General Psychiatry, 62(6),* 617–627.

Kessler, R. C., Chiu, W. T., Jin, R., Ruscio, A. M., Shear, K., & Walters, E. E. (2006). The epidemiology of panic attacks, panic disorder, and agoraphobia in the National Comorbidity Survey Replication. *Archives of General Psychiatry, 63(4),* 415–424.

Kessler, R. C., Mickelson, K. D., & Williams, D. R. (1999). The prevalence, distribution, and mental health correlates of perceived discrimination in the United States. *Journal of Health and Social Behavior, 40(3)*, 208–231.

Ketter, T. A., & Wang, P. O. (2010). Overview of pharmacotherapy for bipolar disorders. In T. A. Ketter (Ed.), *Handbook of diagnosis and treatment of bipolar disorders* (pp. 83–106). Arlington, VA: American Psychiatric Publishing.

Killick, S., & Allen, C. (1997). "Shifting the balance": Motivational interviewing to help behaviour change in people with bulimia nervosa. *European Eating Disorders Review, 5*, 33–41.

Kim, E. (2008). Does traumatic brain injury predispose individuals to develop schizophrenia? *Current Opinion in Psychiatry, 21(3)*, 286–289.

Kinney, D. K., Yurgelun-Todd, D. A., Tohen, M., & Tramer, S. (1998). Pre- and perinatal complications and risk for bipolar disorder: A retrospective study. *Journal of Affective Disorders, 50(2–3)*, 117–124.

Kinney, J. M., & Rentz, C. A. (2005). Observed well-being among individuals with dementia: Memories in the making, an art program, versus other structured activity. *American Journal of Alzheimer's Disease and Other Dementias, 20(4)*, 220–227.

Kirsh, B., & Cockburn, L. (2007). Employment outcomes associated with ACT: A review of ACT literature. *American Journal of Psychiatric Rehabilitation, 10(1)*, 31–51.

Kisely, S., & Campbell, L. A. (2007). Does compulsory or supervised community treatment reduce "revolving door" care? Legislation is inconsistent with recent evidence. *British Journal of Psychiatry, 191(5)*, 373–374.

Klein, D. N., Dougherty, L. R., & Olino, T. M. (2005). Towards guidelines for evidence-based assessment of depression in children and adolescents. *Journal of Clinical Child and Adolescent Psychology, 34(3)*, 412–432.

Klein, D. N., Shankman, S. A., & Rose, S. (2006). Ten-year prospective follow-up study of the naturalistic course of dysthymic disorder and double depression. *American Journal of Psychiatry, 163(5)*, 872–880.

Klerman, L. (2004). *Another chance: Preventing additional births to teen mothers.* Washington, DC: National Organization on Adolescent Pregnancy, Parenting, and Prevention.

Kliem, S., Kröger, C., & Kosfelder, J. (2010). Dialectical behavior therapy for borderline personality disorder: A meta-analysis using mixed-effects modeling. *Journal of Consulting and Clinical Psychology, 78(6)*, 936–951.

Knapp, P. (2006). Evolutionary biology of stress disorders. In P. S. Jensen, P. Knapp, & D. A. Mrazek (Eds.), *Toward a new diagnostic system for child psychopathology: Moving beyond the DSM* (pp. 131–149). New York: Guilford Press.

Knouse, L. E., Bagwell, C. L., Barkley, R. A., & Murphy, K. R. (2005). ADHD evidence from a driving study. *Journal of Attention Disorders, 8(4)*, 221–234.

Koch, J. M., Hinze-Selch, D., Stingele, K., Huchzermeier, C., Göder, R., Seeck-Hirschner, M., et al. (2009). Changes in CREB phosphorylation and BDNF plasma levels during psychotherapy of depression. *Psychotherapy and Psychosomatics, 78(3)*, 187–192. DOI: 10.1159/000209350.

Kolla, N. J., Eisenberg, H., & Links, P. S. (2008). Epidemiology, risk factors, and psychopharmacological management of suicide behavior n borderline personality disorder. *Archives of Suicide Research, 12*, 1–19.

Kolodziej, M. E., Griffin, M. L., & Najavits, L. M. (2005). Anxiety disorders among patients with co-occurring bipolar and substance use disorders. *Drug and Alcohol Dependence, 80(2)*, 251–257.

Korczak, D. J., & Goldstein, B. I. (2009). Childhood onset major depressive disorder: Course of illness and psychiatric comorbidity in a community sample. *Journal of Pediatrics, 155(1)*, 118–123.

Kotler, L. A., Cohen, P., Davies, M., Pine, D. S., & Walsh, B. D. (2001). Longitudinal relationships between childhood, adolescent, and adult eating disorders. *Journal of the American Academy of Child and Adolescent Psychiatry, 40*, 1434–1441.

Kotlyar, M., Dysken, M., & Adson, D. E. (2005). Update on drug-induced depression in the elderly. *American Journal of Geriatric Pharmacotherapy, 3*, 288–300.

Kovacs, M. (2001). Gender and the course of major depressive disorder through adolescence in clinically referred youngsters. *Journal of the American Academy of Child and Adolescent Psychiatry, 40*, 1079–1085.

Kownacki, R., & Shadish, W. (1999). Does Alcoholics Anonymous work? The results from a meta-analysis of controlled experiments. *Substance Use and Misuse, 34*, 1897–1916.

Koyama, T., Tachimor, H., & Osada, H. (2006). Cognitive and symptom profiles in high-functioning pervasive developmental disorder not otherwise specified and attention-deficit/hyperactivity disorder. *Journal of Autism and Developmental Disorders, 36(3)*, 373–380.

Kraaij, V., Arensman, E., & Spinhoven, P. (2002). Negative life events and depression in elderly persons: A meta-analysis. *Journals of Gerontology Series B-Psychological Sciences & Social Sciences, 57B(1)*, 87–94.

Kraft, K., Schubert, K., Pond, A., & Aguirre-Molina, M. (2006). Adolescent treatment services: The context of care. In H. A. Liddle & C. L. Rowe (Eds.), *Adolescent substance abuse: Research and clinical advances* (pp. 174–188). New York: Cambridge University Press.

Kranzler, H., Montejano, L. B., Stephenson, J. J., Wang, S., & Gastfriend, D. R. (2010). Effects of naltrexone treatment for alcohol-related disorders on healthcare costs in an insured population. *Alcoholism: Clinical and Experimental Research, 34(6)*, 1090–1097. DOI: 10.1111/j.1530-0277.2010.01185.x.

Krishnakumar, A., & Buehler, C. (2000). Interparental conflict and parenting behaviors: A meta-analytic review. *Family Relations, 49*, 25–44.

Krishnan, K. R. (2005). Psychiatric and medical comorbidities of bipolar disorder. *Psychosomatic Medicine, 67*, 1–8.

Kuipers, E., Garety, P., & Fowler, D. (2006). Cognitive, emotional, and social processes in psychosis: Refining cognitive behavioral therapy for persistent positive symptoms.

Kumsta, R., Stevens, S., Brookes, K., Schlotz, W., Castle, J., Beckett, C., et al. (2010). 5HTT genotype moderates the influence of early institutional deprivation on emotional problems in adolescence: Evidence from the English and Romanian Adoptee (ERA) study. *Journal of Child Psychology and Psychiatry, 51*, 755–762.

Kupka, R. W., Luckenbaugh, D. A., & Post, R. M. (2005). Comparison of rapid-cycling and non-rapid-cycling bipolar disorder based on prospective mood ratings in 539 outpatients. *American Journal of Psychiatry, 162(7)*, 1273–1280.

Kurtz, M. M., & Mueser, K. T. (2008). A meta-analysis of controlled research on social skills training for schizophrenia. *Journal of Consulting and Clinical Psychology, 76(3)*, 491–504.

Kutchins, H., & Kirk, S. A. (1997). *Making us crazy; DSM: The psychiatric bible and the creation of mental disorders*. New York: The Free Press.

Kymalainen, J. A., & Weisman de Mamani, A. G. (2008). Expressed emotion, communication deviance, and culture in families of patients with schizophrenia: A review of the literature. *Cultural Diversity and Ethnic Minority Psychology, 14(2)*, 85–91.

Lahey, B., & Waldman, I. (2003). A developmental propensity model of the origins of conduct problems during childhood and adolescence. In B. Lahey, T. E. Moffitt, & A. Caspi (Eds.), *Causes of conduct disorder and juvenile delinquency* (pp. 76–117). New York: Guilford Press.

Laidlow, K., Thompson, L., Gallagher-Thompson, D., & Dick-Siskin, L. (2003). *Cognitive behaviour therapy with older people*. Hoboken, NJ: Wiley.

Lam, K. S. L., Aman, M. G., & Arnold, L. E. (2005). Neurochemical correlates of autistic disorder: A review of the literature. *Research in Developmental Disabilities, 27(3)*, 254–289.

Landa, R. J., Holman, K. C., & Garrett-Mayer, E. (2007). Social and communication development in toddlers with early and later diagnosis of autism spectrum disorders. *Archives of General Psychiatry, 64(7)*, 853–864.

Lang, R., Register, A., Lauderdale, S., Ashbaugh, K., & Haring, A. (2010). Treatment of anxiety in autism spectrum disorders using cognitive behaviour theory: A systematic review. *Developmental Neurorehabilitation, 13(1)*, 53–68.

Langley, G. C., & Klopper, H. (2005). Trust as a foundation for the therapeutic intervention for patients with borderline personality disorder. *Journal of Psychiatric and Mental Health Nursing, 12(1)*, 23–32.

Larimer, M., Palmer, R., & Marlatt, A. (1999). Relapse prevention: An overview of Marlatt's cognitive-behavioral model. *Alcohol Research and Health, 23*, 151–160.

Laucht, M., Skowronek, M. H., Becker, K., Schmidt, M. H., Esser, G., Schulze, T. G., et al. (2007). Interacting effects of the dopamine transporter gene and psychosocial adversity on attention-deficit/hyperactivity disorder symptoms among 15-year-olds from a high-risk community sample. *Archives of General Psychiatry, 64*, 585–590.

Lavretsky, H., Nguyen, L. H., & Goldstein, M. Z. (2006). Diagnosis and treatment of neuropsychiatric symptoms in Alzheimer's disease. *Psychiatric Services, 57(5)*, 617–619.

Lawrence, R., Bradshaw, T., & Mairs, H. (2006). Group cognitive behavioural therapy for schizophrenia: A systematic review of the literature. *Journal of Psychiatric and Mental Health Nursing, 13(6)*, 673–68.

Le, H. N., Munoz, R., Ippen, C. G., & Stoddard, J. (2003). Treatment is not enough: We must prevent major depression in women. *Prevention and Treatment*. Retrieved December 31, 2003, from http://80gateway1.ovid.com.proxy.library.vcu.edu/ovidweb.cgi.

Leahy, R. L. (2007). Bipolar disorder: Causes, contexts, and treatments. *Journal of Clinical Psychology, 63(5)*, 417–424.

Ledingham, J. (1999). Children and adolescents with oppositional defiant disorder and conduct disorder in the community: Experiences at school and with peers. In H. Quay & A. Hogan (Eds.), *Handbook of disruptive* behavior disorders (pp. 353–370). New York: Kluwer Academic/Plenum Publishers.

Le Grange, D., Lock, J., Loeb, K., & Nicholls, D. (2010). Academy for eating disorders position paper: The role of the family in eating disorders. *International Journal of Eating Disorders, 43(1),* 1–5.

Lemery, K. S., & Doelger, L. (2005). Genetic vulnerabilities to the development of psychopathology. In B. L. Hankin & J. R. Z. Abela (Eds.), *Development of psychopathology: A vulnerability-stress perspective* (pp. 161–198). Thousand Oaks, CA: Sage Publications.

Lemstra, M., Neudorf, C., D'Arcy, C., Kunst, A., Warren, L. M., & Bennett, N. R. (2008). A systematic review of depressed mood and anxiety by SES in youth aged 10–15 years. *Canadian Journal of Public Health, 99(2),* 125–129.

Lenoir, M. E., Dingemans, P., Schene, A. H., Hart, A. A., & Linszen, D. H. (2002). The course of parental expressed emotion and psychotic episodes after family intervention in recent-onset schizophrenia: A longitudinal study. *Social Psychiatry and Psychiatric Epidemiology, 39(2),* 69–75.

Lenzenweger, M. F., Lane, M. C., Loranger, A. W., & Kessler, R. C. (2007). DSM-IV personality disorders in the National Comorbidity Survey Replication. *Biological Psychiatry, 62(6),* 553–564.

Leonard, B. E. (2003). *Fundamentals of psychopharmacology.* New York: Martin Duwitz.

Leskovec, T. J., Rowles, B. M., & Findlay, R. L. (2008). Pharmacological treatment options for autism spectrum disorders in children and adolescence. *Harvard Review of Psychiatry, 16(2),* 97–112.

Leventhal, T., & Brooks-Gunn, J. (2003). Children and youth in neighborhood contexts. *Current Directions in Psychological Sciences, 12(1),* 27–31.

Levy, F., Hay, D. A., & Bennett, K. S. (2006). Genetics of attention-deficit/hyperactivity disorder: A current review and future prospects. *International Journal of Disability, Development and Education, 53(1),* 5–20.

Levy, R. A., & Ablon, J. S. (Eds.). (2009). *Handbook of evidence-based psychodynamic psychotherapy: Bridging the gap between science and practice.* Totowa, NJ: Humana Press.

Lewinsohn, P. M., Streigel-Moore, R. H., & Seeley, J. R. (2000). Epidemiology and natural course of eating disorders in young women from adolescence to young adulthood. *Journal of the American Academy of Child and Adolescent Psychiatry, 39,* 1284–1292.

Lichtenberg, P. A., Kemp-Havican, J., MacNeill, S. E., & Johnson, A. S. (2005). Pilot study of behavioral treatment in dementia care units. *Gerontologist, 45,* 406–410.

Liddle, H. A. (1999). Theory development in a family-based therapy for adolescent drug abuse. *Journal of Clinical Child Psychology, 28,* 521–532.

Lieberman, J., Stroup, S., McEvoy, J., Swartz, M., Rosenheck, R., Perkins, D., et al. (2005). Effectiveness of antipsychotic drugs in patients with chronic schizophrenia. *New England Journal of Medicine, 353,* 1209–1223.

Lindert, J., von Ehrenstein, O. S., Priebe, S., Mielck, A., & Brähler, E. (2009). Depression and anxiety in labor migrants and refugees: A systematic review and meta-analysis. *Social Science & Medicine, 69,* 246–257. DOI: 10.1016/j.socscimed.2009.04.032.

Linehan, M. M. (1993). *Cognitive behavioral treatment of borderline clients.* New York: Guilford Press.

Lipsey, M. W., Landenberger, N. A., & Wilson, S. J. (2007). Effects of cognitive-behavioral programs for criminal offenders. *The Campbell Systematic Reviews, 2007,* 6.

Liu, X., Paterson, A. D., & Szatmari, P. (2008). Genome-wide linkage analyses of quantitative and categorical autism subphenotypes. *Biological Psychiatry, 64(7),* 561–570.

Livesley, W. J. (2004). Changing ideas about the treatment of borderline personality disorder. *Journal of Contemporary Psychotherapy, 34(3),* 185–192.

Lock, J., Le Grange, D., Agras, W. S., & Dare, C. (2001). *Treatment manual for anorexia nervosa: A family-based approach.* New York: Guilford Press.

Loeber, R., Burke, J. D., Lagey, B. B., Winters, A., & Zera, M. (2000). Oppositional defiant and conduct disorder: A review of the past 10 years, part I. *Journal of the American Academy of Child and Adolescent Psychiatry, 39(12),* 1468–1484.

Loeber, R., Farrington, D., Stouthamer-Loeber, M., & Van Kammen, W. (1998). *Antisocial behavior and mental health problems: Explanatory factors in childhood and adolescence.* Mahwah, NJ: Lawrence Erlbaum.

Loeber, R., Green, S. M., Lahey, B. B., Frick, P. J., & McBurnett, K. (2002). Findings on disruptive behavior disorders from the first decade of the Developmental Trends Study. *Clinical Child and Family Psychology Review, 3,* 37–60.

Lonergan, E., Luxenberg, J., Colford, J., & Birks, J. (2007). Haloperidol for agitation in dementia. *The Cochrane Database of Systematic Reviews,* Issue 1. DOI: 10.1002/14651858.CD002852.

Longabaugh, R., Wirtz, P., Zweben, A., & Stout, R. (1998). Network support for drinking: Alcoholics Anonymous and long term matching effects. *Addiction, 93*, 1313–1333.

López, A., & Birks, J. (2007). Nimodipine for primary degenerative, mixed and vascular dementia. *The Cochrane Database of Systematic Reviews,* Issue 1. DOI: 10.1002/14651858.CD000147.

Lord, C., Risi, S., & Lambrecht, L. (2000). The Autism Diagnostic Observation Schedule—Generic: A standard measure of social and communication deficits associated with the spectrum of autism. *Journal of Autism and Developmental Disorders, 30(3),* 205–223.

Lord, C., Rutter, M., & LeCouteur, A. (1994). Autism Diagnostic Interview—Revised: A revised version of a diagnostic interview for caregivers of individuals with possible pervasive developmental disorders. *Journal of Autism and Developmental Disorders, 24(5),* 659–685.

Lott, L., & Klein, D. T. (2003). Psychotherapeutic interventions. In D. P. Hay, D. T. Klein, L. K. Hay, G. T. Grossman, & J. S. Kennedy (Eds.), *Agitation in patients with dementia: A practical guide to diagnosis and management, Clinical practice series* (pp. 103–118). Arlington, VA: American Psychiatric Publishing.

Lovaas, O. I. (1987). Behavioral treatment and normal education and intellectual functioning in young autistic children. *Journal of Consulting and Clinical Psychology, 55(1),* 3–9.

Lovaas, O. I. (2003). *Teaching individuals with developmental delays: Basic intervention techniques.* Austin, TX: PRO-ED.

Lowe, M. R. (2002). Dietary restraint and overeating. In K. D. Brownell (Ed.), *Eating disorders and obesity* (pp. 88–92). New York: Guilford.

Lowe, M. R., & Timko, C. A. (2004). What a difference a diet makes: Towards an understanding of differences between restrained dieters and restrained nondieters. *Eating Behaviors, 5(3),* 199–208.

Lu, P. H., Masterlund, D. A., Mulnard, R., Cotman, C., Miller. B., Yaffe, K., et al. (2006). Effects of testosterone on cognition and mood in male patients with mild Alzheimer's disease and healthy elder men. *Archives of Neurology, 63(2),* 177–185.

Lu, Y. Y., & Austrom, M. G. (2005). Distress responses and self-care behaviors in dementia family caregivers with high and low depressed mood. *Journal of the American Psychiatric Nurses Association, 11(4),* 231–240.

Luhrmann, T. M. (2010). Review of the protest psychosis: How schizophrenia became a black disease. *American Journal of Psychiatry, 167(4),* 479–480.

Luppino, F. S., de Wit, L. M., Bouvy, P. F., Stijen, T., Cuijpers, P., Penninx, B., et al. (2010). Overweight, obesity, and depression: A systematic review and meta-analysis of longitudinal studies. *Archives of General Psychiatry, 37(3),* 220–229.

Lynch, T. R., Chapman, A. L., & Rosenthal, M. Z. (2006). Mechanisms of change in dialectical behavior therapy: Theoretical and empirical observations. *Journal of Clinical Psychology, 62(4),* 459–480.

Lynch, W. J., Roth, M. E., & Carrol, M. E. (2002). Biological basis of sex differences in drug abuse: Preclinical and clinical studies. *Psychopharmacology, 164,* 121–137.

Mackinnon, D., Potash, J., McMahon, F., & Simpson, S. (2005). Rapid mood switching and suicidality in familial bipolar disorder. *Bipolar Disorders: An International Journal of Psychiatry and Neurosciences, 7(5),* 441.

MacKinnon, D. F., & Pies, R. (2006). Affective instability as rapid cycling: Theoretical and clinical implications for borderline personality and bipolar spectrum disorders. *Bipolar Disorders, 8,* 1–14.

Maddi, S. R. (2007). Personality theories facilitate integrating the five principles and deducing hypotheses for testing. *American Psychologist, 62(1),* 58–59.

Mahoney, D. F., Tarlow, B. J., & Jones, R. N. (2003). Effects of an automated telephone support system on caregiver burden and anxiety: Findings from the REACH for TLC intervention study. *The Gerontologist, 43(4),* 556–567.

Maldonado-Molina, M. M., & Wagenaar, A. C. (2010). Effects of alcohol taxes on alcohol-related mortality in Florida: Time-series analyses from 1969–2004. *Alcoholism: Clinical and Experimental Research, 34(11),* 1915–1921. DOI: 10.1111/j.1530-0277.2010.01280.x.

Malmberg, L., & Fenton, M. (2005). Individual psychodynamic psychotherapy and psychoanalysis for schizophrenia and severe mental illness. *The Cochrane Database of Systematic Reviews, 4.* Art. No. CD001360.

Mandell, D. S., Novak, M., & Zubritsky, L. (2005). The role of culture in families' treatment decisions for children with autism spectrum disorders. *Mental Retardation and Developmental Disabilities Research Reviews, 11(2),* 110–115.

Mandell, D. S., & Palmer, R. (2005). Differences among states in the identification of autistic spectrum disorders. *Archives of Pediatric and Adolescent Medicine, 159,* 266–269.

Mannuzza, S., Klein, R., & Moulton, J. (2002). Young adult outcome of children with "situational" hyperactivity: A prospective, controlled, follow-up study. *Journal of Abnormal Child Psychology, 30,* 191–198.

Mantere, O., Melartin, T. K., Suominen, K., Rytsala, H. J., Valtonen, H. M., Arvilommi, P., et al. (2006). Differences in axis I and axis II comorbidity between bipolar I and II disorders and major depressive disorder. *Journal of Clinical Psychiatry, 67(4)*, 584–593.

Maracek, J. (2006). Social suffering, gender, and women's depression. In C. L. M. Keyes & S. H. Goodman (Eds.), *Women and depression: Handbook for the social, behavioral, and biomedical sciences* (pp. 283–308). New York: Cambridge University Press.

Marangell, L. B., Kupfer, D. J., Sachs, G. S., & Swann, A. C. (2006). Emerging therapies for bipolar depression. *Journal of Clinical Psychiatry, 67(7)*, 1140–1151.

March, J., & Vitiello, B. (2009). Clinical messages from the treatment for adolescents with depression study (TADS). *American Journal of Psychiatry, 166*, 1118–1123.

Markowitz, J. C., Bleiberg, K., Pessin, H., & Skodol, A. E. (2007). Adapting interpersonal therapy for borderline personality disorder. *Journal of Mental Health, 16(1)*, 103–116.

Marriott, R., Neil, W., & Waddingham, S. (2006). Antipsychotic medication for elderly people with schizophrenia. *Cochrane Database of Systematic Reviews, 1*. Art. No. CD005580.

Marshall, M., Crowther, R., Almaraz-Serrano, A., Creed, F., Sledge, W., Kluiter, W., et al. (2006). Natural history and predictors of clinical course. In J. A. Lieberman, T. S. Stroup, & D. O. Perkins (Eds.),*The American Psychiatric Publishing textbook of schizophrenia* (pp. 289–301). Washington, DC: American Psychiatric Publishing.

Marshall, M., & Lockwood, A. (2003). Early intervention for psychosis. *Cochrane Database of Systematic Reviews, 2*. Art. No. CD004718.

Marshall, M., & Rathbone, J. (2006). Early intervention for psychosis. *Cochrane Database of Systematic Reviews, 4*. Art. No. CD004718. DOI: 10.1002/14651858. CD004718.

Martin, M. M., Orsillo, S. M., & Roemer, L. (Eds.). (2001). *Practitioner's guide to empirically based measures of anxiety.* New York: Kluwer Academic Publishers.

Martin-Cook, K., Remakel-Davis, B., Svetlik, D., Hynan, L. S., & Weiner, M. F. (2003). Caregiver attribution and resentment in dementia care. *American Journal of Alzheimer's Disease and Other Dementias, 18(6)*, 366–374

Martino, S., Carroll, K., Kostas, D., Perkins, J., & Rounsaville, B. (2002). Dual diagnosis motivational interviewing: A modification of motivational interviewing for substance-abusing patients with psychotic disorders. *Journal of Substance Abuse Treatment, 23*, 297–308.

Marziali, E. (2002). Borderline personality disorders. In A. R. Roberts & G. J. Greene (Eds.), *Social workers' desk reference* (pp. 360–364). New York: Oxford University Press.

Matson, J. L., & Hess, J. A. (2011). Psychotropic drug efficacy and side effects for persons with autism spectrum disorders. *Research in Autism Spectrum Disorders, 5(1)*, 230–236.

Matson, J. L., & Minshawi, N. F. (2006). *Early intervention for autism spectrum disorders: A critical analysis.* New York: Elsevier Science.

Matson, J. L., Nebel-Schwaim, M., & Matson, M. L. (2007). A review of methodological issues in the differential diagnosis of autism spectrum disorders in children. *Research in Autism Spectrum Disorders, 1(1)*, 38–54.

Matza, L. S., Rajagopalan, K. S., Thompson, C. L., & Lissovoy, G. (2005). Misdiagnosed patients with bipolar disorder: Comorbidities, treatment patterns, and direct treatment costs. *Journal of Clinical Psychiatry, 66(11)*, 1432–1440.

Mayes, R., Bagwell, C., & Erkulwater, J. (2009). *Medicating children: ADHD and pediatric mental health.* Cambridge, MA: Harvard University Press.

McCart, M., Priester, P., Davies, H., & Azen, R. (2006). Differential effectiveness of behavioral parent-training and cognitive-behavioral therapy for antisocial youth: A meta-analysis. *Journal of Abnormal Child Psychology, 34*, 527–544.

McClendon, M. J., Smyth, K. A., & Neundorfer, M. M. (2004). Survival of persons with Alzheimer's disease: Caregiver coping matters. *Gerontologist, 44(4)*, 508–519.

McConachie, H., & Diggle, T. (2007). Parent implemented early intervention for young children with autism spectrum disorder: A systematic review. *Journal of Evaluation in Clinical Practice, 13(1)*, 120–129.

McCrady, B. (2005). Alcohol use disorders and the Division 12 task force of the American Psychological Association. *Psychology of Addictive Behaviors, 14*, 267–276.

McCrady, B. S., Epstein, E. E., Cook, S., Jensen, N., & Hildebrandt, T. (2009). A randomized trial of individual and couple behavioral alcohol treatment for women. *Journal of Consulting and Clinical Psychology, 77(2)*, 243–256.

McCullough, M. E., Larson, D. B., Hoyt, W. T., & Koenig, H. G. (2000). Religious involvement and mortality: A meta-analytic review. *Health Psychology, 19(3)*, 211–223.

McFarlane, W. R. (2002). *Multifamily groups in the treatment of severe psychiatric disorders.* New York: Guilford.

McGee, R., & Williams, S. (1999). Environmental risk factors in oppositional-defiant disorder and conduct disorder. In H. Quay, C. Herbert, & A. Hogan (Eds.), *Handbook of disruptive behavior disorders* (pp. 419–440). Dordrecht, Netherlands: Kluwer Academic Publishers.

McGilloway, A., Hall, R. E., Lee, T., & Bhui, K. S. (2010). A systematic review of personality disorder, race and ethnicity: Prevalence, aetiology and treatment. *BMC Psychiatry, 10,* Article 33.

McGlashan, T. H., Miller, T. J., & Woods, S. W. (2001). Pre-onset detection and intervention research in schizophrenia psychoses: Current estimates of benefit and risk. *Schizophrenia Bulletin, 27(4),* 563–570.

McGovern, C. W., & Sigman, M. (2005). Continuity and change from early childhood to adolescence in autism. *Journal of Child Psychology and Psychiatry, 46(4),* 401–408.

McGrath, P. J., Khan, A. Y., Trivedi, M. H., Stewart, J. W., Morris, D. W., Wisniewski, S. R., et al. (2008). Response to selective serotonin reuptake inhibitors (citalopram) in major depressive disorder with melancholic features: a STAR*D report. *Journal of Clinical Psychiatry, 69,* 1847–1855.

McGuffin, P., Rijsdijk, F., Andrew, M., Sham, P., Katz, R., & Cardino, A. (2003). The heritability of bipolar affective disorder and the genetic relationship to unipolar depression. *Archives of General Psychiatry, 60,* 497–502.

McHugo, G. J., Mooney, D., Racusin, R., Ford, J. D., & Fleischer, A. (2000). Predicting posttraumatic stress after hospitalization for pediatric injury. *Journal of the American Academy of Child and Adolescent Psychiatry, 39(5),* 576–583.

McIntosh, D. E., & Trotter, J. S. (2006). Early onset bipolar spectrum disorder: Psychopharmacological, psychological, and educational management. *Psychology in the Schools, 43(4),* 451–460.

McKay, J. (1999). Studies of factors in relapse to alcohol, drug and nicotine use: A critical review of methodologies and findings. *Journal of Studies on Alcohol, 60,* 566–576.

McLellan, A. T. (2008). Evolution in addiction treatment concepts and methods. In H. D. Kleber & M. Galanter (Eds.), *The American psychiatric publishing textbook of substance abuse treatment* (4th ed.) (pp. 93–108). Arlington, VA: American Psychiatric Publishing

McLeod, B., Weisz, J., & Wood, J. (2007). Examining the association between parenting and childhood depression: A meta-analysis. *Clinical Psychology Review, 27,* 986–1003.

McLeod, B. D., Wood, J. J., & Weisz, J. R. (2007). Examining the association between parenting and childhood anxiety: A meta-analysis. *Clinical Psychology Review, 27,* 155–172.

McMahon, R. J., & Frick, P. J. (2005). Evidence-based assessment of conduct problems in children and adolescents. *Journal of Clinical Child and Adolescent Psychology, 34(3),* 477–505.

McMurtray, A. M., Ringman, J., & Chao, S. Z. (2006). Family history of dementia in early-onset versus very late-onset Alzheimer's disease. *International Journal of Geriatric Psychiatry, 21(6),* 597–598.

McShane, R., Areosa-Sastre, M., & Minakaran, N. (2007). Memantine for dementia. *The Cochrane Database of Systematic Reviews,* Issue 1. DOI: 10.1002/14651858. CD003154.pub5.

Meeks, T. W., Ropacki, S. A., & Jeste, D. V. (2006). The neurobiology of neuropsychiatric syndromes in dementia. *Current Opinion in Psychiatry, 19(6),* 581–586.

Mee-Lee, D., Shulman, G. D., Fishman, M., Gastfriend, D. R., & Griffith, J. H. (2001). *ASAM patient placement criteria for the treatment of substance-related disorders* (2nd ed., rev.). Chevy Chase, MD: American Society of Addiction Medicine.

Melvin, C. L., Carey, T. S., Goodman, F., Oldham, J. M., Williams, J. W., & Ranney, L. H. (2008). Effectiveness of antiepileptic drugs for the treatment of bipolar disorder: Findings from a systematic review. *Journal of Psychiatric Practice, 14(1),* 9–14.

Mercer, D., Douglass, A. B., & Links, P. S. (2009). Meta-analyses of mood stabilizers, antidepressants and antipsychotics in the treatment of borderline personality disorder: Effectiveness for depression and anger symptoms. *Journal of Personality Disorders, 23(2),* 156–174.

Merikangas, K. R., Akiskal, H. S., Angst, J., Greenberg, P. E., Hirschfeld, R. M. A., Petukhova, M., et al. (2007). Lifetime and 12-month prevalence of bipolar spectrum disorder in the national comorbidity survey replication. *Archives of General Psychiatry, 64,* 543–552.

Merikangas, K. R., He, J., Brody, D., Fisher, P. W., Bourdon, K., & Koretz, D. S. (2010). Prevalence and treatment of mental disorders among U.S. children in the 2001–2004 NHANES. *Pediatrics, 125,* 75–81.

Merikangas, K. R., He, J., Burstein, M., Swanson, S. A., Avenevoli, S., Cui, L., et al. (2010). Lifetime prevalence of mental disorders in U.S. adolescents: Results from the National Comorbidity Study-Adolescent Supplement (NCS-A). *Journal of the American Academy of Child and Adolescent Psychiatry, 49(10),* 980–989.

Meyer, O. L., Zane, N., Cho, Y., & Takeuchi, D. T. (2009). Use of specialty mental health services by Asian Americans with psychiatric disorders. *Journal of Consulting and Clinical Psychology, 77(5)*, 1000–1005. DOI: 10.1037/a0017065.

Micali, N., Heyman, I., Perez, M., Hilton, K., Nakatani, E., Turner, C., & Mataix-Cols, D. (2010). Long-term outcomes of obsessive-compulsive disorder: Follow-up of 142 children and adolescents. *British Journal of Psychiatry, 197*, 128–134. DOI: 10.1192/bjp.bp.109.075317.

Michalak, E. E., Murray, G., Young, A. H., & Lam, R. W. (2008). Burden of bipolar depression: Impact of disorder and medications on quality of life. *CNS Drugs, 22(5)*, 389–404.

Middleton, L. E., Barnes, D. E., Lui, L., & Yaffe, K. (2010). Physical activity over the life course and its association with cognitive performance and impairment in old age. *Journal of the American Geriatrics Society, 58(7)*, 1322–1326.

Miklowitz, D. J. (2007). The role of the family in the course and treatment of bipolar disorder. *16(4)*, 192–196.

Miklowitz, D. J., & Otto, M. W. (2006). New psychosocial interventions for bipolar disorder: A review of literature and introduction of the systematic treatment enhancement program. *Journal of Cognitive Psychotherapy, 20(2)*, 215–230.

Miklowitz, D. J., Otto, M. W., & Frank, E. (2007). Psychosocial treatments for bipolar depression: A 1-year randomized trial from the Systematic Treatment Enhancement Program. *Archives of General Psychiatry, 64(4)*, 419–427.

Miklowitz, D. J., Wisniewski, S. M., Otto, M. W., & Sachs, G. S. (2005). Perceived criticism from family members as a predictor of the one-year course of bipolar disorder. *Psychiatry Research, 136(2–3)*, 101–111.

Miller, L., Davies, M., & Greenwald, S. (2000). Religiosity and substance use and abuse among adolescents in the National Comorbidity Survey. *Journal of the American Academy of Child and Adolescent Psychiatry, 39(9)*, 1190–1197.

Miller, T., Nigg, J., & Miller, R. (2009). Attention deficit hyperactivity disorder in African American children: What can be concluded from the past ten years? *Clinical Psychology Review, 29*, 77–86.

Miller, W., & Rollnick, S. (2002). *Motivational interviewing: Preparing people to change addictive behavior* (2nd ed.). New York: Guilford Press.

Miller, W. R., Meyers, R. J., & Tonigan, J. S. (1999). Engaging the unmotivated in treatment for alcohol problems: A comparison of three strategies for intervention through family members. *Journal of Consulting and Clinical Psychology, 67*, 688–697.

Miller-Johnson, S., Coie, J. D., Maumary-Gremaud, A., & Bierman, K. (2002). Peer rejection and aggression and early starter models of conduct disorder. *Journal of Abnormal Child Psychology, 30(3)*, 217–231.

Millon, T. (2010). A sociocultural conception of the borderline personality disorder epidemic. In T. Millon, R. F. Krueger, & E. Simonsen (Eds.), *Contemporary directions in psychopathology: Scientific foundations of the DSM-V and ICD-11* (pp. 111–123). New York: Guilford Press,

Millon, T., & Grossman, S. D. (2006). Goals of a theory of personality. In J. C. Thomas, D. L. Segal, & M. Hersen (Eds.), *Comprehensive handbook of personality and psychopathology, Vol. 1: Personality and everyday functioning* (pp. 3–222). Hoboken, NJ: Wiley.

Milne, B. J., Caspi, A., Harrington, H., Poulton, R., Rutter, M., & Moffitt, T. E. (2009). Predictive value of family history on severity of illness: The case for depression, anxiety, alcohol dependence, and drug dependence. *Archives of General Psychiatry, 66(7)*, 738–747. Retrieved from http://www.archgenpsychiatry.com.

Mineka, S., & Zinbarg, R. (2006). A contemporary learning theory perspective on the etiology of anxiety disorders: It's not what you thought it was. *American Psychologist, 61*, 1–25.

Minuchin, S., Rosman, B. L., & Baker, L. (1978). *Psychosomatic families: Anorexia nervosa in context.* Cambridge, MA: Harvard University Press.

Mirin, S., Batki, S., Bukstein, O., Isbell, P., Kleber, H., Schottenfeld, R., et al. (2002). Practice guideline for the treatment of patients with substance use disorders: Alcohol, cocaine, opioids. *American Psychiatric Association practice guidelines for the treatment of psychiatric disorders: Compendium 2002* (pp. 249–348). Washington, DC: American Psychiatric Association.

Mitchell, A. J., Rao, S., & Vaze, A. (2010). Do primary care physicians have particular difficulty identifying late-life depression? A meta-analysis stratified by age. *Psychotherapy Psychosom, 79(5)*, 285–294.

Mittal, V. A., Ellman, L. M., & Cannon, T. D. (2008). Gene–environment interaction and covariation in schizophrenia: The role of obstetric complications. *Schizophrenia Bulletin, 34(6)*, 1083–1094.

Mizes, J. S., & Palermo, T. M. (1997). Eating disorders. In R. T. Ammerman & M. Hersen (Eds.), *Handbook of prevention and treatment with children and adolescents: Intervention in the real world context* (pp. 238–258). New York: Wiley.

Moffitt, T., Caspi, A., Harrington, H., & Milne, B. (2002). Males on the life-course-persistent and adolescence-limited antisocial pathways: Follow-up at age 26 years. *Development and Psychopathology, 14,* 179–207.

Moffitt, T., Caspi, A., Rutter, M., & Silva, P. (2001). *Sex differences in antisocial behavior: Conduct disorder, delinquency, and violence in the Dunedin longitudinal study.* New York: Cambridge University Press.

Molina, B. S. G., Hinshaw, S., Swanson, J., Arnold, L. E., Vitiello, B., Jensen, P. S., et al. (2009). The MTA at 8 years: Prospective follow-up of children treated for combined-type ADHD in a multisite study. *Journal of the American Academy of Child and Adolescent Psychiatry, 48(5),* 484–500. DOI: 10.1097/CHI.0b013e31819c23do.

Moncrieff, J., Hopker, S., & Thomas, P. (2005). Psychiatry and the pharmaceutical industry: Who pays the piper? *Psychiatric Bulletin, 29,* 84–85.

Moncrieff, J., Wessely, S., & Hardy, R. (2004). Active placebos versus antidepressants for depression. *Cochrane Database of Systematic Reviews, 1,* 1–2.

Mond, J. M., Hay, P. J., Rodgers, B., & Owen, C. (2006). An update on the definition of "excessive exercise" in eating disorders research. *International Journal of Eating Disorders, 39,* 147–153.

Morano, C. L. (2003). Appraisal and coping: Moderators or mediators of stress in Alzheimer's disease caregivers. *Social Work Research, 27(2),* 116–128.

Moreno, C., Laje, G., Blanco, C., Jiung, H., Schmidt, A. B., & Olfson, M. (2007). National trends in the outpatient diagnosis and treatment of bipolar disorder in youth. *Archives of General Psychiatry, 64(9),* 1032–1038.

Mosconi, L. Berti, V., Glodzick, L., Pupi, A., De Santi, S., & de Leon, M. (2010). Pre-clinical detection of Alzheimer's disease using FDG-PET, with or without amyloid imaging. *Journal of Alzheimer's Disease, 20(3),* 843–854.

Mueser, K. T., Bond, G. R., Drake, R. E., & Resnick, S. G. (1998). Models of community care for severe mental illness: A review of research on case management. *Schizophrenia Bulletin, 24,* 37–74.

Mueser, K. T., Corrigan, P. W., Hilton, D. W., Tanzman, B., Schaub, A., Gingerich, S., et al. (2002). Illness management and recovery: A review of the research. *Psychiatric Services, 53(10),* 1272–1284.

Mufson, L., Dorta, K. P., Moreau, D., & Weissman, M. M. (2005). Efficacy to effectiveness: Adaptations of interpersonal psychotherapy for adolescent depression. In E. Hibbs & P. Jensen (Eds.), *Psychosocial treatments for child and adolescent disorders: Empirically based strategies for clinical practice* (2nd ed.) (pp. 165–186). Washington, DC: American Psychological Association.

Muise, A., Stein, D., & Arbess, G. (2003). Eating disorders in adolescent boys: A review of the adolescent and young adult literature. *Journal of Adolescent Health, 33,* 427–435.

Mulvany, F., O'Callaghan, E., Takei, N., Byrne, M., & Fearon, P. (2001). Effects of social class at birth on risk and presentation of schizophrenia: Case-control study. *British Medical Journal, 323(7326),* 1398–1401.

Mungas, D., Beckett, L., Harvey, D., Tomaszewski-Farias, S., Reed, B., Carmichael, O., et al. (2010). Heterogeneity of cognitive trajectories in diverse older persons. *Psychology and Aging, 25(3),* 606–619.

Muroff, J., Edelsohn, G. A., Joe, S., & Ford, B. C. (2008). The role of race in diagnostic and disposition decision making in a pediatric psychiatric emergency service. *General Hospital Psychiatry, 30(3),* 269–276.

Murphy, K. R., & Adler, L. A. (2004). Assessing attention-deficit/hyperactivity disorder in adults: Focus on rating scales. *Journal of Clinical Psychiatry, 65(3),* 12–17.

Murray, J., Irving, B., Farrington, D. P., Colman, I., & Bloxsom, C. A. J. (2010). Very early predictors of conduct problems and crime: Results from a national cohort study. *Journal of Child Psychology and Psychiatry, 51(11),* 1198–1207. DOI: 10.1111/j.1469-7610.2010.02287.x.

Murray, R. M., Jones, P. B., & Susser, E. (2003). *The epidemiology of schizophrenia.* New York: Cambridge University Press.

Musicco, Massimo (2010). Gender differences in the occurrence of Alzheimer's disease. *Functional Neurology, 25(2),* 89–92.

Nakash-Eisikovitz, O., Dierberger, A., & Westen, D. (2002). A multidimensional meta-analysis of pharmacotherapy for bulimia nervosa: Summarizing the range of outcomes in controlled clinical trials. *Harvard Review of Psychiatry, 10,* 193–211.

National Institute of Mental Health. (2007). *Autism spectrum disorders: Pervasive developmental disorders.* Washington, DC: National Institute of Health.

Neale, B. M., Medland, S. E., Ripke, S. Asherson, P., Franke, B., Lesch, K. P., et al. (2010). Meta-analysis of genome-wide association studies of attention-deficit/hyperactivity disorder [Abstract]. *Journal of the American Academy of Child and Adolescent Psychiatry, 49(9),* 884–897.

Nelson-Zlupko, L., Kauffman, E., & Dore, M. M. (1995). Gender differences in drug addiction and treatment: Implications for social work intervention with substance-abusing women. *Social Work, 40,* 45–54.

Nemeroff, C. B. (2000). An ever-increasing pharma-copoeia for the management of patients with bipolar disorder. *Journal of Clinical Psychiatry, 61*(Suppl. 13), 19–25.

Newman, C. F. (2006). Bipolar disorder. In F. Andrasik (Ed.), *Comprehensive handbook of personality and psychopathology: Vol. 2: Adult psychopathology* (pp. 244–261). Hoboken, NJ: Wiley.

Newton-Howes, G., Tyrer, P., North, B., & Yang, M. (2008). The prevalence of personality disorder in schizophrenia and psychotic disorders: Systematic review of rates and explanatory modeling. *Psychological Medicine, 38,* 1075–1082.

Ni, X., Chan, K., & Bulgin, N. (2006). Association between serotonin transporter gene and borderline personality disorder. *Journal of Psychiatric Research, 40(5),* 448–453.

Nigg, J., & Huang-Pollock, C. (2003). An early-onset model of the role of executive functions and intelligence in conduct disorder/delinquency. In B. Lahey, T. E. Moffitt, & A. Caspi (Eds.), *Causes of conduct disorder and juvenile delinquency* (pp. 227–253). New York: Guilford Press.

Nigg, J. T., Nikolas, M., Friderici, K., Park, L. Y., & Zucker, R. A. (2007). Genotype and neuropsychological response inhibition as resilience promoters for ADHD, OCD, and CD under conditions of psychosocial adversity. *Developmental Psychopathology, 19,* 767–786.

Nock, M. K., Kazdin, A. E., Hiripi, E., & Kessler, R. C. (2006). Prevalence, subtypes, and correlates of DSM-IV conduct disorder in the National Comorbidity Survey Replication. *Psychological Medicine, 36(5),* 699–710.

Nolen-Hoeksema, S. (2002). Gender differences in depression. In I. H. Gotlib & C. Hammen (Eds.), *Handbook of depression* (pp. 492–509). New York: Guilford Press.

Norcross, J., Beutler, L., &Levant, R. (Eds.). (2006). *Evidence-based practices in mental health.* Washington, DC: American Psychological Association.

Northway, R. (2005). Case management, care coordination, and managed care. In W. M. Nehring (Ed.), *Health promotion for persons with intellectual and developmental disabilities: The state of scientific evidence.* (pp. 235–263). Washington, DC: American Association on Mental Retardation.

Nose, M., Cipriani, A., Biancosino, B., Grassi, L., & Barbui, C. (2006). Efficacy of pharmacotherapy against core traits of borderline personality disorder: Meta-analysis of randomized controlled trials. *International Clinical Psychopharmacology, 21(6),* 345–353.

O'Connell, B., Gardner, A., Takase, M., Hawkins, M. T., Ostaszkiewicz, J., Ski, C., et al. (2007). Clinical usefulness and feasibility of using reality orientation with patients who have dementia in acute care settings. *International Journal of Nursing Practice, 13(3),* 182–192.

O'Farrell, T., & Fals-Stewart, W. (2006). *Behavioural couples therapy for alcoholism and drug abuse.* New York: Guilford Press.

Ohan, J., & Johnston, C. (2005). Gender appropriateness of symptom criteria for attention-deficit/hyperactivity disorder, oppositional-defiant disorder, and conduct disorder. *Child Psychiatry and Human Development, 35,* 359–381.

Olfson, M., Blanco, C., Liu, L., Moreno, C., & Laje, G. (2006). National trends in the outpatients treatment of children and adolescents with antipsychotic drugs. *Archives of General Psychiatry, 63,* 679–685.

Olfson, M., & Marcus, S. C. (2009). National patterns in antidepressant medication treatment. *Archives of General Psychiatry, 66(8),* 848–856.

Olfson, M., Marcus, S. C., Druss, B., Elinson, L., Tanielian, T., & Pincus, H. A. (2002). National trends in the outpatient treatment of depression. *Journal of the American Medical Association, 287,* 203–209.

Olfson, M., Marcus, S. C., Tedeschi, M., & Wan, G. J. (2006). Continuity of antidepressant treatment for adults with depression in the United States. *American Journal of Psychiatry, 163,* 101–108.

Olsen, C. E., Poulsen, H. D., & Lubline, H. K. F. (2005). Drug therapy of dementia in elderly patients: A review. *Nordic Journal of Psychiatry, 59(2),* 71–77.

Onder, G., Orazio, Z., & Ezio, G. (2005). Reality orientation therapy combined with cholinesterase inhibitors in Alzheimer's disease: Randomized controlled trial. *British Journal of Psychiatry, 187(5),* 450–455.

O'Neill, S. (2003). African American women and eating disturbances: A meta-analysis. *Journal of Black Psychology, 29,* 3–16.

Orwin, R., Maranda, M., & Brady, T. (2001). *Impact of prior physical and sexual victimization on substance abuse treatment outcomes.* Report prepared under Contract No. 270-97-7016 for the Center for Substance Abuse Treatment. Fairfax, VA: Caliber Associates.

Oswald, D. P., & Sonenklar, N. A. (2007). Medication use among children with autism-spectrum disorders. *Journal of Child and Adolescent Psychopharmacology, 17(3),* 348–355.

Ownby, R. L., Crocco, E., Acevedo, A., John, V., & Loewenstein, D. (2006). Depression and risk for Alzheimer's disease. *Archives of General Psychiatry, 63,* 530–538.

Ozer, E., Best, S., Lipsey, T., & Weiss, D. (2003). Predictors of posttraumatic stress disorder and symptoms in adults: A
meta-analysis. *Psychological Bulletin, 129,* 52–73.

Ozonoff, S., Goodlin-Jones, B. L., & Solomon, M. (2007). Autism spectrum disorders. In E. J. Marsh & R. A. Barkley (Eds.),*Assessment of childhood disorders* (4th ed.) (pp. 487–525). New York: Guilford Press.

Ozonoff, S., Iosif, A., Baguio, F., Cook, I. C., Hill, M. M., Hutman, T., et al. (2010). A prospective study of the emergence of early behavioral signs of autism. *Journal of the Academy of Child & Adolescent Psychiatry, 49(3),* 256–266.

Ozonoff, S., Rogers, S. J., & Hendren, R. L. (Eds.). (2003). *Autism spectrum disorders: A research review for practitioners.* Arlington, VA: American Psychiatric Publishing.

Padilla-Walker, L. M., Harper, J. M., & Jensen, A. C. (2010). Self-regulation as a mediator between sibling relationship quality and early adolescents' positive and negative outcomes. *Journal of Family Psychology, 24(4),* 419–428.

Papassotiropoulos, A., Fountoulakis, M., Dunckley, T., Stephan, D. A., & Reiman, E. M. (2006). Genetics, transcriptomics, and proteomics of Alzheimer's disease. *Journal of Clinical Psychiatry, 67(4),* 652–670.

Pappadopulos, E., Woolston, S., Chait, A., Perkins, M., Connor, D. F., & Jensen, P. S. (2006). Pharmacotherapy of aggression in children and adolescents: Efficacy and effect size. *Journal of the Canadian Academy of Child and Adolescent Psychiatry, 15(1),* 27–39.

Paris, J. (2003). *Personality disorders over time: Precursors, course, and outcome.* Washington, DC: American Psychiatric Publishing.

Paris, J. (2005). The diagnosis of borderline personality disorder: Problematic but better than the alternatives. *Annals of Clinical Psychiatry, 17(1),* 41–46.

Pasco, J., Williams, L., Jacka, F., Ng, F., Henry, M., Nicholson, G., et al. (2008). Tobacco smoking as a risk factor for major depressive disorder: Population-based study. *British Journal of Psychiatry, 193,* 322–326.

Peat, M., Mitchell, J., Hoek, H., & Wonderlich, S. (2009). Validity and utility of subtyping anorexia nervosa. *International Journal of Eating Disorders, 42,* 590–594.

Pelham, W. E., Fabiano, G. A., & Massetti, G. M. (2005). Evidence-based assessment of attention deficit hyperactivity disorder in children and adolescents. *Journal of Clinical Child and Adolescent Psychology, 34(3),* 449–476.

Penza, K., Heim, C., & Nemeroff, C. (2006). Trauma and depression. In C. L. M. Keyes & S. H. Goodman (Eds.), *Women and depression: Handbook for the social, behavioral, and biomedical sciences* (pp. 360–381). New York: Cambridge University Press.

Perkins, D. O., Miller-Anderson, L., & Lieberman, J. A. (2006). Natural history and predictors of clinical course. In J. A. Lieberman, J. A. Stroup, & D. O. Perkins (Eds.), *The American Psychiatric Publishing textbook of schizophrenia* (pp. 289–301). Washington, DC: American Psychiatric Publishing.

Perlis, R. H., Welge, J. A., Vornik, M. S., Herschfeld, R. M. A., & Keck, P. E. (2006). Atypical antipsychotics in the treatment of mania: A meta-analysis of randomized, placebo-controlled trials. *Journal of Clinical Psychiatry, 67(4),* 509–516.

Perrin, S., Smith, P., & Yule, W. (2000). Practitioner review: The assessment and treatment of post-traumatic stress disorder in children and adolescents. *Journal of Child Psychology and Psychiatry and Allied Disciplines, 41(3),* 277–289.

Perry, J. C., Banon, E., & Ianni, F. (1999). Effectiveness of psychotherapy for personality disorders. *American Journal of Psychiatry, 156,* 1312–1321.

Peterson, K., McDonagh, M. S., & Fu, R. (2008). Comparative benefits and harms of competing medications for adults with attention-deficit hyperactivity disorder: A systematic review and indirect comparison meta-analysis. *Psychopharmacology, 197(1),* 1–11.

Petrakis, I., Gonzalez, G., Rosenheck, R., & Krystal, J. (2002). Comorbidity of alcoholism and psychiatric disorders: An overview. *Alcohol Research and Health, 26,* 81–90.

Petticrew, M., & Roberts, H. (2006). *Systematic reviews in the social sciences: A practical guide.* Malden, MA: Blackwell Publishing.

Pfammatter, M., Junghan, U. N., & Brenner, H. D. (2006). Efficacy of psychological therapy in schizophrenia: Conclusions from meta-analyses. *Schizophrenia Bulletin, 32(S1),* S64.

Pham, A. V., Carlson, J. S., Kosciulek, J. F. (2010). Ethnic differences in parental beliefs of attention-deficit/hyperactivity disorder and treatment. *Journal of Attention Disorders, 13(6),* 584–591.

Pharoah, F., Mari, J., Rathbone, J., & Wong, W. (2010). Family intervention for schizophrenia. *Cochrane Database of Systematic Reviews,* Issue 12. Art. No. CD000088. DOI: 10.1002/14651858.CD000088.pub3.

Pharoah, F. M., Rathbone, J., Mari, J. J., & Streiner, D. (2003). Family intervention for schizophrenia.

Cochrane Database of Systematic Reviews, 3. Art. No. CD000088.

Phillipe, T., Lalloue, F., & Preux, P. (2006). Dementia patients' caregivers' quality of life: The PIXEL study. *International Journal of Geriatric Psychiatry, 21(1),* 50–56.

Phillips, L. J., Francey, S. M., Edwards, J., & McMurray, N. (2007). Stress and psychosis: Towards the development of new models of investigation. *Clinical Psychology Review, 27(3),* 307–317.

Phillips, N. K., Hammen, C. L., Brennan, P. A., Najman, J. M., & Bor, W. (2005). Early adversity and the prospective prediction of depressive and anxiety disorders in adolescents. *Journal of Abnormal Child Psychology, 33,* 13–24.

Pilling, S., Bebbington, P., Kuipers, E., Garety, P., Geddes, J., Martindale, B., et al. (2002). Psychological treatments in schizophrenia: II. Meta-analysis of randomized controlled trials of social skills training and cognitive remediation. *Psychological Medicine, 32(5),* 783–791.

Pilowsky, D. J., Wickramaratne, P. J., Rush, A. J., Hughes, C. W., Garber, J., Malloy, E., et al. (2006). Children of currently depressed mothers: A STAR*D ancillary study. *Journal of Clinical Psychiatry, 67(1),* 126–136.

Pinikahana, J., Happell, B., & Keks, N. A. (2003). Suicide and schizophrenia: A review of literature (1990–1999) and implications for mental health nursing. *Issues in Mental Health Nursing, 24,* 24–27.

Pinquant, M., & Sorensen, S. (2006). Ethnic differences in stressors, resources, and psychological outcomes of family caregiving: A meta-analysis. *Gerontologist, 45,* 90–106.

Pliszka, S. R., Crismon, M. L., Hughes, C. W., Conners, C. K., Emslie, G. J., Jensen, P. S., et al. (2006). The Texas children's medication algorithm project: Revision of the algorithm for pharmacotherapy of attention-deficit/hyperactivity disorder. *Journal of the American Academy of Child and Adolescent Psychiatry, 45(6),* 642–657.

Polderman, T. J., Derks, E. M., Hudziak, J. J., Verhulst, F. C., Posthuma, D., & Boomsma, D. I. (2007). Across the continuum of attention skills: A twin study of the SWAN ADHD rating scale. *Journal Child Psychology and Psychiatry, 48,* 1080–1087.

Pollard, J., Hawkins, D., & Arthur, M. (1999). Risk and protection: Are both necessary to understand diverse behavioral outcomes in adolescence? *Social Work Research, 23,* 145–158.

Pompili, M., Mancinelli, I., Girardi, P., Ruberto, A., & Tatarelli, R. (2004). Suicide in anorexia nervosa: A meta-analysis. *International Journal of Eating Disorders, 36,* 99–103.

Posey, D. J., Erickson, C. A., Stigler, K. A., & McDougle, C. J. (2006). The use of selective serotonin reuptake inhibitors in autism and related disorders. *Journal of Child and Adolescent Psychopharmacology, 16(1–2),* 181–186.

Post, R. M., Leverich, G. B., King, Q., & Weiss, S. R. (2001). Developmental vulnerabilities to the onset and course of bipolar disorder. *Development and Psychopathology, 13(1),* 581–598.

Pot, A. M., Bohlmeijer, E. T., Onrust, S., Melenhorst, A. S., Veerbeek, M., & De Vries, W. (2010). The impact of life review on depression in older adults: A randomized controlled trial. *International Psychogeriatrics, 22(4),* 572–581.

Potvin, S., Sepehry, A. A., & Strip, E. (2006). A meta-analysis of negative symptoms in dual diagnosis schizophrenia. *Psychological Medicine, 36(4),* 431–440.

Powers, M. B., Vedel, E., & Emmelkamp, P. M. G. (2008). Behavioral couples therapy (BCT) for alcohol and drug use disorders: A meta-analysis. *Clinical Psychology Review, 28,* 952–962.

Prasad, K. M. R., Shirts, B. H., Yolken, R. H., Keshavan, M. S., & Nimgaonkar, V. L. (2007). Brain morphological changes associated with exposure to HSV1 in first—episode schizophrenia. *Molecular Psychiatry, 12(1),* 105–113.

Pratt, B. M., & Woolfenden, S. R. (2003). Interventions for preventing eating disorders in children and adolescents (Cochrane Review). *The Cochrane Library,* Issue 1. Oxford: Update Software.

Prendergast, M., Podus, D., & Change, E. (2000). Program factors and treatment outcomes in drug dependence treatment: An examination using meta-analysis. *Substance Use and Misuse, 35,* 1931–1965.

Project MATCH Research group. (1997). Matching alcoholism treatments to client heterogeneity: Project MATCH posttreatment drinking outcomes. *Journal of Studies on Alcohol, 58,* 7–29.

Punnoose, S., & Belgamwar, M. (2006). Nicotine for schizophrenia. *Cochrane Database of Systematic Reviews, 1.* Art. No. CD004838.

Purdie, N., Hattie, J., & Carroll, A. (2002). A review of the research on interventions for attention deficit hyperactivity disorder: What works best? *Review of Educational Research, 72(1),* 61–99.

Qin, P., Mortensen, P. B., & Pedersen, C. B. (2009). Frequent change of residence and risk of attempted and completed suicide among children and adolescents. *Archives of General Psychiatry, 66(6),* 628–632.

Ramtekkar, U. P., Reiersen, A. M., Todorov, A. A., & Todd, R. D. (2010). Sex and age differences in attention-deficit/hyperactivity disorder symptoms and diagnoses: Implications for DSM-V and ICD-11. *Journal of the American Academy of Child and Adolescent Psychiatry, 49(3)*, 217–228.

Rathod, S., Phiri, P., & Kingdon, D. (2010). Cognitive behavioral therapy for schizophrenia. *Psychiatric Clinics of North America, 33(3)*, 527–536.

Reichenberg, A., Gross, R., Weiser, M., Bresnahan, M., Silverman, J., Harlap, S., et al. (2006). Advancing paternal age and autism. *Archives of General Psychiatry, 63(9)*, 1026–1032.

Reid, H. M., & Zborowski, M. J. (2006). Schizophrenia—proneness, season of birth and sleep: Elevated schizotypy scores are associated with spring births and extremes of sleep. *Personality and Individual Differences, 41(7)*, 1185–1193.

Rice, C. (2007). *Prevalence of autism spectrum disorders—Autism and developmental disabilities monitoring network, 14 sites, United States, 2002.* Retrieved 2007, from CDC MMWR surveillance summaries, 56(SS01), 12–28.

Rief, W., Nestoriuc, Y., Weiss, S., Welzel, E., Barsky, A. J., & Hofman, S. G. (2009). Meta-analysis of the placebo response in antidepressant trials. *Journal of Affective Disorders, 118*, 1–8.

Riggs, P., & Whitmore, E. (1999). Substance use disorders and disruptive behavior disorders. In R. Hendren (Ed.), *Disruptive behavior disorders in children and adolescents, Vol. 18, No. 2. Review of psychiatry series* (pp. 133–173). Washington, DC: American Psychiatric Publishing.

Robin, A. L., Siegel, P. T., & Moye, A. (1995). Family versus individual therapy for anorexia: Impact on family conflict. *International Journal of Eating Disorders, 17(4)*, 313–322.

Robin, A. L., Seigel, P. T., Moye, A. W., Gilroy, M., Barker Dennis, A., & Sikand, A. (1999). A controlled comparison of family versus individual therapy for adolescents with anorexia nervosa. *Journal of the American Academy of Child and Adolescent Psychiatry, 38*, 1482–1489.

Robins, C. J., & Chatman, A. L. (2004). Dialectical behavior therapy: Current status, recent developments, and future directions. *Journal of Personality Disorders, 18(1)*, 73–89.

Rogers, S. J., & Vismara, L. A. (2008). Evidence-based comprehensive treatments for early autism. *Journal of Clinical Child and Adolescent Psychology, 37(1)*, 8–38.

Rolstad, S., Nordlund, A., Eckerstrom, C., Gustavsson, M. H., Blennow, K., Olesen, P. J., et al. (2010). High education may offer protection against tauopathy in patients with mild cognitive impairment. *Journal of Alzheimer's Disease, 21(1)*, 221–228.

Romano, C. J. (2004). Posttraumatic stress disorder—A continuing controversy in neuropsychiatry. *Neuropsychiatry Reviews, 5*, 9–12.

Rome, E., & Ammerman, S. (2003). Medical complications of eating disorders: An update. *Journal of Adolescent Health, 33*, 418–426.

Root, R. W. II., & Resnick, R. (2003). An update on the diagnosis and treatment of attention-deficit/hyperactivity disorder in children. *Professional Psychology: Research and Practice, 24*, 34–41.

Rose, S., Bisson, J., Churchill, R., & Wessely, S. (2002). Psychological debriefing for preventing post traumatic stress disorder (PTSD). *Cochrane Database of Systematic Reviews, 2002, 2*.

Rosenberg, P. B., Onyikel, C. U., Katz, I. R., Porsteinsson, A. P., Mintzer, J. E., Schneider, L. S., et al. (2005). Clinical application of operationalized criteria for "Depression of Alzheimer's Disease." *International Journal of Geriatric Psychiatry, 20*, 119-127.

Rosenthal, R., & Westreich, L. (1999). Treatment of persons with dual diagnoses of substance use disorder and other psychological problems. In B. McCrady & E. Epstein (Eds.), *Addictions: A comprehensive guidebook* (pp. 439–476). New York: Oxford University Press.

Rosner, S., Leucht, S., Lehert, P., & Soyka, M. (2008). Acamprosate supports abstinence, naltrexone prevents excessive drinking: Evidence from a meta-analysis with unreported outcomes. *Journal of Psychopharmacology, 22(1)*, 11–23.

Ross, S., & Peselow, E. (2009). Pharmacotherapy of addictive disorders. *Clinical NeuroPharmacology, 32*, 277–289.

Rothe, E. (2005). Considering cultural diversity in the management of ADHD in Hispanic patients. *Journal of the National Medicine Association, 97*, S17.

Rückinger, S., Rzehak, P., Chen, C., Sausenthaler, S., Koletzko, S., Bauer, C., et al. (2010). Prenatal and postnatal tobacco exposure and behavioral problems in 10-year-old children: Results from the GINI-plus Prospective Birth Cohort Study. *Environmental Health Perspectives, 118(1)*, 150–154. DOI: 10.1289/ehp.0901209.

Rudolph, K. (2002). Gender differences in emotional responses to interpersonal stress during adolescence. *Journal of Adolescent Health, 30*, 3–13.

Rugulies, R. (2002). Depression as a predictor for coronary heart disease: A review and meta-analysis. *American Journal of Preventive Medicine, 23*, 51–61.

Runyan, D. K., Hunter, W. M., Socolar, R. R., Amaya-Jackson, L., English, D., Landsverk, J., et al. (1998).

Children who prosper in unfavorable environments: The relationship to social capital. *Pediatrics, 10,* 12–20.

Rush, A. J., Sackeim, H. A., & Marangell, L. B. (2005). Effects of 12 months of vagus nerve stimulation in treatment-resistant depression: A naturalistic study. *Biological Psychiatry, 58(5),* 355–363.

Rush, A. J., Trivedi, M. H., Wisniewski, S. R., Stewart, J. W., Nierenberg, A. A., Thase, M. E., et al. (2006). Bupropion-ST, sertraline, or venlafaxine-XR after failure of SSRIs for depression. *Archives of General Psychiatry, 354,* 1231–1242.

Rutter, M., Bailey, A., Berument, S., LeCouyeur, A., Lord, C., et al. (2003). *Social Communication Questionnaire (SCQ) manual.* Los Angeles: Western Psychological Services.

Ryan, M. M., Lockstone, H. E., & Huffaker, S. J. (2006). Gene expression analysis of bipolar disorder reveals downregulation of the ubiquitin cycle and alterations in synaptic genes. *Molecular Psychiatry, 11(10),* 965–978.

Ryle, A. (2004). The contribution of cognitive analytic therapy to the treatment of borderline personality disorder. *Journal of Personality Disorders, 18(1),* 3–35.

Sachs, G. S., Printz, D. J., Kahn, D. A., Carpenter, D., & Docherty, J. P. (2000). *Medication treatment of bipolar disorder. Expert consensus guideline series.* New York: McGraw-Hill.

Sackett, D., Straus, S., Richardson, W., Rosenberg, W., & Haynes, R. (2000). *Evidence-based medicine: How to practice and teach EMB* (2nd ed.). London: Churchill Livingstone.

Saczynski, J. S., Beiser, A., Seshadri, S., Auerbach, S., Wolf, P. A., & Au, R. (2010). Depressive symptoms and risk of dementia: The Framingham Heart Study. *Neurology, 75(1),* 35–41.

Safran, S. P. (2008). Why youngsters with autistic spectrum disorders remain underrepresented in special education. *Remedial and Special Education, 29(2),* 90–95.

Safren, S. A., Sprich, S., Mimiaga, M. J., Surman, C., Knouse, L., Groves, M., et al. (2010). Cognitive behavioral therapy vs relaxation with educational support for medication-treated adults with ADHD and persistent symptoms: A randomized controlled trial. *Journal of the American Medical Association, 304(8),* 867–874. DOI: 10.1001/jama.2010.1190.

Sander, J. B., & McCarty, C. A. 2005. Youth depression in the family context: Familial risk factors and models of treatment. *Clinical Child Family Psychology Review, 8(3),* 203–219.

Sansone, R. A., Rytwinski, D., & Gaither, G. A. (2003). Borderline personality and psychotropic medication prescription in an outpatient psychiatry clinic. *Comprehensive Psychiatry, 44(6),* 454–458.

Sareen, J., Cox, B. J., Clara, I., & Asmundson, G. J. (2005). The relationship between anxiety disorders and physical disorders in the U.S. National Comorbidity Survey. *Depression and Anxiety, 21,* 193–202.

Sareen, J., Cox, B. J., Goodwin, R. D., & Asmundson, G. (2005). Co-occurrence of posttraumatic stress disorder with positive psychotic symptoms in a nationally representative sample. *Journal of Trauma and Stress, 18,* 313–322.

Sax, L., & Kautz, K. J. (2003). Who first suggests the diagnosis of attention-deficit/hyperactivity disorder? *Annals of Family Medicine, 1(3),* 171–174.

Schachter, H. M., Pham, B., King, J., Langford, S., & Moher, D. (2001). How efficacious and safe is short-acting methylphenidate for the treatment of attention-deficit disorder in children and adolescents? A meta-analysis. *Canadian Medical Association Journal, 165(11),* 1475–1488.

Schatzberg, A. F., & Nemeroff, C. B. (Eds.). (2001). *The American Psychiatric Publishing Press textbook of psychiatry* (2nd ed.). Washington, DC: American Psychiatric Publishing.

Scheeringa, M. S., Peebles, C. D., Cook, C. A., & Zeanah, C. H. (2001). Toward establishing procedural, criterion, and discriminant validity for PTSD in early childhood. *Journal of the American Academy of Child and Adolescent Psychiatry, 40(1),* 52–60.

Scheeringa, M. S., Zeanah, C. H., Drell, M. J., & Larrieu, J. A. (1995). Two approaches to the diagnosis of posttraumatic stress disorder in infancy and early childhood. *Journal of the American Academy of Child and Adolescent Psychiatry, 34(2),* 191–200.

Schenkel, L. S., West, A. E., Harral, E. M., Patel, N. B., & Pavuluri, M. N. (2008). Parent–child interactions in pediatric bipolar disorder. *Journal of Clinical Psychology, 64(4),* 422–437.

Schnurr, P. P., Friedman, M. J., & Bernardy, N. C. (2002). Research on posttraumatic stress disorder: Epidemiology, pathophysiology, and assessment. *JCLP/In Session: Psychotherapy in Practice, 58,* 877–889.

Scholz, J. K., & Levine, K. (2000). The evolution of income support policy in recent decades. *Focus, 21(2),* 9–15. Madison, WI: University of Wisconsin-Madison, Institute for Research on Poverty.

Schreibman, L., Stahmer, A. C., & Akshoomoff, N. (2006). Pervasive developmental disorders. In M. Hersen (Ed.), *Clinical handbook of child behavioral assessment* (pp. 503–524). San Diego: Elsevier Academic Press.

Schulte-Herbrüggen, O., Ahlers, C. J., Kronsbein, J., Rüter, A., Bahri, S., Vater, A., et al. (2009). Impaired sexual function in patients with borderline personality disorder is determined by history of sexual abuse. *Journal of Sexual Medicine, 6(12)*, 3356–3363.

Scott, J., Colom, F., & Vieta, E. (2007). A meta-analysis of relapse rates with adjunctive psychological therapies compared to usual psychiatric treatment for bipolar disorders. *International Journal of Neuropsychopharmacology, 10(1)*, 123–129.

Scott, J., McNeil, Y., & Cavanaugh, J. (2006). Exposure to obstetric complications and subsequent development of bipolar disorder: Systematic review. *British Journal of Psychiatry, 189*, 3–11.

Scott, K. M., Smith, D. R., & Ellis, P. M. (2010). Prospectively ascertained child maltreatment and its association with DSM-IV mental disorders in young adults. *Archives of General Psychiatry, 67*, 712–719.

Seeman, M. V. (2003). Gender differences in schizophrenia across the life span. In C. I. Cohen (Ed.), *Schizophrenia into later life: Treatment, research, and policy* (pp. 141–154). Washington, DC: American Psychiatric Publishing.

Seida, J. K., Ospina, M. B., Karkhaneh, M., Hartling, L., Smith, V., & Clark, B. (2009). Systematic reviews of psychosocial interventions for autism: An umbrella review. *Developmental Medicine and Child Neurology, 51(2)*, 95–104.

Sektnan, M., McClelland, M. M., Acock, A., & Morrison, F. J. (2010). Relations between early family risk, children's behavioral regulation, and academic achievement. *Early Childhood Research Quarterly, 25(4)*, 464–479. DOI: 10.1016/j.ecresq.2010.02.005.

Selten, J.-P., Cantor-Graae, E., & Kahn, R. S. (2007). Migration and schizophrenia. *Current Opinion in Psychiatry, 20(2)*, 111–115.

Seng, J. S., Graham-Bermann, S. A., Clark, M. K., McCarthy, A. M., & Ronis, D. L. (2005). Posttraumatic stress disorder and physical comorbidity among female children and adolescents: Results from service-use data. *Pediatrics, 116(6)*, 767–776.

Serretti, A., & Olgiati, P. (2005). Profiles of "manic" symptoms in bipolar I, bipolar II and major depressive disorders. *Journal of Affective Disorders, 84(2–3)*, Special issue: Bipolar Depression: Focus on Phenomenology, 159–166.

Shanmugham, B., Karp, J., Drayer, R., Reynolds, C. F., & Alexopoulos, G. (2005). Evidence-based pharmacologic interventions for geriatric depression. *Psychiatric Clinics of North America, 28(4)*, 821–835.

Shapiro, F. (1995). *Eye movement desensitization and reprocessing: Basic principles, protocols and procedures.* New York: Guilford Press.

Shattuck, P. T., Durkin, M., Maenner, M., Newschaffer, C., Mandell, D. S., Wiggins, L., et al. (2009). Timing of identification among children with an autism spectrum disorder: Findings from a population-based surveillance study. *Journal of the American Academy of Child and Adolescent Psychiatry, 48(5)*, 474–483.

Shattuck, P. T., & Grosse, S. D. (2007). Issues related to the diagnosis and treatment of autism spectrum disorders. *Mental Retardation and Developmental Disabilities, 13*, 129–135.

Shear, K., Jin, R., & Ruscio, A. M. (2006). Prevalence and correlates of estimated DSM-IV child and adult separation anxiety disorder in the National Comorbidity Survey Replication. *American Journal of Psychiatry, 163(6)*, 1074–1083.

Sheehan, T., & Owen, P. (1999). The disease model. In B. McCrady & E. Epstein (Eds.), *Addictions: A comprehensive guidebook* (pp. 268–286). New York: Oxford University Press.

Shelton, J. F., Tancredi, D. J., & Hertz-Picciotto, I. (2010). Independent and dependent contributions of advanced maternal and paternal ages to autism risk. *Autism Research, 3(1)*, 30–39.

Shepard, B., Carter, A., & Cohen, J. (2000). Attention-deficit/hyperactivity disorder and the preschool child. In T. E. Brown (Ed.), *Attention-deficit disorders and comorbidities in children, adolescents, and adults* (pp. 231–295). Washington, DC: American Psychiatric Publishing.

Sher, L. (2003). Daily hassles, cortisol, and the pathogenesis of depression. *Medical Hypotheses, 62(2)*, 198–202.

Shin, S. H., Edwards, E. M., & Heeren, T. (2009). Child abuse and neglect: Relations to adolescent binge drinking in the national longitudinal study of Adolescent Health (AddHealth) Study. *Addictive Behaviors, 34*, 277–280.

Shirk, S., Talmi, A., & Olds, D. (2000). A developmental psychopathology perspective on child and adolescent treatment policy. *Development and Psychopathology, 12*, 835–855.

Siebenbruner, J., Englund, M. M., Egeland, B., & Hudson, K. (2006). Developmental antecedents of late adolescence substances use patterns. *Development and Psychopathology, 18*, 551–571.

Siegel, B., & Hayer, C. (1999). *Detection of autism in the 2nd and 3rd year: The Pervasive Developmental Disorders Screening Test (PDDST).* Presented at the Society for Residential Child Development, Albuquerque, NM.

Sierra, P., Livianos, L., Arques, S., Castello, J., & Rojo, L. (2007). Prodromal symptoms to relapse in bipolar disorder. *Australian and New Zealand Journal of Psychiatry, 41*, 385–391.

Siller, M., & Sigman, M. (2002). The behaviors of parents with children with autism predict the subsequent development of their children's communication. *Journal of Autism and Developmental Disorders, 32(2)*, 77–89.

Silva, R., & Kessler, L. (2004). Resiliency and vulnerability factors in childhood PTSD. In R. Silva (Ed.), *Posttraumatic stress disorders in children and adolescents: Handbook* (pp. 18–37). New York: W.W. Norton.

Silva, R. R., Gabbay, V., & Minami, H. (2005). When to use antidepressant medication in youths. *Primary Psychiatry, 12(9)*, 42–50.

Simon, N., Otto, M. W., Wisniewski, S. R., Fossey, M., Sagduyu, K., Frank, E., et al. (2004). Anxiety disorder comorbidity in bipolar disorder patients: Data from the first 500 participants in the systematic treatment enhancement program for bipolar disorder. *American Journal of Psychiatry, 161*, 2222–2229.

Simon, V., Czobor, P., Balint, S., Meszaros, A., & Bitter, I. (2009). Prevalence and correlates of adult attention-deficit hyperactivity disorder: Meta-analysis. *British Journal of Psychiatry, 194*, 204–211.

Skodol, A. E. (2005). The borderline diagnosis: Concepts, criteria, and controversies. In J. G. Gunderson, P. D. Hoffman (Eds.),*Understanding and treating borderline personality disorder: A guide for professionals and families* (pp. 3–19). Arlington, VA: American Psychiatric Publishing.

Skodol, A. E., Gunderson, J. G., Shea, M. T., McGlashan, T. H., Morey, L. C., Sanislow, C. A., et al. (2002). The borderline diagnosis II: Biology, genetics, and clinical course. *Biological Psychiatry, 51(12)*, 951–963.

Skodol, A. E., Gunderson, J. G., Shea, M. T., McGlashan, T. H., Morey, L. C., Sanislow, C. A., et al. (2005). The collaborative longitudinal personality disorders study (CLPS): Overview and implications. *Journal of Personality Disorders, 19(5)*, 487–504.

Smith, T., Magyar, C., & Arnold-Saritepe, A. (2002). *Autism spectrum disorder.* New York: Wiley.

Smolak, L., & Murnen, S. K. (2002). A meta-analytic examination of the relationship between child sexual abuse and eating disorders. *International Journal of Eating Disorders, 31*, 136–150.

Soloff, P. H. (2005). Somatic treatments. In J. M. Oldham, A. E. Sokil, & D. S. Bender (Eds.), *The American Psychiatric Publishing textbook of personality disorders* (pp. 387–403). Washington, DC: American Psychiatric Publishing.

Solomon, D. A., Leon, A. C., Coryell, W. H., Endicott, J., Li, C., Fiedorowicz, J., et al. (2010). Longitudinal course of bipolar disorder: Duration of mood episodes. *Archives of General Psychiatry, 67(4)*, 339–347.

Spaulding, W., & Nolting, J. (2006). Psychotherapy for schizophrenia in the year 2030: Prognosis and prognostication. *Schizophrenia Bulletin, 32*(Suppl. 1), S94–S105.

Steen, R. G., Mull, C., McClure, R., Hamer, R. H., & Lieberman, J. A. (2006). Brian volume in first-episode schizophrenia: Systematic review and meta-analysis of magnetic resonance imaging studies. *British Journal of Psychiatry, 188*, 510–518.

Stein, D. J., Zungu-Dirwayi, N., Van der Linden, G. J. H., & Seedat, S. (2003). Pharmacotherapy for posttraumatic stress disorder (Cochrane Review). *The Cochrane Library*, Issue 1. Oxford: Update Software.

Stein, L. I., & Test, M. A. (1980). Alternative mental hospital treatment: I. Conceptual model, treatment program, and clinical evaluation. *Archives of General Psychiatry, 37*, 392–397.

Stein, M. B., Sherbourne, C. D., Craske, M. G., Means-Christensen, A., Bystritsky, A., Katon, W., et al. (2004). Quality of care for primary care patients with anxiety disorders. *American Journal of Psychiatry, 161*, 2230–2237.

Steinberg, L. (April 1, 2000). We know some things: Parent–adolescent relations in retrospect and prospect. Presidential address, The Society for Research on Adolescence, Chicago, IL. Retrieved March 25, 2004, from http://astro.temple.edu/~lds/sra.htm.

Steinberg, M., Corcoran, C., Tschan, J. T., Huber, C., Welsh-Bohmer, K., Norton, M. C., et al. (2006). Risk factors for neuropsychiatric symptoms in dementia: The Cache County Study. *International Journal of Geriatric Psychiatry, 21(9)*, 824–830.

Stevens, S. E., Sonuga-Barke, E. J. S., Kreppner, J. M., Beckett, C., Colvert, E., Castle, J., et al. (2008). Inattention/overactivity following early severe institutional deprivation: Presentation and associations in early adolescence. *Journal of Abnormal Child Psychology, 36*, 385–398.

Stice, E. (2002). Risk and maintenance factors for eating pathology: A meta-analytic review. *Psychological Bulletin, 128(5)*, 825–848.

Stinson, F. S., Grant, B. F., Dawson, D. A., Ruan, W. I., Huang, B., & Saha, T. (2005). Comorbidity between DSM-IV alcohol and specific drug use disorders in the United States: Results from the National Epidemiologic Survey on Alcohol and Related Conditions. *Drug and Alcohol Dependence, 80(1)*, 105–116.

Stockdale, S. E., Lagomasino, I. T., Siddique, J., McGuire, T., & Miranda, J. (2008). Racial and ethnic disparities in the detection and treatment of depression and anxiety among psychiatric and primary health care visits, 1995–2005. *Medical Care, 46*, 668–677.

Stone, M. H. (2006). Relationship of borderline personality disorder and bipolar disorder. *American Journal of Psychiatry, 163(7)*, 1126–1128.

Stone, W. L., Coonrod, E. E., & Ousley, O. Y. (2000). Screening Tool for Autism Two-Year-Olds (STAT): Development and preliminary data. *Journal of Autism and Developmental Disorders, 30(6)*, 607–612.

Storch, E. A., Merlo, L. J., Larson, M. J., Geffken, G. R., Lehmkuhl, H. D., Jacob, M. L., et al. (2008). Impact of comorbidity on cognitive-behavioral therapy response in pediatric obsessive-compulsive disorder. *Journal of the American Academy on Child and Adolescent Psychiatry, 47(5)*, 583–592.

Storr, C. L., Ialongo, N. S., Anthony, J. C., & Breslau, N. (2007). Childhood antecedents of exposure to traumatic events and posttraumatic stress disorder. *American Journal of Psychiatry, 164(1)*, 119–125.

Striegel-Moore, R. H. (1993). Etiology of binge eating: A developmental perspective. *International Journal of Social Psychiatry, 32*, 383–387.

Striegel-Moore, R. H., & Cachelin, F. M. (1999). Body image concerns and disordered eating in adolescent girls: Risk and protective factors. In N. G. Johnson, M. C. Roberts, & J. Worell (Eds.), *Beyond appearance: A new look at adolescent girls* (pp. 85–108). Washington, DC: American Psychological Association.

Striegel-Moore, R. H., Franko, D. L., Thompson, D., Barton, B., Schreiber, G. B., & Daniels, S. R. (2005). An empirical study of the typology of bulimia nervosa and its spectrum variants. *Psychological Medicine, 35*, 1563–1572.

Strunk, D. R., Brotman, M. A., DeRubeis, R. J., & Hollon, S. D. (2010). Therapist competence in cognitive therapy for depression: Predicting subsequent symptom change. *Journal of Consulting and Clinical Psychology, 78(3)*, 429–437.

Substance Abuse and Mental Health Services Administration. (2006). *Results from the 2005 National Survey on Drug Use and Health: National Findings.* Rockville, MD: Office of Applied Studies, NSDUH Series H-30, DHHS Publications No. SMA 06-4194.

Substance Abuse and Mental Health Services Administration. (2007, June 14). The DASIS Report: Facilities Offering Special Treatment Programs or Groups: 2005. Rockville, MD: SAMHSA Office of Applied Studies.

Substance Abuse and Mental Health Services Administration. (2009, October 8). *Mental Health Support and Self-Help Groups* (NSDUH Report No. NSDUH09-1008). Rockville, MD: SAMHSA Office of Applied Studies. Retrieved from http://store.samhsa. gov/product/NSDUH09-1008.

Sullivan, P. F., Neale, M. C., & Kendler, K. S. (2000). Genetic epidemiology of major depression: Review and meta-analysis. *American Journal of Psychiatry, 157(10)*, 1552–1562.

Swann, A. C. (2006). Neurobiology of bipolar depression. In R. S. El-Mallakh & N. S. Ghaemi (Eds.), *Bipolar depression: A comprehensive guide* (pp. 37–68). Washington, DC: American Psychiatric Publishing.

Swann, A. C., & Ginsberg, D. L. (2004). Special needs of women with bipolar disorder. *CNS Spectrums, 9(8)*, 1–11.

Swanson, J. (1992). *School based assessments and interventions for ADD students.* Irvine, CA: KC.

Swanson, J., Schuck, S., Mann, M., Carlson, C., Hartman, K., Sergeant, J., et al. (2001). Categorical and dimensional definitions and evaluations of symptoms of ADHD: The SNAP and SWAN ratings scales. Retrieved 2007, from http://www.adhd.net.

Szapocznik, J., & Williams, R. A. (2000). Brief strategic family therapy: Twenty-five years of interplay among theory, research and practice in adolescent behavior problems and drug abuse. *Clinical Child and Family Psychology Review, 3*, 117–135.

Szentagotai, A., & David, D. (2010). The efficacy of cognitive-behavioral therapy in bipolar disorder: A quantitative meta-analysis. *Journal of Clinical Psychiatry, 71(1)*, 66–73.

Tannock, R., & Brown, T. E. (2000). Attention-deficit disorders with learning disorders in children and adolescents. In T. E. Brown (Ed.), *Attention-deficit disorders and comorbidities in children, adolescents, and adults* (pp. 231–295). Washington, DC: American Psychiatric Publishing.

Tantillo, M., Bitter, C. N., & Adams, B. (2001). Enhancing readiness for eating disorder treatment: A relational/motivational group model for change. *Eating Disorders, 9*, 203–216.

Task Force on Research Diagnostic Criteria: Infancy and Preschool. (2003). Research diagnostic criteria for infants and preschool children: The process and empirical support. *Journal of the American Academy of Child and Adolescent Psychiatry, 42*, 1504–1512.

Taylor, R. J., Ellison, C. G., Chatters, L. M., Levin, J. S., & Lincoln, K. D. (2000). Mental health services in faith communities: The role of clergy in black churches. *Social Work, 45*, 73–87.

Taylor, V., & MacQueen, G. (2006). Associations between bipolar disorder and metabolic syndrome: A review. *Journal of Clinical Psychiatry, 67,* 1034–1041.

Teri, L., McCurrry, S. M., Logsdon, R., & Gibbons, L. E. (2005). Training community consultants to help families improve dementia care: A randomized controlled trial. *Gerontologist, 54(6),* 802–811.

Tharyan, P., & Adams, C. E. (2005). Electroconvulsive therapy for schizophrenia. *Cochrane Database of Systematic Reviews, 2.* Art. No. CD000076.

Thomas, C., & Corcoran, J. (2001). Empirically based marital and family interventions for alcohol abuse: A review. *Research on Social Work Practice, 11,* 549–575.

Thompson, L. A., & Kelly-Vance, L. (2001). The impact of mentoring on academic achievement of at-risk youth. *Children and Youth Services Review, 23(3),* 227–243.

Thompson-Brenner, H., Glass, S., & Westen, D. (2003). A multidimensional meta-analysis of psychotherapy for bulimia nervosa. *Clinical Psychological Science Practice, 10,* 269–287.

Tondo, L., Albert, M. J., & Baldessarini, R. J. (2006). Suicide rates in relation to health care access in the United States: An ecological study. *Journal of Clinical Psychiatry, 67,* 517–523.

Torrey, E. F., Buka, S., Cannon, T. D., Goldstein, J. M., Seidman, L. J., Liu, T., et al. (2009). Paternal age as a risk factor for schizophrenia: How important is it? *Schizophrenia Research, 114(1–3),* 1–5.

Tozzi, F., Thornton, L. M., Klump., K. L., Fichter, M. M., Halmi, K. A., Kaplan, A. S., et al. (2005). Symptom fluctuation in eating disorders: Correlates of diagnostic crossover. *American Journal of Psychiatry, 162,* 732–740.

Treasure, J., Katzman, M., Schmidt, U., Troop, N., Todd, G., & de Silva, P. (1999). Engagement and outcome in the treatment of bulimia nervosa: First phase of a sequential design comparing motivation enhancement therapy and cognitive behavioural therapy. *Behaviour Research and Therapy, 37,* 405–418.

Treasure, J., & Ward, A. (1997). A practical guide to the use of motivational interviewing in anorexia nervosa. *European Eating Disorders Review, 5,* 102–114.

Treatment for Adolescents with Depression Study (TADS) Team (2006). The Treatment for Adolescents with Depression Study (TADS): Predictors and moderators of acute outcome. *Journal of American Academy of Child and Adolescent Psychiatry, 45,* 1427–1439.

Treatment for Adolescents with Depression Study (TADS) Team (2007). The Treatment for Adolescents with Depression Study (TADS): Long-term effectiveness and safety outcomes. *Archives of General Psychiatry, 64,* 1132–1144.

Trierweiler, S. J., Neighbors, H. W., Munday, C., Thompson, E. E., Binion, V. J., & Gomez, J. P. (2000). Clinician attributions associated with the diagnosis of schizophrenia in African American and non-African American patients. *Journal of Consulting and Clinical Psychology, 68(1),* 171–175.

Trivedi, M. H., Fava, M., Wisniewski, S. R., Thase, M. E., Quitkin, F., Warden, D., et al. (2006). Medication augmentation after the failure of SSRIs for depression. *New England Journal of Medicine, 354,* 1243–1252.

Trivedi, M. H., Rush, A. J., Wisniewski, S. R., Nierenberg, A. A., Warden, D., Ritz, L., et al. (2006). Evaluation of outcomes with citalopram for depression using measurement-based care in STAR*D: Implications for clinical practice. *American Journal of Psychiatry, 163,* 28–40.

Twamley, E. W., Jeste, D. V., & Lehman, A. F. (2003). Vocational rehabilitation in schizophrenia and other psychotic disorders: A literature review and meta-analysis of randomized controlled trials. *Journal of Nervous and Mental Disease, 191(8),* 515–523.

Tyrer, P. (1999). What is the future of assertive community treatment? *Epidemiologia e Psichiatria Sociale, 8(1),* 16–18.

Tyrer, S. (2006). What does history teach us about factors associated with relapse in bipolar affective disorder? *Journal of Psychopharmacology, 20*(Suppl. 2), 4–11.

Uddin, M., Aiello, A. E., Wildman, D. E., Koenen, K. C., Pawelec, G., de Los Santos, R., et al. (2010). Epigenetic and immune function profiles associated with posttraumatic stress disorder. *Proceedings of the National Academy of Sciences of the United States of America, 107(20),* 9470–9475.

U.S. Department of Health and Human Services. (1999). *Mental health: A report of the surgeon general.* Retrieved 2007, from http://www.surgeongeneral.gov/library/mentalhealth/home.html.

U.S. Department of Health and Human Services. (2001). *Culture, race, and ethnicity: A supplement to mental health: A report of the surgeon general.* Retrieved 2007, from http://www.surgeongeneral.gov/library/mentalhealth/cre/.

van Boeijen, C. A., Van Balkom, A. J., Van Oppen, P., Nettie Blankenstein, N., Cherpanath, A., & van Dyck, R. (2005). Efficacy of self-help manuals for anxiety disorders in primary care: A systematic review. *Family Practice, 22(2),* 192–196.

Van Citters, A. D., Pratt, S. I., Bartels, S. J., & Jeste, D. V. (2005). Evidence-based review of pharmacologic and nonpharmacologic treatments for older adults with schizophrenia. *Psychiatric Clinics of North America, 28(4),* 913–939.

van Hoeken, D., Veling, W., Sinke, S., Mitchell, J., & Hoek, H. (2009). The validity and utility of subtyping bulima nervosa. *International Journal of Eating Disorders, 42*, 595–602.

van Os, J., Rutten, Bart, P. F., & Poulton, R. (2008). Gene-environmental interactions in schizophrenia: Review of epidemiological findings and future directions. *Schizophrenia Bulletin, 34(6)*, 1066–1082.

Veenstra-Vanderweele, J., & Cook, E. H. (2003). Genetics of childhood disorders: XLVI. Autism, part 5: Genetics of autism. *Journal of the Academy of Child and Adolescent Psychiatry, 42(1)*, 116–119.

Velting, O., Setzer, N., &Albano, A. M. (2004). Update on and advances in assessment and cognitive-behavioral treatment of anxiety disorders in children and adolescents. *Professional Psychology: Research and Practice, 35*, 42–54.

Verdoux, H., Geddes, J. R., Takei, N., Lawrie, S. M., Bovet, P., Eagles, J. M., et al. (1997). Obstetric complications and age at onset in schizophrenia: An international collaborative meta-analysis of individual patient data. *American Journal of Psychiatry, 154(9)*, 1220–1227.

Vernooij-Dassen, M., Vasse, E., Zuidema, S., Cohen-Mansfield, J., & Moyle, W. (2010). Psychosocial interventions for dementia patients in long-term care. *International Psychogeriatrics, 22(7)*, 1121–1128.

Vieta, E., & Suppes, T. (2008). Bipolar II disorder: Arguments for and against a distinct diagnostic entity. *Bipolar Disorders, 10*, 163–178.

Vink, A. C., Birks, J. S., Bruinsma, M. S., & Scholten, R. J. (2007). Music therapy for people with dementia. *The Cochrane database of Systematic Reviews, 1*, New York: Wiley.

Vinton, L., & Wambach, K. (2005). Alcohol and drug use among elderly people. In C. A. McNeese & D. DiNitto (Eds.), *Chemical dependency: A systems approach* (pp. 484–502). Boston: Pearson.

Vita, A., Silenzi, C., & Dieci, M. (2006). Brian morphology in first episode schizophrenia: A meta-analysis of quantitative magnetic resonance imaging studies. *Schizophrenic Research, 82(1)*, 75–88.

Vitiello, B., & Towbin, K. (2009). Stimulant treatment of ADHD and risk of sudden death in children. *American Journal of Psychiatry, 166*, 955–957. DOI: 10.1176/appi.ajp.2009.09050619.

Volk, D. W., Morine, S., Tew, J. D., Hosanagar, A., Travis, M. j., & Lewis, D. A. (2008). Schizophrenia and related psychoses. In D. J. Kupfer, M. S. Horner, D. A. Brent, D. A. Lewis, C. F. Reynolds, M. E. Thase, & M. J. Travis (Eds.), *Oxford American handbook of psychiatry* (pp. 203–269). New York: Oxford University Press.

Volkmar, F., Charwanda, K., & Klin, A. (2004). Autism in infancy and early childhood. *Annual Review of Psychology 56*, 315–336.

Volkmar, F. R., Lord, C., Bailey, A., Schultz, R. T., & Klin, A. (2004). Autism and pervasive developmental disorders. *Journal of Child Psychology and Psychiatry, 45(1)*, 135–170.

Vreeburg, S. A., Hoogendijk, W. J., Pelt, van J., Derijk, R. H., Verhagen, J. C., Dyck, van R., et al. (2009): Major depressive disorder and hypothalamic-pituitary-adrenal axis activity: Results from a large cohort study. *Archives of General Psychiatry, 66*, 617–626.

Wachs, T. (2000). *Necessary but not sufficient.* Washington, DC: American Psychological Association.

Wadsworth, M. E., & Achenbach, T. M. (2005). Explaining the link between low socioeconomic status and psychopathology: Testing two mechanisms of the social causation hypothesis. *Journal of Consulting and Clinical Psychology, 73(6)*, 1146–1153.

Waldemar, G., Dubois, B., Emre, M., Georges, J., McKeith, G., Rossor, M., et al. (2007). Recommendations for the diagnosis and management of Alzheimer's disease and other disorders associated with dementia: EFNS guidelines. *European Journal of Neurology, 14*, 1–26.

Waldman, I. D., & Gizer, I. R. (2006). The genetics of attention deficit hyperactivity disorder. *Clinical Psychology Review, 26(4)*, 396–432.

Waldron, H. B., & Turner, C. W. (2008). Evidence-based psychosocial treatments for adolescent substance abuse. *Journal of Clinical Child and Adolescent Psychology, 37*, 238–261.

Walitzer, K., Dermen, K., & Conners, G. (1999). Strategies for preparing clients for treatment: A review. *Behavior Modification, 23*, 129–151.

Walitzer, K. S., & Dearing, R. L. (2006). Gender differences in alcohol and substance use relapse. *Clinical Psychology Review, 26*, 128–148.

Walsh, J. (2010a). *Psychoeducation in mental health.* Chicago: Lyceum Books.

Walsh, J. (2010b). *Theories for direct social work practice* (2nd ed.). Pacific Grove, CA: Brooks/Cole.

Walters, G. (2002). The heritability of alcohol abuse and dependence: A meta-analysis of behavior genetic research. *American Journal of Drug and Alcohol Abuse, 28*, 557–584.

Wang, J., Nansel, T. R., & Iannotti, R. J. (2011). Cyber and traditional bullying: Differential association with depression. *Journal of Adolescent Health, 48*, 415–417.

Wang, P. S., Berglund, P., Olfson, M., Pincus, H. A., Wells, K. B., & Kessler, R. C. (2005). Failure and delay in initial treatment contact after first onset of mental disorders in the National Comorbidity Survey Replication. *Archives of General Psychiatry, 62,* 603–613.

Wang, P. S., Lane, M., Olfson, M., Pincus, H. A., Wells, K., & Kessler, R. C. (2005). Twelve-month use of mental health services in the United States. *Archives of General Psychiatry, 62,* 629–640.

Warren, S., Huston, L., Egeland, B., & Sroufe, L. A. (1997). Child and adolescent anxiety disorders and early attachment. *Journal of the American Academy of Child and Adolescent Psychiatry, 36,* 637–644.

Waslick, B. D., Kandel, B. A., & Kakouros, B. S. (2002). Depression in children and adolescents: An overview. In D. Shaffer & B. D. Waslick (Eds.), *The many faces of depression in children and adolescents* (pp. 1–36). Washington, DC: American Psychiatric Publishing.

Wechsberg, W. M., Craddock, S. G., & Hubbard, R. L. (1998). How are women who enter substance abuse treatment different than men? A gender comparison from the drug abuse treatment outcome study (DATOS). *Drugs and Society, 13,* 97–115.

Wei, W., Sambamoorthi, U., Olfson, M., Walkup, J. T., & Crystal, S. (2005). Use of psychotherapy for depression in older adults. *American Journal of Psychiatry, 162,* 711–717.

Weinstein, D., Staffelbach, D., & Biaggio, M. (2000). Attention-deficit hyperactivity disorder and posttraumatic stress disorder: Differential diagnosis in childhood sexual abuse. *Clinical Psychology Review, 20(3),* 359–378.

Weiss, G., & Hechtman, L. T. (1993). *Hyperactive children grown up: ADHD in children, adolescents, and adults* (2nd ed.). New York: Guilford Press.

Weiss, M., & Weiss, J. (2004). A guide to the treatment of adults with ADHD. *Journal of Clinical Psychiatry, 65*(Suppl. 3), 27–37.

Weissman, M. M., Markowitz, J. C., & Klerman, G. L. (2000). *Comprehensive guide to interpersonal psychotherapy.* New York: Basic Books.

Weissman, M. M., Wickramaratne, P., Nomura, Y., Warner, V., Pilowsky, D., & Verdeli, H. (2006). Offspring of depressed parents: 20 years later. *American Journal of Psychiatry, 163,* 1001–1008.

Wells, K., Klap, R., Koike, A., & Sherbourne, C. (2001). Ethnic disparities in unmet need for alcoholism, drug abuse, and mental health care. *American Journal of Psychiatry, 158,* 2027–2032.

Wenzel, A., Chapman, J. E., Newman, C. F., Beck, A. T., & Brown, G. K. (2006). Hypothesized mechanisms of change in cognitive therapy for borderline personality disorder. *Journal of Clinical Psychology, 62(4),* 503–516.

Werner, E. (2000). Protective factors and individual resilience. In J. Shonoff & S. Meisels (Eds.), *Handbook of early childhood intervention* (2nd ed.) (pp. 115–133). Cambridge: Cambridge University Press.

Werner, E. E., & Smith, R. S. (2001). *Journeys from childhood to midlife: Risk, resilience, and recovery.* Ithaca, NY: Cornell University Press.

Westen, D. (2005). Patients and treatments in clinical trials are not adequately representative of clinical practice. In J. C. Norcross, L. E. Beutler, & R. F. Levant (Eds.), *Evidence-based practices in mental health: Debate and dialogue on the fundamental questions* (pp. 161–171). Washington, DC: American Psychological Association.

Wetherell, J. L., Lenze, E. J., & Stanley, M. A. (2005). Evidence-based treatment of geriatric anxiety disorders. *Psychiatric Clinics of North America, 28(4),* 871–896.

Wethington, H. R., Hahn, R. A., Fuqua-Whitley, D. S., Sipe, T. A., Crosby, A. E., Johnson, R. L., et al. (2008). The effectiveness of interventions to reduce psychological harm from traumatic events among children and adolescents. *American Journal of Preventive Medicine, 35,* 287–313.

Whaley, A. L. (2001). Cultural mistrust: An important psychological construct for diagnosis and treatment of African Americans. *Professional Psychology: Theory and Practice, 32(6),* 555–562.

Whitaker, T. (2009). *The results are in: What social workers say about social work.* Washington, DC: National Association of Social Workers.

White, J. (2000). The prevention of eating disorders: A review of the research on risk factors with implications for practice. *Journal of Child and Adolescent Psychiatric Nursing, 13,* 76–78.

White, M., & Epston, D. (1990). *Narrative means to therapeutic ends.* New York: W.W. Norton.

Whittal, M., Agras, W. S., & Gould, R. (1999). Bulimia nervosa: A meta-analysis of psychosocial and pharmacological treatments. *Behavior Therapy, 30,* 117–135.

Whittington, C. J., Kendall, T., Fonagy, P., Cottrell, D., Cotgrove, A., & Boddington, E. (2004). Selective serotonin reuptake inhibitors in childhood depression: Systematic review of published versus unpublished data. *Lancet, 363,* 1341–1345.

Wiggins, L. D., Baio, J., & Rice, C. (2006). Examination of the time between first evaluation and first autism spectrum diagnosis in a population-based sample. *Journal of Developmental and Behavioral Pediatrics, 27*(Suppl. 2), S79–S87.

Wildes, J. E., & Emery, R. E. (2001). The roles of ethnicity and culture in the development of eating disturbance and body dissatisfaction: A meta-analytic review. *Clinical Psychology Review, 21(4),* 521–551.

Wildgust, H. J., Hodgson, R., & Beary, M. (2010). The paradox of premature mortality in schizophrenia: New research questions. *Journal of Psychopharmacology, 24*(11, Suppl. 4), 9–15.

Willer, M. G., Thuras, P., & Crow, S. J. (2005). Implications on the changing use of hospitalization to treat anorexia nervosa. *American Journal of Psychiatry, 162,* 2374–2376.

Williams, J., & Brayne, C. (2006). Screening for autism spectrum disorders: What is the evidence? *Autism, 10(1),* 11–35.

Williams, N. L., Reardon, J. M., Murray, K. T., & Cole, T. M. (2005). Anxiety disorders: A developmental vulnerability-stress perspective. In B. L. Hankin & J. R. Z. Abela (Eds.), *Development of psychopathology: A vulnerability-stress perspective* (pp. 289–327). Thousand Oaks, CA: Sage Publications.

Willoughby, M. T., Curran, P. T., Costello, E. J., & Angold, A. (2000). Implications of early versus late onset of attention-deficit/hyperactivity disorder symptoms. *Journal of the American Academy of Child and Adolescent Psychiatry, 39(12),* 1512–1514.

Wilson, G., Heffernan, K., & Black, C. (1996). Eating disorders. In E. Mash & R. Barkley (Eds.), *Child psychopathology* (pp. 541–571). New York: Guilford Press.

Wilson, G. T. (1999). Eating disorders and addictive disorders. In C. Fairburn & K. D. Brownell (Eds.), *Eating disorders and obesity: A comprehensive handbook* (pp. 199–203). New York: Guilford Press.

Wilson, G. T., Grilo, C. M., & Vitousek, K. M. (2007). Psychological treatment of eating disorders. *American Psychologist, 62,* 199–216.

Wilson, G. T., & Sysko, R. (2009). Frequency of binge eating episodes in bulimia nervosa and binge eating disorder: Diagnostic considerations. *International Journal of Eating Disorders, 42,* 603–610.

Wilson, S., Lipsey, M., & Soydan, H. (2003). Are mainstream programs for juvenile delinquency less effective with minority youth than majority youth? A meta-analysis of outcomes research. *Research on Social Work Practice, 13,* 3–26.

Wilson, S. J., & Lipsey, M. W. (2007). School-based interventions for aggressive and disruptive behavior: Update of a meta-analysis. *American Journal of Preventive Medicine, 33(2),* S130–S143.

Wilson, T. G., Loeb, K., Walsh, T. B., Labouvie, E., Petkova, E., Xinhua, L., et al. (1999). Psychological versus pharmacological treatments of bulimia nervosa: Predictors and processes of change. *Journal of Consulting and Clinical Psychology, 67(4),* 451–459.

Wolff-Menzler, C., Hasan, A., Malchow, B., Falkai, P., & Wobrock, T. (2010). Combination therapy in the treatment of schizophrenia. *Pharmacopsychiatry, 43(4),* 122–129.

Wolraich, M. L., Bard, D. E., Stein, M. T., Rushton, J. L., & O'Connor, K. G. (2010). Pediatricians' attitudes and practices on ADHD before and after the development of ADHD Pediatric Practice Guidelines. *Journal of Attention Disorders, 13(6),* 563–572. DOI: 10.1177/1087054709644194.

Wonderlich, S., Gordon, K., Mitchell, J., Crosby, R., & Engel, S. (2009). The validity and clinical utility of binge eating disorder. *International Journal of Eating Disorders, 42,* 687–705.

Wong, H. H. L., & Smith, R. G. (2006). Patterns of complementary and alternative medical therapy use in children diagnosed with autism spectrum disorders. *Journal of Autism and Developmental Disorders, 36(7),* 901–909.

Woods, M. E. (1999). Personality disorders. In F. J. Turner (Ed.), *Adult psychopathology: A social work perspective* (pp. 374–429). New York: Free Press.

Xie, P., Kranzler, H. R., Poling, J. Stein, M. B., Anton, R. F., Brady, K., et al. (2009). Interactive effect of stressful life events and the serotonin transporter 5-HTTLPR genotype on posttraumatic stress disorder diagnosis in 2 independent populations. *Archives of General Psychiatry, 66(11),* 1201–1209. Retrieved from http://www.archgenpsychiatry.com.

Xue, Y., Leventhal, T., & Brooks-Gunn, J. (2005). Neighborhood residence and mental health problems of 5- to 11-year-olds. *Archives of General Psychiatry, 62(5),* 554–563.

Yager, J., Anderson, A., Devlin, M., Egger, H., Herzog, D., Mitchell, J., et al. (2002). Practice guideline for the treatment of patients with eating disorders. In *American Psychiatric Association practice guidelines for the treatment of psychiatric disorders: Compendium 2002* (2nd ed.) (pp. 697–766). Washington, DC: American Psychiatric Publishing.

Yehuda, R. (2006). *Psychobiology of posttraumatic stress disorders: A decade of progress* (Vol. 1071). Malden, MA: Blackwell Publishing.

Yen, S., Shea, M. T., Sanislow, C. A., Grilo, C. M., Skodol, A. E., Gunderson, J. G., et al. (2004). Borderline personality disorder criteria associated with prospectively observed suicidal behavior. *American Journal of Psychiatry, 161,* 1296–1298.

Young, A. S., Klap, R., Sherbourne, C. D., & Wells, K. B. (2001). The quality of care for depressive and anxiety disorders in the United States. *Archives of General Psychiatry, 58,* 55–61.

Young, K., Greenwood, C. E., Van Reekum, R., & Binns, M. A. (2004). A randomized, crossover trial of high-carbohydrate foods in nursing home residents with Alzheimer's disease: Associations among intervention response, body mass index, and behavioral and cognitive function. *Journal of Gerontology: Series A: Biological Sciences and Medical Sciences, 60A(8),* 1039–1045.

Young, R. C. (2005). Evidence-based pharmacological treatment of geriatric bipolar disorder. *Psychiatric Clinics of North America, 28,* 837–869.

Youngstrom, E. A., Findling, R. L., Youngstrom, J. K., & Calabrese, J. R. (2005). Toward an evidence-based assessment of pediatric bipolar disorder. *Journal of Clinical Child and Adolescent Psychology, 34(3),* 433–448.

Yu, W., Ren, X. S., Lee, A. F., Herz, L., Huang, Y.-H., & Kazis, L. E. (2006). Association of co-morbidities with prescribing patterns and cost savings: Olanzapine versus risperidone for schizophrenia. *PharmacoEconomics, 24(12),* 1233–1248.

Zabala, M. J., Macdonald, P., & Treasure, J. (2009). Appraisal of caregiving burden, expressed emotion and psychological distress in families of people with eating disorders: A systematic review. *European Eating Disorders Review, 17,* 338–349. DOI: 10.4002/erv.925.

Zammitt, S., Lewis, G., Dalman, C., & Allebeck, P. (2010). Examining interactions between risk factors for psychosis. *British Journal of Psychiatry, 197,* 207–211.

Zanarini, M. C., Frankenburg, F. R., Hennen, J., Reich, B., & Silk, K. R. (2004). Axis I comorbidity in patients with borderline personality disorder: 6-year follow-up and prediction of time to remission. *American Journal of Psychiatry, 161(11),* 2108–2114.

Zanarini, M. C., Frankenburg, F. R., Reich, D. B., & Fitzmaurice, G. (2010). Time to attainment of recovery from borderline personality disorder and stability of recovery: A 10-year prospective follow-up study. *American Journal of Psychiatry, 167,* 663–667.

Zanarini, M. C., & Jager-Hyman, S. (2009). Dissociation in borderline personality disorder. Paul F. Dell & John A. O'Neil (Eds.), *Dissociation and the dissociative disorders: DSM-V and beyond* (pp. 487–493).

Zaretsky, A., Lancee, W., Miller, C., Harris, A., & Parikh, S. V. (2008). Is cognitive-behavioural therapy more effective than psychoeducation in bipolar disorder? *Canadian Journal of Psychiatry, 53 (7),* 441–448.

Zarit, S. H., & Femia, E. E. (2008). A future for family care and dementia intervention research? Challenges and strategies. *Aging and Mental Health, 12(1),* 5–13.

Zeltzer, B. B., & Kohn, R. (2006). Mental health services for homebound elders from home health nursing agencies and home care agencies. *Psychiatric Services, 57(4),* 567–569.

Ziabreva, I., Perry, E., & Perry, R. (2006). Altered neurogenesis in Alzheimer's disease. *Journal of Psychosomatic Research, 61(3),* 311–316.

Zientz, J., Rackley, A., & Chapman, S. B. (2007). Evidence-based practice recommendations for dementia: Educating caregivers on Alzheimer's disease and training communication strategies. *Journal of Medical Speech-Language Pathology, 15(1),* 3–14.

Zimmerman, M., & Galione, J. (2010). Psychiatrists' and nonpsychiatrist physicians reported use of the DSM-IV criteria for major depressive disorder. *Journal of Clinical Psychiatry, 71(3),* 236–239.

Zimmerman, M., Galione, J., Attiullah, N., Friedman, M., Toba, C., Boerescu, D. A., et al. (2010). Underrecognition of clinically significant side effects in depressed patients. *Journal of Clinical Psychiatry, 71(4),* 484–490. DOI: 10.4088/jcp.08m04978blu.

Zimmerman, M., McGlinchey, J. B., Young, D., & Chelminski, I. (2006). Diagnosing major depressive disorder IV: Relationship between number of symptoms and the diagnosis of disorder. *Journal of Nervous and Mental Disease, 194(6),* 450–453.

Zito, W., Greig, T. C., Wexler, B. E., & Bell, M. D. (2007). Predictors of on-site vocational support for people with schizophrenia in supported employment. *Schizophrenia Research, 94(1–3),* 81–88.

Index

Page numbers followed by "*b*" indicate a box; and those followed by "*t*" indicate a table.